CHRONOLOGICAL CHART OF EAST [ ] HISTORY

D0640473

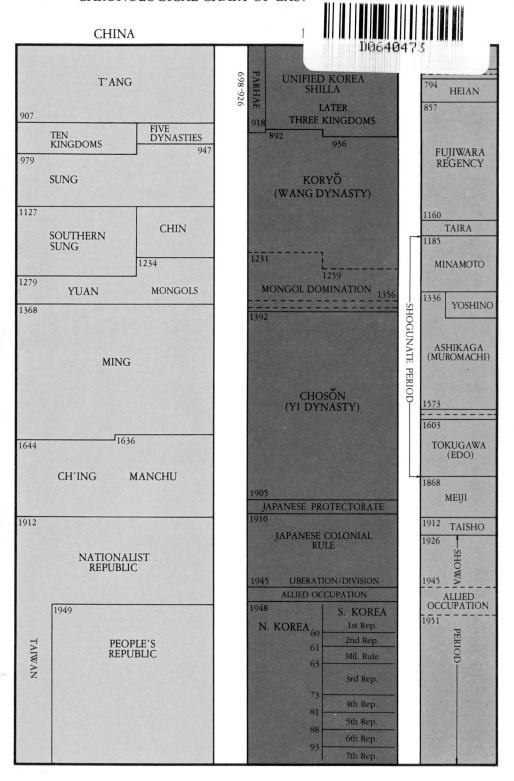

CHINA

T'ANG	
907	
TEN KINGDOMS	**FIVE DYNASTIES**
	947
979	
SUNG	
1127	
SOUTHERN SUNG	**CHIN**
	1234
1279	
YUAN	**MONGOLS**
1368	
MING	
1644	1636
CH'ING	**MANCHU**
1912	
NATIONALIST REPUBLIC	
1949	
TAIWAN	**PEOPLE'S REPUBLIC**

KOREA

698-926 PARHAE

918 **UNIFIED KOREA SHILLA**

LATER THREE KINGDOMS

892 · 936

KORYŎ (WANG DYNASTY)

1231 · 1259

MONGOL DOMINATION · 1356

1392

CHOSŎN (YI DYNASTY)

1905 **JAPANESE PROTECTORATE**

1910 **JAPANESE COLONIAL RULE**

1945 **LIBERATION/DIVISION**

ALLIED OCCUPATION

1948 **N. KOREA** — **S. KOREA**

	1st Rep.
60	2nd Rep.
61	Mil. Rule
63	3rd Rep.
73	4th Rep.
81	5th Rep.
88	6th Rep.
93	7th Rep.

JAPAN

794 **HEIAN**

857

FUJIWARA REGENCY

1160 **TAIRA**

1185 **MINAMOTO**

1336 **YOSHINO**

ASHIKAGA (MUROMACHI)

1573

1603

TOKUGAWA (EDO)

SHOGUNATE PERIOD

1868 **MEIJI**

1912 **TAISHO**

1926 *SHOWA*

1945 **ALLIED OCCUPATION**

1951 *PERIOD*

Traditional
Korea
A Cultural History

A HISTORY OF KOREAN CIVILIZATION

韓國傳統文化史

改正增補版

趙 宛 濟　著

崔 鴻 圭　改正增補

中央大學校　教授

株式會社　翰林出版社

大韓民國　서울

Traditional
Korea
A Cultural History

A HISTORY OF KOREAN CIVILIZATION

Revised Edition

by Wanne J. Joe
Revised & edited
by Hongkyu A. Choe

HOLLYM

ELIZABETH, NJ · SEOUL

Revised Edition, 1997
Second printing, 1998
by Hollym International Corp.
18 Donald Place, Elizabeth, New Jersey 07208 USA
Phone: (908)353-1655 Fax: (908)353-0255
http://www.hollym.com

Published simultaneously in Seoul, Korea
by Hollym Corporation; Publishers
13-13 Kwanchol-dong, Chongno-gu, Seoul 110-111, Korea
Phone: (02)735-7551~4 Fax: (02)730-5149, 8192
http://www.hollym.co.kr

ISBN: 1-56591-072-9
Library of Congress Catalog Card Number: 97-71675

Printed in Korea

PREFACE

This is my first book on the history of Korean civilization. It is meant to provide the general readers and the students in Korean studies with an understanding of the unique story of the Korean people up to the 19th century. That story, like all other histories, embraces the whole of what constitute life itself : economic, social, intellectual, religious, and aesthetic as well as political and military. I have endeavored to make my discussions as accurate and balanced as possible in terms of their total composition. While the method of truth-telling is yet to be developed, I have taken full advantage of the interdisciplinary approach for my purpose.

For transcribing Korean words and names, I have made use of the McCune-Reischauer system of romanization as best as I could and for Chinese and Japanese the Wade-Giles and Hepburn systems, respectively.

The bibliographical basis of the book is works published mostly in Seoul ; it is with my greatest indebtedness to their authors and publishers that I have listed those works at the end of the book. I am also greatly indebted to various friends, colleagues, and other scholars in the field for their valuable corrections and textual comments. My special thanks go to the following professors.

Byung Chul Kim, Yong Duk Kim and Kwang U Nam of Chung Ang University; Won Young Kim, Sung Nyung Lee, Jae Sup Byun, Byoung Do Lee and Woo Keon Han of Seoul National University; Dong Uk Kim and Paw Key Sohn of Younsei University; Chun Yop Kim, Ki Chun Cho and Song Ui Park of Korea University; Sun Ken Lee, Kye Hyon Ahn and Yo In Song of Dongguk University; Hong Sop Chin of Ehwa Womens University; Yu Song Lee and Hong Nyol Yu of Sunggyungwan Uniersity; and Hae Chong Chun of Sogang University.

I am also deeply indebted to the members of the staff of the Chung Ang University Library, Sunggyungwan University Library, and Seoul National University Library for their unfailing help and conveniences accorded to me during the research period.

Wanne J. Joe
Chung Ang Universtiy
Seoul, Korea

PREFACE

THE REVISED EDITION

The passage of two decades calls for a revised edition of *Traditional Korea : A Cultural History,* and the temptation to alter the main text has been resisted. This new edition suggests a few comments and reflections.

A few changes have been made in format and some new material has been added. In the listing of chapters, the titles of those which were designed to supply information about the history of thought and of the instruments of culture have now been revised. The master plan of the work may thus be seen more clearly, it is hoped, as a cultural history of Korea rather than as a merely factual history. The view of history as the aesthetic expression of the general culture of a people in a given time and place was, from the start, an axiom in the thinking of the editor. Rejecting the theory that history of any kind is merely a chronological record of objective facts, the editor adopted an organic view of culture as the record of human experience and of its history as the portrait of a people, designed from the curves of its cultural cycles and the colors of its rich and unique life.

I have endeavored to follow the original text as closely as possible, and at the same time to present the living union of diction and thought. To aid the understanding of the reader, this edition includes the addition of many new pictures and illustrations. It is my wish that this book will help the reader understand traditional Korean culture and history and serve as a reference for students and scholars who are concerned with Korean studies. I especially wish to thank Executive Vice President Ham Ki-man and his staff at the Hollym Publishers in Seoul., Korea.

Hongkyu A. Choe
Professor of Humanities
Chung Ang University
Seoul, Korea
September 1997

INTRODUCTION

Traditional Korea : A Cultural History examines the history of Korean civilization. It ranges over the whole context of cultural, intellectual, religious, economic and political aspects. The author, the late Prof. Wanne J. Joe at Chung Ang University endeavored to make his dicussions as accurate and balanced as possible in terms of historical integrity. Prof. Joe's method is inter-disciplinary, with greater emphasis on certain significant individuals, events, and areas of discussions which are most essential to the understanding of the Korean culture. He takes into account as many aspects of it as possible and synthesizes them into this book.

The book consists of eight chapters covering from the beginning of early Korea through the latter Yi Dynasty of the 19th century. It presents innova-tive scholarship and commentary that looks critically at the past and its history from a non-sectarian perspective. It is a unique combination of a descriptive core of information and a thorough examination of the development of con-servatism and nationalism in Korea. It contains a thorough discussion of our historical past and continues to develop the historical themes throughout the text, covering all of the key areas in history.

The author shows us through the faculty of understanding an appendage to the faculty of acting, a more complex and supple adaptation of the con-sciousness of historical beings to the conditions of existence that are made for them. In this book we would indeed feel that no single one of the categories of our history—unity, multiplicity, mechanical casuality, intelligent finality, etc.— totally encapsulates our history.

Throughout our history certain powers reside that are complementary to our understanding, powers of which we have only an indistinct feeling when we remain shut up in ourselves, but which become clear and distinct when we read this book. We will thus learn in what direction we must intensify or expand our research.

A theory of history that is not accompanied by a criticism of culture is obliged to accept culture as it stands. It is necessary that history and culture join each other in a circular, synergetic process. Thogether they may prove to be a method more sure, bringing the great problems that history poses nearer to experience. For, if they should succeed in their common enterprise, they would show us the formation of the intellect, and thereby the genesis of that matter of which our history traces its general configuration.

Like Korea's phenomenal upsurge in the economic field over the last few decades, the increasing interest in the Korean tradition and culture, which has already resulted in a tremendous volume of scholarly output, is an academic phenomenon of rare proportions. The widened horizon of Korean studies includes a large amount of multi-dimensional materials which the customary approach of established disciplines may find themselves inadequate to deal with in attempting to present a whole picture.

This book is is an attempt at the study of the total culture of Korea as patterns of interrelated experiences by applying the disciplines of history, literature, art, philosophy, and social sciences. As a history, it contains refreshing, new perspectives and interpretations based on scholarly research in a wide range of fields, combined with a presentation which sustains the reader throughout.

For important and varied reasons, the investigations of Korean culture as a viable discipline urgently needs new perspectives and analyses and confidence in the bright future. In terms of these needs, the book is a landmark the kind of which has never appeared before in Korean studies.

Hongkyu A. Choe
Professor of Humanities
Chung Ang University
Seoul, Korea
September 1997

Contents

Buddhism in Koguryŏ and Paekche
Buddhism in Silla
Scholastic and Sectarian Buddhism

Koguryŏ Painting
Paekche Sculpture
Art in Silla

Part 4 *Disintegration and Re-Centralization*

The Royal Power
The Provincial Growth
The Foreign Trade

Social Changes
Sŏn Buddhism
The Theory of Wind and Water

Organs of the Central Government
Provincial and Military Organizations
Economic Policies

Part 5 *Society and Culture Under Koryŏ*

2. **The Nature of Koryŏ Aristocracy** ······························· 157

3. **Education and the Examination System** ······················· 159

4. **The Development of Buddhism** ································· 163

    The Unity Movement and Ŭich'ŏn

5. **Geomantic Theories and Politics** ······························· 168

6. **Pattern of International Dealings** ······························· 170

7. **Printing** ·· 175

8. **Literature** ·· 177

9. **Art** ··· 181

    Buddhist Art
    Ceramic Art

Part 6 *The Late Koryŏ Period*

2. **The Triumph of the Military in Government** ·················· 194

    Succession of Coups d'Etat
    The Government of the Ch'oe Family
    Social Unrest and Changes
    Mongol Invasions
    The Revolt of the Sambyŏlch'o

King Tangun. The father of Korea.
According to Tangun legend, he founded
'Old Korea' in B.C. 2333. The capital city
was Asadal. The Old Korea lasted for
2200 years.

Part 1

Early Korea

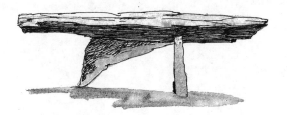

1
The Beginning

The Geographical Setting

The "importance" of the geographical location of Korea has often been spoken of. That "importance" being from the strategic point of view of contending continental and Pacific powers that surround the Peninsula, it is doubtful that the Korean people themselves have placed any appreciable value on their country's location, for it has been throughout their history a constant source of the national stress that at times amounted to tragic proportions. The important matter is to see how the Koreans have reacted to political and military problems arising primarily from the fact of Korea's geographical location.

The Korean Peninsula that projects about 600 miles from Manchuria toward "the heart of Japan" lies between 43° N. and 34° N. latitudinally and within the longitudinal limit of from 125° to 130°, thus roughly in the center of Northeast Asia. The rabbit-shaped Peninsula, about 85,285 square miles, bears a number of physical features which somehow make it distinguishable from the rest of the Northeast Asian land. Roughly corresponding with the rabbit's backbone, the T'aebaek Range stretches along the east coast with Mt. Paektu as the starting point. A series of associated mountain ranges, all branching out southwest from the T'aebaek Range toward the west coast, rib the rabbit, as it were. Between these mountain chains run rivers of varying lengths carrying the alluvial material from the uplands to form the lowland basins that make up most of the arable one-fifth of the Peninsula. The Yellow Sea, to the west, into which principal rivers empty, has an extensive continental shelf and the unusually-high tidal range of, at places, thirty feet, hence outstretched tidal flats and many offshore islands on the west coast. On the other hand, the Eastern Sea, also known as the Sea of Japan, is deeper, the continental shelf there ending rather bluntly, and has a tidal range of only a few feet yet few natural harbors. In sharp contrast to the east coast, the coast lines of the west and especially the south with a penchant for indentation delineate an endless sequence of beaches, bays, gulfs, promontories, minipeninsulas, etc. intermingling with innumerable offshore islands. And the generally moderate, humid, and monsoonal climate, strongly affected by continental as well as maritime influences, brings the most distinct seasonal weather with abundant precipitation in the summer months.

Since the Peninsula was initially peopled by immigrants from modern Manchuria and Central Asia, northern Korea holds a special place for the early cultures of Korea and even Japan. The land mass of northern Korea, covering provinces of P'yŏng'an and Hamgyŏng, is in many respects continental. Its forbidding, mountainous interior where the temperature ranges from an average of -6° F. in January to relatively warm 72° F. in July is linked geographically with Manchuria. Politically too, southeastern Manchuria was in fact Korean territory until the demise of Koguryŏ in the seventh century. The present-day natural boundary that Korea shares with China and Russia is demarked by the deeply-entrenched, meandering rivers, Amnok (Yalu) and

JANUARY AIR TEMPERATURE
(in degress Centigrade)

Tuman (Tumen), with Mt. Paektu, 9,000 feet in height, as their common source. The massive Mt. Paektu, literally White Head Mountain, embracing a crater lake at the summit surrounded by snow covered ridges, is the holiest of the mountains to the Koreans of the traditional period. Extending south and southwestward from the middle reaches of the Amnok River and the Mt. Paektu area, a series of ridges interlocking the major mountains of the northern interior divides the northwestern and northeastern regions; the provincial boundary between P'yŏng'an and Hamgyŏng is drawn along this natural divide. The northwestern region contains the two important river systems of the Ch'ŏngch'ŏn and the Taedong, and a few mountain ranges parallel them, trending from the interior region. It was on those fertile plains created by the two rivers where the earliest historic settlements occurred. Settlements in the northeastern region in historic times, however, were along the narrow strip of coastal plain east of the mountain escarpments which are favored by the moderating maritime influence. Isolated from the rest of the country by the interior mountain stretch whose southern tip chokes the rabbit's neck, this sparsely populated region, with a relatively large basin around Wŏnsan, had tended to form a self-sufficient economic and cultural unit up until modern times.

Central and southern Korea shows a notable difference in both climate and terrain from the north. Mountains and ranges are not so forbidding and well-defined as in the northern interior. The T'aebaek Range, complex masses of hills and mountains which contain most of the mineral resources of southern Korea, subsides at the rabbit's tail. It has a branch trending southwest and culminating in the Mt. Chiri massif, that is, the Sobaek Range which provides the backdrop to southwestern Korea. And fortunately the central and southern Peninsula, except a few high level inland areas, is favored with a mild climate which makes winter cropping possible. The average January temperatures at Seoul and Pusan are $24°$ F. and $35.6°$ F., respectively, whereas at P'yŏngyang it is a little above $17°$ F.; nor is the cold season in southern Korea longer in duration.

As in the northeastern region, the abrupt eastern escarpments of the T'aebaek Range physiographically sets off a narrow strip of the east central coastal plain, most of Kangwŏn Province, which, if not of agricultural potential, offers an impressive landscape quite different from those of the rest of the Peninsula. The most agriculturally productive regions of the whole country are plains in the west central, southwestern, and southeastern regions. On the gradual slope extending toward the west coast from the T'aebaek and Soback Ranges, covering the entire west central and southwestern part of the Peninsula, run several drainage systems which have built extensive alluvial plains in these regions. The Han River basin, where Seoul, Kaesŏng, and Kanghwa Island are situated, has been the political and cultural center of the country for centuries, and its importance is even more pronounced today. The agricultural plains irrigated by the Kŭm, the Sŏmjin, and other lesser river systems in the provinces of South Ch'ungch'ŏng and Chŏlla, blessed with double cropping, are by far the most suited to agriculture and rightly regarded as the granaries of Korea.

The southeastern region drained by the Naktong River is also agriculturally important. The region's terrain is characterized by hilly slopes which make it necessary to resort to dry or terraced farming more than in other regions. Somewhat isolated from the rest of the country by protective wings of the T'aebaek and Sobaek Ranges, the region that embraces the whole of Kyŏngsang Province, the territory of old Silla, has been a distinct political and cultural unit that tended to resist foreign influence. Of the innumerable offshore islands, the volcanic island of Cheju, about fifty miles off the southwestern coast, is the largest and warmest in the country. Having been a semi-independent state once in the remote past, it offers some interesting areas of cultural study, and of late, its economic potential is being explored. Some eighty miles off the eastern coast are Ullŏng Island and its tributary, the uninhabited island of Tokto which together provide maritime bases in the Eastern Sea today.

Cultural and physiographical diversity — regional diversity in culture as well as in terrain is a theme in Korean Studies which is intriguing when considered with special reference to the size of the country. If it is understood that the Koreans are a homogeneous people racially and culturally, the marginal cultural differences according to geographical localities can be relevantly studied. Comments have been made on the matter by scholars, notably since the Yi dynasty. The most graphic demonstration of the cultural difference is the existence of clearly discernible dialects corresponding with the traditional eight provinces and Cheju Island. Although the dialectal difference between Ch'ungch'ŏng Province and Kyŏnggi (Capital) Province whose tongue is made standard Korean is difficult to discern even to the Korean ear, the P'yŏng' an dialect, for instance, is not only pronouncedly different from that of the Kyŏngasang people but also from the neighboring one of Hamgyŏng Province. The same thing can be said of the difference between the dialects of Kyŏngsang and Chŏlla provinces, which are divided only by the breadth of the Sŏmjin River. Cultural differences in general are being eroded rapidly now through the vigorous governmental modernization programs.*

The physiographical diversity of the Peninsula, which is undoubtedly the principal cause for the cultural one, is even more striking. The rugged topog-

---

* The cold problem in this connection is the one arising from the artificial division of the country. The deepening cultural gap between the democratic South and the Communist North may eventually become the stumbling block toward unification of the country.

raphy of the Peninsula is not the product of a single geologic action but of many and confused catastrophic movements in different directions, levels, times, and places resulting in extremely variegated structural deformation. Terrain characteristics, which vary almost from district to district in some regions, consist of a tremendous variety of features. Upthrown, then eroded blocks, welled-up lava sheets, metamorphosed limestones and shattered granite in contorted earth folds, superimposed faults, narrow valleys, and sharp divides are covered by the equally diverse fauna and flora distributed in vertical and directional zonation. And deeply entrenched rivers and streams wind leisurely around these physical features.

Startled at the poetic surprisingness of their land, the Koreans fittingly describe it as "the embroidered tapestry of three thousand ri," † which is, however, only one dimensional description. While they became more and more intimately related with wonders and failures of nature, especially in connection with agriculture, the early Koreans, it is interesting to note, also came to think of certain mysterious forces, if not geologic forces, as existing underground, which created "the embroidered tapestry." They developed elaborate theories on these mysterious, subterranean forces, which we shall discuss again later. Thus the natural forces above and below, as the economic and religious life of the early Koreans became inextricably involved with these forces, came to profoundly permeate the Korean culture during the traditional period.

Paleolithic Life

Paleolithic Korea is still in the developmental stage. Until recently, little Paleolithic life was thought to have existed in the Korean Peninsula, but a series of scientific excavations since 1964 have brought up under the sun again hundreds of thousands of Paleolithic tools and other evidences, including human hair and boulders on which pictures, a harpoon, etc., were carved. A piece of charcoal from a site in the Kongju area of Ch'ungch'ŏng Province, measured by the carbon 14 method, was found to be 30,690 years old. As a number of new excavation sites are proposed, the study of Paleolithic Korea seems to have a bright future.*

---

† A ri is about 1/4 mile.

* The Yonsei University excavation team under Professor Pow Key Sohn has been most active in this field.

Neolithic Life : *Chŏlmun Pottery People*

The first major Neolithic culture in the Peninsula, known as the Chŏlmun or Comb-Marked Pottery culture, is conjectured to have appeared in the third millennium B. C. The Chŏlmun people have left relatively abundant remains, among which the most representative are "comb-marked" pots. This pottery, hand-made of fine dirt mixed with mica and asbestos, usually has an egg-shaped or narrower bottom and occasionally, in later phases, a handle. The upper half of its surface is decorated with a series of short parallel lines and dots marked by something like a comb, hence the name "comb-marked." This type is closely related in design to pottery found in northern Europe and Siberia.

Distribution of these pots and other stone implements shows that the Chŏlmun people lived in coastal zones and along rivers, and it is interesting to note that the remains found in the northeastern coastal zone are cruder : the people there were the last to emerge from the Stone Age. The Chŏlmun people in general seem to have eked out their livelihood mainly from fishing and hunting. They dwelt in caves or more often in round or square sunken pits with thatched roofs clustered together in small groups. Inside they enjoyed the fireplace. In later stages, they produced such refined necessaties of life as stone sickles, bone needles, saddle querns, stone ploughshares, spindles, etc. They certainly knew how to knit and weave, and they wore crude clothes made of hemp and decorated with trinkets. At least in the last stage of their culture, these Neolithic people knew of agriculture : evidence shows that they ate, among other things, grains of some kind of millet. And immigration of North Asian people into the Peninsula seems to have occurred from Neolithic times or even before, Mongols and Tungus being the major racial stocks that peopled the Korean Peninsula and partly the Japanese islands.

Geometric design pottery, Neolithic Age;
from excavations at Amsa-dong, Seoul.

Bronze Culture : Mumun Pottery People

In the early first millennium B. C., a new wave of cultural development based on bronze and agriculture occurred. The introduction of the new ingredients was clearly from the north : bronze works found in the northwestern region show a linkage with those of the Tagar culture centering around Minusinsk in Siberia. The new cultural wave, which seems to have originated on the Peninsula in modern North P'yŏng'an Province, soon assimilated the Chŏlmun culture and started the Yayoi culture in western Japan. The dominant type of pottery for the new culture, known as Mumun culture, is the one that lacks the surface design, hence *mumun*, or literally no design. The Mumun pottery in general was shaped simply by fumbling fingers, but it was made convenient to handle. It shows considerable freedom in shape and size, indicating versatility as well as many sources of influence. The Mumun pottery has been found widely distributed, with major concentration in hilly areas, unlike the Cholmun pottery. Coexisting in this period with the Mumun pottery was the Hongdo or Red pottery which has been found in modern Hamgyŏng Province. This pretty pottery is painted with oxidized iron and polished to a shine with pebblestones.

The bronze implements found so far, largely weapons and vessels, have been brought up in P'yŏng'an Province and to a lesser degree in the southern part of the Peninsula. Bronze weapons might have been used for hunting as well as in war against the Chŏlmun people. Much more abundantly found relics of the Mumun culture are a variety of polished stone and bone works, of which farming tools such as the stepped adze and the stone knife in the shape of a half moon show Chinese origin. Although their racial composition is not clear, the Mumun people were beneficiaries of the Scytho-Siberian culture of the north and the agricultural culture of North China. By the time that the great wave of iron culture from China reached Korea around the fourth century B. C., the Mumun people not only cast bronze wares themselves but also became better versed in rice cultivation. It is apparent that such a society must have developed a high degree of political organization.

The rulers of this society have been credited with the construction of huge tombs, namely, dolmens. A dolmen consists of two parts : chamber and protective roof. On the top of the square chamber which is assembled with four or more large stone slabs, a huge flat stone is placed like the lid over a square bowl. Lid stones, in many cases, are as large as ten meters in length. Construction of these structures and transportation of such large pieces over a long distance must have required a great number of workers, who were themselves content with cists and urns. Dolmens, usually in groups, are concentrated notably in the northwestern parts of the Peninsula. Some groups, arranged in a vaguely discernible pattern of forty or fifty dolmens, give out an air of certain mysterious and barbaric grandeur, suggesting that the Mumun people's was an aristocratic society. As this method of tomb building spread toward the south and on to Japan, it became considerably modified, and there its use extended well into the historic period and in Japan even later.

Most of the Mumun people were, however, users of stone implements, and they lived in the sunken pits and thatched dwellings of the Chŏlmun people, though with much improvement. The depth of the pit became shallower, and more frequently it had a heating system, probably the prototype of the present day *ondol,* or hot floor. The Mumun people, whose life now seemed to have become more sedentary, built houses in hilly areas clustered together in hamlets and villages. A Mumun village was one big family related in blood which, as the evidence strongly suggests, seemed under a matriarchal head at least in earlier times. As the farming, religious worship, and recreational sports, all strictly group activities of the village, expanded in tribal scope, the patriarchal leadership inevitably emerged and ultimately yielded its allegiance to a tribal authority or leader who might well have been hereditary. It must have been these tribal leaders who were buried in the dolmens. And there seem to have been among these tribes certain vaguely defined systems of exchange of goods and intermarriage.

Religious belief was at first primitive animism which in time became a mixture of demonology and nature worship, the basis from which Shamanism was to be developed through the introduction of magic later. The Mumun people believed in spirits, both benevolent and malignant, that filled the unseen world. They considered large trees and rocks to be dwelling places of these spirits and unfathomable phenomena of nature to be workings of deities. The sun and ancestral spirits were universally worshipped as benefactors of the living, as could be seen in genetic legends.

2

The Early States

Korea's Bronze Age seems to have been rather brief, with its peak covering about two hundred years from the sixth century B.C. The Iron Age that followed in Korea is largely the result of the Chinese influence that was markedly felt from about the fourth century B.C., even though Scytho-Siberian bronze wares continued to cross the Amnok(Yalu) River. The century-old, hegemonic struggle between the nomadic Hsiung-nu and the sedentary Chinese, that came to a climax in favor of the latter around the second century B.C., seems to have helped the influx of the two cultures into Korea. It is interesting to note that the bronze and iron wares seem to have been first received by early Koguryŏ tribes before making their way across the Amnok River at its middle reaches into the fertile plains irrigated by the Ch'ŏngch'ŏn and Taedong Rivers in modern P'yŏng'an Province, the cultural heartland of early Korea.

Of the ironwares from China, the most important were farming implements which, probably of southern Chinese origin, advanced the peninsular agriculture to a new high ; use of domesticated animals in the period is also evident. The general improvement of economy is indicated by abundant remains of the knife money of Yen, a small state in North China, which point to the existence then of quite intensive trade with that area. Of the metal remains which Koreans cast for themselves, however, those of Scytho-Siberian origin in design are more abundant than those of Chinese derivation : bronze daggers, *tongt'aek* (*tŏtaku* in Japanese), bronze mirrors, etc., unquestionably of nomadic derivation, are more conspicuous items among the relics of this period. And also improvements in this period in housing and horse equipment were to leave permanent marks on Korean folk art.

The resplendently-decorated, horse riding warrior was the undisputed master of the Iron Age society which vigorously assimilated the two major foreign cultures of the period. As military and economic consolidation on a larger scale necessitated political reorganization, several tribes in some areas organized themselves into loosely formed federations and in others tribal states with kings who might have been either hereditary or elective. In southern Korea, however, the life that was characteristic of the Neolithic and Mesolithic periods persisted much longer ; the flow of cultural influence up to the sixth century A.D. was constantly from the north to the south and to western Japan.

The Tan'gun Legend and Old Chosŏn

Formation of tribal states produced in its wake a series of genetic legends, of which the most important is the story of Tan'gun. In the *Ancient Record*, it states :

In olden times, there was Hwan Ung, a son of Hwan In, the celestial being. Hwan Ung always desired for earthly power with a view to governing human society. The father, knowing his son's intention, looked down at Mt. T'aebaek, one of three high mountains and trusted that *the mankind is worthy of wide benefits*. Thereupon, he gave his son three talismanic seals and let him go. Hwan Ung, leading three thousand followers, descended to under the trees around the holy altar on the top of Mt. T'aebaek(or Mt. Myohyang) and called the place the Holy City. Commanding the Lord of Wind, the Master of Rain, and the Master of Cloud, he attended to the planting of grains, the regulation of life, sickness, and punishment and judged good and evil. Thus, directing more than three hundred and sixty affairs, he civilized human society and regulated the workings of nature.

At this time, there lived together in a cave a bear and a tiger who always prayed to God Ung that they might be transformed into human beings. Ung casually gave them a stalk of miraculous wormwood and twenty cloves of garlic. He instructed them to eat those and to shun the sunlight for one hundred days ; then, they would acquire human form. The bear and the tiger took and ate them and sat in retreat for three times seven days. The bear acquired the body of a woman, but the tiger, unable to shun(the sunlight), failed to obtain a human body. Since the bear-woman could find no one to marry, she again prayed under the trees around the altar that she might be with young ; thereupon, Ung changed his form and married her. She became pregnant and bore a son, and his name was Tan'gun Wanggŏm. In the fiftieth year after Yao ascended the throne (of China), (that is, 2333

B.C.,] Tan'gun Wanggŏm established his capital at P'yŏngyang and called his kingdom Chosŏn [or Morning Freshness]. He ruled Chosŏn for one thousand five hundred years.*

So goes the foundation legend of Korea. The legend of Tan'gun Wanggŏm, which is noticeably of North Asian type, is thought to have been created by a theocratic tribe whose totemic symbol was bear. The name Tan'gun Wanggŏm, analyzed etymologically, is a combination of two words : Tan'gun denotes sacerdotal head and Wanggŏm is the appellation for secular, political leader. Thus Tan'gun may be regarded as the head of the bear tribe in the theocratic period or in prehistoric times, in whom these two functions were vested.

It is worth noting that, in various other foundation legends also, the marriage of celestial and mundane elements, the light, and, as in those of Koguryŏ and Silla, a large egg are brought in to play essential roles in the mythological makeup. By the time the foundation legends, which had been handed down in written form and orally, were re-collected in the *Samguk yusa* or *Memorabilia of the Three Kingdoms* written in the early 1280's by a Buddhist monk, Iryŏn(1206-1289), they had been seasoned with Buddhist, Taoist, and Confucian sauces ; this is especially true with the Tan'gun legend. Because Tan'gun Wanggŏm's Chosŏn is believed to have been the first kingdom in the Peninsula, roughly covering modern P'yŏng'an Province, the region which is indeed the cradleland of ancient Korean culture, it was the Tan'gun legend that gained national currency as *the* genetic story of Korea, and its contents centering around such ideals as, "the mankind is worthy of wide benefits," have been given much philosophical elaboration.

Tan'gun's legendary Chosŏn extends into historic times around the fourth century B.C. when its territory expanded to southern Manchuria up to the Liao River, sharing common boundaries with Yen, one of the "warring states" in North China. This enlarged, historic state, which seems to have grown out of a tribal state, is called Old Chosŏn, probably as against the Chosŏn that Yi Sŏng Kye, the first king of the Yi dynasty, founded in 1392. The king of Old Chosŏn seems to have had some serious border problems with Yen and planned on sending an expeditionary force against Yen. The plan, which was somewhat reckless considering Old Chosŏn's only recent adoption of ironwares, was killed by Minister Ye. Apparently pressed by the threat posed by Old Chosŏn, Yen moved to strike first and incorporated most of Old Chosŏn's western territory ; accordingly, Old Chosŏn shrank to the

---

* The Tan'gun legend is recorded in Monk Iryŏns's *Memorabilia of the Three Kingdoms*. The *Ancient Record* from which the legend was quoted in the *Memorabilia* is not extant. It may be just an ancient record, instead of being a book.

territory south of the Amnok River. Ch'in, that unified China in 221 B.C., pushed Old Chosŏn's western border even further inside the Peninsula, probably as far as the Taedong River. When Ch'in was displaced by the Han in 207 B.C., Han Kao Tzu, who briefly revived the feudal system, placed the old Yen territory under one of his old friends, Lu Kuan. But soon learning of Han Kao Tzu's intention to purge him, Lu Kuan fled into the Hsiung-nu country, leaving his principality to be occupied by Han Kao Tzu's troops. Thus the chaotic conditions which were created in Old Chosŏn's immediate neighbor by incessant wars and political changes since China's Warring States period sent a steady flow of refugees and adventurers into the Peninsula looking for new opportunity.

Wiman Chosŏn

Among the groups of latest refugees was one led by Wiman, a Korean who probably had been in Lu Kuan's service. With his group of more than 1,000, the politically astute Wiman induced King Chun of Old Chosŏn to appoint him to a military post responsible for the defense of the northwestern border. There he organized the stream of refugees into his own power base from which to eventually launch a surprise attack upon the court of King Chun. He usurped the throne sometime between 194 and 180 B.C. King Chun fled south to Chin'guk, a loose tribal federation south of the Han River.

The power structure of Old Chosŏn under Wiman, or Wiman Chosŏn, seems to have been a confederation of local tribal powers. Leaders of these tribal groups, some of whom were still of dolmen building society, were appointed to governmental posts and local commanderies according to their actual economic and numerical strengths. The Wiman court was immediately recognized by the Han on the condition that King Wiman keep local tribal groups along the Han border from engaging in predatory activities but not hinder them from trading with the Han. In return, Wiman received military support from the Han with which he consolidated surrounding tribal states into his rule which soon extended over the territory north of the Han River. By the late second century B.C., Wiman Chosŏn was a cocky state. King Ugŏ, Wiman's grandson, welcomed refugee-immigrants by providing political protection against the Han, while intent upon a middleman's profits he interfered with tribute missions to the Han court from Chin'guk and others. He also seems to have had control over parts of southern Manchuria.

Han naturally became apprehensive of Ugŏ's hostile policy which might develop into Wiman Chosŏn's alliance with the Hsiung-nu. About this time,

Ye, a tribal federation strategically located north of the middle reaches of the Amnok River through which, as we have seen, bronze and ironwares seeped toward Old Chosŏn, became prosperous to such an extent that it embraced a population of "two hundred and eighty thousand households." Ye's King Namnyŏ, probably vexed with King Ugŏ's interference, voluntarily surrendered to the Han in 128 B.C. Han welcomed this move and set up a commandery in Ye to check Ugŏ's expansion, but the Han was forced to abandon this outpost in a few years largely because of difficulties in road construction. It was also from this international tension resulting from Ugŏ's expansionist policy that Yŏkkyegyŏng, one of Ugŏ's ministers, fled south into Chin'guk with his tribal followers of 2,000 households.

Han reached its apogee of power under Wu Ti (Martial Emperor) who ruled from 141 to 87 B.C. Throughout his long reign, Han Wu Ti pursued his policy of expansion with such an unremitting tenacity that his wars of conquest lasted for decades even after his death. His major military campaigns were concentrated against the Hsiung-nu ; consequently, the Hsiung-nu territory over the vast steppes and deserts north of the Great Wall was incorporated into Han. As part of the strategy of these campaigns, Han Wu Ti chose to strike recalcitrant Wiman Chosŏn in order to outflank the Hsiung-nu. One of Wu Ti's emissaries to King Ugŏ's court, probably frustrated in his pretext-seeking peace mission, assassinated a Korean officer at the border on his way back, and he was in turn killed by a Korean retaliatory expedition sent to his headquarters in Liaotung. In 109 B.C., Han's expedition, consisting of about 50,000, hit Ugŏ's capital P'yŏngyang in a pincers attack with a contingent dispatched across the Yellow Sea from the Shantung Peninsula and the other marched overland through southern Manchuria. The confrontation soon ran into a stalemate which lasted for a year with intermittent battles and attempts at negotiation. In the end it was the enemy within that undid Wiman Chosŏn. King Ugŏ was assassinated by one of the ministers who advocated peace. But Minister Sŏnggi alone, urging on his exhausted troops, fought to death. It was Korea's first test of nationhood in which it kept the world's largest empire at bay for a whole year. The price of the test was high enough : the most developed area of the Peninsula was made a Chinese colony for more than four centuries.

The Chinese Commanderies

In 108 B.C., the year Wiman Chosŏn collapsed, Han Wu Ti set up four commanderies that administered Wiman Chosŏn proper and the tribal areas formerly under Wiman Chosŏn's control. It soon became clear that the military-backed Chinese colony, purporting to be a military outpost against the

KOREA IN THE FIRST CENTURY A. D.

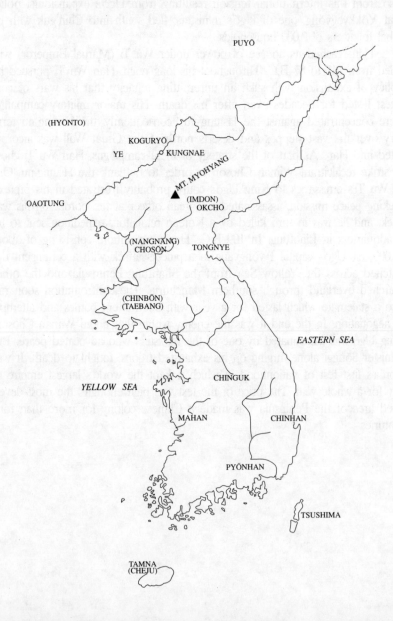

PUYŎ

(HYŎNTO)

KOGURYŎ

YE   ○KUNGNAE

MT. MYOHYANG

OAOTUNG

(IMDON)
OKCHŎ

(NANGNANG)
CHOSŎN   TONGNYE

(CHINBŎN)
(TAEBANG)

EASTERN SEA

CHINGUK

YELLOW SEA

MAHAN   CHINHAN

PYŎNHAN

TSUSHIMA

TAMNA
(CHEJU)

Hsiung-nu, now turned to be a military output against the Hsiung-nu, now turned to the economic exploitation of the native societies. The commercial traffic between China and Korea financed by the Chinese since the Yen times had been heavy indeed. Reviving this trade, the Chinese turned the colony in this remote but strategic location into a commercial outpost whose influence encompassed southern Korea and Japan. They embarked upon commercial ventures with zeal and skill, while undermining the political development of the peninsular societies.

Four Chinese commanderies, each subdivided into a number of prefectures, covered the northern half of the Peninsula : Lo-lang(Nangnang in Korean) Commandery embraced most of the former territory of Wiman Chosŏn ; Chen-p'an (Chinbŏn in Korean), modern Hwanghae ; Lin-t'uen (Imdun), modern South Hamgyŏng Province ; and Hsuan-t'u(Hyŏnt'o), the eastern half of North P'yŏng'an Province and the T'ung-chia(Tongga in Korean) River basin in Manchuria. Of the four the Nangnang Commandery was the political and economic center as this area was before. The Chinese seem to have gone to great lengths to secure the political stability of this region. They uprooted local political organizations, thus creating an exodus of people into the south where refugee-immigrants stimulated political and social development there. The Chinbŏn Commandery to the south served as a buffer zone between the Nangnang and Chin'guk. Another commandery whose importance was second only to Nangnang was Hyŏnt'o strategically situated straddling the middle reaches of the Amnok River ; this region was the link between Liaotung and Nangnang for the Chinese, but it was also the country where the fast-growing Koguryŏ people were wringing regional hegemony from the Yemaek people. The Imdun Commandery, facing the Eastern Sea with Wŏnsan as its center, was the eastern terminal for Chinese merchants. Its local societies were the most underdeveloped and later were subjected to the political control by Koguryŏ. Chinbŏn and Imdun, because of their unimportant geographical locations and negligible economic potential, were made subservient to Nangnang and Hyŏnt'o, respectively. These inter-commandery relations obviously reflected the relationships of the local tribal states and federations of the pre-Han commandery period.

In the face of growing native hostility, however, the Chinese were forced to make a series of organizational changes in the commanderies. In 82 B.C., Chinbŏn and Imdun were disestablished, and their important prefectures were re-attached to the nearest commanderies, Nangnang and Hyŏnt'o. In 75 B.C., the Hyŏnt'o Commandery itself had to be moved northwest to the Hŭng-gyŏng-Nosŏng (Hsing-king-Liao-ch'eng in Chinese) area, probably because Koguryŏ stepped up its hostility. In the early first century A.D., when the Later Han was still in political turmoil in the wake of Wang Mang's downfall, a native rebellion occurred in Nangnang. A local mighty named Wang Cho, having killed the Chinese viceroy of Nangnang, usurped the title and dictated to the Commandery until 30 A.D. when the newly-appointed Chinese commander suppressed the rebellion.

After this incident, he Chinese did away with all but seven of the prefectures around the periphery of the original Nangnang Commandery ; the discarded administrative units were then placed under local political leaders. In the north the Hyŏnt'o Commandery in the early second century A.D. had for the second time to be moved further north because of Koguryŏ's expansion under King T'aejo. In the south, Chin'guk, while absorbing the dislocated people from the Nangnang area, began pushing its boundaries northward around the middle of the second century A.D. The birth and growth of Paekche, which eventually displaced Chin'guk, was noteworthy in this period. During the late second century A.D., when the Later Han, reaching the end of its "dynastic circle," lapsed into the period of "rival military chiefs," Kung-suen Tu, the viceroy of Liaotung, achieved a degree of independent statehood. And he brought the Nangnang Commandery under his hegemony with a view to containing Koguryŏ, while creating a new commandery in the old Chinbŏn territory to check the flow of emigrants southward from Nangnang. But now without a centralized political authority comparable to the Han's, the Chinese colony as a military and commercial outpost declined in power and prestige. Finally, in 313 A.D., it was obliterated by the onslaught of Koguryŏ.

Koguryŏ and Its Neighbors

Koguryŏ's recapture of the Old Chosŏn area was an important event for the ambitious tribal state which was destined to become a great empire in few centuries. It should be noted that Koguryŏ's location in the Tongga (T'ung-chia in Chinese) River basin in Manchuria just north of the middle reaches of the Amnok River was the same region through which the Neolithic culture passed into the Ch'ŏngch'ŏn and Taedong River basins, and it was also the birthplace of one of the earliest tribal federations, namely, the Ye of "two hundred and eighty thousand households" which existed in the second century B.C. Although Koguryŏ enjoyed cultural stimulation from various sources, it lacked productive land. To secure food which they had to seek from elsewhere, Koguryŏ chose war rather than diplomacy. Its ruling class, like nomadic warriors in Central Asia, regimented themselves into military groups – usually five – in peace as well as in war. The victory in war, which was to them a means of production, indeed brought land, labor force or prisoners, and other spoils of war.

Puyŏ, Koguryŏ's northern neighbor, from which Koguryŏ seems to have stemmed, was agricultural, however. The Puyŏ people, of about "eighty thousand households," lived on arable land and pastures on the plains drained by the upper reaches of the Sungari River with probably Ning-an(Nong'an in Korean) as its political center. Beset by hostility from surrounding seminomadic Hsien-pei and Hsiung-nu tribes and even of Koguryŏ to the south, the Puyŏ formed a close relationship with China. And China in turn used the Puyŏ for "playing one barbarian off against another," the traditional Chinese foreign policy motto which they more skillfully pursued in this early period. In the northeastern region of the Peninsula, which later became the territory of the Imdun Commandery, there were two tribal groups of the same racial strain as the Koguryŏans. Tongnye was located over the southern part of modern South Hamgyŏng Province around Wŏnsan, and the Okchŏ society covered the rest of that province. These two peoples, though stout and hardworking, were politically underdeveloped largely due to geographical isolation and, therefore, susceptible to foreign exploitation, notably by Koguryŏ later.

By the very early first century A.D., Koguryŏ, a tribal federation comprised of five tribes, probably had an elected king, a mark of Koguryŏ's growth as a state. Wang Mang of Hsin, shortly after his usurpation of the Han throne in 8 A.D., distributed customary official seals as a token of China's alleged overlordship over "barbarian" states ; Koguryŏ was not strong enough yet to refuse the seal. A few years later, Wang Mang, unable to finance his military operations against the Hsiung-nu, ordered Koguryŏ to mobilize its troops as part of Hsin's punitive expedition against that country. Koguryŏ did send some troops, but taking advantage of Hsin's military weakness they sacked some of Hsin's border towns instead. Enraged Wang Mang could do nothing more than to proclaim that Koguryŏ would be thenceforth called Haguryŏ (or Low-guryŏ rater than Koguryŏ or High-guryŏ).

Koguryŏ seems to have come of age, in many respects, under King T'aejo or Grand progenitor (53-ca. 121 A.D.) with whom Koguryŏ's kingship became hereditary and political authority more centralized. Koguryŏ was now ready to strike outward toward the great river basins of the Liao to the west, the Sungari to the north, and the Ch'ŏngch'ŏn and the Taedong to the south, and to the coastal areas of Tongnye and Okchŏ to the southeast.

King T'aejo often clashed with the Chinese commanderies of Liaotung and Hsuan-t'u (Hyŏnt'o) ; the latter, constantly harassed by Koguryŏ assaults, was moved further north for the second time. T'aejo subjected Okchŏ to Koguryŏ's control and pressed south toward the Ch'ŏngch'ŏn River basin. The Later Han, apprehensive of Koguryŏ's expansiveness, anxiously played Hsien-pei tribes and Puyŏ against it. Presently, in 136 A.D., the king of Puyŏ himself visited Loyang, the capital of the Later Han and was lavishly entertained. In the declining years of the Later Han, Kung-suen Tu, the viceroy of the Liaotung Commandery who became a quasi-independent power in that area, formed an alliance with Puyŏ through marriage, and in 206 his son Kung-suen K'ang set up the T'aebang Commandery in what was formerly the Chinbŏn territory.

During the reign of King Sansang(197-226) of Koguryŏ, the King's brother, Palgi fled with his followers to the Kung-suen family of Liaotung after failing in a power struggle. Koguryŏ, on the other hand, moved to form close relations with Wu and Wei, two of the three Chinese kingdoms that were destined to displace the Later Han in 219 ; Koguryŏ helped Wei with troops in its attempt to integrate the Liaotung area into its regime in 238. But when Wei brought the Nangnang Commandery under its control, thus expanding its border toward Koguryŏ, the old pattern of conflicts developed. In 242 Koguryŏ made the initial assault into Hsianp'ing, one of the strategic towns in Liaotung. In retaliation, Wei sacked Koguryŏ's capital Kungnae two years later, and in another expedition the next year the Wei force almost captured King Tongch'ŏn (227-247) of Koguryŏ who escaped into Okchŏ. Throughout these wars, Puyŏ sent provisions to Wei who had inherited the traditional alliance relations with Puyŏ from the Kung-suen family. Thus to be successful in struggles with China for occupation of the Old Chosŏn and other important regions, Koguryŏ was still to take more than a half century.

Puyŏ, through the alliance with whichever Chinese state occupied the Liaotung Peninsula, could indeed successfully protect itself from Koguryŏ's predatory excursions into its northern neighbor. It was, however, the semi-nomadic Hsien-pei that quite frequently delivered hard blows to Puyŏ and Koguryŏ as well in the late third century. In the disintegrating years, that is, from 290 on, of the Chin (265-317) that had briefly united China, taking the place of the three kingdoms, the "five barbarian" states of nomadic origin descended upon the agricultural Chinese and made the marches of North China a veritable "stage for survival of the fittest." The Hsien-pei, one of the "five barbarians," invaded Puyŏ in 285 and killed its king in the first of the series of blows that, lasting until 346, seriously weakened Puyŏ. Koguryŏ, while repelling the Hsien-pei incursions, was now determined to take advantage of the weakened Chin also, and in 311 it captured the prefecture of Hsianp'ing in Liaotung and took the Nangnang and T'aebang Commanderies in 313, thus putting an end to the four centuries of Chinese rule in northern Korea.

Koguryŏ's capture and possession of the Old Chosŏn area constituted the most important change in power configuration in the combined areas of the Peninsula and southern Manchuria for the next few centuries. Before Koguryŏ could fully avail itself of the newly-acquired productive land and better-developed social resources, however, it had to continue struggles for survival with the "barbarian" states of North China and fast-growing Paekche to the south which had as much territorial aspiration of its own. The Hsien-pei who had competed successfully with Koguryŏ for the prizes of the Hyŏnt'o and Liaotung areas since 293, now at the heyday of its power in the early fourth century, made its way eastward again. The Hsien-pei tribes were probably the most powerful and ruthless of the "five barbarians" that created sixteen kingdoms, each only of ephemeral duration, in North china in the fourth century.

In 342 the Mu-jung horde of the Hsien-pei, that was soon to found the Earlier Yen in the northeast of North China, attacked Koguryŏ and in the ensuing classical nomadic plunder reduced the capital to a garbage dump. The nomads burnt palaces and houses, looted ancestral treasures, desecrated royal tombs, and captured the king's mother as a hostage. Then, in 346, they turned for more to Puyŏ, now helpless because Chin (or Western Chin), its North Chinese ally, had long been engulfed by the "barbarian" inundation. In addition to the customary pillage, the invading Mu-jung tribe took the king and 50,000 people of Puyŏ as prisoners.

Koguryŏ kept peace with the Hsien-pei or the Earlier Yen until 370 when it ended its existence. While the Earlier Yen's successors generally held hegemony over the Liaotung area, Koguryŏ faced yet another enemy from the south. Paekche had been chipping off the Old Chosŏn area that Koguryŏ wrung from the Chinese. In 371, having tied Japan down to an alliance with itself, Paekche attacked Koguryŏ's southernmost stronghold at P'yŏngyang, from which Koguryŏ was expected to launch a southward thrust. In this critical battle Koguryŏ lost King Kogukwŏn, if not the city itself. Koguryŏ seemed to have fallen upon evil days.

Paekche and Its Neighbors

As the bronze culture of dolmen builders spread southward and transformed the Mumun society, there emerged in the area south of the Han River, around the second century B.C., a loosely organized tribal state called Chin'guk into which, as we have seen, luminaries of the north fled with their tribal followers. Although there is some evidence that Chin'guk seems to have exerted some sort of political authority over other tribal groups in the south, its coercive power was so tenuous that, by the early third century, it disappeared in the midst of social changes created by immigrant northern tribal groups carrying the iron culture. It should be noted that these northern tribal groups, uprooted by the impact of the rise and fall of Wiman Chosŏn and the Chinese commanderies there, were welcomed by the host society which, however, could not integrate them but instead, it seems, let itself disintegrate into a new political and social order ; this came to be called Sam Han or

Three Han, namely, Ma Han, Chin Han, and Pyŏn Han.

Ma Han, the largest of the three, covered modern Kyŏnggi, Ch'ungch'ŏng, and Chŏlla Provinces, which in the early third century contained fifty-four "countries." Chin Han held the eastern half of Kyŏngsang Province, conterminously sharing the Naktong River with Pyŏn Han which spread over the western half of that province. Each contained twelve "countries." A "country" was a tribal political group consisting of several thousand or less households, and some of these "countries" in many cases seem to have organized themselves into a tribal federation or "large country" embracing 10,000 or more households. These "countries," still retaining institutions reminiscent of the theocratic past, did not have kings as such but chiefs of various titles indicating the physical size and strength of their "countries." Social order was maintained by paternalistic customs and tribal taboos. They had not yet developed cities where the chief of the state might hold court ; instead he lived among his people. Although they had certain intertribal relations in terms of hegemonic order, these "countries" stood more or less by themselves, independent of one another. It seems that at a certain stage of political development toward a stronger statehood in these regions, the strong political influence from the Han colonies and elsewhere disrupted their normal developmental process. Indeed, this lack of the centralized authority, as we shall see later, can be attributable to the Chinese colonial policy pursued to that end.

As the Chinese influence was diminished with the decline of the Later Han, the Sam Han Koreans, especially the people in the Ma Han area immediately south of the modern Hwanghae area in which was located the Chinbŏn and later T'aebang commandery, began to show a political consciousness. Indicative of this incipient political growth was a clash with the Chinese in 246. Wei, one of the three kingdoms which ruled North China and also the colonies in northern Korea then, attempted an administrative realignment in the T'aebang. Backed by the army that had been back from an expedition through Koguryŏ and Tongnye, the Chinese partitioned the commandery so as to put the T'aebang-controlled eight local "countries" under the jurisdiction of the Nangnang Commandery. to the Korean point of view, this represented a "divide and rule" policy designed to undermine the growth of unified political power. Korean offence was not mitigated by an interpreter's error, the blunder traditionally held as the cause of the conflict. Noteworthy is not so much the intensity of the short-lived rebellion, in which the viceroy of the T'aebang was killed in action, as the scope of participation in it. "Several ten countries," that is, nearly the entire Korean population seems to have joined in the fight. Another measure of the Sam Han's political growth is the frequency with which many states in the area dispatched envoys directly to the Chin court, sidestepping Nangnang ; in the late third century the direct contact with China became routine for Sam Han.

From this background Paekche emerged in the fertile Han River basin as the most powerful state of Sam Han, and under the leadership of its eighth King Koi (234-285), Paekche rapidly consolidated surrounding tribes into an enterprising state. The tribe that founded Paekche is thought to have been made up of late first century B.C. refugees from Koguryŏ. Unlike Koguryŏ or Puyŏ whose statehood was based on the contractual cooperation of major tribes, Paekche, with its superior knowledge of government and technology, seems to have conquered neighboring tribes in its adopted land, the Han River basin. Its *sŏul* (or capital) was probably in the site of modern Seoul or the Kwangju area just south of Seoul. In many respects, Paekche was the most advanced of the early states, including even Koguryŏ. In the twenty-seventh year of his reign(260), King Koi set up six ministries and divided court ranks into sixteen grades. In the next year, the ceremonially-dressed King gave audience to the government officials and appointed five of the six ministers. In 262 King Koi promulgated a law that government officials found guilty of bribery and people of stealing would be subjected to confiscation of property three times the amount of the bribe received or things stolen and to forfeiture of the right to serve the government for the rest of their life.

Paekche, now a remarkably centralized state, expanded in all directions to control all of Ma Han, and by the early fourth century it encountered Koguryŏ in the old T'aebang territory. King Kŭnch'ogo (346-374), the great conqueror, brought Paekche to its height of territorial expansion over the entire western half of the southern part of the Peninsula, including the T'aebang. It was King Kŭnch'ogo who humiliated Koguryŏ in the battle of P'yŏngyang in 371 and extended diplomatic relations to Japan and the Eastern Chin, Western Chin's successor in South China.

Paekche's southeastern neighbors in Chin Han and Pyŏn Han in modern Kyŏngsang Province were also rounding out their territories. Silla, which was destined to unify the entire Peninsula in the seventh century, was the most underdeveloped of the early states up until the fourth century. Silla's introduction to the iron culture was more than a century later than that of Koguryŏ and Paekche was. It started as a tribal federation-type group called Saro, one of the twelve "countries" of Chin Han in the eastern Kyŏngsang region. Saro consisted of six "villages" or tribes around the Kyŏngju area, of which three tribes, Sŏk, Pak, and Kim–the last two being the most common family names today–were the most powerful in the beginning. Leadership was provided by these three families alternately through the unanimous agreement of the six tribes. Through stages of organizational development not found in other early states, Silla emerged as a power and made appearance on the international scene under the leadership of Namul Maripkan (365-401) ; Maripkan was the designation for kingship which Namul made hereditary for the Kim family.

The international power relations which Silla now faced, however, were not conducive to the growth of the fledgling kingdom. Paekche, with its penchant for diplomacy, had aligned Japan and South China to its support and was bent on enlarging its territory at the expense of Silla as well as Koguryŏ and Kaya. Japan posed as serious a threat to Silla. It was under such circumstances that Silla turned for protection to Koguryŏ which, around 400, became a full-fledged military nation. Annoyed by Paekche encroachment on its southern border, Koguryŏ readily provided Silla with military support against Paekche and Japan.

Another federation-type state, Kaya, along the Naktong River between Silla and Paekche, was in geographical terms like Okchŏ and Tongnye in the north : it was hedged off by stronger states hampering its growth. But, unlike Okchŏ and Tongnye, Kaya was not a cultural backwater ; in fact, it seems to have been more developed than Silla in the beginning, as its cultural relics show. And it was a prosperous trade center which produced iron as the mainstay of its export from the second century B.C. on when the presence of the Chinese commanderies in northern Korea enhanced the importance of iron. Kaya's iron was exported by sea to Nangnang, Koguryŏ via Tongnye, and Japan.

Kaya's early cultural, if not military, advancement over the surrounding areas, including Japan's cultural cradle in northern Kyŏshŏ and the western tip of Honshú, is an interesting phenomenon which is also important for understanding the early history of Korean-Japanese relations. Kaya kept close trade and cultural ties with Nangnang, and Kaya's iron, in turn, was an important item for the Nangnang economy. Some household utensils of Nangnang economy. Some household utensils of Nangnang origin and other items of iron age technology among the Kaya relics attest to this. Kaya, occupying one of the most fertile plains of the Peninsula and with its direct sea access to Nangnang, forged ahead in such fields as agriculture, weaving, and pottery. Kaya's achievement in pottery is noteworthy : before the fourth century Kaya produced a distinctly new type of vessel, the hardness of which suggests the use of a tunnel kiln. Kaya pottery is known also as Kimhae pottery after its site, which was taken over and developed further by Silla later. It also seems to have been Kaya where Korean sculptural art was originated.

Probably even before the third century, Kaya eased itself out of Chin'guk control and organized a tribal federation, like early Silla, comprised of six tribes. The most powerful tribes, Pon Kaya situated in the modern Kimhae area at the mouth of the Naktong River and Tae Kaya in the Koryŏng area in northwestern Kyŏngsang Province, formed a kind of axis of the Kaya confederation. This political development in the Kaya area can be assumed to have antedated the similar developmental stage of Silla. It might just as well have been Kaya that absorbed Silla and Paekche. Despite its high degree of cultural attainment, however, Kaya had neglected the development of martial arts, a fact that proved to be tragic for Kaya. Long before it was conquered by Silla in 562, or even before King Kŭnch'ogo of Paekche, Kaya, much plagued by attacks by Silla and Paekche, seems to have either been occasionally helped by the Japanese or diverted the Japanese attack upon itself against its enemies, capitalizing on the Japanese position which was economically and culturally linked with it.

Many ingredients of the Japanese culture as well as people were transmitted through the Peninsula, particularly through Kaya. Kaya also provided Japan with iron, as has been noted, textile fabrics, grains, and ornamental stones. Research in comparative linguistics strongly suggests that the "mother land", or "root land" that appears in the old Japanese records was indeed the designation of place in the Kaya area, namely, Koryŏng, the capital of Tae kaya. Although the Japanese had had contact with China during their tribal period, the Peninsula remained the more immediate source of cultural and commercial inspiration until long after the formation of their statehood, as we shall see. It was, therefore, vitally important for the Japanese to maintain liaison with Korea, whose people, after all, manned many of their political and social institutions. It was for this reason that the Japanese did their utmost to keep closer relations with Kaya, even with arms which eventually proved harmful to Kaya and a constant threat to Silla.

Flying fairy, a Koguryŏ tomb mural, circa
6th-7th century A.D.

3

The Growth Process of Early States

Since the Neolithic times, a village, it can be reasonably assumed, was a consanguineous society which maintained close ties with a near-by village or villages as partners for economic exchange and intermarriage. Several villages or more, through such kinship relations, formed a larger political and social unit which is usually called a *sijok*, which was internally a group of different clans. Several *sijok* joined together in a still larger political group or *pujok* that can be translated appropriately as tribe. The leader of a *pujok* and, probably of *sijok* also, was hereditary from the beginning and responsible for both religious and political affairs of the society. Tan'gun seems to have been such a leader ; the early leaders of Silla and other tribal states were of the same nature. And the degree of internal development of *sijok* and *pujok* societies varied according to their locality. In Tongnye, when it developed into a *pujok* society in the early iron age, for instance, each *sijok*, still strongly independent, maintained its own sphere of life, and members of different *sijok* were not permitted to engage in productive activities within one another's border. Transgressors were liable for reparation. The *pujok* control, in whatever from, seems to have been very nebulous there.

When several or more *pujok*, were combined into a political arrangement or tribal federation, we have an incipient early state. In a tribal federation state, member tribes, assuming their physical strength to be equal to one another, were bound strictly by a contractual agreement as in Puyŏ, Koguryŏ, and Silla, Corollary to this is that a stronger *pujok* might conquer weaker neighbors as in the case of Paekche. The head of a tribal federation, who now at least partly renounced sacerdotal duties, was in the beginning elective, and later an elected leader of strong personality, as his federation expanded under his leadership, claimed hereditary kingship for his family.

The Ture. The *ture*, probably the earliest social organization, seems to have come into existence when agriculture replaced hunting as the dominant mode of life. Agriculture, not only in early times but also, more or less, throughout the traditional period, was a group activity. Although it is impossible to ascertain its precise organizational relations to the early clan-centered society, the *ture* seems to have provided a kind of organized labor force. And it might have also played the main role in other communal activities such as religious and recreational gatherings, which had an inseparable relation with agricultural life.

The Influence of the Han Commanderies

Once having established themselves firmly in northern Korea after the conquest of Wiman Chosŏn allegedly to outflank the Hsiung-nu, the Chinese veered from military to economic exploitation of the native societies, as already noted. In addition to salt and iron ore, the two monopoly items of the Han government, timber, agricultural produce, marine produce, and the native labor force were the main objects of Chinese exploitation. To secure the maximum economic gain, the Chinese, while assuming an attitude of meeting the Koreans halfway, inaugurated a series of political policies that were even in the modern eyes extemely sophisticated. They eschewed, whenever possible, the use of military means to suppress or destroy local political powers, but they chose instead to disintegrate them or to retard their further growth. With superior military means and taking advantage of the native desire for cultural contact, the Chinese tamed local political leaders through dispensing, on an individual basis, trade permits in the form of official titles and ranks and corresponding court attires and head gears which symbolized the vassalage to the Han empire. The Chinese conferred official titles upon even inspired individuals who had something to trade with the Chinese, thus preventing the Koreans from developing political and economic relations with one another, while collecting what they could from the native economy.

To keep the Koreans under control without resorting to the military might was to keep their colonies prosperous and splendid. No doubt, the Chinese were in the Peninsula to stay. They even dedicated a shrine to a native god in the Nangnang Commandery around 85 A.D. Each commandery was governed by a viceroy assisted by civil and military lieutenants. When all four commanderies were at their apogee, there were about forty to fifty prefectures. Nangnang, the pivotal one of the four, alone boasted a population of 400,000 at its peak prosperity. This figure, though which must have included the local populace, is indeed indicative of the Chinese colonial success. Traffic was heavy in trade and people, including ruffians and scholars, between China and Nangnang, the center that absorbed the commercial flow from the rest of Korea and Japan also.

Nangnang Commandery had its administrative capital near P'yŏngyang in a rather small but well-planned walled city with paved streets, the drainage system, and the cemetery. Among the Nangnang remains reminiscent of a golden age are an elaborate lacquer work, mirrors, and a gold filigree which surpasses in finesse the best of the contemporary Han works of the kind. Even a sheet of tile or a piece of brick was decorated with artistic designs or Chinese characters in ornamental calligraphy. Although for some of these artistic works found in Nangnang the continental provenance is difficult to be established, thereby indicating the possible participation of some native crafts-men in their production, it is equally difficult to claim them as part of the Korean heritage. At any rate, the historical significance of the Nangnang cul-ture is that it undoubtedly constituted the aesthetic gravity that kept a con-stant pull upon cultural aspirations of the contemporary Koreans and, to a lesser degree, the Japanese. The native yearning for contact with the Chinese culture was a great asset, greater than military power, to the Chinese control of the Koreans, which the Chinese fully exploited.

The devastating effect of the Chinese influence was more strongly felt among the relatively backward Sam Han societies. The leaders of large and small political groups from the Sam Han areas submitted to the Nangnang authorities in order to trade or to "get naturalized." Moreover, more than, 1,000 individuals from these areas received Chinese titles and investitures, or rather trade permits, along with local mighties. Under such circumstances political disintegration was almost inevitable, with the social changes immedi-ately following Chinese penetration reinforced by the technological advance of the Chinese. The easy access to the prosperous outpost of Han civilization brought coveted items of ironwares within the reach of Koreans even in the remote areas. The discovery of iron ore and the technique for smelting soon followed, resulting in the manufacturing of, among other things, farm imple-ments in greater number. As productive capacity led to the wider availability of improved farming methods and tools, individual families, rather than larger groups of *sijok* (clans), tended to become economic units. The emergence of *homin* or patriarchal heads of large families, with newly-acquired economic power in the second and third centuries, represented a notable change in political leadership, breaking up tightly-knit *sijok* societies, particularly in the regions where the Chinese political grip was strongest.

As has been noted, some states like Koguryŏ successfully resisted the malignant Chinese political manipulation, while importing Chinese goods and institutions with which to develop their own societies. The internal political development of Puyŏ that was far less influenced by the Chinese is of historical importance. As a state with a king, Puyŏ embraced many *pujok* (tribes) and *sijok* which together had households totalling "eighty thousands" living on an agricultural and pastoral economy of over "two thousand square ri" territory in northeastern Manchuria. A *pujok*, with the strength of about 10,000 households, was a recalcitrant political unit. The *pujok* seem to have more often than not reached decisions through brawls or even by force among themselves. The king's lot, even though he was allowed to live in a palace which included warehouses and a prison, was no better than that of a *pujok* leader. In the beginning he was elected by powerful *pujok* leaders and unseated or even sentenced to death when the country was hard hit by a natural disaster. * By the early third century, however, Puyŏ's kingship seems to have become hereditary, even though its power was still far short of being dictatorial. Five most powerful *pujok* divided the country into five provinces as administrative districts among themselves, and a fifth, as a kind of capital province in the center, was for the *pujok* that produced the king. Still, the king was occasionally dominated by the most powerful *pujok*, while the heads of the four *pujok* sat on the king's council largely to restrain the royal authority. And the internal structure and the size of the royal government was about the same as those of *pujok* leaders'. It is possible, however, that before Puyŏ was absorbed by Koguryŏ the royal government and power had been much enlarged.

Koguryŏ, which was the most successful of early states in nation-building, had to wage a three dimensional campaign : conquest of neighboring tribes, fighting-off of Chinese political manipulations, and constant revamping of the internal political structure to cope with expansion. The major territorial objective for Koguryŏ in its early stage of development was to wrest the Nangnang area from the Chinese. While making frequent forays into surrounding Chinese commanderies, Koguryŏ is said to have subjected Okchŏ to its control as early as the late first century A.D. The Okchŏ people were made to supply Koguryŏ with various goods produced in Okchŏ, including "beautiful women." The horse-riding warriors, who formed the aristocratic layer of the Koguryŏ society in its later stage, seem to have had a remarkably long-sighted scheme for expansion which they pursued with unusual vigor.

In their trading with the Chinese, the Koguryŏans were very cautious. In the early second century, the more centralized government under King

---

* Such Puyŏconcept of monarchal relations with the universe was later strengthened by introduction of the Confucian doctrine of the Mandate of Heaven.

T'aejo, for example, made a list of traders-*sijok* leaders and other individuals–
who had received official Chinese court attires and headgears and forbade
them to trade with the Chinese commanderies on an individual basis, but only
as representatives of Koguryŏ as a state. The Koguryŏ government allowed a
designated number of traders to go to the commanderies at a designated
time. Tenaciously sticking to the ritual aspect of commercial exchanges, the
Chinese commanderies, it is interesting to note, thereupon, built small walled
posts near their borders where the vestments were kept for Koguryŏ traders
to wear as Chinese vassals while in Chinese territories.

Koguryŏ's internal development from a tribal federation to an early
state was completed in the first century A.D. when King T'aejo became the
first hereditary king. Yet the tribal legacy was strongly at work. The political
backbone of the state was made up of five major tribal groups : Kerubu,
Sonobu, Chŏllobu, and so on, which resisted giving up their tribal privileges.
The office of the Taedaero, a kind of prime minister who also served as a
check upon the royal authority, was elective ; usually the strongest group
seems to have had its way in election. The hereditary kingship, which in the
beginning passed from brother to brother, was not always secure. King T'aejo
was formerly chief of the Kerubu who wrested the central leadership from
the Sonobu ; the Sonobu, who never renounced pretensions to the throne,
continued the maintenance of the temple of Heaven which belonged only to
the royalty. When King Sansang (197–226) grappled with his brother Palgi for
the royal succession, the Sonobu staked their fortune on the race by siding
with Palgi. Upon Palgi's defeat, part of the Sonobu group broke away from
Koguryŏ and surrendered themselves of Kung-suen K'ang of Liaotung. After
the incident, the royal authority became greatly strengthened. Father-to-son
succession became the rule, and the Chŏllobu became allied with the royal
family against other groups by becoming the exclusive supply source of
queens.

At about the same time, a profound administrative change occurred.
The tribal territories of the five major political groups, including the king's,
were reorganized into the five administrative provinces, as in Puyŏ, which
were given the impersonal designations devoid of tribal hint such as East,
West, South, North, and Center, the last being the capital province. While the
leaders of lesser tribes were, or might have been, given local administrative
posts, the upper layers of the five major groups were gradually coaxed into
residing in the capital which was also divided into five administrative districts.
The royal governments was enlarged over those of other groups, and the
Chŏllobu and the still powerful Sonobu were placated with honorary titles.
Although these political groups, with their own power structures and high
offices in the royal government, still presented a powerful check, the general
tide was in favor of the centralization of power under the monarchy. The ter-

ritorial expansion, which inevitably resulted from the Koguryŏ warriors' belligerence, further promoted the concentration of power in the central government. Furthermore, kings, under whose control newly conquered people and land were placed, found their authority enlarged as the territory expanded, and the appetite for more conquest grew.

In the Sam Han region where political consciousness was awakened much later than in the north, Paekche seems to have gone through its early stages, unencumbered by tribal competition because its original group, refugees from the north, was more or less a single tribe. Silla, however, went through its own unique stages of development after the iron culture reached it. Silla, as we have seen, was made up of six tribes, three of which, Pak, Sŏk, and Kim first provided the elected leadership. Eventually, Kim, the native tribe, was to gain supremacy over all others : Pak and Sŏk tribes seem to have been refugee-immigrant groups who made their headway in tribal politics. With regard to Silla's internal evolution up until the establishment of the hereditary kingship, less evidence is available than on that of Koguryŏ.

The most interesting evidence in this connection is a series of title designations given to the head of state. They are, in chronological order, Kŏsŏgan, Ch'ach'aung, Nisagŭm, Maripkan, and king. The first few heads of state were called Kŏsŏgan that simply meant a big man ; Ch'ach'aung is believed to have been a kind of Shaman or theocratic leader ; Nisagŭm meant a successor ; and the title Maripkan seems to have been a designation for hereditary kingship, as, for instance, King Namul (365-402), who laid the foundation of Silla Kingdom, was called Namul Maripkan.

Like Silla, Kaya was also made up of six Kaya or tribes and was annexed by Silla just before it could firmly establish itself as a kingdom. It is worth noting that Kaya's relations in terms of internal structure and growth to Silla in the south was in some respects what Puyŏ was Koguryŏ in the north.

4

The Early Life

The prehistoric Koreans' adoption of agriculture and metal artifacts, the two basic elements in the Korean traditional cultural configuration, constituted the most profound turnabout in Korean life from the nomadic to the sedentary mode of life, which determined that particular groove along which the subsequent Korean history was to develop. No less important in determining the nature of Korean civilization is the Korean penchant for grouping together according to consanguinity and geographical locality. Organization of early groups such as *ture* was initially prompted by agricultural needs, and their functions were extended for social, religious, and military purposes. These early groups had a strict hierarchy that prescribed individual places in organization. Groupism, as appeared in the early characterological process of the Koreans as a people, is indeed the most persistent social trend in the Korean history. Another characteristics of the early life of the peninsular people was the convergence upon their societies of rough, often malignant, foreign influences from divergent origins, making much more vigorous and dynamic the social mobility, horizontal as well as vertical, which was created by migrations of uprooted tribal groups and establishments of new states.

Economic and Social Life

Agriculture was rapidly developed in the third century B.C. when the Chinese refugees from their "warring states" brought with them agricultural technology and iron implements. In the Old Chosŏn region where the result of the Chinese contact was most immediate, the firm establishment of patriarchal authority and the accumulation of private wealth brought notable political and social changes from the tightly-knit communal life of the previous period. The life just prior to the establishment of the Han commanderies was graphically shown in "the eight articles of the folk laws of Old Chosŏn," three of which are extant :

1) A person who committed homicide should be immediately sentenced to death.
2) A person who inflicted bodily injury upon another should be made to compensate him with grains.
3) A person who stole should made slave to the victim, along with his entire family ; to atone for the crime he should be required to pay five hundred thousand coins per person.

An observation was made concerning the third article that even if the guilty could atone through indemnification, (which must have been virtually impossible, considering the sum,) he would be still unable to find himself a spouse. No one, therefore, took the risk of stealing ; consequently, no one bothered to shut the door at night. And women were expected to be chaste.

Puyŏ had similar folk laws :

1) A person who committed homicide should be put to death, and his family made slaves.
2) A person who stole should be required to make restitution twelve times the property stolen.
3) A woman who committed adultery should be put to death.
4) A jealous woman should be also put to death, and her body left at the top of the south hill. To recover the body her children should be made to pay in the form of cattle and horse.

Koguryŏ hade equally severe laws that suggest where the social emphasis was laid. These laws, however, seem to have been generally applied to the ruling class. The lower class and slaves, inasmuch as they fulfilled their duties to the ruling body, seem to have remained relatively free from the severity of the laws. They enjoyed, for instance, a remarkable degree of sexual freedom. It is possible that the laws' harshness upon women might have been of transitory nature, a reflection of the new social order of the strenuous Iron Age that called for undisputed patriarchal leadership and at the same time diminution of feminine power.

We have seen the Old Chosŏn society crumbling after the establishment of the Han colonies. Aside from its political disintegration, its social stability and morality were deeply disturbed by the unscrupulous Chinese civilians.

Petty Chinese merchants and riffraff rubbed the wide-open Korean households for thievery at night. Some Koreans, on the other hand, actively followed Chinese ways. The upshot all this was that the eight articles of the Old Chosŏn folk laws swelled to sixty in number. Puyŏ and Koguryŏ maintained their political and social order, guarding against unofficial contacts with the Chinese.

In Puyŏ and Koguryŏ, class distinctions were more noticeable than in other regions. The majority of the population seems to have been called *haho*, or lower family, just above slaves. The *haho* classes, who seem to have been originally the conquered people, were engaged in agriculture and animal husbandry, and in time of war they served as transport corps without weapons. In Koguryŏ, the *haho* are believed to have become tenant farmers in the later part of the second century. In 194, the Koguryŏ government inaugurated the grain control system to relieve the tenant farmers of food shortage. Landowners, consisting of government and tribal officials and heads of local families, usually possessed warehouses or barns for storage. To supplement scanty domestic supplies, Koguryŏ had to import foodstuff from the newly-acquired territories. Okchŏ, as noted, served as a kind of rear supply depot for Koguryŏ's struggle with the Nangnang, with the *haho* as carriers of provisions, including grains and salt. The circulation of goods through commercial activities in Koguryŏ was evidenced by the existence of a certain medium of exchange, which is more or less true of all other early states.

The extent of manual industry in Puyŏ and Koguryŏ is shown partly by the quality of weapons and dresses of the ruling class. Bows and arrows were made in great quantity ; Koguryŏan handicraftsmen seem to have been especially good at making them. Puyŏan aristocrats wore white garments and leather shoes and also had excellent tablewares for daily use. When going abroad, they wore outfits specially made of silk and furs and, in case of high officials, headgears decorated with gold and silver.

The general character of life in the Sam Han states was quite different from that of the northern states. Socially, the class cleavage does not seem to have been so noticeable as in the north. The *haho* people in the north knelt down when addressing their superiors, but there was no such standard of conduct in Sam Han. Although some powerful tribal leaders, even during the Han occupation of the Old Chosŏn area, laid down some harsh laws, possessed fortresses, and could mobilize a mass of work forces at their command, still a large number of lesser leaders reportedly had to be content with living among people without much social distinction nor even actual authority. In

---

* The cold problem in this connection is the one arising from the artificial division of the country. The deepening cultural gap between the democratic South and the Communist North may eventually become the stumbling block toward unification of the country.

the productive field, however, the Sam Han people made much headway in some respects. Discovery of iron ore around the lower reaches of the Naktong River brought technical advances in iron smelting and tool making. The techniques of weaving textile fabrics and of forging sword and armor were greatly developed and aptly copied by the Japanese. Commercially, Kaya, which used pieces of iron as the medium of exchange, seems to have been particularly enterprising. Abundant amounts of the money--the type of money used by Wang Mang's Shin and the "knife money" of even earlier periods--discovered in Kimhae attest to Kaya's prosperous foreign commerce. However, it was in agriculture that the Sam han, blessed with many fertile river basins and abundant precipitation, were most productive. Great numbers of water reservoirs were constructed in Sam Han, some of which are still in use today, and carbonized grains of rice found in Kimhae show the extent of rice cultivation.

On a deeper level too, it was the agricultural life that unified the self-contained early Korean societies in the Peninsula and in southeastern Manchuria. The most important of the social customs born of the agricultural economy was the annual thanksgiving festival. Puyŏ held the festival in December and Koguryŏ, Tongnye, and Sam Han in October. Today, it is observed on the fifteenth day of August by the lunar calendar. With only slight variations in celebration, the early states offered sacrifices to deities and guardian spirits, released convicts, and enjoyed themselves dancing and singing, transcending social distinctions. In the Sam Han, another festival was held in May after the rice planting at which villages vied in group performances of dancing and weaving which remain popular today. These festival programs are at once of social, recreational, and religious import. The dominant theme was to renew the communal spirit and to secure the universal harmony.

Religious Life

Dealing with the unseen, the early Koreans believed that all natural objects possessed indwelling souls whose conscious life was expressed in natural phenomena. Spirits of great mountains, rivers, trees, and stones were treated with proper care. The sun and other celestial bodies were worshiped as beneficial gods who brought mankind productivity and happiness. In time, evil spirits, who took delight in disturbing the harmony of the human world, came into existence. They were placated, or diverted from their mischievous

---

† A ri is about 1/4 mile.

* The Yonsei University excavation team under Professor Pow Key Sohn has been Most active in this field.

intentions, through magic incantation and exorcism. The maintenance of harmony in the spiritual world was usually assigned to the rulers, in addition to their temporal responsibilities. The rulers, however, tended to delegate their sacerdotal duty to special officials. In the Sam Han region, the head of sacrificial affairs, as opposed to the political leader, was called Ch'ŏn'gun. The Ch'ŏn'gun, literally the Ruler of Heaven, probably comparable with the Japanese Tennŏ (Ch'ŏnhwang in Korean) or the Emperor of Heaven, established himself in a seperate town called *sodo* where sacrificial rituals were performed with bells and drums. Although the Ch'ŏn'gun's relations with the secular leader are not clear, he seems to have been given privileged immunity from political encroachment. Even criminals who took refuge into the *sodo* were immune from temporal punishment.

Animism and Shamanism constitute the intractable core of the Korean religious mind. Rationale and rituals derived from them were applied to the ancestor worship which was to command the intensive religious devotion of the Korean people, as we shall see later. Archetypal father figures were presented in the shroud of variant tribal myths, of which common ingredients are invariably heaven, the sun, and their attributes such as roundness and brightness. According to Koguryŏ's founding legend, Chumong, the founding father of Koguryŏ, "came out from an egg as the sun light shined upon it." The ancestors of the six tribes of Kaya were transformed from six golden eggs. The mythical births of the Pak, Sŏk, and Kim tribes of Silla are stories of similar ingredients, and the Tan'gun legend in which the son of the heavenly god consorts with the bear woman can be seen of the heavenly god consorts with the bear woman can be seen in this light also. These tribal ancestors were later deified and enshrined as the protectors of the state, and the rulers, unlike those of the earlier Shamanistic tribal period, took responsibility for sacrificial rites to these deities with the assistance of their officials.

While these deities attained the godhood for collective worship, individual families became more and more devoted to their own immediate ancestors. In peaceful Puyŏ, filial homage was expressed by burying the dead parents with costly treasures, as in other regions, and, in some cases, with live servants by "the hundred." Less powerful families paid their respect simply by not interring the body at all until forced to by olfactorically-irritated neighbors. In the Sam Han region the dead were given the wings of large birds presumably for use in flight to the new residence in heaven. While some of these forms of ancestor worship were discarded, others were reinforced later by the logic of Confucian doctrines.

Vaguely comparable with the Confucian heaven, *Ch'ŏnji snmyŏng* or God-Light of Heaven and Earth was the supreme god that could be invoked, usually in time of distress. *Hananim* or Heavenly God, the god of a wider constituency, was interchangeable in function with *Ch'ŏnjisinmyŏng* ; they were created in these primitive times as the supreme gods of all purposes. Whereas *Ch'ŏnji sinmyŏng* was invoked more often for supplication, *Hananim* was regarded as the supreme god that presided over the affairs of heaven, earth, and human world. Below *Hananim* was later developed a pantheon of polytheistic gods largely by spirit-worshipping Shamanistic priests or *mudang* under the heavy influence of Buddhism and Taoism. Characteristically, the hierarchy of the pantheon of Shamanistic gods was not rendered rigid, and rituals varied from cult to cult. This primitive religion, generally known as Singyo, comparable with Japan's Shintŏism, has been an integral part of the religious mind of the Korean people from the earliest times.

Korean Singyo and Japanese Shintŏ, both originally of a haphazard amalgam of animistic and Shamanistic nature worship, ancestor worship, and accompanying rituals, were formless and had no doctrinal structures. Doctrines which they took on by piecemeal later were largely of foreign origin and came short of holding the native religions in systematic theology. Before they developed into viable religions, a full-fledged foreign religion, namely, Buddhism, swept the spiritual world of the Koreans and the Japanese and retarded the growth of their infant religions. The impact of the foreign religion was especially harsh on Korean Singyo which was hardly able to grow above the primitive level throughout the traditional period. The emergence of Japanese Shintŏ with a semblance of national religion is a pretty recent affair.

Sot'tae ; Totem pole with a wooden dragon or bird on its top. The poles are usually set up at the entrance way or road of the village.

Dolmen (table style), Bronze Age. Unyul country, Hwanghae Province.

Part 2

Three Kingdoms and Unification

1

The Three-Way War and Diplomacy

As champions of unification in the inevitable course of centralization of the Peninsula, Koguryŏ, Paekche, and Silla emerged with varying degrees of maturity in administrative and military strengths. They had shown dynamic abilities in war and diplomacy needed to cope with ever-changing balances of power. Against the strongest the weaker two usually formed an alliance, from which neither hesitated to extricate itself as a new situation required. In periods of peace, they endeavored with equal dynamism to attain the internal growth that was to bring about a new level of cultural synthesis. Indeed, this was one of the most strenuous periods in the Korean history.

Warlike Koguryŏ

Despite its occupation of the Nangnang region after expelling the Chinese in 313, Koguryŏ was much weakened. Even Paekche could invade Koguryŏ and kill its king with impunity. The reason for this was that Koguryŏ relied largely on hit-and-run tactics based on the prowess and ingenuity of individual warriors, which had worked well so far in dealing with semi-nomadic tribes of Tungus and in guerrilla-like assaults against Chinese defense lines. But now facing the Chinese armies on the offensive with superior weapons and battle formations usually in phalanx, Koguryŏ's conventional method of war was clearly incongruous. Koguryŏ, now a growing kingdom which had trebled its territory, needed not only military and political reorganizations but also inauguration of up-to-date institutional policies.

King Sosurim (371–383) did much to solidify the institutional foundation of Koguryŏ. A year before King Kogukwŏn, Sosurim's father, was killed by the Paekche army under King Kŭnch'ogo, the Hsien-pei Earlier Yen, Koguryŏ's long-time enemy in North China, was wiped out by the Earlier Ch'in, a powerful Tibetan state that briefly reunified North China. Koguryŏ immediately entered into friendly relations with the Earlier Ch'in. In 372 the Earlier Ch'in sent to Koguryŏ a Buddhist monk with *sutras* an statuettes who was whole-heartedly welcomed by the Koguryŏ court. King Sosurim erected a Buddhist temple for the monk, an act that was tantamount to recognition of Buddhism as the national religion. In the same year, King Sosurim instituted a Confucian college with a view to recruiting government officials, and in the next year he promulgated "the law." The maintenance of good relations with the Earlier Ch'in was understandably of paramount importance to Koguryŏ's security, for it dissipated the menace from the west. Possibly, for this political reason, Buddhism made such easy headway in Koguryŏ without encountering the slightest resistance. Koguryŏ's, which moved to establish close ties with Silla, introduced Silla to the Earlier Ch'in. Meanwhile, Koguryŏ made frequent assaults upon Paekche. Against the Koguryŏ-Silla alignment, Paekche strengthened its position with the Japanese and, in 372, started diplomatic relations with the Eastern Chin in South China, which introduced Buddhism to Paekche in 384.

When in 384, the Mu-jung tribe of the Hsien-pei set up the Later Yen in the North China, one of the successor states that sprung up after disintegration of the Earlier Ch'in, Koguryŏ again fell into the situation where it had to deal with two enemies. But under King Kwanggaet'ŏ (391–412) Koguryŏ was on its way to becoming a great empire. King Kwanggaet'ŏ, whose name literally means territorial enlargement, started at the age of eighteen to enlarge his territory. He first took the northern half of the Han River basin, the most strategic area of the Peninsula coveted by all three kingdoms, from Paekche. During this campaign, Koguryŏ tremendously impressed Paekche with improved troop maneuvers. Undoubtedly, this was a hard blow to Paekche, which also found itself in a precariously-isolated political position, with fledgling Silla having entrusted itself to Koguryŏ's protection by sending Prince Silsŏng to Koguryŏ as a hostage. Under these circumstances, Paekche desperately sought military help from Japan to which it sent Prince Chŏnji as a hostage. In 399 Japan obligingly dispatched a force to encroach on Silla's southern borders. The Japanese force was completely destroyed by Koguryŏ's army of 50,000 that came to Silla's rescue. In 404 Japan made another expedition this time into the southern part of Koguryŏ and was again badly mauled.

With Paekche and its ally Japan beaten back, King Kwanggaet'ŏ's army now turned west toward the Later Yen, which, taking advantage of

Koguryŏ's preoccupation with the southward movement, had taken the "seven hundred square ri" of Koguryŏ's western territory. King Kwanggaet'o retook in less than a few years not only the lost territory but also the entire area east of the Liao River, which had been territory of Old Chosŏn until taken by the Yen in the third century B. C. In 407 one Ko Un, a Koguryŏan in Chinese service, usurped the throne of the Later Yen, and Kwanggaet'o immediately recognized the new but short-lived regime. Then, King Kwanggaet'o turned to conquer the Tungusic tribes of Suksin (Hsi-shen in Chinese) in northeastern Manchuria. Together with Suksin, most parts of Puyŏ, which had by now been reduced to a nondescript entity, were incorporated into Koguryŏ. Koguryŏ now came to cover the northern half of the Peninsula from Han River to the southeastern and northeastern plains of Manchuria. As King Kwanggaet'ŏ's biography records in 1,800 Chinese characters carved in intaglio over a giant stele still standing to the height of twenty-two feet in modern T'onggu, the old Koguryŏ capital in southern Manchuria, the great king conquered sixty-four walled fortresses and 1,400 towns and villages until his death at the age of thirty-nine.

King Changsu, or literally Long Life, unlike his short-lived father, lived to ninety-eight years of age, ruling and expanding his empire from 413 to 491. King Changsu extended contact with the Chinese states. He formed diplomatic relations not only with the Northern Wei founded by the T'o-pa Hsienpei that wiped out the Later Yen and other states in North China in the early fifth century, but also with its rival Juan-juan empire in the northern steppes. He also exchanged embassies with the Eastern Chin and Liu Sung in South China. His foreign policy was one of "pitting one barbarian against another." It effectively neutralized Paekche's special relations with the South Chinese states. His active foreign interest indicates that King Changsu, like everyone else in North Asia, seems to have entertained the idea of making an expeditionary thrust into China.

With the western front thus stabilized, King Changsu in 427 moved his capital from Kungnaesŏng or modern T'onggu to P'ŏngyang. The direct impact was great upon Paekche, which previously had been forced to retreat to the area south of the Han River and, to a less or degree, upon fast-growing Silla, which was now trying to ease itself out of Koguryŏ's influence. The two neighbors were pressed, by 433, into an alliance initially proposed by Paekche. Koguryŏ, however, made no large scale invasions against this alliance, except scattered forays along its southern borders, for nearly four decades which were probably intended for internal administrative consolidations. But, in 475, King Changsu dispatched an expeditionary force of 30,000 that took Paekche's capital Hansansŏng south of modern Seoul. King Kaero(455-474) of Paekche was killed in the battle just as King Kogukwŏn of Koguryŏ was killed in the battle of P'yŏngyang a century before.

In a series of campaigns that followed, Koguryŏ pushed its southern frontier as far south as the southern edge of the Gulf of Namnyang (Inch'ŏn) on the west and the Chungnyŏng Pass on the east, thus crowding Paekche, Silla, and Kaya into a southern third of the Peninsula. In 494 it also absorbed what was left of Puyŏ in the north. Turning internally, King Changsu effected an administrative reorganization. He established two more capitals, Kungnaesŏng (the old capital) and Hansŏng in modern Hwanghae Province, auxiliary to the main capital at P'yŏngyang and reorganized the country into five provinces. Koguryŏ, by the end of Changsu's reign, was ready for a confrontation with no less a power than united China itself.

Sophisticated Paekche

Paekche in the southwest was a kingdom that followed a unique path. Since it was founded by a single immigrant group from the north and thus unburdened by serious intertribal rivalry, Paekche was able to develop a well organized government system earlier than any other group in the Peninsula. Paekche naturally set out on wars of conquest, but it curiously lacked the martial spirit which Koguryŏ had. During the reign of King Kŭnch'ogo who pushed Paekche's northern frontier up to the southern periphery of the Taedong River basin in the fourth century, it looked for a while as if Paekche were on its way to the conquest of the Old Chosŏn area. In the face of warlike Koguryŏ that presented an indomitable block on its road to expansion, however, Paekche seems to have become increasingly preoccupied with the question of survival and cultural growth rather territorial expansion.

Paekche-Japan Relations. It is interesting to note that Paekche's utilization of Japanese military resources and Japan's establishment of cultural relations with Paekche started quite early. The first dispatch by Japan of troops against Silla at the inducement of King Kŭnch'ogo (346–374) occurred in 369. The Japanese expedition dampened Silla's territorial aspirations on Kaya, from which the Japanese attacks were made, and with the frequent Japanese raids on southern coastal areas King Kŭnch'ogo brought those areas under his administrative grasp. It was about this time, that is, in the reign of King Kŭn'gusu (375–383) that a Paekche scholar, Wang In (Wani in Japanese), was sent to Japan to teach Chinese classics at the Yamato court. This was the official beginning of cultural transmission from Paekche to Japan which went on with a remarkable constancy, culminating in the flowering of the Asuka culture of seventh century Japan, an outstanding variant of Paekche culture, especially in art. In any case, as Paekche called on Japan for its defense, Japan responded with active support for economic and cultural reasons on its part.

During the period when Koguryŏ was at its peak of power in the fifth century, Paekche, in a somewhat precarious alliance with Silla, seriously sought Japanese participation in the peninsular conflicts, if only as a safeguard against Silla's expansion. Around this time or even earlier, Yamato Japan seems to have agreed to the dispatchment of a force stationed probably in Tsushima in cooperation with Paekche which thus expected a speedier response from the Japanese. This was the period in which the Yamato, the strongest tribe in Japan, began actively strengthening its ties with Paekche because, in addition to economic and cultural rewards, the Korean contacts brought to its court the political prestige needed for unification of various tribal groups. It was under these circumstances that "the Yamato court lent its military force for the Paekche scheme." The intriguing nature of this Tsushima-based Japanese force is that, although it was placed more or less under Paekche's control, it could in a certain situation come to terms with Silla or even act independently of Paekche or the Yamato government itself. *

When King Changsu's army of 30,000 descended on Paekche's capital in 475, King Kaero (455–474) of Paekche seems to have been aware of the invasion beforehand. In 472 King Kaero sent an emissary to the Northern Wei in a serious effort to induce a Wei expedition against Koguryŏ, but without avail. Yet King Kaero was more interested in depleting his coffers, constructing palaces and temples, than in military preparations. He eventually lost the Han River basin and his own life to Koguryŏ ; reinforcements dispatched by Silla failed to arrive in time.

Paekche was forced to move its capital south to Ungjin, modern Kongju in South Ch'ungch'ŏng Province, and a brief period of confusion followed, in which the royal prestige sank with the assassination of the king by brawling ministers. But Tongsŏng (479–500) again asserted the strong leadership under which Paekche was on its way to recovery. Through marriage, he reinforced the alliance with Silla that emphasized mutual military support against Koguryŏ, while building defense facilities along his borders ; not the least important of these were a fortress and a palisade on T'anŏh, east of modern Taejŏn, against Silla itself. Internally, he enlarged his capital, appointed princes and other members of the royal family to provincial military and administrative posts, and tightened control over T'amna (Cheju Island), then an independent state.

In general, the early sixth century witnessed a relatively long lull among the warring kingdoms, and the period was marked by the growth of the agricultural economies of both Paekche and Silla. King Sŏng (523–553), one of

---

*The debates on the relationship between Korea and Japan in this period has by no means been settled. To get a more accurate picture, fresh interdisciplinary researches are needed ; in fact, they are going on in both countries.

the great kings of Paekche, brought Paekche to a new height of cultural maturity. He moved the capital about twenty miles southwest from Kongju to the more strategically located Sabi, modern Puyŏ, and effected the further administrative consolidation through which Paekche's government system reached its final stage.

King Sŏng encouraged the import of Confucian and Buddhist cultural materials and other practical learning from the Liang dynasty, then ruling South Chinese dynasty. By this time, Japan came completely under Paekche's cultural influence. At Japanese request, King Sŏng sent successive groups of scholars and teachers in such diverse fields as Confucianism, Buddhism, divination, astronomy, medicine, and music to stay at the Japanese court probably for a prearranged period of time until the next one arrived ; this went on for a period of time during the late sixth century.

With the military strength resulting from the economic improvement, Paekche looked to the recovery of its lost territory. This appeared a distinct possibility in the light of the fact that Koguryŏ now became much weakened by internal power struggles among ruling aristocrats. Although Paekche's alliance with Silla became increasingly precarious because of Silla's own territorial ambitions, King Sŏng launched a series of campaigns against Koguryŏ. By 551 King Sŏng succeeded in retrieving the western half of the Han River basin, only to be snatched away by Silla ; Silla had occupied the eastern half of the Han River region while fighting alongside Paekche against Koguryŏ and then turned to the west to take the other half from Paekche. Enraged at this wanton betrayal by Silla of a century old friendship, King Sŏng, in cooperation with the Tae Kaya, attacked Silla's Kwansan Fortress at modern Okch'ŏn with a vengeance, but this move ended in his own death by a Silla ambush. This unexpected turn of events reshuffled the three rivals into a new alignment which combined Paekche with Koguryŏ against Silla a century later.

Dynamic Silla

The erstwhile *protégé* of Koguryŏ had come a long way now to compete with the combined forces of Paekche and Koguryŏ. Silla's economic growth in the late fifth century was indicated by a series of improvements made by the government : construction and repair of roads, establishment of a postal network in 487 and of markets and shops in its capital Kyŏngju in 490 and 509, and, most importantly, introduction of cows for ploughing in 502. It was also around this period or even earlier that Silla's unique process of centralization began.

As the royal power and prerogatives were strengthened, Silla's original six tribal groups found themselves organized into an aristocratic status system consisting of six vaguely defined status groups with each residing in a certain administrative section of the capital. They were stripped of the tribal equality in the state council which had required the unanimity of all six tribal groups for major government actions. The formation of this status system seems to have been based on the political and military strengths of each group at the time ; that is, the most powerful was assigned to the highest status. However, it is not clear actually how many layers in the status system there were, how rigid the status lines were, or what were the relations of the six tribal groups to the royal court in this formative period of the Silla status system. Evidently, each group's political strength was most important in the formation of social organization. Similarly, local tribes were organized on same basis, and their leaders, while being allowed to maintain control over their own tribes, might have been required to live in the capital to prevent the growth of local power.

This status system when matured was called *Kolp'um* or Bone Rank system which was formalized probably during the reign of King Pŏphŭng (514–539). The Bone Rank system was a vertical alignment of the existing political groups in five grades in accord with their relative political strengths. As we shall see later, the Bone Rank system, as it was made hereditary, became the most important institution that determined the nature of the Silla society.

King Pŏphŭng also inaugurated a series of notable government and institutional system. As a means of reinforcing the royal authority, he made the powerful Pak family the exclusive source of queens, thus allying that family and its tribal following with his Kim family. He promulgated "the law" in 520 and established diplomatic relations with the Liang dynasty in South China with Paekche's help. He also set up a new ministry for military affairs and a system of court uniforms for officials with rank differences marked by color arrangement. It was probably under him also that Silla's seventeen-grade rank system for officials was instituted, as was Paekche's in 260. It is worthwhile to note that Silla had another rank system under which conquered people could be recruited into the low-echelon government and military service in provinces. Although Silla drew a line between the original Silla people and those from the newly-incorporated lands, it dealt with the problem of integrating non-Silla people into its social structure more seriously than Koguryŏ and Paekche did.

Another significant event under King Pŏphŭng was that the official sanction was given to Buddhism in 527. Buddhism had been clandestinely practiced among the common people to a certain extent. Unlike in Koguryŏ and Paekche, the official recognition of Buddhism in Silla was delayed by the aristocratic opposition in the court. Once adopted as the national religion, however, Buddhism, that is Mahayana Buddhism (or Greater Vehicle), which considered individual salvation and national welfare to be compatible with each other, was used as a vehicle for the advancement of national spiritual unity under the royal authority. And, like King Kwanggaet'o of Koguryŏ, Kingŏ Pŏphŭng adopted his own year period in Chinese style.

The Silla king who could really emulate King Kwanggaet'o in territorial conquest was King Chinhŭng (540-575). It was under King Chinhŭng that, as has been noted, Silla came to occupy the Han River basin, one of the most fertile regions in the Peninsula, which was also to serve as a corridor leading directly to China. King Chinhŭng pushed northward along the eastern coast, claiming from Koguryŏ the Tongnye-Okchŏ area in the southern half of modern South Hamgyŏng Province. In the south, he incorporated Tae Kaya, modern Koryŏng, into Silla in 562, thus bringing under his rule the entire Naktong River basin and with it the whole of the rich Kaya culture.

Through these conquests, King Chinhŭng joined two illustrious predecessors, King Kŭngch'ogo (346-374) of Paekche and King Kwanggaet'o (391-412) of Koguryŏ in a triad of great expansionist of the Three Kingdoms period. Like King Kŭnch'ogo who made a great pile of large rocks dozens of feet high near the Sugok Fortress at modern Sin'gye to commemorate his conquest of the eastern half of the Peninsula south of the Taedong River, and like King Changsu who raised the magnificent stele for King Kwanggaet'o, King Chinhŭng erected huge stone monuments at key points along his borders that tell the stories of his conquests today.

The important institutional development that occurred during the reign of King Chinhŭng was the emergence of youth organizations known as

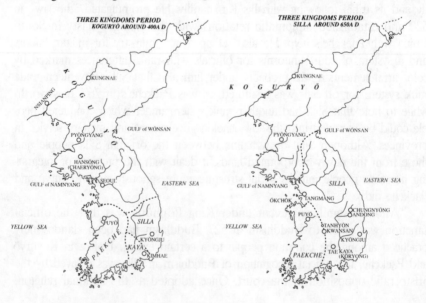

Hwarang *to*, or Hwarang groups. The Hwarang, literally Flower Youths, grouping themselves together under a leader, strove to discipline themselves through group activities for the ultimate purpose of serving the kingdom. In 576 these voluntary youth groups were formally organized into a nationally coordinated orders under government leadership. As we shall see later, the Hwarang *to*, while they served the national war efforts often as elite troops, as evidence shows, eventually became a source of cadres that manned the government and social institutions.

By far the most important of King Chinhǔng achievements, as noted above, was the conquest and the continued occupation of the whole region drained by the Han River, despite the constant military pressures from both Koguryǒ and Paekche. As mentioned previously, Silla was introduced to dynasties in North and South China by its northern and western neighbors, respectively. Silla seems to have realized quite early a potentially important role China could play in its national expansion. It was indeed through the full exploitation of this Chinese potential that Silla was to win a united Korea. The maintenance of the Han valley corridor that guaranteed the direct communication with China for Silla, a backwater in the international community of that day, therefore, was of paramount importance to Silla's national growth. Immediately following his conquest, King Chinhǔng built the Tanghang Fortress abutting on the Gulf of Namnyang (Inch'ǒn) and other strongholds in the area manned by garrison troops. Indeed, the greatly increased flow of cultural exchanges between Silla and the Chinese dynasties followed.

Koguryǒs Episodes with Sui and T'ang

Koguryǒ and Paekche, bitter rivals for nearly two centuries, now had a common cause, namely, the elimination of Silla from the Han River basin. They frequently attacked Silla's garrison troops along their borders and at times converged upon the Tanghang Fortress that protected Silla's gate to China. But with the rise of the Sui dynasty that reunited China in 589, after four centuries of political division, the power balance in Korea was recomposed. The burden of the new power situation naturally fell upon Koguryǒ which had enjoyed relative peace in its Yodong (Liaotung) territory through diplomatic manipulation of rival states in North China. Sharing borders with the Sui along the Liao River, Koguryǒ now had to concentrate more of its attention on the western defense, leaving Paekche most of the fighting against Silla, which was the main beneficiary of the new international balance of power.

Before long a conflict developed between Koguryǒ and the Sui over

Koguryŏ's refusal to allow the semi-nomadic Khitans and the Malgal in its border areas to have direct contact with the Chinese. The Sui in turn threatened Koguryŏ's security in the Yodong area. In 598 Koguryŏ made the first thrust against the Sui. This move was also intended to instigate the T'u-chŭeh, former vassels of the Juan-juan, who had built a large empire in Central Asia in the late sixth century to encroach upon the Sui, Sui immediately retaliated with a 300,000 force, but without the expected result. Sui had managed to subdue the Easten and Western T'u-chŭeh, but Koguryŏ constantly tried to disturb the Sui-T'u-chueh relations.

Sui Yang Ti who, like Ch'in's First Emperor, liked to undertake grandiose projects such as digging of the Grand Canal, decided upon the subjugation of recalcitrant Koguryŏ with an expeditionary force befitting his extravagant schemes. In 612, after five years of preparation, Sui Yang Ti personally led army of 1,133,800 plus a transport corps of 2,000,000 against Koguryŏ. The troop procession is said to have stretched out 960 ri. Actually, this was the climax of a long series of Sui conquests of its peripheral states.

The great waves of the Chinese army rapidly engulfed the scattered Koguryŏ fortresses in the Liaotung Peninsula, but the garrison forces, with inclement weather and rough terrain on their side, fought the invaders to a standstill. Thereupon, the Sui dispatched a detachment of 300,000 to try a direct thrust at P'yŏngyang. This formula of sidestepping frontier fortresses when they could not be obliterated and marching directly to the capital was frequently resorted to by invading armies throughout the traditional period. The Sui detachment had almost reached its destination when it realized that it had been lured into a trap laid by General Ŭchi Mundŏk. The weary enemies hurriedly took to retreat, running the gauntlet of Koguryŏ soldiers in ambush. When the Chinese were half way across the Ch'ŏngch'ŏn River, General Ŭlchi let loose his main troops who descended on the thoroughly demoralized enemies, claiming the lives of all but 2,700. Another force dispatched by sea from the Shantung Peninsula met with a similar fate. The recklessly planned and executed campaign imposed indescribable hardships and privations on the surviving Sui soldiers, a traumatic experience that was expressed in a folk song urging not to waste life in the Liaotung thereafter. The egocentric personality of Sui Yang Ti was not the kind that would listen to the Song's counsel, however.

So, in 613, the Sui emperor again personally led an invasion army that laid siege to Koguryŏ's fortresses and walled cities in Liaotung. Sui Yang Ti's personally supervised attack on Yodong-sŏng, Koguryŏ's main castellated city in the area, took an appalling toll from the Chinese. A serious rebellion at home, which was only one of many sings of the seething discontent that eventually ended the dynasty itself, forced the Chinese withdrawal.

After suppression of the rebellion at home, Sui Yang Ti, in 614, made the third attempt at Koguryŏ. Koguryŏ, however, responded this time with a peace proposal and returned Yang Ti's Vice Minister of War who had surrendered himself to Koguryŏ in the previous year. The disintegrating situation on the home front again forced Yang Ti to accept the proposal. Frustrated in three expeditions, and with his imperial pride hurt, the Chinese ruler vented his ire upon his hapless Vice Minister of War. The minister's body was torn apart and then boiled ; the remaining bones were cremated ; ashes were blown away. Sui Yang Ti himself was assassinated amid the crumbling empire in 618.

With the rise of the T'ang in 618, a period of cautious peace between Koguryŏ and the new dynasty ensued. The exchanges of prisoners of war and cultural amenities between the two seemed to assure friendship at least for a while, thus releasing Koguryŏ for dealing with its peninsular adversaries. But as T'ang T'ai Tsung (627–650), one of the ablest of the Chinese monarchs, restored the central administration and launched ambitious programs for wars of conquest, the subjugation of Koguryŏ again loomed large in his overall scheme.

Long aware of the Chinese ambitions, Koguryŏ, in 631, undertook one of its most ambitious defense projects, namely, the construction of a 1,0000 *ri* wall along its western border from modern Ning-an down to the Gulf of Pohai ; the project took sixteen years. General Yŏn Kaesomun, who was supervising the construction project, seized power through a *coup* d'*état* in 642 in a political change that was to have a direct bearing upon subsequent international developments. General Yŏn Kaesomun, a man of strong personality, was as uncompromising in international politics as despotic in domestic affairs.

In the meantime, sporadic clashes between Silla and Paekche had been going on, climaxing in King Ŭija's offensive in 642 which claimed forty fortresses from Silla. So desperate was Silla that it sent Kim Ch'unch'u, the royal prince, to no other than Koguryŏ for help. Yŏn Kaesomun responded by imprisoning the prince for a while and demanded the return of Koguryŏ's southeastern territory which King Chinhŭng took almost a century before. Moreover, Koguryŏ in cooperation with Paekche attempted the destruction of the Tanghang Fortress in order to block Silla's access to the T'ang. T'ang, to whom Silla then appealed for help, thereupon, dispatched an envoy to Koguryŏ to mediate between the warring states, but Yŏn Kaesomun imprisoned him too.

A T'ang expedition against Koguryŏ, long in preparation, was thus given an excuse. In 645 T'ang T'ai Tsung, like Sui Yang Ti before him personally led an invasion force of 170,000. The Chinese force under T'ai Tsung, a far better tactician, took all major Koguryŏ defenses, including Yodongsŏng, in a few months and converged on Ansisŏng, the last strategic but small walled city built upon a steep mountain in the Yodong (Liaotung) Peninsula. A reinforcement of 150,000 sent to the beleaguered city was dispersed by the Tang troops. Koguryŏ's desperation at this time was indicated by the fact that Koguryŏ's even tried to persuade the Syrtardus tribe in Outer Mongolia to strike at the rear of the T'ang, but without success. Under an able commander, however, Ansisŏng proved to be a tough knot that even T'ang T'ai Tsung was unable to undo. The invaders tried every conceivable offensive tactics, but they were met with the correspondingly improvised defenses. The Chinese built an earth mound to equalize the ground level of attack with the fortress's wall, taking 500,000 men for two months, but the defenders simply built the wall higher to maintain the advantageous height. Tsung, suddenly sobered down by the supply shortages, human losses, and above all the cold weather that was coming by stealth, reluctantly ordered the withdrawal of his army. Upon seeing the Chinese retreat, the general of the Korean garrison appeared on the wall and bade farewell. The Chinese monarch, deeply on the wall and bade farewell. The Chinese monarch, deeply moved by the heroic defenders, sent a hundred bolts of silk as a token of his respect. T'ang T'ai Tsung made two more attempts at Koguryŏ in 647 and 648, but without much result.

Silla Succeeds in Unification

Since the middle of the sixth century when Silla occupied the Han River region, making its forces spread thin, Silla had been forced onto the defensive. Paekche's frequent encroachments on Silla's borders posed a serious threat at times. Especially during the T'ang invasion of Koguryŏ, when Silla was obligingly harassing Koguryŏ's rear, Paekche, with Japan behind it, stepped up its offensive against Silla.

Prince Kim Ch'unch'u set out on his diplomatic mission ; in 647 he went to Japan to blunt its military help to Paekche and nest year to the T'ang. Prince Kim, who lost his daughter and a son-in-law in one of the Paekche attacks, persuaded T'ang T'ai Tsung to subjugate both Paekche and Koguryŏ. The Chinese emperor, though not completely recovered from the Koguryŏ fiasco, nevertheless, promised him to do so, and further he offered to recognize Silla's territorial rights over the Peninsula south of P'yŏngyang. This was a great diplomatic triumph for Silla who had probably been entertaining just such an idea. Indeed, Silla's subsequent relations with the T'ang were firmly riveted to this Kim Ch'unch'u-T'ang T'ai Tsung agreement. Silla, probably to reciprocate the T'ang's favor, pointedly adopted some of T'ang's government systems. Queen Chindŏk (647–653), the feminine ruler of Silla at the time, personally embroidered a laudatory poem on silk as a gift for Tang Kao Tsung, then on the throne.

But Silla did not rest content with the exchanges of promises and romantic gestures. Silla steadily built up its defenses and particularly its navy, which came to surpass those of Koguryŏ, Paekche, and Japan and commanded control of the Yellow Sea. With the advance in navigation and shipbuilding and its own determination to maintain contact with China at any cost, Silla gained an early momentum in maritime expansion, which gave it hegemony over the Northeast Asian seas for centuries to come.

In 655 Koguryŏ and Paekche again in concert invaded Silla, and King T'aejong, the former Prince Kim Ch'unch'u, requested military assistance from the T'ang. T'ang Kao Tsung tried three minor expeditions against Koguryŏ between 655 and 659 only to find Koguryŏ strong in defense as ever. It was Silla T'aejong's idea that Paekche, the weaker of the two, should be knocked off first. Silla's long lobbying at the T'ang court finally bore fruit. T'ang Kao Tsung dispatched an expeditionary force of 13,000 by sea to Paekche in 660. The overall strategy was that the T'ang force, joined by the Silla navy at Tŏkchŏk Island in the Gulf of Namnyang (Inch'ŏn), would approach the Paekche capital Puyŏ along the Kŭm River, while the Silla army under General Kim Yu Sin would hit it from the east. Paekche under King Ŭija's misrule was at a nadir of internal dissension and fell an easy prey to the Silla-T'ang allies. The loyal Paekche General Kye Paek is said to have killed his family by his own hand before leaving for the front. As the General thus foresaw it, his handpicked 5,000–man force was badly mauled by General Kim Yu Sin's Silla army, and Paekche collapsed within a few months.

No sooner had King Ŭija surrendered than Paekche started a revival movement under Prince P'ung who had returned from Japan. With the active support of Koguryŏ and Japan, Paekche's new army quickly gathered momentum and isolated the T'ang garrison troops in Puyŏ from the rest of the invasion forces which were now heading toward Koguryŏ. Paekche's revival movement was also helped by Silla's lukewarm attitudes toward the complete subjugation of Paekche at this time. But the movement collapsed after three years due to lack of leadership.

In 661 the T'ang army, while still fighting the Paekche revivalists, attacked its main target, Koguryŏ, from both sides. A fresh Chinese force marched toward P'yŏngyang through the Yodong Peninsula where it bypassed the Koguryŏ garrisons. This reinforcement joined the Chinese army at P'yŏngyang that had been laying siege to the city. Although the Silla army did their part in transportation of food for the allies, the overall food supply soon fell short of need because Koguryŏ's garrison forces in the Yodong effectively disrupted the Chinese supply line. In the face of the determined defense by Yŏn Kaesomun's army, the Silla-T'ang allies were forced to retreat, and the expedition seemed again doomed to failure.

During the lull created by this setback, the T'ang busied itself with implementing its scheme on Paekche. It established its own administrative system in Paekche with Prince Yung, the former crown prince of Paekche, as the head of occupied Paekche and imposed, though only on paper, a similar setup upon Silla itself with the king of Silla as its appointed head. Moreover, in 665, the T'ang made Prince Yung and King Munmu of Silla enter into a covenant of friendship, thus reducing Silla to an equal footing with the conquered and voiding T'ang T'ai Tsung's promise to recognize Silla's sovereignty over the Peninsula south of P'yŏngyang. So far as Koguryŏ remained a strong enemy in the north, Silla was not to challenge the T'ang militarily, however.

Koguryŏ had become weakened by continuous foreign invasions since Sui, and even though it still could repulse the combined forces of Silla and the T'ang, signs appeared that portended its demise. The dictator Yŏn Kaesomun died at this critical time. Soon a feud developed among Kaesomun's three sons, resulting in the surrender by Namsaeng, the eldest and heir to the dictatorial position, to the T'ang. And Yŏn Chaengt'o, Kaesomun's brother, surrendered to Silla with his troops.

In 667, at Silla's initiative the allies approached P'yŏngyang in a pincers movement. The T'ang force this time easily demolished the Koguryŏ's defenses in the Yodong Peninsula. The ease with which the T'ang waded through Yodong was due less to its in creased military might than to the fact that Koguryŏ's political confusion loosened its grip over Khitans, the Malgal, and slaves in the provinces. Their revolts and desertion from military service severely weakened frontier defenses. The pincers movement that consisted of the T'ang army from Yodong to the north, the navy from the west, and the Silla army from the south converged on P'yŏngyang in 668. The city fell within a month, signifying the dissolution of the seven century old dynasty.

Although some Koguryŏ cities in the north were still in hostility against it, the T'ang went ahead with administrative reorganization of the conquered territory which was, as usual, largely a declaration on paper. But it stationed a considerable number of troops in P'yŏngyang, Puyŏ, and other strategic cities. With troops in P'yŏngyang, Puyŏ and other strategic cities. With Koguryŏ, its indomitable adversary, now gone, Silla faced the Chinese cautiously, but, as subsequent maneuvers show, with a determination to materialize its sovereignty over the agreed-upon territory. Silla quietly began to take advantage of, and instigate, the revival movement of koguryŏ. Silla welcomed Prince Ansŭng of Koguryŏ who surrendered to Silla with his followers comprising 4,000 households in 669 and appointed him the King of Koguryŏ as a symbol of continuity. When General Kŏm Mojam revolted against the T'ang in the northwest in 670, Silla dispatched reinforcements of 10,000 men to help him.

Although General Kŏm Mojam's movement was ill-fated, thereby ending the armed revival movement, "King" Ansŭng remained under Silla's protection as the rallying point for Koguryŏ refugees from T'ang rule.

Silla's main area of concentration was, however, Paekche where King Munmu (661–680) now resorted to the overt military action. By 671 Silla had established its own military administration in the old Paekche capital which governed the Paekche territory as a province of Silla. Silla's unilateral action in Paekche and its overall accentuation of armed clashes with the T'ang in the Peninsula, provoked the wrath of T'ang Kao Tsung. In 672, T'ang Kao Tsung dispatched reinforcements, and their main force was assigned to the defense of P'yŏngyang.

With swiftness and determination, Silla countered the Chinese move. While sending an envoy to the T'ang capital to propitiate the emperor's ire, Silla confronted the Chinese army in and around the Han River region now for control of the Peninsula. At the same time, Silla's war preparation rose to a sudden pitch. Five new army corps were activated, including one formed exclusively with Paekche recruits and another corps of lance for the defense of Kyŏngju. At least ten walled fortresses were built or repaired, fanning out from the capital ; locations of these defense facilities show that every possible direction of enemy approach to the capital was considered.

Probably more significant than Silla's military preparations for confrontation with the Chinese was its administrative preparedness for the integration of the Koguryŏ and Paekche peoples into its political and social systems as functioning members of society with a full sense of participation. The appointment system, for instance, of non-Sillans as government officials, that had been improvised under King Pŏphŭng more than a century before, was now fully developed. Non-Sillans could be appointed to Silla's tow parallel official rank systems, central and provincial, but under some artificial disadvantages Paekche men when appointed to a central post, could be promoted no higher than the tenth rank or the fourth in the provincial officialdom. Koguryŏ men were allowed to attain up to the seventh rank in the central government. Men of nobility and ministerial rank seem to have been given exceptional treatment.

As the critical last act of the unification drama unfolded, Silla proved itself a worthy opponent of the T'ang. The Silla army in colorful armored uniforms over which insignias dangled and the navy also spread out in the familiar theatre of war. They won several scores of bitterly fought battles until, finally in 677, they forced the Chinese completely out of the Peninsula.

How then Silla came short of possessing the entire Peninsula, let alone the whole of Koguryŏ territory, can only be surmised. Possibly, Silla may have resisted its own momentum of northward expansion in deference to its 649 agreement with T'ang T'ai Tsung. Furthermore, P'yŏngyang, thoroughly sacked by Chinese in 668, was a ruined city completely unattractive to Silla. In fact, the erstwhile political and cultural center for a millennium remained gutted until the Koryŏ dynasty repeopled it in the tenth century.

The T'ang dynasty itself could not extend its jurisdiction over the Koguryŏ territory for long, for there emerged a new kingdom known as Parhae (P'o-hai in Chinese) founded in 699 by a former Koguryŏ general named Tae Choyŏng. Parhae, its people consisting of the Koguryŏans and the Tungusic tribes, was to enjoy centuries of prosperity until 926. The Gulf of Pohai, the northern arm of the Yellow Sea, bears the name of the ancient kingdom today.

Tomb of Gen, Kim Yu-shin.

2

The Internal Structure

The formation of the Three Kingdoms was a long process of political and cultural growth from the tribal stage. Internally, war played the most important role in this process : it added new lands and people, necessitating the development of larger and more sophisticated government institutions. The foreign, that is, Chinese, influence presented a constant problem of how much of it should be allowed or rejected, a problem that was in the last analysis more *political* than cultural, as we shall see. The Chinese political and military involvement in the peninsular states, though it was generally malignant, undeniably fomented vague tribalism into an incipient national consciousness which constituted a spiritual basis for unification.

The difference in political and social makeup among the Three Kingdoms, inasmuch as they went through similar stages of development, is worth nothing. Koguryŏ attached a high value to the warlike prowess of individual warriors and the tribal tradition in government. Yet it showed a great degree of flexibility in international politics, coupled with the unquestionable military strength which withstood the determined attempts at its subjugation by the two great empires, Sui and T'ang. It was, in more ways than otherwise, fortunate for Paekche, Silla, and, to a lesser degree, Japan to have such a great breakwater against the raw influences of China.

Paekche, though of the same origin as Koguryŏ's, adopted a much developed form of government earlier than the others, and probably because of its geographical location and the influence from South Chinese dynasties, it acquired the peaceful and sophisticated national character that can be readily detected in its arts. Latecomer Silla's dynamic self-assertion, which is in every respect remarkable, seems to have been motivated more strongly by its desire to grow out of its geographical isolation, a heavy handicap in international race for peninsular hegemony that drove Silla proportionately harder.

Developmental Stages

With these different circumstances and experiences, Three kingdoms went through distinctly similar developmental stages. In general, the first strong king appearing in a transitory period from tribal federation to early statehood would strengthen the royal authority and prerogatives by combining the royal family with another powerful house through marriage, thus eliminating or weakening other contending houses for the throne. Then, leaders of political groups were made aristocratic central officials with ranks given on the basis of their tribal strengths. In this Paekche, which was founded by a single tribe, was an exception, even though it had a number of aristocratic families in its ruling class : they seem to have descended from local leaders.

The coming of Buddhism represented the most important event in the second stage. Buddhism, aptly utilized for political purposes from the begin-

stage	Koguryŏ	Paekche	Silla
I	**King Taejo(6th King—53—121)** * Tribal groups brought under his control. * Hyŏnt'o Commandery moved for the second time. * Okchŏ brought under Koguryŏ's control.	**King Koi(8th King—234—285)** * Official ranking system and uniforms established. * Statutory laws promulgated. * Control of the established.	**King Namul(11th King—356—401)** * The title Maripkan (king) adopted. * The Kim family achieved hereditary kingship. * The first envoy
II	**King Sosurim (17th—371—383)** * Buddhism adopted. * Central and provincial schools established. * Official ranking system organized. * Statutory laws promulgated. * Histroy thought to be compiled in this reig.	**King Kŭnch'ogo (12th—346—374)** * Territorial expansion up to the Taedong River. * Histroy compiled.	**King Pŏphŭng (23rd—514—539)** * Buddhism adopted. * Statutory laws promulgated. * Official uniforms
III	**King Kwanggaet'o (19th—391—412)** * Great expansion took place. * Cultural activities encouraged.	**King Ch'imnyu (14h—383—384)** * Buddhism adopted.	**King Chinhŭng (23th—540—575)** * Territorial expansion : control of the Han River * Kaya annexed. * History compiled.

ning, did much to enlarge the spiritual perspective from a tribal to a national viewpoint. Then, in the third stage, each kingdom took off, so to speak, for expansion through conquest. The compilation of national histories followed.

Throughout the three stages, which are necessarily tentatively set here, Silla's development is about 250 years behind that of Koguryŏ in the first stage and 150 years behind in the second and third stages. Paekche comes somewhere in-between with one exception : Paekche's territorial expansion came before came before the adoption of Buddhism. Without assigning undue importance to the interrelationship between the adoption of Buddhism and the territorial expansion, the Chinese influence may have accounted for Paekche's earlier expansion. With the elimination of the Chinese commanderies whose political influence had subtly wrought disintegration of local tribal powers into family or clan centered societies in the Ma Han region, Paekche, the most ambitious group, encountered little resistance in its attempts to control the whole region and areas formerly under Chinese rule.

The Distribution of Land and Labor Force

The concept of land labor force as productive as well as financial resources was developed with a view to strengthening the royal power. Transfer of communal ownership of land and also of labor which had been provided by social groups such as *ture* under the communal auspices to royal ownership was achieved through successive transformations of society. As the patriarchal leaders of local political power groups were reoriented to become the privileged aristocracy or government officials in the royal government, their political grip over *sijok* or *pujok* was gradually, if not wholly, severed in favor of the royal authority. In this process the private ownership of land appeared ; aristocratic officials came to own goodly slices of land. The land not owned privately, however, came generally under the control of the monarch as the patriarch of the state.

Although successive monarchs justified the royal ownership of all land by resorting to power and theorization, the force that worked for private ownership never completely died. In fact, swings of these two forces centering on the ownership of land constituted a persistent undercurrent which created turbulent surface phenomena on many occasions during the traditional period. Monarchs of many occasions during the traditional period. Monarchs of the traditional period, with their economic resources less diversified, were dependent upon the distribution of land and labor force to assure themselves of the loyalty of the subjects, who still held considerable influence over their former followers. Wars of unification were no doubt prompted greatly by this immediate desire for land.

The land and people newly acquired through wars during the period in question were managed, of course, to a productive end largely in support of the ruling family and the newly formed aristocracy. Beside a vast expanse of field for government revenue, there was land allocated for the purpose of maintaining royal facilities such as detached palaces, ancestral shrines, and tombs ; this category of land increased as did the royal power. The aristocracy — civil and military officials — obtained land mostly, at least in the beginning, through the royal bestowal in recognition of their meritorious service in wars and on other occasions.

After the suppression of a revolt in Kaya in 562, King Chinhŭng gave General Sa Taham, the most meritorious in the campaign, two hundred prisoners and a large tract of land, which the humble general in turn divided among his soldiers. Chesu of Koguryŏ received ten *kun* (a unit of weight ; about 600gm.) of gold and 1,000 furrows of field from the grateful king for his recovery from a rive of the body of a drowned prince. The largest grant of land was called *sig'ŭp* which covered a vast spread of land with a town in it. In 532 when King Kŭmguae of Kŭmgwan Kaya voluntarily surrendered to Silla, King Pŏphŭng assigned a part of Kŭmguae's old domain to him as *sig' ŭp*. A *sig' ŭp* might be under the administrative control of the central government, but its assignees were given right to levy taxes in produce and labor service on people in the area. And in 657 King Ŭija of Paekche granted a *sig' ŭp* to each of forty-one princes.

Land reclamation was also an important mode of transferring land into private possession. Paekche in its later period, when it was contained by powerful Silla, understandably turned within itself for new arable land. There are evidences that Koguryŏ, too, had its share of extensive reclamation over its pastures and hunting grounds. In Silla, aristocratic families were often ordered, for the purpose of defense and cultural dissemination, to migrate to strategic towns, where they came to possess a great deal of land by clearing. In these instances of reclamation, small land owners whose land happened to be within projected areas seem to have been forced out of their land or to sell it.

The Buddhist church was another recipient of a tremendous amount of land. The church, regarded as one of the most important national institutions, was accorded unsparing economic support by both the government and inspired individuals. In fact, the government made it a rule to bestow a certain amount of land upon a newly erected Buddhist temple, and wealthy families also lavished land and other gifts on temples. Buddhist monasteries emerged soon as great landowners second only to the royal family and kept up that status which posed a serious threat at times to government revenue, all monasterial properties being tax-exempt. In 664 King Munmu had to prohibit the donation of land and other properties to monasteries. Such prohibition, though intermittently declared thereafter, was never effectively enforced until the very end of the Koryŏ dynasty.

The labor force tilling the soil, after the *sijok* and the *pujok* disappeared as independent political units, consisted mostly of small farmers. Their numbers, however, were diluted by the wars of conquest ; some were called into military and *corě* duties ; others were made to bear heavy taxation, resulting in their dislocation. Drifting farmers most often ended up in voluntary or forced servitude to powerful houses in return for personal protection. This phenomenon appeared recurrently under similar conditions throughout the traditional period. To replace the lost farm labor, the government transplanted groups of war prisoners in villages or other localities. Such a method of peopling certain areas for the purposes of production and defense was often resorted to later. Even aristocratic families were not immune from such forced migration, as we shall see.

Although the general populace was thus roughly treated in various services to the government, they seem to have enjoyed the ownership of slaves. Such cases seem to have been quite prevalent, indicating that, as free farmers decreased in number, domestic and field slaves, who were reduced to that status because of crime, debt, or being foreigners-taken-prisoners, increased, comprising the majority of the productive classes during the last days of the Three Kingdoms period. These slaves seem to have received somewhat "dehumanized" treatment ; yet they were allowed to retain their own households. Nevertheless, it would be a mistake to draw a clear-cut class distinction between free farmers and field or domestic slaves in this period.

While the demise of Paekche and Koguryŏ was caused as much by internal decay, it seems probable that internal decay was caused by economic stagnation, that is, the inability to secure more land and people to distribute among the upper class because their frontiers were either fixed or even pushed back. In Paekche, amid the brawls of aristocratic officials, King Ŭija sank deep in debauchery, even in the face of the Silla-T'ang armies fast approaching the capital. In Koguryŏ the internal disintegration set in as the culmination of a long period of institutional contradictions. It is significant to note that Yŏn Kaesomun personally encouraged the practice of Taoism which won the popularity over Buddhism then. Given the general climate of pessimism that prevailed in Koguryŏ during its last days, the encouragement by the actual ruler, and the popularity among the ruling class, of cynic Taoism might have been more of a confession of failure in government than a cultural concern.

In victorious Silla, right after the fall of Koguryŏ, in 669 King Munmu distributed land and slaves among those who had performed meritorious military service. The local political leaders were also carefully handled with due share of the national wealth. It is doubtful that without generous dispensation of wealth the Silla royalty, still far from maturity, would have been allowed to claim as much power and authority as it gained in this period.

Organs of the Central Governments

Seen through the official ranking systems, Koguryŏ's government does not seem to have been developed as much as its early achievement of a nationhood might suggest. In the fourteen-grade rank system finalized probably in the reign of King Changsu, the highest was called Taedaero, a kind of an elective official with a political purpose of holding the royal power in check. The triennial election of the Taedaero by Sangga or political leaders of major tribes in the early period of nationhood was more often than not an affair of military contest. When failed by peaceful means, the election seems tto have been settled by naked force. The king was not supposed to intervene. Thus the office of the Taedaero, that Yŏn Kaesomun was, retained much of tribal tradition.

Another characteristic in Koguryŏ's ranking system was the predominance of ranks whose designations included the letter *hyŏng* or elder brother and *saja* or messenger. The concept of *hyŏng* in ranking was born of the consanguineous hierarchy of the patriarchal society. When leaders of tribal groups were organized into the royal government as officials, they were given ranks of *Tae Hyŏng*, (*Big Hyŏng* or big brother), So *Hyŏng*, (*Small Hyŏng* or small brother), etc. in accordance with their political strengths.

Similarly-given appellations, *Big Saja, Higher Saja*, etc., seem to have been offices of tax administrators posted in provinces and smaller administrative units, respectively. Koguryŏ stationed a *saja* (messenger) in the newly subjugated Okchŏ whose duties were, among other things, the supervision of the Okchŏ people in supplying Koguryŏ with tribute materials, salt, fish, and "beautiful women," as noted. The importance of the *saja* must have increased as Koguryŏ's territory expanded because, as mentioned previously, Koguryŏ needed food supplies from non-Koguryŏ subjects.

As indicated by the abundance of *hyŏng* ranks (five) and s*aja* ranks (four) in the fourteen-grade rank system, the structural development of the Koguryŏ government seems to have evolved from two most important needs : integration into the royal government of local tribal leaders and establishment of a tax and tribute collection system.

Although Paekche established the administrative divisions similar to Koguryŏ's and named places after those in Koguryŏ, it developed a government organization quite different from Koguryŏ's. It had sixteen official ranks divided into three groups in vertical order with uniforms distinguished by three different colors ; the eleventh and twelfth ranks belonged to different groups but had bands of the same color.

The so-called Six Chwap'yŏng were responsible for six ministries : Royal Secretariat, Defense, Rites, Treasury, Justice, and Royal Guards ; they served immediately under the king. To these six ministries were added new ministerial departments as necessitated later. By the time Paekche moved its capital to Puyŏ, a total of twenty-two Chwap'yŏng posts came into being. The fact that no less than twelve of them were for management of the royal household affairs and that the ministerial increase was not accompanied by territorial expansion seem to constitute a clear internal contradiction. It seems probable that bickering central mighties, whose military energy should have best been channeled into foreign conquests, were placated instead with ministerial ranks and offices.

Silla's Bone Ranks and Government. With completion in 674 of the eleven-grade provincial ranking system in parallel with the seventeen rank system for the central officials developed much earlier, Silla perfected its government organization. The method of ranking provincial officials, which had developed since the time of King Chinhŭng in the late sixth century, was in conformity with that of central officials. The provincial ranks, too, were given in consideration of the politico-military strengths of candidates' power groups in relation to one another. This vertical grouping of local powers based on their actual strengths was the very formation of social status also. Indeed, the two parallel officialdoms, central and provincial, were locked, as it were, into a social status system called *Kolp'um*. The *Kolp'um*, literally meaning the quality of bone, is usually translated Bone Ranks, which amounted to a caste system, though within the officialdom, when it was rigidly kept.

The "qualities of the bones" were classified into five grades. The highest bone grade or rank was the *Sŏnggol* or Holy Bone who could qualify for kingship. The second highest, *Chin'gol* or True Bone included the Pak family and the members of the Kim or royal family except those of the Holy Bone. The third highest bone rank was the *Ruktup'um* or literally Six Head Quality ; then there was the Five Head Quality ; the lowest bone rank was the Four Head Quality. Those Kims of the Holy Bone had to be born of mother from the Pak family, but this rule was abandoned when Prince Kim Ch'unch'u, of the True Bone, was installed on the throne as King T'aejong. The majority of local leaders seem to have been assigned to the Five or Four Head Quality. The Bone Rank system in time became hereditary, and one's life was much dictated by its stipulations.

As shown in the following diagram, the True Boners can advance from the lowest rank through the top ; the Six Head Quality men can advance only up to the sixth rank ; the Five Head Quality up to the tenth or the provincial fourth ; the Four Head Quality up to the twelfth or the provincial

Bone Ranks (Holy Bone omitted)				Ranks for Central Officials			Ranks for Provincial Officials		Uniforms in Colors
True Bone	Six Head Quality	Five Head Quality	Four Head Quality	Ordinals	Designations of Ranks	Remarks	Ordinals	Designations of Ranks	
				1	(Designations of ranks omitted)				Purple
				2					Purple
				3					Purple
				4					Purple
				5					Purple
	←			6		The sixth rank has four grades of its own			Red
				7			1	(Designations of ranks omitted)	Red
				8			2		Red
				9			3		Red
		←		10			4		Blue
			←	11	The tenth rank has eight grades of its own	The eleventh rank has six grades of its own,	5		Blue
				12			6		Yellow
				13			7		Yellow
				14			8		Yellow
				15			9		Yellow
				16			10		Yellow
←				17			11		Yellow

sixth. For the expediency of promoting one official higher than the upper limit of his Bone Rank, the court created, in three cases, a few more ranks on top of his last rank which were, however, regarded as belonging within his Bone Rank. When, however, regarded as belonging within his Bone Rank. When, for instance, a Six Head Quality man attained to the sixth rank, his upper limit, he had three more ranks through which he could be promoted on merit, but still falling below the fifth rank which was reserved for True Bone men. Similarly, the tenth and eleventh ranks for the Five Head Quality families together contained the equivalent of fourteen subranks as remarked in the diagram.

By and large, the True Bone people, truly aristocratic in the strict sense of that term (or as shown by the purple color of their uniform), monopolized all key positions of the government and enjoyed a disproportionately large portion of the wealth of the kingdom. The Bone Rank system also imposed restraints upon the social life of the official class with various limitations applicable to each rank. Houses, vehicles, and tablewares are said to have been regulated for size, decoration, etc., according to the Bone Ranks of their owners.

The highest office in the Silla government was that of the Sangdaedŭng created in 531 on top of the seventeen rank system of the central government. The Sangdaedŭng presided over meetings of the leaders of the central aristocracy on the important matters of the state in name of the king. Politically, the Sangdedŭng, even though he was appointed by the monarch, represented the interests of the aristocracy and tribal tradition.

By the time of unification, Silla had established nearly twenty ministries, courts, and directorates. The Ministry of Defense, created long before the office of the Sangdaedŭng, was by far the most important department of the government, especially in the most important department of the government, especially in the period of military growth, that is, during the reigns of King Pŏphung (514–539) and King Chinhŭng (540–575). As the unique ministerial level office of the government in the sixth century, the Ministry of Defense also functioned as the royal secretariat and the royal household management in addition to its main business of war-making, and later it served as the organ for bracing the royal authority against the office of the Sangdaedŭng.

King Chinp'yŏng (579–631) instituted a few more ministries in his long reign, the most important of which were the Ministries of Personnel, Revenue, Rites, and Royal Household Affairs. Then, in 651, Queen Chindŏk (647–653) established the *Chipsasŏng*, a top organ of the central government, which transmitted the royal orders to the governmental departments and supervised their implementations. The establishment of the *Chipsasŏng* marked a bureaucratic solidarity strengthened in favor of the royal authority *vis-ă-vis* the aristocratic power represented by the Sangdaedŭng. With the establishment of the Left Ministry of Justice in 651 and the Right in 667 and of the Ministry of Public Works in 686, Silla completed the administrative divisions of the government which were to be streamlined into Six Ministries and related departments of later dynasties.

These bureaucratic establishments, which signified the royal domination over the traditional power groups, may be viewed also in the context of some significant political and social changes. King T'aejong's ascension to the throne in 654, though more than a decade before unification, actually marked the beginning of a new era for Silla. King T'aejong, first True Bone king who made Silla open to the political influence of T'ang China, was instrumental in creating, in many respects, an aristocracy of merits to which, as we have seen, much of the nation's wealth was alloted. Such powerful and prestigious positions in the royal family as king's brothers and queen's father were gradually relegated to under the shadow of the king, a tendency that was to be reinforced in later dynasties.

Provincial Administration

Koguryŏ, as has been noted, was divided into five provinces, each of which was divided into five provinces, each of which was administered by a governor who resided in a large walled city. Beside the provincial capitals, there were about 170 walled cities and towns in the country where government officials assisted by military deputies carried out their administrative responsibilities. The capital was also divided into five districts ; so was the capital province where each of five traditional hereditary patriarchs with military forces of their own seems to have governed a district assigned to him. This administrative setup of tribal origin seems to have continued to the last days of Koguryŏ. After Koguryŏ moved its capital to P'yŏngyang, it named Kungnae, its old capital, and Hansŏng, modern Chaeryŏng in Hwanghae Province, subsidiary capitals whose significance was military rather than administrative.

Paekche's provincial administrative system was completed after its capital was moved to Puyŏ for the last time. Until then twenty-two large walled cities in the country seem to have been administrative and military centers. Like Koguryŏ, Paekche had divided the country into five provinces and the capital area into five districts. Each of the five provinces, which together contained 200 fortified cities and towns, was administered by a governor who had a force of 700 to 1,200 men under his command. A province consisted of seven to ten counties, each of which was under three military officers commanding a certain number of soldiers.

Silla started with two provinces and added new ones as it acquired new territories. After unification, in 685 the government set up nine provinces which were in turn divided into prefectures and subprefectures ; this administrative division into nine provinces of the country, since it was simply modeled on the T'ang's nine provinces, seems to have lacked geographical logic. At first, military men were appointed heads of provincial administrative units, but they were gradually replaced by civilian officials.

The salient features of Silla's provincial administration system were the specially-established five subsidiary capitals and the thoroughly administered village level units. The capital Kyŏngju, located in the southeastern corner of the Peninsula, was now clearly not in a position to command the entire country. Consequently, there was a movement to transfer the capital to modern Taegu, but it was frustrated by conservatives. To compensate for Kyŏngju's disadvantageous location, five strategic cities were set up as subsidiary capitals. These small capitals were meant to be exact replicas of Kyŏngju in city planning and population composition. Some aristocratic families of Kyŏngju were forced to emigrate to these cities for a two-fold purpose. They served as a kind of cultural or educational service corps who were expected to exercise influence over local people, particularly those formerly under Paekche and Koguryŏ rule, and for many powerful houses in crowded Kyŏngju, on the other hand, such transplantation of people was a release.

Village chiefs were usually political leaders whose wealth and power were traditionally rooted in the areas of their jurisdiction. The government, mindful of their political growth, required them or their close relatives to sojourn in Kyŏngju for an alternative period of time in liaison and advisory capacities on local administrative matters, or, in more realistic parlance, as political hostages. By the early eighth century, the government's administrative penetration of villages became surprisingly thorough. The village households were classified into nine grades according to wealth ; the people were grouped into twelve categories according to sex and age for purposes of taxation, *corvée* labor, military duty, and land allocation. Numbers of domestic animals, cone pine trees, catalpa trees, Numbers of domestic animals, cone pine trees, catalpa trees, mulberry trees, the area of dry and paddy fields and hemp field, and also the boundary of the village were meticulously recorded. These administrative records were triennially reviewed for changes.

Beside these villages of tax-paying *p'yŏngmin* or commoners, there were three categories of forced settlements called *hyang, so,* and *pugok* where, as has been noted, agricultural serfs, former prisoners of war, and families of rebels and traitors were herded together in groups. Although the differences among these types of forced settlements are not clear, each was required to engage in specified productive activities such as farming, stock raising, and manual work which included the weaving of wicker baskets.

The Military Organization

The fact that possession of sufficient military strength was of paramount importance in harsh realities of the Three Kingdoms period is shown by the military orientation of administrative arrangement. Administration seems to have been more of military affairs. Indeed, military might was not only for foreign conquests but also for domestic use. Internal security, partly because of the general lack of national spirit on the part of the people as a whole, was maintained by the military grip over them. Understandably, it was on military training and organization that the Three Kingdoms alike concentrated the best of their energy and genius. Koguryŏ and Paekche are known to have defeated soldiers executed as traitors. No less severe was the martial spirit of Silla, about which we know more.

Silla, in its final phase of military establishment around the middle of the seventh century, had twenty-odd categories of army corps organized for different purposes and at different times as the national defense called for. The serious reorganization of the army began while in confrontation with the T'ang. The mainstay of the reorganized army was nine Sŏdang and ten Chŏng, which not only constituted the elite core of the Silla army but, more importantly, showed, in its organizational intent and components, the confidence and purposefulness with which Silla mastered the Peninsula.

The Sŏdang were primarily the royal guards stationed in Kyŏngju and served as a striking force in war. A Sŏdang unit was manned by 135 officers with ranks ranging over twenty-one of the thirty-one military ranks of the Silla army. The Sŏdang were distinguished from one another by the color of the collars on the soldiers' uniforms. All but two of the nine Sŏdang were activated after 668, and the last one was organized in 687, as shown in the diagram on the right. The Jade and Red Collar Sŏdang were the followers of Prince Ansŭng of Koguryŏ who surrendered to Silla. When, after a try at the Koguryŏ revival, the Prince was brought to Kyŏngju and enrolled in the True Bone rank and his followers were separately settled in the old Paekche territory, they revolted. Thereupon, they too were brought to the capital and organized into the said two Sŏdang.

Ten Chŏng were stationed in nine provinces one each except in militarily important Han Province (modern Kyŏnggi Province), where two Chŏng were placed. Much smaller than a Sŏdang in size, a Chŏng, with cavalry as its backbone, served as the local police and patrol. Silla's defense posture, illustrated in the Sŏdang-Chŏng deployment over the country, was to become the prototype after which later dynasties patterned their defense.

The Hwarang. Although, as we have seen, Hwarang organizations were not part of the army as such, they contributed tremendously towards the maintenance of general vitality and strength of the Silla army. As a social institution, which strongly influenced Silla culture particularly in its formative years, however, the role of the Hwarang (Flower Youth) took on a many dimensional significance. Groups of unmarried youths, gathered for physical and spiritual cultivation. naturally attracted the eyes of the expansion-minded government which, thereupon, began taking a direct hand in their organiza-

Units Name	Regional and Racial Background	Rear of Activation	Remarks
Green Collar Sŏdang	Silla	583	
Purple Collar Sŏdang	Silla	625	
Dark Red Collar Sŏdang	Silla	672	A long lance unit
White Collar Sŏdang	Paekche	672	
Yellow Collar Sŏdang	Koguryŏ	683	
Black Collar Sŏdang	Malgal (Jurched)	683	The predecessors of the Manchus
Jade Collar Sŏdang	Koguryŏ	686	The followers of Prince Ansŭng
Red Collar Sŏdang	Koguryŏ	686	The followers of Prince Ansŭng
Blue Collar Sŏdang	Paekche	687	

tional growth ; this has been thought to be about the middle of the sixth century in the reign of king Chinhŭng.

The government first appointed two beautiful girls as *wŏnhwa* or literally source flower, symbolizing leadership around which the Flower Youths were to rally. Soon, the godesses of beauty became jealous of each other, resulting in the murder of one and the execution of the other. Thereafter, a young man of good family was placed to lead each youth group. To coordinate their activities, a high-ranking official was later appointed, who was called *hwaju* or master flower. Thus, under the government encouragement, the Hwarang organizations rapidly increased in number and social prestige, growing into several hundred groups during the seventh century.

As the Hwarang movement, essentially a social phenomenon, was thus nationalized, its ideology was also formulated to fit the needs for training the leaders of the kingdom. The spiritual prop of the Hwarang was, in the beginning, beliefs in the gods of Sinkyo : the *Ch'ŏnji sinmyŏng* (God-Light of Heaven and Earth), spirits of the holy mountains, dragon kings of great rivers and seas, and ancestral spirits were some of the divine guardians whom the Hwarang (or the Silla people in general) worshiped. And the Hwarang so often confined themselves in mountain retreats for prayer and *suyang* or mental cultivation.

More importantly, the Hwarang developed ideals of conduct based on human relations born of the group-and family-centered social life. They were embodied in the so-called Five Commandments for Mundane Life written for the Hwarang by a Buddhist monk, Wŏn'gwang Pŏpsa (Teacher of Law

Wŏn'gwang) during the reign of King Chinp'yŏng (579–631). The Five Commandments, which included elements of the current foreign religious teachings of Buddhism and Confucianism, taught ; to serve one's sovereign with loyalty and one's parents with filial piety, to associate with one's friends with sincerity, not to retreat in battle, and not to destroy life, human or animal, aimlessly. One's sense of humility and moral obligation toward society was also emphasized.

Actual training consisted of a variety of programs in physical and mental cultivation. The Hwarang were drilled in such martial skills as horsemanship, swordmanship, javelin and stone throwing, football, and climbing up and down ladders. Through group discussions, appreciation of songs and music, and pilgrimage to the holy mountains, they fostered the magnanimity and infinitude of soul. Thus they were expected to become brave soldiers and officers in war and loyal officials and leaders of government in peace. The government severely punished anyone, regardless of social status, who did injury to the Hwarang, and soon they acquired social prestige of enormous proportions. People in general looked up to the Hwarang as a Maitreya, or "next Buddha," who, having attained buddhahood himself, postponed entering Nirvana in order to help others achieve salvation.

Parhae

Silla's unification of the Three Kingdoms, when fully considered, was less than complete. It was unable to integrate all of the vast territory of Koguryŏ and its people. Silla's failure eventually gave birth to the kingdom of Parhae (P'o-hai in Chinese), it was founded by Koguryŏans in 699, fully three decades after the demise of Koguryŏ. This delay was caused mainly by the T'ang's animosity toward its old foe preventing its revival. The T'ang carried off as prisoners more than 200,000 people, as has been noted, leaving P'yŏngyang virtually empty. Against T'ang's various maneuvers, the Koguryŏ remnants rallied around General Tae Choyŏng, and, using eleven fortified cities which had never surrendered to the T'ang as their power base, aligned themselves with the Tungusic Malgal tribes, predecessors of the Jurched of Manchuria. By 698 they were able to break out of the T'ang control and build an empire covering the forested northern regions of former Koguryŏ territory. Its capital, Tuen-hua in modern Chinlin Province in Manchuria, commanded the fertile Sungari River basin, the cradle of the Puyŏ culture whose elements subsequently were much retained by the new state.

Parhae, at its peak of prosperity, ruled the territory from the Gulf of Wŏnsan up to the Amur River region. Its economy was based on traditional livestock raising, agriculture, and trade with the T'ang and Japan. In cultural endeavors, Parhae seems to have made a new departure from those of its predecessors. Bound less by tradition, it more actively adopted the T'ang culture. Its capital layout, for instance, was a replica of T'ang's Ch'ang-an, and the government was also patterned after that of the T'ang, though with some modifications. Although there were occasional skirmishes among Parhae, the T'ang, and Silla, peaceful relations among them were generally maintained. Some remains of Parhae art suggest that it was indeed the "Prosperous State of East" as the Chinese called it.

Parhae and Silla, however, remained rather cool to each other like two disenchanted brothers. Their consanguinity became evidenced only when a stream of Parhae refugees flowed into the Peninsula, following the overthrow of Parhae by the Khitans in 926.

Roof tiles with surface design in Paekche period.

Dragon-headed, Turtle-bodied Kettle.

Part 3

Cultural Endeavors

1

The Native Religion

In the cultural history of Korea, religion has played the most important, genetic role ; as in other civilizations, the major cultural activities were evolved from religious ideas. But, as we shall see, before the Koreans could fully develop a religion of their own, highly developed foreign religions made their way into the Peninsula and overwhelmed the native religion whose gods were only in an incipient stage of growth. As the Koreans began to absorb these foreign religious doctrines and elaborate outlooks on life and cosmology, the whole fabrics of spiritual and social life were gradually transformed into a new cultural synthesis. The cultures of the Three Kingdoms can be regarded as the result of the first such synthesis, which was further matured into the United Silla culture.

Peace and Harmony as the Early Ideals

The early religious cults of nature worship and ancestor worship, whose primary purpose was to assuage man's primitive fear of unusual natural phenomena, were not yet contained in an enduring doctrinal framework as such, but they were tied in with agricultural activities, providing a spiritual basis for management of the early life as a whole. In this primitive stage of spiritual development, the early Koreans sought peace and harmony as the ideals of life and the universe.

They created the Sun God or, in Koguryŏ's case, Sun-and-Moon God, along with the *Ch'ŏnji sinmyŏng*, to whom the origin of ancestral myths could be traced and the agricultural productivity attributed. Although they began to develop vague organic relations among a multitude of gods, the early Koreans usually dealt with their gods and spirits individually for a specific purpose which might be soliciting help for one's soul or family welfare. The usual mode of contact with these supernatural beings was one of pampering, lest they should cause natural or social disasters.

Religious manifestations of the early ideals in the agricultural life took various forms which were at once aesthetic and recreational, but the central theme was on realization of the harmonious workings of universe that brought the abundant yields of nature in the autumnal field. The harvest was the measure with which to judge the degree of universal harmony for the year. Early kings released criminals from jails when a natural disaster hit the kingdom, for fear of possible involvement of innocents in punishment that might have disturbed the orderly workings of the universe.

Thus, profound preoccupation with, and emphasis on, the agricultural economy, often at the expense of other fields of production, became firmly rooted in the Korean mind. Technological stress for agriculture has been evinced as in the skill for construction of water reservoirs for which especially the Sam Han Koreans were well known, but technology as a field of human endeavor was less important for the early Koreans. The agricultural activities as a whole provided a frame of reference with which to create new knowledge and values and above all the method of life itself which was important.

In government the ideals of harmony and peace became the unanimity of opinions in the strict sense of that term. From the period of tribal confederation, all major governmental actions were taken on the basis of unanimity in political council held by the leaders of power groups and the government. A failure in obtaining the unanimity resulted in resort to armed settlement, which was another method of acquiring unanimity at the expense of peace temporarily.

In Silla the ideal of unanimity was institutionalized in the Hwabaek system, under which a single nay on the matter under deliberation meant rejection by all. To assure the utmost fairness and the proper procedure, the deliberating body, as. a rule, chose as the meeting place mountains traditionally held holy. Paekche had a more sophisticated system of "voting" which was not much different in spirit from modern voting. In choosing a minister, a box containing the names of several candidates would be placed on a lagre rock called Chŏngsaam or Rock of Government Matters. Later, the candidate who had received the "mark on his mame" was appointed minister. A number of inferences can be drawn from this elementary information, but it is doubtful that any concept of majority was involved in the "voting."

The Hwabaek meeting and the Chŏngsaam "voting" should not be referred in any significant sense to modern democracy, which is based primarily on individualism. The Korean concept of unanimity was born of the preference for harmonization of power groups in which individual was a part. An individual maintained his identity as a purposeful part of a group, though not as "a cogwheel of the society" as a whole. Political groups such as *sijok* and *pujok*, social groups such as family and clan, socio-economic groups such as *ture*, military-educational groups such as Hwarang, status groups such as Bone Rank class and prisoner-reduced serf masses, all as group, played an important role in the formative period of the Korean culture. Although they changed their forms through the vicissitudes of time, the concept of group as something which facilitated unanimity and which made individual existence meaningful became intractably fixed in the configuration of the Korean culture. We are less sure, however, for want of historical records, of the organizational procedure and the internal structure of these early groups. The role of individual was to make himself a harmonious and organic part of the group to which he belonged ; but, to initiate a move by an individual within the group was to disrupt its order.

The realization of oneself, therefore, was not in the area of revolutionary or materially productive activities as such but in excellence of one's endeavors in such fields as morals, arts, and scholarship and in military service in defense of the existing order. As seen in the Tan'gun legend, Old Chosŏn's folk laws, or in other fragmentary records scattered in early Chinese histories, the early Koreans came to highly value the "wide service to mankind," chastity, loyalty, filial piety, social decorum, beauty and music, etc., all pointing to universal harmony and peace, and they came to show infinite capacity for practice of these ideals and virtues. Confucianism, the first foreign thought which the Koreans slowly assimilated, was to provide the native religious ideals and social relations with metaphysical framework and organizational rationale.

2

Confucius and Confucianism

The beginning of the fourth century B.C., when the first light of civilized life dawned on the Peninsula, signified for China the political end of a brilliant period of cultural achievement based on the agricultural economy. The Chinese had over a millennium developed the bronze culture and, in the sixth century B.C. or earlier, began using ironwares toward a greater productivity. As the Koreans settled down to agricultural life, they were, therefore, destined to come under Chinese influence. Disintegration of the Chou dynasty into the Warring States period actually set in motion the Chinese cultural inroads into the Peninsula in the fourth century B.C., which in fact never ceased until modern times. Indeed, what and how the Koreans absorbed and assimilated of Chinese culture constituted, to a substantial degree, the stuff which tempered the development of Korean history.

The cultural indebtedness to China of the early Koreans is symbolically found in such cultural myth as the coming of Kija (Chi-tzu in Chinese). Kija, a nobleman of the Shang dynasty of China, is said to have come to Korea around 1,000 B.C. and taught the peninsular people a civilized way of life. Of what the Koreans acquired from the Chinese culture, by far the most important, that proved also the most durable in the Korean culture, was Confucianism.

The Warring States period, a period of political disintegration and war roughly covering from the fifth century B.C. to the middle of the third century B.C., was actually one of the most vigorous intellectual outbursts in the Chinese history. It witnessed a proliferation of philosophical teachings known as the Hundred Schools. Of the "hundred schools," which were really six major schools of thought, the worth-mentioning here, because of their subsequent influence on Korean thought, are about three. First, the *yin-yang* (*ŭmyang* in Korean) school was founded on a cosmological theory of *yin* and *yang*. *Yin* representing the female principle and *yang* the male principle are thought to produce all universal phenomena through their mutual interaction. Secondly, the *Tao-te* school, literally school of Way and Power known in the West as Taoism(Togyo in Korean), was based on that mystical concept of Tao or Way of the universe, the idea that man can achieve his salvation by obeying the Way or the underlying principle of the universe. Then there was the school of *ju*, meaning weaklings (as against men of sword) or literati, that came to be known as the Confucian school.

Literati, well versed in the Six Classics and the ways and philosophy of rites and ceremonies discussed in them, made their living by, and their mission of, teaching and preserving these ancient cultural legacies. K'ung-fu-tzu or Master K'ung, known as Kongja in Korea and Latinized as Confucius in the West, represented this tradition of the early Chinese scholars and much more, as we shall see.

The life of Confucius has been rather prosaic outwardly and often pathetic in his long quest for securing an appointment in government. He was born in about 551 B.C., and died in 479 B.C. A native of the state of Lu located in modern Shantung Province, he served in minor capacity in the government of Lu until his surviving mother died in his middle twenties. After three years of mourning and a longer period of repose in which he overcame the personal tragedy, he was able to hold a cabinet post in the same government but soon was forced to resign through political intrigues. All these years, however, with unfailing enthusiasm and skill, he taught and interpreted for his disciples not only the Six Classics but also ancient Chinese institutions and customs. Eager students, from all over the country whose number is said to have been "three thousands," flocked around the Master. Seventy-two of these disciples were later elevated to the position of reverence for their own virtues and scholarship.

Through indefatigable teaching and convincing interpretation of the cultural heritage, Confucius achieved his fame and has been regarded as *the* teacher or even the divinely-appointed inheritor and perpetrator of the ancient civilization. He answered the questions put by inspired disciples at any given moments and commented on random subjects and events. These educational "conversations" went on even during his hazardous ten year journey seeking a government office from one state after another, accompanied by a train of disciples, but without success. His idea of government, highly charged with moralism, was invariably rejected by the practical politicians of the time, a fact which, as one of his disciples said, was the mark of a true gentleman.

He came home with experiences and revelations which only a virtuous man could have and spent his last years in retirement on the highest level of spiritual attainment. One needs only read a few pages of the *Lun yu* or *Conversation* to feel his well-rounded sagely personality strike forth. His impeccable moralism, warm humanism, transcendental lightheartedness, and genuine interest in sport and music, all seem to have been so well blended to make a great man, indeed the greatest man China has ever produced.

Chinese Classics

The sources of Confucian scholarship and moralism are ancient classics totalling thirteen. The six of the thirteen classics, generally thought to have been written before the time of Confucius and somehow survived Ch'in *Shih Huangti*'s book burning campaigns, are most important and venerated works. Of the six, the *Book of Music*, however, was either lost or included as an essay in the *Book of Rites*, and the number became five which came to be called the Five Classics.

The first of the Five Classics in traditional order is the *Book of Songs* (*Shih ching ; Sigyŏng* in Korean). The *Book of Songs* or *Poetry* contains 305 songs which were selected by Confucius, as the tradition claims, from among 3,000 songs dating from the tenth to the seventh century B.C. Of the 305 songs, many are charming folk songs, while others are political poems and ritual hymns used on governmental ceremonial occasions.

The *Book of History* (*Shu ching ; Sŏgyŏng* in Korean) consists of historical and semi-historical documents such as short announcements and oral reports supposedly made by the rulers and their officials, dating from early Chou times. This Book has two versions : the "modern text" which, as the original text was thought to have been burnt by the Ch'in government, was reconstructed by a Confucian scholar named Fu Sheng (ca. 180 B.C.) through his memory. Later appeared the "old text" which was supposedly found in the old residence of Confucius. The "old text" contains sixteen essays more than the "modern text" and has been claimed by many as the original text. Scholarly debates on the authenticity of the two texts have been going on until recent times somewhat in favor of the "old text."

The *Book of Changes* (*I ching ; Yŏkkyŏng* in Korean) is also known as the *Book of Divination* because it was used for divination. Divination was a widely practiced art in traditional China and Korea. In China, bones and tortoise shells were used for divination but later substituted with the stalks of milfoils to make various trigrams and hexagrams, as shown below. Referring to the latter method of divination, the *Book of Changes* contains clues to, and interpretations of, variant combinations of the eight trigrams and sixty-four hexagrams, appendices, and philosophical comments on the significance of those interpretations which are additions made by later scholars.

A trigram is composed of three broken or unbroken lines (or, in actual practice, short milfoil stalks), and through different combinations of these lines, a trigram changes in eight possible ways as follows : ☰☱☲☳☴☵☶☷ . By the same method, a hexagram makes sixty-four possible combinations. The two component lines, the unbroken symbolizing the *yang* or positive force of nature and the broken the *yin* or negative force, are believed to have created the universe through their mutual, complementary, and balancing actions. A random combination of *yang* and *yin* in trigram or hexagram represents a particular phenemenon in nature at a given moment. The *Book of Changes* served as a handbook which supplied the interpretative answer to that phenomenon.

The *Book of Rites* (*Li chi ; Yegi* in Korean), the most Confucian of the Five Classics, is a compilation of miscellaneous materials on ritual matters, dating from Chou times. The compilation of this book, also known as *Record of Rituals*, in its present form was made in the second century B.C. ; most of the *Book of Rites* was written by scholars after Confucius.

The last of the Five Classics, *Ch'un ch'iu* or *Spring and Autumn Annals* is a brief and concise chronicle of major events which took place in Confucius' native state of Lu for the period covering from 722 to 481 B.C. Tradition has credited Confucius with the authorship of the *Spring and Autumn Annals*, which was believed by the Confucianists to be an entirely factual history. In any case, the book is replete with moralistic meaning read into it, thus setting a Confucian tradition in historical writing which was followed up by successive Chinese and Korean historians.

As these Classics were gradually revered as bibles of the Confucian school of thought, the ardent Confucian scholars of later generations came to claim Confucius to be the writer or partial editor of all Five Classics. But the truth is that these so-called Five Classics, with which Confucius and his followers, with an unusual interest in the past, developed their school of thought.

As Confucianism grew, lesser but often better composed works, most of them elaborately written as commentaries and philosophical expositions on the Five Classics, were added to the classics list which, by T'ang times, counted thirteen, including Five Classics. The first three newly added to the Thirteen Classics are commentaries on the *Spring and Autumn Annals* written sometime between the early fifth and early second centuries B.C. : *Commentaries of Kung-yang* (*Kung-yang chuan ; Kongyang chŏn* in Korean) and *Commentaries of Ku-liang* (*Ku-liang chuan ; Kogyang chŏn* in Korean) are exegetical works on the *Annals ; Commentaries of Tso* (*Tso chuan* ; *Chwa chŏn* in Korean), a thirty-chapter work, contains many historical informations and is extremely well written ; probably for this reason, it has been widely read.

Related to the *Book of Rites* are two works dating from the second century B.C. : Ceremonies and Rituals (*I li ; Ŭirye* Korean) and *Rites of Chou (Chou li ; Churye* in Korean). The former deals mainly with ceremonies and rituals on one's coming-of-age, marriage, funeral, and sacrificial rites of Chou times, and the latter is an idealized operation of the Chou government institutions, which, for the most part, involves rituals and ceremonies in reference to the cycle of the seasons.

The *Lun yu* or *Conversation* is the best known of the Confucian classics in Korea, usually rendered *Analects (Nonŏ* in Korean). The *Nonŏ*, the most important source of the biographical materials on Confucius, is in the main a collection of laconic and instructive sayings of Confucius given during conversations with his disciples. The greater portion of the book consists of usually two or three line statements removed from the background ; inspire of, or probably because of, this, the salient points made in these lines drive home to the heart of readers.

The *Book of Mencius (Meng-tzu ; Maengja* in Korean) contains the sayings and writings of Mencius (372–289 B.C.), the great Confucian thinker after Confucius, who explored the Confucian teachings with a philosophical viewpoint, as we shall see later. The two other works complete the Thirteen Classics. The *Book of Filial Piety (Hsiao ching ; Hyogyŏng* in Korean) was composed in the third or second century B.C. of materials on the subject selected from the *Book of Rites*, and it became a principal text for instruction of the children on that virtue. Finally, the *Erh ya (Ia* in Korean), compiled in the third century B.C., is a collection of glosses on names of plants and animals and on those in astronomy, geography, music, etc. which appear in the classical texts.

Another system of classification, which appeared much later, singles out the *Analects*, the *Mencius*, the *Great Learning (Ta hsüeh ; Taehak* in Korean), and the *Doctrine of the Mean (Chung yung ; Chung yong* in Korean) as embracing the most profound philosophical essence of Confucianism ; these are the so-called Four Books. The last two of these books were originally two chapters from the *Book of Rites* and made two separate books. In Korea, along with the Four Books, the *Book of Songs*, the *Book of History*, and the *Book of Changes* were grouped together as the Three Classics. The Four Books and the Three Classics were musts for a Confucian gentleman during the Yi dynasty.

Confucian Ideals

In his role of transmitting the wisdom of China's past, Confucius also gave his own views on, and interpretations of, man and society, their relations, and things in general. This was extremely helpful to the contemporary Chinese who lived in an age of moral and political confusion. Indeed, the greatness of Confucius lies in his placing things of spiritual value in proper order for the first time in the Chinese history. It is worth noting that in his thought, which was devoid of otherworldliness, the government was regarded as being in the best position to bring about the ideal society which he believed to have existed in antiquity.

His was, however, an idealized society in which the people were bound by ethical relations and a set of virtues with T'ien (Heaven) as representing the unseen yet purposeful force of nature beyond man's control. The basic human relations as the foundation of the ideal society were five : the ruler and the ruled with loyalty, parents and children with filial piety, husband and wife with obedience, the elder and the younger with respect, and friend and friend with trust. Always looking back to the pseudo-historical days of Yao and Shun or to the heyday of the Chou dynasty as the model society, Confucius urged the rulers to return to the ancient way or to follow that exemplary age when hereditary kings governed a simple agricultural society not by means of force but through their virtues. He held that the paramount consideration for a ruler should be to create a right spiritual climate in which every member of the society would be able to live in accord with their station in society. Confucius said ; "The ruler let be a ruler and the subject a subject ; the father let be a father and the son a son."

The Rectification of Names. In Confucius' political and social philosophy, the so-called rectification of names is of far-reaching significance. The concept was born against the background of rampant social and intellectual chaos that perverted semantics. Names and words contain meanings which constitute the reality to which they are assigned. A prince can be called a prince only when he performs the duties and responsibilities assigned to a prince. Things in actuality must conform to their ideal meanings attached to them by names and words. In other words, "theory should correspond to reality or, as the Confucians really meant it, reality should be made to conform with theory." *

This concept, while it was useful in reinvigorating the morals of Confucius' day or even later periods, had a deleterious effect on Korea in its relations to China. The Son of Heaven of the Middle Kingdom, that is, the Chinese king, stipulated that all kings of "barbarian" or peripheral nations, in their intercourse with China, should enter into its vassalage, a condition that Confucianism sanctified as international propriety. Silla showed a remarkable

---

* John K. Fairbank,Edwin O. Reischauer, East Asia : *The Great Tradition*, p. 70.

freedom from the restraint of this propriety, as we have seen. But when the Confucian gentlemen of the Yi dynasty ruling class, who lost the dynamic flexibility of Silla, assumed the junior partnership with all assigned roles going with it in Korea-China relations, they honestly behaved like a junior or a vassal. The result was a voluntary servitude in many respects.

The Will of Heaven. Another important concept in Confucian ideals is that of Heaven. Heaven in Confucian thought is not suprahuman, anthropomorphic being as such ; Confucius was never interested in just such an entity. Indeed, he took delight in performing religious ceremonies and recognized at one time or another the existence of spirits. But his invariably-discriminating attitudes toward the spirits seem to show that he could not simply disown them which had been part of the past. Instead, confucius conceived Heaven as an impersonal yet willful force in nature and society. And this natural and social force which was beyond human control could not be made to accord with man-made theory. This was a higher reality to which man must conform. This Confucius called T'ien-ming, the will of Heaven. To know the will of Heaven, which is of great importance in the Confucian life, is to acquiesce in one's fate or to accept the limit of one's capacity or social status.

The Confucian Virtues

In the spectrum of Confucian morality, the foremost item is *jen* (*in* in Korean), usually translated love or human-heartedness. Loving others can be in essence a universal love ; however, Confucian love is minutely regulated and gradated in accordance with one's social relations to the recipients of that love. One imparts his love through the form of *li* (*ye* in Korean), variously rendered ceremony, social decorum, propriety, or etiquette. One's love to his father, uncle, first cousin, second cousin, friend, stranger is made artificially different in its outward manifestation. This artificiality in *li* produced many knotty problems as in the Yi dynasty period when the outward form of *li* came to be more emphasized as a unique means of ensuring orderly society and government.

I (*ŭi* in Korean) or righteousness also is an important virtue that a gentleman ought to possess. Righteousness is "oughtness of a situation" which must be translated into action, regardless of difficult conditions, whether they may be temptation to personal profit or even danger of death. When the purity of righteousness is stressed, the result becomes uncompromising, obdurate attitudes or often eruptions of violence. human-heartedness might be brought in to balance this extreme ; a more useful virtue in such cases, however, is *shu* (*sŏ* in Korean), reciprocity, altruism, or mutual consideration which is in Confucius' own words in the *Analects*, "What you do not want done to yourself, do not do to others." The more positive aspect of the virtue is *chung* (*ch'ung* in Korean), which is considerateness to others or loyalty. One ought to serve his father as he wants his son to serve him ; an unloving father, on the other hand, ought not to expect to enjoy filial piety from his son.

The Sage-Gentleman. A perfect man by the Confucian standards is called sage-gentleman as against small or inferior man whose action is always motivated by personal "profit." In a sage-gentle-man's conduct, the Confucian ideals and virtues are embodied in perfectly balanced form. The sage-gentleman is also conscious of the will of Heaven ; therefore, he is completely at ease with society and universe. Reflecting on his own spiritual development, Confucius neatly sums up in the *Analects* : "At fifteen I set my mind 'on learning. At thirty I could stand firmly. At forty I had no doubt. At fifty I knew the decrees of Heaven. At sixty I was obediently listening to them. At seventy I could follow what my heart desired without overstepping the boundaries of what was right."

Mencius and Hsün-tzu

Confucius' teachings and sayings were to develop into a vast system of philosophy. The first great step in that direction was made by two contrasting philosophers during the third century B.C. Mencius developed the optimistic and idealistic side, while Hsün-tzu (ca. 298–237 B.C.) emphasized the somewhat pessimistic and realistic wing of Confucianism.

Mencius, with a deep psychological perceptive, held that man's innate nature was good, a conception that became an unquestioned premise in orthodox Confucianism. One of analogies Mencius used to support his theory is man's instinctive response to a child about to fall into a well. Regardless of his status, whether a sage or a thief, he would feel alarm and distress at the sight because he was born human-hearted, that is, with the faculty of *jen* or humanity. But this innate goodness of man, he pointed out, can be corrupted by adverse living conditions. If man's innate goodness is fostered unhindered of improper environs and provided with proper education, it would realize into the Confucian virtues, that is, ultimately becoming one with the universe just as a plant, if properly preserved, would grow into expected size and beauty. The perfectibility of man is not far to seek in Mencius, if a certain mystic element in his philosophy is understood.

Man's external conditions, therefore, in Mencius' view, were no less important than his innate goodness in realization of the Confucian virtues in society. In fact, he placed an extraordinary emphasis on the society well-ordered in accordance with the five human relations as a preliminary step leading directly to actualization of the ideal society of Yao and Shun, which he tirelessly expounded for the benefit of "profit"-motivated kings of contemporary China. When the people were well fed and clothed according to their age and status, there would be peace and virtuous living. A ruler's paramount duty was to see to it that they were materially well provided for and morally well led by his moral leadership, for which he was given the Mandate of Heaven in the first place. For a son who neglects his filial duties, the ruler should be blamed, whose moral influence was obviously not strong enough among his people. The government, in the last analysis, is a moral institute under a moral leader assisted by morally impeccable bureaucrats. Lack of moral leadership on the part of the ruler, who, for instance, exploits his people for personal "profit," can result in the forfeit of his mandate to rule, and the subsequent rebellion may be justified.

True to the style of Confucius, Mencius wandered from state to state, seeking an opportunity to put his political philosophy into practice, but without avail. Like the Master, it was also as a teacher that Mencius was acclaimed as the great sage-gentleman next only to Confucius himself. The *Mencius*, a collection of his philosophical essays and dialogues with disciples and rivals, was, as has been noted, included, along with the *Analects*, in the Four Books, which were rightly regarded as "the supreme embodiment of the Confucian teachings." Indeed, Confucianism might as well be called the Way of Confucius and Mencius.

Much more successful as a government official and as a teacher also in his days than Mencius, Hsün-tzu approached Confucianism from quite a different angle. With a "realistic" evaluation of man and society, he rationalized that man's nature was essentially evil. Yet Hsün-tzu believed in man's ability and intelligence to possess virtues, which could be perfected through emulating the life of ancient sage-gentlemen. He also pushed aside the moralistic concept of Heaven and social force, and in the process he dealt havoc with a host of superstitious beliefs of the time. Reestablishment of the glorious society of the past which he envisioned with Mencius, therefore, he argued, was possible through education and government not by a moralistic ruler but by one who punished misdemeanors by law. Such a cold view of humanity of Hsün-tzu's was much exploited by "realists" like the Legalist, one of the Hundred Schools.

Hsun-tzu's emphasis on education as a means of correcting man's wickedness was a reconfirmation of social and educational necessity of *li* or rules of conduct as prescribed in the *Book of Rites, Ceremonies and Rituals*, and other classics. Although Hsün-tzu was rejected by later Confucian humanists for his blunt appraisal of man's nature as evil, his brand of realistic rationalism, affirming the necessity of social restraint and education as the only means of harnessing the animal nature of man, added another dimension to Confucianism as a whole. How these aspects of Confucianism came to influence Korean thinking we shall see later.

Noja.   Gongja.

3

Taoism

Next to Confucianism, the most persistent Chinese idea that prevailed in Korea was Taoism. Probably, Taoism, with its mystic and naturalistic inclination, was more appealing than Confucianism's dry formalism to the early Koreans that longed for such ecstatic dabbling in the unknown. Like Confucianism it found the congenial soil, and slowly took roots, in the depth of Korean mind. In the process, however, Taoism in Korea was less successful in maintaining itself as a systematic philosophy because of the very formless and negative nature of it ; it rather tended to become attenuated into other bodies of thought such as Buddhism, Shamanism, and Confucianism, and its dominant ideas were freely truncated and appropriated by artists, poets, escapists, cynics, or experimenters in mysticism.

Taoist Philosophy

The philosophical formation of Taoism occurred during the fourth century B.C., helped in no small measure by Confucian thinkers who turned their back on society then in chronic turmoil. Unquestionably, there was in Taoism a stark element of revolt against the conventional society from its birth. Yang Chu, a fourth century philosopher-recluse, who figures prominently in the early stage of Taoism, is thought to have said that he would not pluck a single hair from his shank, even if he would be given the whole world for it. Some others took to advocating the repudiation of knowledge and values, which they felt were the cause of social conflicts and individual anxiety, and the return to man's original state of anarchy. Although such unconventional outbursts was undoubtedly the result of the intellectual ferment of the period, revolting thinkers had no intention of formulating a systematic philosophy to found a school of thought, much less policies for institutional reform. But Taoism, inspite of itself, developed into a unified body of thought which enriched Chinese and other Northeast Asian cultures.

The primary books of Taoism, unlike Confucian classics, are not many. The *Lao-tzu* (*Noja* in Korean), also known as *Tao te ching* (*The Way and Power Classic ; Todŏkkyŏng* in Korean) and the *Chuang-tzu* (*Changja* in Korean) are the chief source of Taoist thought. The *Tao te ching* is attributed to Lao-tzu, literally Old Master, presumably the first Taoist sage who, according to tradition, lived in the late sixth century B.C. and is said to have once conversed with young Confucius. While the historicity of the Old Master is still held in doubt, the *Tao te ching*, in its present version, seems to be a creation of the third century B.C. The book is full of poetic passages and paradoxically balanced lines in laconic, often cryptic prose.

The *Chuang-tzu* consists of thirty-three lively essays, a substantial number of which were written by its namesake, a Taoist philosopher-recluse who lived in the late fourth century. The book as a whole, sharing with the *Lao-tzu* (*Tao te ching*) in expounding the Tao centrality, represents a substantial step forward from the *Lao-tzu* in the development of Taoism. But the no less enduring feature of the *Chuang-tzu* is its extensive use of entertaining allegories, parables, and poetic imageries, which make a delightful reading.

As the opening lines of the *Tao te ching* acknowledge, it is difficult to explain the Way, essence of Taoism, which sustained extreme antisocial attitudes of the Taoists. It is formless, nameless non-being shrouded in cosmic mystery, yet it is "the origin of heaven and earth ; " from which all changeable things come into being. This process of things coming into being, reaching one extreme, reversing from it, and then again returning may be called the "motion," or the very nature of the *Tao* (Way). Success is achieved from calamity which in turn "rests" upon success. Similarly, diminish a thing, it will increase, then again in reverse. The circular flow from one extreme to the other of the *Tao*, as in the *yin-yang* movement, is quiet and beguiling and may be detected only by sagely intuition.

The sage who understands the relativity of nature of things, therefore, in the moral realm, is able to transcend emotions and enjoy the serenity of soul. Since the absolute truth or absolute good, that is, the *Tao*, is wrapped in unreachable mystery even to the wise man, the Taoist sage let things and

---

* John B. Noss, *Man's Religions*, p. 321.

events come to pass ; attempt to change the flow of things is to disturb harmony. He would not even try to know what is right or wrong or what is good or bad. But he will identify himself with the way things are. By becoming one with the Way of universe, he transcends the invidious lines between the self and the world and between the "nameless" and the "nameable." Since the sage is one with the *Tao*, the essence of universe which never ceases to be, he, too, never ceases to be. His life is eternal.

Like the will of Heaven (*T'ien-ming*) in Confucianism, the *Tao* (Way) of Taoism is an impersonal force, but it lacks purpose. Therefore, the Taoist's is a society founded on such static and primitive idealism, which implements no program. The Taoists longed for a society where man could do without distinction between good and bad or virtue and vice. Wisdom, Knowledge, and law which man created contributed nothing toward his welfare but merely served to pollute his inborn nature. Let people follow what is natural in themselves and live in inactivity without desire like an unspoiled infant. Let no government meddle into the life of people, and let no production exceed a bare minimum of need. Only then, the Taoist utopia can be realized.

The Taoist ruler does not arouse the material desire or the social ambition of the people but rules them by doing nothing, for the Old Master said ; "Do nothing, and there is nothing that is not done." Then, the people, as those in the village-state pictured in the *Tao te ching*, will live contented in peace and harmony. Happy with their full bellies and simple customs, (and probably, with empty heads also), the Taoist people "will only look at the country over the border, will hear the cocks crowing and the dogs barking there, but right down to old age⋯, they will not trouble to go there." * If indeed contented with everything at home, one would wish to go and see the world. But then he would be a deviate in the Taoist culture.

The Taoist Movement. After a lively beginning as a philosophy, Taoism soon took a kind of supernatural turn, in metamorphosis or more in perversion, toward geomancy, thaumaturgy, and then a religion. As time progressed, the mythical aspect, rather than philosophical revitalization, of Taoism got the upper hand in China and came to attract the imagination of the common people. By the Six Dynasties period, it culminated in a spectacular religious movement. Pursuing the course of organized Buddhism, the Taoists developed a tremendous pantheon and built a large number of monasteries and convents under imperial sanction. Although Taoism as an organized religion in China fell far short of winning the heart of intellectuals, it served, through its transfiguration into theism, as a vehicle of mobilizing religious resources into an ecclesiastical movement on the glass roots level, which has been an experience of great significance in the Chinese history.

The profounder role of Taoism, however, was providing psychological freedom in a restrictive Confucian society. Its wholehearted offer of the mystical union with eternal nature made man drunken with ecstasy, creating an infinite possibility of aesthetic expression. It served as a carefree retreat for the alter ego of the Confucianist weary of prosaic routines and social responsibilities ; thus it was kept alive among the educated class. At the same time, its apocryphal statements and superhuman anecdotes that abound in Taoist classics gradually gave rise to pseudo-scientific beliefs which spawned a variety of occult arts and imaginations.

Chuang-tzu relates a marvelous story of a Lieh-tzu, reputedly a contemporary philosopher. "Lieh-tzu could ride upon the wind. Sailing happily in the cool breeze, he could go on for fifteen days before his return." "Yet," Chuang-tzu adds, "although Lieh-tzu could dispense with walking, he would still have to depend upon the wind. As to one who is charioted upon the eternal fitness of Heaven and Earth, driving before him the changing elements as his team to roam through the realms of the Infinite, upon what, then, would such a one have need to depend ?" * Chuang-tzu's flying imagination was not new, to be sure, but now so convincingly told by a sage-philosopher, flying was a distinct possibility.

This possibility may have spurred would-be occultists on to study of the magic art of contracting space, comparable with that of the seven-league boots. Buddhism had its share of such flight. It was also familiar with Koreans. As we have seen, the Sam Han people believed in the air-borne journey to Heaven of their dead ancestors, for whose use they buried the wings of large birds. It seems that the celestial traffic was heavy those days. Confucians, however, bogged down in such earthly matters as rituals and ceremonies, had no idea of offering such luxury as "roaming through the realm of the Infinite."

The Theories of the Yin-Yang and the Five Elements

A set of ideas to explain the workings of the universe but without didactic purpose was the *yin-yang* dualism. It was an attempt to explain the structure and workings of the universe in terms of certain cosmic principles. The *yang* force (*yang* meaning light) represents male, heat, activity, hardness, etc., and the *yin* force force (*yin* meaning dark) stands for female, cold, inactivity, softness, etc. These two forces are supposed to be in the eternal process of harmonious interaction through which all phenomena of nature are created. The way they interact is seen, for example, in the alternation of day and night or in the succession of four seasons. A burning piece of wood is the

---

* Ibid, p. 328..

yang forces in the wood overwhelming the *yin* at the moment. These cosmic forces or principles, which are also energy-modes, are thought to be coexistent, and at any given moment one force is dominating the other.

Another non-moralistic concept absorbed into the early Korean culture is that of five elements or agents, (or even power,) which was developed independently of the *yin-yang* theory. Only in the much later date were the five elements thought to be produced by the *yin-yang* interaction. The five elements are wood, metal, fire, water, and earth. These are the primary elements or essences which, through their various combinations, make up the universe. They are supposed to work in a sequence generating and destroying each other in accordance with a certain natural law. Thus, fire creates earth, as in the case of burning wood above, earth is to produce metal, metal to generate water, and water to beget wood, which in turn makes fire. The sequence can be turned back in a destroying order.

In the beginning, the five elements were thought to be physical substances as, for instance, in five planets, Jupiter, Mars, Saturn, Venus, and Mercury, which were believed to have the dominant elements of wood, fire, earth, metal, and water, respectively. Later, the five elements were made to manifest in every matter and thing in the universe : colors, animals, grains, tastes, virtues, numbers, medicine, succession of rulers, and so on. Every object and aspect of life were assigned one or another of the five elements. Theories of the *yin-yang* and the five elements, which are non-moralistic, hence probably of non-Chinese origin, are indeed rationalistic or "scientific" in many respects, even though they have generated many superstitious beliefs. Before long, they were absorbed into the philosophical systems of Confucianism and Taoism.

Through the liberal application of the *yin-yang* and five elements theories, a wide variety of pseudo-science such as numerology, astrology, physiognomy, and geomancy were developed. The geomantic theory of *feng-shui* (*p'ungsu* in Korean) was a widely practiced art particularly in Korea. The central idea of the *p'ungsu*, literally wind and water, is that man as part of the universe must conform to the cosmic workings of *yin-yang* and live in harmony with the five elements. One's house or burial place, for instance, must be properly arranged so as not to disturb the free flow, as it were, of these universal forces. The *p'ungsu* theory came into vogue during the Koryŏ dynasty. Equally popularized throughout the traditional period were the so-called "ten heavenly stems" and "twelve earthly branches" used for marking time. They are two sets of calendar signs combined in sequence to form sixty pairs of characters representing a sixty day cycle and a sixty year cycle. Each "stem" and "branch" are also associated with a particular direction, hour, each of five agents, and so on.

4

Scholarship and Education

With Chinese thought came the Chinese characters that by Han times had from simple pictographs of the Shang period evolved into a perfect writing system. It was this Han writing system that spread to Korea and Japan where Han and China were synonimous. It is worth noting that Korean, an "agglutinative" Altaic language, despite its geographical proximity to China, contrasts most sharply its geographical proximity to China, contrasts most sharply with tonal and non-inflecting Chinese. Obviously, this linguistic difference has been one of the major elements that maintained the cultural distinctiveness between the Koreans and the Chinese. The early Koreans and Japanese who were yet to develop literature of their own naturally turned to appropriate the Chinese characters for expression of their thought, a fact that has been proved not always blessing for them.

The Korean use of the Chinese writing system might have been rapidly extended during the period of Han occupation of the northern Peninsula. in 372 Koguryŏ set up a national college in its capital, patterned after the Chinese model, where the Five Classics, the *Historical Records* of Ssu-ma Ch'ien, the *History of the Han*, and other literary anthologies as well as the military art were taught to the aristocratic youth. In its later years, Koguryŏ extended the establishment of educational institutions to provinces where they were called Kyŏngdang. The Kyŏngdang, provincial school for the children of the common people with emphasis on Chinese classics and archery, seems to have been the institutional equivalent of Silla's Hwarang education. Paekche established the *paksa* system quite early, probably in the middle of the fourth century. A *paksa*, meaning scholar who knows widely, (the term is used for a doctor of philosophy today,) was appointed in each of the Five Classics and in other fields such as arithmetic, law, medicine, etc. It was these *paksa* who were sent to Japan to teach. Silla, drawing its first law code in 520, was, as usual, late in wider use of the Chinese writing system.

The emergence of scholarship, as in China, was first seen in the field of history-compilation usually at the order of a development conscious king. In Koguryŏ a *paksa* named Yi Mun Chin, in 600, compiled the five volumes of the *Sinjip* or *New History*, actually an abridged form of the *Yugi* or *Memorable Records* written earlier in 100 volumes. In Paekche Paksa Kohŭng compiled the *Sŏgi* or *Historical Records* during the reign of King Kŭncho' go (346-374). There were also a few other histories : the *History of Paekche*, the *Main History of Paekche*, and the *New History of Paekche* which were repeatedly quoted in the *Nihon shoki* or *History of Japan* compiled in 720. In Silla General Kŏch'ilbu coordinated scholars in compilation of a history of Silla at the order of King Chinhŭng in 545.

Unfortunately, all these early histories have been lost. A prototypal form of early historical writings can be seen in that large stele erected in 414 to commemorate the achievements of King Kwanggaet'o of Koguryŏ. The monumental inscription, consisting of some 1,800 Chinese characters, begins with Koguryŏ's foundation myth featuring Chumong, the legendary founder born of the Heavenly Emperor and Lady Yuhwa, and, before getting down to the story of the King's conquests, it describes his personal merit with quotations from the *Book of History* jammed in.

The ruling classes of the Three Kingdoms, by the early seventh century, seem to have been well versed in major Chinese classics and other literary anthologies. United Silla, as it set out in earnest for the cultural advancement through contact with the T'ang made belated efforts to promote education in Chinese thought. It established a central college in 682 and enshrined Confucius and his seventy-two disciples at the college in 717. A number of *paksa* and assistants taught three classes of students under the curricula that consisted of : the *Book of History* and the *Literary Anthology*, written by a sixth-century Liang dynasty prince, for the first class ; the *Commentaries of Tso* and the *Book of Poetry* for the second class ; the *Book of Rites* and the *Book of Changes* for the third class ; and the *Analects* and the *Book of Filial Piety* were required of all students. Instruction in arithmetic as a separate field was offered only when feasible. The students were recruited from the children of low ranking officials in the nine to thirty age-bracket for the maximum period of nine years for graduation.

A serious attempt at the selection of officials on the basis of scholarly merit was made in 788 when a civil service examination system was instituted. Candidates were classified into three categories, according to their comprehension of Chinese classics : those who were thoroughly familiar with the *Analects* and the *Book of Filial Piety* and could read the *Commentaries of*

Tso, the *Book of Rites,* and the *Literary Anthology* were classified as the upper grade ; those who mastered a chapter from the *Book of Rites* called "Ch'uli" ("Kog'ye" in Korean) dealing with personal deportment and public ceremonies, the *Analects*, and the *Book of Filial Piety* were grouped as the middle grade ; the low grade was given to those who could comprehend the *Book of Filial Piety* and the above chapter from the *Book of Rites.*

A Candidate who showed a full knowledge of the Five Classics, three histories, that is, *Historical Records*, the *History of the Han*, and the *History of the Later Han,* and the philosophical works of the Hundred Schools was supposedly accorded a special priority in appointment. But the scholarship shown either in the college or through the examination had no particular relationship to actual appointment and promotion which were still quite rigidly controlled by the Bone Ranks.

Partly because of this rigid status system at home, a remarkably large number of United Silla students, who were not blessed with the True Bone rank, aspired to Chinese studies in the T'ang. Along with Buddhist monks, they braved a long hazardous journey to the T'ang capital ch'ang-an, probably the greatest center of learning in the contemporary world. The majority of theses students were sponsored jointly by the Silla and T'ang governments, the former paying for their travel and books and the latter for room, board, and clothing. They were allowed to take T'ang's civil examination specially administered for the foreign students. During the United Silla period, at least fifty-eight Silla students served in the T'ang government via the examination before their return home. Ch'oe Ch'i Wŏn (857- ?), a great scholar-literatus of Silla, was better known for his literary works in the T' ang than in Silla. Kang Su (? -692), Sŏl Ch'ong, an eighth century scholar, and his contemporary Kim Tae Mun were some of the great names in United Silla scholarship.

Taoism, like Confucianism, quietly seeped into the Peninsula, and, by the early seventh century, it seems to have been quite extensively popularized particularly in Koguryŏ, even though Taoism as religion made little headway. In Koguryŏ a Taoist meeting in 624 is said to have attracted an audience of "several thousands," including the king himself. Taoism, as has been noted, was encouraged by the government at the expense of Buddhism, with unhappy Buddhist monks fleeing the country. In Paekche Taoism seems to have been known before Buddhism and provided artistic motif as in Koguryŏ, as we shall see. Silla's Hwarang life was much influenced also by Taoism, and United Silla saw a further popularization of Taoism along with Buddhism.

5

Buddhism

As Buddhism took root in Korea, it produced many ideas and concepts which proved extremely useful to the growing societies of the Peninsula. The absorption and eventual naturalization of the Indian religion into Korean culture were a matter of long process. Although Buddhism far surpassed any of native beliefs in theological and ecclesiastical maturity, its triumph in Korea, for that matter, in China and Japan also, may be explained in terms of its ready accommodation with native religions. Buddhism' pliancy, or it might be said leniency as manifest in the image of Buddha, made this completely foreign religion palatable to Korean tastes. Furthermore, Buddhism, as the early Koreans and Japanese knew, had already been much seasoned at the Chinese hand.

The Basic Teachings of Buddhism

Unlike Confucius, Mencius, or Chuang-tzu who looked at life in relation to sociopolitical realities, Sakyamuni, the founder of Buddhism, probed it in terms of psychological truth. Unlike Confucius and Mencius who sought a responsible position in government to practice their teachings, Sakyamuni, who was born and educated in the thick of it, renounced it to find life's truth for its own sake. He was a crown prince of a small kingdom in northern India who lived around 500 B.C. or earlier. On that fateful day when he saw "the four passing sights," the aged, the sick, the dead, and an ascetic, he embarked on a six-year course of the most intensive asceticism and meditation. What he was finally enlightened to in meditation under that tree of knowledge or Bo-tree was the supreme peace of high Nirvana, which was embodied in the Four Noble Truths.

The Four Noble Truths, the most basic of the Buddhist teachings, are : that life is essentially suffering ; that the cause of this suffering is craving ; that the cessation of suffering can be brought about only by abandoning that craving ; lastly, that the way to achieve this goal is to follow the course carefully prescribed in the Noble Eightfold Path. The Noble Eightfold Path is right belief, right aspiration, right speech, right meditation, etc., The Three intoxications, the Five Hindrances, the Ten Fetters, and so on are other prescriptions that help one surcease from all desires and awaken to Nirvana, that is becoming Buddha.

Nirvana, Buddhism's final goal, holds no organic relationship to the human world. Nirvana is not only the state of peace of mind but also that of nothingness ; yet it is not mere emptiness, for it is the state of eternal being, or "supreme bliss." The obstacle to Nirvana, which is most difficult to remove, is the chain of causation, or laws of *karma*, the concept that sees a human act inexorably tied to another. These human acts in nexus are operated by desire ; sexual desire, for instance, brings birth, death, and rebirth. Each nexus, however, is not permanent. Man can and must break the chain of causation because all events in the human world, which are the aggregation of five components—that is, body, feeling, perception, psychic disposition, and consciousness—are transient. They can be, therefore, resolved back, like a light being blown out, into the impersonal state of constant flux, a state of becoming which is eternal, or even meaningless because there is no central planning in that state. Nirvana is such a state.

The path to Nirvana through denial of the desires, supported by such a callous philosophy, naturally failed to render itself attractive to the masses, but Sakyamuni as the man who was so compassionately human became the fountainhead from which Buddhism as a religion for the masses was eventually developed. Through social turmoil, dynastic changes, and above all the deep spiritual need of the common masses in India, the religious development of Buddhism went on. In the process, monastic orders sprang up ; new mythologies were created ; oral traditions and theories were committed to writing into Pali and Sanskrit.

These writings, including scholastic elaborations, in time amounting to a tremendous volume, became Buddhism's sacred literature which came to be called the Tripitaka or Three Baskets : They are the *Vinayas* or monastic rules (*yul* in Korean ; *lü* in Chinese ; *ritsu* in Japanese), the *Sutras* or teachings (*kyŏng* in Korean ; *ching* in Chinese ; *kyō* in Japanese), and the *Abhidharmas* or commentaries on those teachings (*lon* or *non* in Korean ; *lun* in Chinese ; *ron* in Japanese). By the first century B.C., the religious transformation of early Buddhism was nearly complete. It had grown out of the world-denying, negativistic philosophy into a well-rounded religion now offering the optimists as well as the pessimists the answers for ultimate salvation to their liking. The transcendental, all-inclusive form of Buddhism came to be known as Mahayana, the Greater Vehicle as against strenuous original Buddhism which the Mahayanists came to call Hinayana, the Lesser Vehicle. What made Mahayana greater was that it made available to a greater number of people the more agreeable provision for entrance to Nirvana. Mahayana Buddhism had created most compassionate, humane Buddhas of all kinds to the very limit of man's imagination, and they were only too glad to help believers in all human situations. As many heavenly regions where different categories of gods dwelt were discovered, as it were, the concept of the most livable paradise came into being, and earthly mortals were accorded open invitation on account of either storing up personal good deeds or help given by a myriad altruistic god. Enlightenment into Nirvana now became synonymous with personal salvation through faith as well as ascetic practice.

Influential Gods of Mahayana Buddhism. Of the celestial residents, some are more popular and enjoy a greater religious reality. Bodhisattvas (Posal in Korean), the most prominent group in the Buddhist pantheon, receive the entreaties of the greatest number of the believers. A Bodhisattva is the one who, having built up imponderable reservoirs of merits enough to entitle him to the full status of Buddha, indefinitely postponed his entrance to Nirvana in order to help suffering humanity. Thus, Bodhisattvas most anxiously respond to needy people. Bodhisattva Maitreya (Mirŭk in Korean ; Mi-lo in Chinese) is the Buddha-in-the-making who awaits the appropriate time to come to the world where he is expected to do good things for mankind. The Silla people regarded the Hwarang as the incarnation of Maitreya.

Avalokitesvara (Kwanŭm in Korean ; Kwan-yin in Chinese ; Kannon in Japanese) is another Bodhisattva who aids man in a wide range of his needs from averting moral dangers or physical pains to bestowing a child upon an imploring woman. Avalokitesvara, the personification of divine compassion, in time, more appropriately changed his sex to female and became the most approachable Goddess of Mercy, upon whom both believers and artists lavished their love and talents.

Munjusri (Munju in Korean ; Wen-yu in Chinese) is a princely looking Bodhisattva who, with a sword and a book, promotes dissemination of Buddhist laws. Amitabha (Amida in Korean and Japanese ; O-mi-t'o in Chinese), one of Dyhani buddhas, is, along with Bodhisattva Kwanŭm, the most commonly invoked god in Mahayana countries. Amita or Amitabul resides in the Western Paradise popularly known as Pure Land (Chaengt'o in Korean) as its presiding lord and stands most ready to admit into his Paradise anyone who does as much as invoking his sacred name in the hour of death.

Whereas Bodhisattvas take care of man's needs here and now, Amitabha makes sure of his future bliss. As these mythologies were being created, sophisticated theological ideas and metaphysical systems were also developed, which were written into the ever swelling volumes of the Tripitaka. Thus, the vast body of Mahayana literature, containing an infinite variety of religious ideology, opened up immense vistas for the religious growth and physical expansion of Buddhism.

The Coming of Buddhism

As the Indian religion spread along its northern vista toward China and fourth century Korea, it was the wheels of the Greater Vehicle that conveyed the gospels of Buddhism. To fledgling Korean kingdoms amid the gospels of Buddhism. To fledgling Korean kingdoms amid the enterprising programs of nation building, the cosmology of the new religion, with its intellectual and aesthetic appeals and magic, seemed something that was indeed portentous—something that at least could be made use of for secular as well as spiritual purposes.

The official introduction of Buddhism first to Koguryŏ in 372 occurred as part of diplomatic transaction. Emperor Fu Chien, an ardent Buddhist, of the Earlier Ch'in, one of the Sixteen Kingdoms in North China, included in his goodwill mission to Koguryŏ, which helped him overthrow the Earlier Yen, a Buddhist monk Shuen Tao (Sundo in Korean) with Buddhist *sutras* and images. Two years later another monk, Ado, supposedly a Koguryŏan, returned from China. King Sosurim provided them with temples and other conveniences for promulgation of their teachings. King Kwanggaet'o also built ten temples in P'yŏngyang and encouraged the missionary work of Monk T'an Shih (Tam Si in Korean) who came from the Eastern Chin with a large number of Buddhist *sutras*. In 384 a "barbarian" monk, Mo-luo-nuo-t'uo (Maranant'a in Korean) came, or probably was sent by the Eastern Chin, to Paekche. King Ch'imnyu (383-384) placed him at a newly built temple in Mt. Namhan where he ordained ten monk-priests. King Asin (392-404) also gave Buddhism a boost in Paekche.

In Silla, however, Buddhism fared somewhat differently. In the face of united resistance presented by the ruling class, an attempt at the propagation of Buddhism among the masses seems to have surreptitiously been made in the early fifth century under the leadership of the Koguryŏan monk Ado, but without much progress. It seems to have been again through diplomatic channel that Buddhism established a foothold in Silla first among families of a few courtiers and the royalty, but still the majority of the officials could not tolerate the foreign religion with strange sacerdotal robes and shaven heads of monks. The religious controversy climaxed in 527 when King Pŏphŭng seemed forced to execute Ich'adon, the devout Buddhist, who bore the brunt of the attacks of officials. Tradition has it that upon beheading Ich'adon the "blood as white as milk" gushed out from his neck and a roaring thunder was heard in the blue sky. This "miracle of Ich'adon" awed the opposition into submission to Buddhism.

Once having overcome the human hindrance, Buddhism in Silla found far less trouble in bringing the gods of the native religion under its influence or at least to acquiescence. A theory advanced in this undertaking was that various native gods were a kind of apparitions into which Buddhist gods had temporarily projected themselves. Certain Shamanistic gods and the God of Road who was believed to protect travellers, for instance, were made Bodhisattvas incarnate. And other gods, changing their godhead, were simply converted to Buddhism and became disciples of Buddha.

Thus, the spiritual world reordered ; as the evidence shows, its method was suspiciously similar to that of the political integration of various tribal groups under the royal authority. This does not, however, mean that Buddhism integrated all native gods into its pantheon. Singyo, for its part, remained much the same as before, only having reinforced its theological contents under the influence of Buddhism.

At first, teaching Buddhism to the common masses was little different from elementary moral training : man receives rewards in accord with his deeds ; therefore, man should promote his virtues and abandon vices. Buddhism with its vividly portrayed paradises and hells seems in the beginning to have held firmer sway over the masses than the royal decrees had done, a situation that was exploited by monarchs to a political end. This was done primarily by centralization of the ecclesiastical hierarchy under the royal authority, and this arrangement was continuously strengthened and remained a feature of Korean Buddhism.

Buddhism in Koguryŏ and Paekche

In one instance, we read a prayer inscribed on the backside of the nimbus of a golden Three Kingdoms period Amidabul statuette but addressed to the Maitreya. The religious knowledge and understanding of Buddhism, however, deepened naturally as time progressed. By the early sixth century Koguryŏ monks came to immerse themselves in scholastic Buddhsim that included studies of Sarvāstivādin (Sŏrilchŏryubu in Korean), Trisāstravādin (Samnon in Korean), Ch'ŏnt'ae hak (T'ien-t'ai hsüeh in Chinese), and so on.

The most notable in this context was Sŭngnang (ca. 450 to 550) whose scholarship in Trisāstravādin or Thee-Treatise doctrine (Samnon ; San-lun in Chinese) was widely acclaimed in China. The interest in the Three-Treatise school, a Mahayana philosophy, became apparent after that great missionary-translator of Buddhist scriptures into Chinese, Kumārajīva (344-413) rendered available to Chinese readers the Middle Doctrine consisting of three Idian works, the philosophical basis of the Indian Madhyamika. (Middle Doctrine) school of Nāgārjuna (ca. 100 to 200 A.D.). Nāgārjuna is said to have founded the Madhyamika school in order to refute the Sarvāstivādins, a Hinayana school.

Nāgārjuna maintained that the ultimate real is the chain of events or essential elements of existence, extending throughout the "three existence," all phenomenal objects that we perceive occurring around that chain is unreal and empty. He placed a pointed emphasis on the emptiness of the ultimate reality, or the absolute truth. All phenomenal beings, which may have reality for those who perceive, will be eventually superseded by, or passed the ultimate Emptiness is the transcendental and all embracing truth which, however, exists together with the phenomenal beings and can be perceived only by the mind completely shed of ignorance through meditation.

Sŭngnang of Koguryŏ was the major exponent of the Three Treatise school in China. During his long sojourn in China, he laid the philosophical basis of the Three-Treatise school upon which, later, Chi-tsang (549-623) founded the San-lun sect. At the same time, Sŭngnang, who was also thoroughly conversant with the doctrine of Hwaŏm (Hua-yen in Chinese) through his exposition of the Middle Doctrine, made havoc of the Sarvāstivādin and the Ch'eng-shih (Sŏngsil in Korean), another Hinayana school which flourished in fifth century South China. Sil Pŏpsa (Teacher of Law Sil) and In Pŏpsa of Koguryŏ, contemporaries of Chi-Tsang, also contributed much to the philosophical elaborations of the San-lun sect in China.

In Paekche, Monk Kyŏmik went directly to the original source of Buddhism itself. In India, he mastered Sanskrit and for five years delved into the *vinayas* or disciplinary aspect of Buddhism. In 526 Kyŏmik, accompained by an Indian monk named Paedaldasamjang (in Korean), returned with books containing the disciplinary doctrines of probably five of the Hinayana schools in India. King Sŏng of Paekche, who welcomed the remarkable monk, summoned an ecclesiastical council of twenty-eight monk who under Kyŏmik's leadership translated them into Chinese in seventy-two volumes. Later two monks wrote thirty-six volumes of commentaries on them, and the King is believed to have written the preface to the books. This was the beginning of the Yul (discipline) sect which, due to the zeal and authority of Kyŏmik, became the strongest sect in Paekche.

The decline of Buddhism in Koguryŏ set in already in the early seventh century when the ruling class turned to Taoism. With the demise of Koguryŏ and Paekche in 660's, the ecclesiastical aspect of Buddhism in the two kingdoms broke up in pieces. A great number of monks and nuns found themselves in Japan where they joined their predecessors in development of Japanese Buddhism and Buddhist art. Hyegwan, a Koguryŏ monk, landed in Japan via China in 602, and there he pioneered in philosophical Buddhism with Kwannŭk, a Paekche monk. He was eventually regarded as the founding father of the Sanron sect in Japan and appointed the second Sōjō, Sōjō being the highest priest in the hierarchy of Japanese Buddhism ; Kwannŭk had been the first.

Another Koguryŏ monk, Hyeja (? -622) taught that great reformer, Prince Shōtoku of Taika Japan and with Hyech'ong, a Paekche monk, was thought to be "treasures" of Japanese Buddhism. Tamjing, a Koguryŏ monk-artist, has been credited with creation of the wall paintings in the Golden Hall of the Hōryūji near Nara. Tojang, a Paekche monk, is said to have either introduced or strengthened Sŏngsil (Jōjitsu in Japanese) philosophy in Japan in 680's. These are a few memorable personalities and events in the growth of Japanese Buddhism after it was transmitted there by Paekche in 552. As Korea benefited from the accelerated influx of the iron culture from North China during the Warring States period, Japan was the cultural beneficiary of the political disintegration in seventh century Korea.

Buddhism in Silla

Silla, the latecomer also in Buddhism, having once accepted it in 527 just a century and a half after its two neighbors did, plunged headlong into building a Buddhist kingdom with a vigor that was matched by neither of them. Monks were especially astute in proselytizing the whole kingdom. With a kind of religious licence, they created myths at short notice. According to Chajang, an early seventh century monk, Buddhism once flourished in Silla long before : therefore, it was not a foreign religion. Chajang is said to have believed that 10,000 Munjusri, those princely Bodhisattvas, had been living in Mt. Odae in the northern part of modern Kangwŏn Province, and he built a temple there to get acquainted with them. The holy or well-known mountains were one after another renamed in Buddhist style, and temples were "rebuilt" in those holy places in the belief that they had formerly stood there, while the resident mountain gods were given due recognition by the temples.*

The monarchal patronage of the new religion was no less ardent, but only more purposive politically. The Hinayana ideal of individual salvation through monastic discipline was well tolerated, but the paramount emphasis was placed on building a kingdom of Mahayana Buddhism, in which the monarch was the rallying center flanked by a hierarchy of monks that administered the laws of Buddha in the name of the king. Temples and monasteries were often dedicated to the cause of national security. The six kings starting with Pŏphŭng were particularly enthusiastic believers bent upon enlightening the entire people on the Buddhist truths and virtues. They adopted Buddhist-style names and titles ; one of them appears to have abdicated in order to enter a holy order.

On the level of the common masses, Mahayana Buddhism's influence was most strongly felt largely through two large-scale Buddhist gatherings : *Paekchaganghoe* and *P'algwanhoe*. The two gatherings, the most important of early Korean Buddhist events which were socially institutionalized and officially sponsored until the end of the Koryŏ dynasty, were inaugurated probably by Hyeryŏng, a Koguryŏ monk in Silla. In 551 Hyeryŏng followed General Kŏch'ilbu, then the commander of an invading Silla army in Koguryŏ, to Silla where he was appointed the Sŭngt'ong, the highest priest, by King Chinhŭng.

The *Paekchaganghoe* was a Buddhist prayer meeting highlighted by social programs held at the royal palace in winter. Royal longevity and the national welfare were the main themes of the prayer meeting, which was followed by a program of singing and dancing. The *P'algwanhoe* was a similar assemblage, purporting to refresh the eight commandments : thou shalt not kill, not steal, not commit adultery, etc. These occasions attracted tens of thousands of bonzes and lay people in a mood of great social festivity, that the two occasions were indeed.

Scholastic and Sectarian Buddhism

Silla Buddhism's organizational and intellectual maturity came with Silla's normalization of relations with the T'ang. The T'ang was Silla's major foreign source of learning in Buddhism. Silla monks who studied T'ang Buddhsim counted several hundreds ; scores of them became great masters of Silla Buddhism. More spirited ones sought the great teachings directly from India. Starting with Paekche's Kyŏmik, at least twleve Korean monks braved the long hazardous pilgrimage to the birthplace of Buddha. Hyech'o, an

---

* Some Korean Christians have said, in a similar vein, that "God, Jesus, and the Holy Ghost are counterparts of Hwan In, Hwan Ung, and Tan'gun." Comparing Mary to the bear woman who bore Tan'gun, they elaborated the Tan'gun myth from the viewpoint of Christian trinitarianism in their "religious saga thesis." Spencer J. Palmer, *Korea and Christianity*, p. 14.

eighth century Silla monk, is the most well-known of this group because of his five volumes of travelogue, one of the great sagas in religious pilgrimage, which also became a precious document for histories of Buddhism and India.

The concentration on the philosophical study of the Buddhist canons, which in many cases not only different from, but also contradictory to, one another, resulted in division of theological views, each representing one particular aspect of Buddhism. Some viewed one particular scripture or a set of scriptures as most central to true Buddhism, while others believed one particular method of practice of the religion to be essential to achieving enlightenment. The sectarian tendency inherent in Indian Buddhism came to flower, in China developing into nearly twenty sects during the seventh and eighth centuries.

An incipient sectarian movement was existent in Koguryŏ and in Paekche as in Kyŏmik's institution of the Yul sect. In Silla about thirteen sects came into existence by the end of the eighth century ; a half of these, as in China, enjoyed only ephemeral career. The Koreans were never interested too deeply in sectarian movement. Their sectarian assertion was always countered by an ecumenical force. The most constant tenor of Korean Buddhism has been kept by its service to the state and the society through which Buddhism penetrated the domain of individual soul.

Probably the first sectarian movement in Silla was initiated by a late sixth century monk, Hyŏn'gwang, a close disciple of Hui Ssu who was the acclaimed patriarch of the T'ien-t'ai (Ch'ŏnt'ae in Korean) sect in China. The Chinese T'ien-t'ai sect, with its principle of the Perfectly Harmonious Threefold Truth contained in the *Scripture of the Lotus of the Wonderful Law,* represents an intellectual effort to reconcile the philosophical study of scriptures with the method of religious meditation in order to facilitate sudden enlightenment. Hyŏn'gwang Pŏpsa, who was as a pupil of Hui Ssu placed above Chi K'ai, the Grand Master of the T'ien-t'ai sect, in scholastic contribution, taught the sectarian doctrine of the T'ien-t'ai to Silla monks. This marked the beginning of study of the Ch'ŏnt'ae thought in Korea.

Chajang, who, as has been noted, did much to the socialization of Buddhism in Silla, was ordered back home from the T'ang in 643 and was appointed the Taegukt'ong or highest priest of the state. He then set about inaugurating a series of disciplinary programs. Chajang Yulsa (Teacher of Discipline Chajang), adopting the *vinaya* ideas of early Indian Buddhist orders, put in force the rules for the bimonthly confession before the assembled chapter and the biannual examination for the monks and nuns on their scholarship. The taegukt'ong made all clergymen receive their ordination on the "diamond ordination platform" before a relic of Sakyamuni at the T'ongdosa in modern South Kyŏngsang Province. Thus Silla's Kyeyul sect was instituted. That the first sect founded in Paekche and Silla had to be the disciplinary sect may be understood in the context of contemporary national endeavors.

About this time the Chinŏn or True Word sect came into vogue in Silla. With its esoteric doctrine derived mainly from Indian Tantrism, the sect was characterized by invocation through magic formulas, secret rites, and incantation of certain Buddhist gods for various purposes ranging from curing sickness to entreating supernatural intervention in foreign invasion. The True Word sect might have been an aspect of Buddhism which was especially vulnerable to the degenerative influences of Shamanistic and other superstitious beliefs. Understandably, its religious appeal seems to have been strong in the early stage of Silla Buddhism. When Monk Ŭisang returned from the T'ang in 671 and informed King Munmu of the Tang's intention of dispatching reinforcements against Silla, the King, so tradition has it, betook himself to Myŏngnang Pŏpsa, the founder of the Sinin sect, a branch of the True Word school, which stressed the efficacy of magic formulas. On the recommendation of Myŏngnang Pŏpsa, the great Sach'ŏnwangsa was built in dedication to the intercessive grace of Buddha in such an impasse. The temple's foundation, which remains today, is regarded as important in the study of Silla Buddhist architecture

Of the rationalist schools, the most articulate was the Hwaŏm (Hua-yen in Chinese) sect founded by the patriotic Ŭsiang (625-702), who was usually called Ŭisang Taesa (Great Teacher Ŭisang). The main tenet of the sect was based on the *Avatamsaka Sutra*, which sees the teachings of Gautama Buddha as the historical manifestation of the greater Buddha, Vairochana. In its all inclusive syncretism, it taught that all phenomenal existences partake of the Realm of Law which is the ultimate reality ; even every instance of thought-moment is rooted in eternity. It assures the universal salvation in the end with the help of Bodhisattva Pohyŏn (P'u-hien in Chinese) whose position was specially enhanced by the Hwaŏm sect.

The Hwaŏm doctrine, like that of the Ch'ŏnt'ae, as we shall see later, classified all Buddhist sects into five levels of truth and regarded itself as the last synthesis in the development of metaphysical Buddhism which embraced all others. Ŭisang Taesa, under the patronage of King Munmu, built ten great temples as major centers of the Hwaŏm sect including the Pusŏksa in Yŏngju, North Kyŏngsang Province where he taught "three thousand" disciples the Hwaŏm doctrine.

The Consciousness-Only school, an idealistic system of thought, appeared in the first half of the seventh century, that is, in almost the same period as it did in China. Its philosophical premise is graphically presented in the experience of the famous monk Wŏnhyo (617-686). Wŏnhyo was on his way with his friend, Ŭisang, to the T'ang for a period of study around 650. Just before embarkation for China, the two monks happened to sleep in an old tomb.

Prompted by the extreme thirst in the middle of the night, Wŏnhyo drank a bowl of water which he unconsciously reached in the dark. Upon discovery of truth in the next moring that what he drank was the decayed water collected in a cranium, he felt unbearable nausea. At the same time, he was enlightened into the world of the Consciousness-Only : all sense perceptions as such have no objective reality ; it is the mind or the consciousness of the perceiver that "holds" or "contains" the universe. Wŏnhyo no longer needed to go to the T'ang. Ŭisang alone went on.

Unlike the Three-Treatise school (Samnon), an earlier idealist philosophy which holds that the ultimate truth is Emptiness or Void, the Consciousness-Only school sets the percipient mind as complete and ultimate. The ultimate consciousness is "that which is such as it is," or, in short, "Suchness" or "Thusness" which is identical with Nirvana. The great champion of this idealism was Wŏnch'ŭk, a contemporary of Wŏnhyo, who, studying in China like Sŭngnang of Koguryŏ before him, contributed greatly to the development of the Fa-hsing (Pŏpsang in Korean) sect founded upon the Consciousness-Only philosophy. The Pŏpsang sect as a distinct sectarian movement in Silla was, however, established by Chinp'yo, an eighth century monk who was also well known as the Teacher of Yul.

The number of major sects in Silla has been said to be five or seven, depending on classifiers. But by far the great majority of monks and laymen remained believers to whom any scripture or legend represented a certain level of truth. The general disinterested attitudes toward sectarianism, in fact, characterized Silla Buddhism.

Wŏnhyo. Most closely personifying Silla Buddhism in its early stage that set the subsequent tone of Korean Buddhism as a whole was Wŏnhyo, one of all-time greats in the Mahayana world. Wŏnhyo elaborated on nearly all important aspects of Buddhism of his time without regard to sectarian differences in his 240 odd volumes written after that nocturnal episode. It is because of this catholicity of scholarly interest that he was thought to be the founder of several sects or the unifier of them.

Wŏnhyo's religious philosophy in its sectarian form was closer to that of the Hwaŏm sect. But, more importantly, his cardinal concern was to synthesize all sectarian truths into T'ong Pulgyo or One Unified Buddhism which was, to him, the final summation of humanity. The *Simmunhwajaeng non* or *Treatise on the Harmonization of Ten Schools,* considered the most important of his works, deals with the themes which are eminently ecumenical. The teachings of Buddha, "if opened," unfold itself into an infinitude of meanings, as the individual and sectarian interpretations of the *sutras* show. Those meanings, if treated with the supreme fairness and impartiality of Buddha, can be reduced to one truth. With this conviction, Wŏnhyo in his *Treatise* analyzed the ten most controversial metaphysical problems in Buddhism, that is, T'ong

Pulgyo. Thus, Wŏnhyo's became the avowed ideal of Korean Buddhism throughout the traditional period.

Wŏnhyo, leaving his philosophical speculation in his later years, turned to awakening the spiritual life of the masses, to whom the winds of doctrines were beyond their grasp. Resorting to Pure Land salvationism, he set out to perpetuate Buddha's grace among the common people. He reminded them of a kind of "short cut" to the Chaengt'o or Pure Land where Amitabul or Amitabha Buddha was now ready to grant anyone admission to his Paradise, if solicited in good faith. They might forgo the scriptural studies ; nor was it always necessary to lead a life of good work. Faith in the saving grace of Amitabul alone, as expressed in simple invocation of Amitabul's name, was all sufficient. A powerful, articulate preacher, that he was to the educated, aristocratic audience, Wŏnhyo now made his way among the common masses, dancing and singing with his gourd begging bowl as a musical instrument.

As he had thus ventured through the depth and breadth of Buddhism, Wŏnhyo, reportedly a handsome man, seemed to have come to realize himself to a fuller humanity, namely, from a celibate monk to a married man. One day, according to tradition, he was walking along a Kyŏngju street, singing :

> Who would lend me an ax without handle ?
> Because I'll fell a pillar,
> That would support the Heaven.

The message of the song, couched apparently in a Freudian symbolism, somehow got through to T'aejong, who thereupon arranged Wŏnhyo's meeting with Princess Yosŏk, then a widow. Out of this union produced was Sŏl Ch'ong, a great name in Silla literature.

6

Literature

Attempt at vernacular expression in writing was first made through appropriation of Chinese characters. A handy way was to line up Chinese characters for their ideographic value in the word order of Korean language for a given sentence. Korean and Chinese being categorically different from each other in almost every linguistic aspect, this method called *Haengch'al* was at best awkward and incomplete. Lack of inflections, postpositions, auxiliary verbs, etc. in Chinese made well-nigh impossible the Korean expression with a degree of subtlety in *Haengch'al*. A more comprehensive method developed was to use Chinese characters for both their phonetic and ideographic values. Addition of a phonetic use of Chinese characters for transliteration of Korean words was a great step forward in the development of Korean literature. This method was called the *Idu* which Sŏl Ch'ong helped complete. Using the *Idu* system he could render, for instance, Chinese classics more readable to Korean readers. Although it was still difficult of Chinese characters was a prerequisite for its use, the *Idu* system had been the unique vernacular writing system among the educated class until 1446 when the *Han'gŭl* was officially put to use.

The Saenaennorae

Korean literature, like many other literatures. has its origin that is as old as society itself. Songs were sung, needless to say, where life was ; group singing occurred at tribal festival such as thanksgiving gathering under the auspices of the *ture* or at inter-village competitions for weaving by girls. These songs of the tribal period were mostly of incantatory, Shamanistic origin and supposed to have certain magical power with which they could manipulate spirits. Prodigies such as comet, for instance, were to disappear by the word-magic of incantatory hymns. By the time that these primitive hymns became blended with Buddhist psalmody, their functions were extended from magical to laudatory and didactic, cultivating both the individual mind and the unifying spirit of the people.

Around the time of unification, a distinct poetic pattern emerged with structure, rhythm, and meter. This literary *genre* was called *Saenaennorae*, also known as *Hyangga*, which dominated the literary scene, probably until the twelfth century. One of the notable cultural undertakings in this connection was the compilation in 888 of the *Samdaemok or Category of Three Generations* which, now lost, is thought to have contained 1,000 to 1,500 *Saenaennorae*, elegies, and odes, A glimpse of the characteristics of the *genre*, however, can be had from the twenty-five *Saenaennorae* which exist as they were originally written in the *Idu* letters.

Of the twenty-five *Saenaennorae*, the oldest is believed to be the "Song of Mattung"("Sŏdong yo") written in *Idu* probably during the reign of Chinp'yŏng (579-631), long before Sŏl Ch'ong completed the *Idu* writing system. The tradition as to the background of the song has it that King Mu (600-640) of Paekche in his youth heard of the extraordinary beauty of Princess Sŏnhwa, daughter of King Chinp'yŏng and decided to marry her. The two countries being in hostility, Mattung, the Paekche prince then, smuggled himself into the Silla capital where he befriended neighborhood urchins and imporvised a scandalous song for them to sing :

> Princess Sŏnhwa,
> Hoping for a secret marriage,
> Went away at night,
> With Mattung in her arms. *

The disreputable allegation rapidly spread and soon reached the court, resulting, as hoped for by its author, in the expulsion of the innocent princess from the royal palace. Prince Mattung met and brought her to Paekche. Although its historicity is in doubt, the poem, read from a literary angle, shows creative imagination. What seemed an impossible love is achieved through the Prince's ingenious trick in such casual and primitive simplicity.

Beside the above form of a four-line stanza, which is the prototype of

---

* Translated by Peter H. Lee in his book, *Studies in the Saenaennorae : Old Korean Poetry,* p. 53.

nursery songs, folk songs, and the like, there are in the *Saenaennorae* two more forms : two stanzas of four lines each and two stanzas of four lines each followed by another stanza of two lines. Of the *Saenaennorae* of the former category, the form that represents the middle phase in the Saenaennorae's structural development, the "Song of Ch'ŏyong" ("Ch'ŏyong ka,") written during the reign of King Hŏn'gang (875-885), is best known for its literary merit.

Ch'ŏyong, a powerful Silla aristocrat, who was believed to be a son of the Dragon King of the Eastern Sea, returned home drunken from a carousal one night, to find his wife in bed with another man. Faced with this situation, Ch'ŏyong sang :

> Having caroused far into the night,
> In the moonlit capital,
> I return home and in my bed,
> Behold, four legs.
>
> Two have been mine ;
> Whose are the other two ?
> Two had been mine ;
> NO, no they are taken. *

The last line may be rendered, instead ; "But what now since they are taken ?"

Ch'ŏyong chose a magnanimous resignation rather than a violent solution for the monstrous problem, when social morality would have acquiesced in the latter. Ordinary mortals do not usually possess such magnanimity. As noted, Ch'ŏyong was not an ordinary mortal ; in fact, he was a son of the Dragon King who could dispatch the adulterous man right there and then. The disposal of the man representing evil spirit would not end evil itself, however. The problem before Ch'ŏyong was not easy one. What Ch'ŏyong did by resorting to the poetic unconventionality was enhancement of a seemingly conventional argument on social moralism to a transcendental realm where a distinction between good and evil was neutralized, a situation in which the evil certainly could not thrive but was made even good in a way The evil spirst was completly perplexed and embarrassed by Ch'ŏyong's unexpected deed which was in fact a most unbearable challenge to him. As tradition the has it, the evil spirit disappeared of its own accord. And Ch'ŏyong's composure and honor were saved. It is worth noting that the magical power of the "Song of Ch'ŏyong" has been used in Shamanistic rituals to help expel the spirits of houses.

---

* Ibid., p. 79.

The last form of the *Saenaennorae* consists ten lines. The last two lines function as summing-up of idea expressed in the previous two four-line stanzas. This summing-up technique and other poetic devices such as alliteration, assonance, onomatopoeia, simile, etc. which were already integral parts of the *Saenaennorae*, were further refined by the poets of similar *genres* in later periods. Eighteen of the existing twenty-five *Saenaennorae* belong to this perfected form, and eleven of the eighteen were composed by the great tenth century Monk Kyunyŏ (923-973).

Kyunyŏ's poems are all religious and beautiful, and they were intended to propagate the Buddhist gospel among the common people. Kyunyŏ's face was never uglier. A Chinese envoy, who knew of Kyunyŏ's saintliness, entreated the king to let him meet Kyunyŏ, but the king as well as Kyunyŏ refused the request lest his facial ugliness should shatter the envoy's expectation. If indeed his religious purity and poetic mind were the reality that endure to eternity, as they do in the immortal song that follows, his physical unloveliness was illusory and certainly temporary.

> To the boundless throne of Buddha
> In the realm of dharma,
> I fervently pray
> For the sweet rain of truth.
>
> Disperse the fever of affliction
> Rooted deep in the ignorant soil,
> And wet the mind's field,
> Where good grasses scarcely grew.
>
> The mind is a moonlit autumn field,
> With the ripe gold fruit of knowledge. *

With the powerful imageries of the rain of truth and the wasteland of mind in dramatic juxtaposition, the poem enlightens one of the final "fruit of knowledge" which is the "supreme Light" of Buddha. As told in the *Biography of Kyunyŏ* published in 1075, the people posted his *Saenaennorae* on the walls of their houses to lead the life of purity, and the divine religious power contained in the songs healed the sickness of devout readers. No less significant is the fact that the Confucian writer of that *Biography* took pains to translate Kyunyŏ's poems into Chinese, with the avowed purpose of having them read among the Chinese people.

Music. Thus the early songs, with their magic power, were sung or

---

* Ibid., p. 91.

chanted for religious purification or the Shamanistic purpose of exorcising evil spirits from the house. With the development of musical instruments, however, music became a distinct field of art. Some musical instruments were originally developed for accompaniment of Shamanistic rituals. They were now for the sake of music art, and music came to the written specific instruments.

Koguryŏ had fourteen to seventeen kinds of musical instruments such as flutes, strings, and drums. The well-known name in Koguryŏ music was Minister Wang Sanak, who was credited with remodeling a seven-string lute of Chinese origin around 552. Wang Sanak also wrote 100-odd pieces of music for the instrument which he named *hyŏnhakkŭm* or black stork lute. According to tradition, black storks would come around and dance to the tune when he played the instrument. * Paekche had instruments similar in kind and number to those of Koguryŏ and exerted influence over Japanese music, as we have seen.

Silla's major musical instruments consisted of : three kinds of lutes, namely, the *Kayagŭm*, the *Kŏmun'go* which was renamed from the *hyŏnhakkŭm*, and the *pip'a* ; three kinds of bamboo-flutes, large, medium, and small ; large double-skinned drums ; and clappers. The twelve-string *Kayagŭm* was the lute of Kaya. Urŭk, the famous Kaya master of the instrument, when his country was annexed to Silla in 562, found an ardent musical patron in King Chinhŭng and popularized the use of the *kayagŭm* in Silla, which is the most beloved traditional musical instrument today. There were for the *kayagŭm* 197 pieces of music, including the twelve which Urŭk wrote. The *kŏmun'go* was also popularly used in Silla. Ok Pogo, the first Silla master of *kŏmun'go* who lived in the first half of the eighth century, taught and composed thirty pieces of music ; his disciples are said to have written 187 pieces. For the *pip'a* there were 210 pieces of music. The bamboo-flutes were also popular instruments. The *taegŭm* or large bamboo-flute had a range of tones covering two and a half octaves. For all large, medium, and small bamboo-flutes, a total of 867 pieces of music are said to have been composed in this period. From the seventh century on, we hear of stately arrays of musicians, dancers, and singers in orchestral performance on various occassions.

---

* Some modern storks—flamingos—are, it is interesting to note, trained to dance to music.

Plate 13. Bodhisattva of Sǒkkuram (p. 119). Granite. Height : 7ft. Sǒkkuram, Kyǒngju. Silla, 8th century.

Plate 14. Arahat of Sǒkkuram (p. 119). Granite. Height : 7ft. Sǒkkuram, Kyǒngju. Silla, 8th century.

Plate 15, 16. Ǔnjin Mairteya (p. 182). Height : 60 ft. Kwanch'oksa, Nonsan, South Ch'ungch'ǒng Province. Koryǒ, late 10th century. Stone Lantern of Kwanchoksa (p. 182). Height : 20 ft. Kwanch'oksa, Nonsan, South Ch'ungch' ong Province. Koryǒ, late 10th century

Plate 12. Sakyamuni of Sŏkkuram. (p. 119). Granite. Height: 10 ft. 8 in. Sokkuram, Kyŏngju. Silla, 8th century.

Plate 11. Tabot'ap (Pagoda of Tabo Buddha). (p. 118). Height : 34 ft. Pulguksa, Kyŏngju.

Plate 9. The Ch'ŏmsŏngdae (Stone Observatory). (p. 118) Height: 28 ft. Kyŏngju, North Kyŏngsang Province. Silla, 7th century

Plate 10. Sŏkkat'ap (Pagoda of Sakyamuni). (p. 118). Height: 25 ft. Pulguksa, Kyŏngju. Silla, 7th, 8th century

Plate 7. Gold Crown from the Gold Crown Tomb. (p.117). Gold and jade ornaments. Height : 1 ft. 5¹/₂ in Silla, 5th-6th century. National Museum of Korea.

Plate 8. Gold Belt from the Gold Crown Tomb. (P. 117). Length : 5ft. 3³/₄ in. Silla, 5th-6th century. National Museum of Korea.

Plate 5. Chŏngimsa Pagoda (p.116). Height :
28 ft. South Ch'ungch'ŏng Province. Paekche, 7th
century.

Plate 6. Stamped Brick (p. 116). Gray Paste.
Height : 11 in.; width : 11 in. Paekche, 7th century National Museum of Korea.

Plate 3. The Paekche Kwanŭm (Kudara Kannon) (p.115). Wood. Height : 9 ft. Hōryūji, Nara, Japan. Paekche, late 6th century.

Plate 4. Bodhisattva Maitreya. (p.115). Gilt bronze. Height : 3 ft. $^{13}/_{16}$ in. Paekche, early 7th century. National Museum of Korea.

Plate 1. Hunting Scene in the Tomb of Dancers Mural (p. 114). Painting on Plaster. Kungnae (T'ung-kou), Manchuria Koguryŏ, 4th-6th centruy.

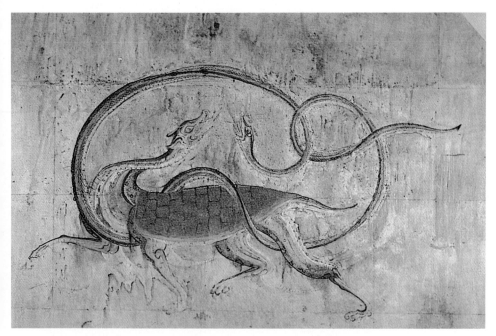

Plate 2. Black Tortoise and Snake in the Great Tomb Mural (p.114). Painting on Plaster. Height : 3 ft.; width 5ft. South P'yŏng'an Province. Koguryŏ, 6th-7th century.

7

Art

A wide variety of art-remains of the Three Kingdoms period show a high degree of aesthetic achievement on the basis of religioartistic motifs and materials available then ; in general, they give an impression of youthful maturity. The existing art works consist mainly of personal appurtenances, vessels, weapons, and fresco paintings, architecture. pagodas and sculptures of Buddhist motif, and so on. A large number of these are works of great magnititude, manifesting the characteristics in aesthetic propensity of the peoples of the Three Kingdoms, which can be also tangibly studied in the context of their historical experiences.

Koguryŏ Painting

The horse-riding, castle-building Koguryŏans maintained northern vigor and stamina. They tenaciously held on to their masculine tribal tradition throughout their dynastic history. The dominant artistic manifestation of these trends is seen in delineation of power and movement. The art of Koguryŏ, as seen through its scanty remnants today, is best represented by the late fourth to early seventh century fresco paintings found on the walls of tombs. Most of these tombs that contain paintings are scattered by the thousands mainly around Koguryŏ's two capitals, Kungnae and P'yŏngyang. The Koguryŏ tombs were built above the ground in the form of stepped-pyramid and, later, of mound with entrance, thus making themselves susceptible to looting. In fact, they were thoroughly looted, except mural paintings.

Mural themes range from depiction of the life of warrior-aristocrats and supranatural beings to picture of decorative figures of geometric and floral designs in such deep primary colors as red, blue, green yellow, and black. Some of chinese features in painting and cosmological thought of Han times were worked through sophisticated and masterly rendition into the unmistakably Koguryŏ painting.

In the fifth-century Tomb of Dancers, so named from the pictures of dancing girls, which has a rectangular antechamber and a square main room covered by a corbeled ceiling, the remarkably well-preserved murals show the dead as the center of the universe. The corbeled dome, eight storied in this particular tomb, was painted as the firmament containing constellations in their proper positions amid the various decorations of supramundane motif. On the wall are shown secular activities of the dead is portrayed as seated on the stool with two monks in front of him. On the eastern wall is a scene of entertainment, its main feature being the five dancers in action. On the opposite, that is, on the western wall depicted is hunting in full swing. Stylized mountains in dark yellow whose repeated contour lines are echoed on the bodily lines of running animals, particularly on the black and yellow stripes of a fleeing tiger. A warrior making a Parthian shot turning backward in his saddle is sensitively rendered with a thematic awareness of powerful, swift movement and internal coherence *(Plate 1)*.

This sense of power and movement is again embodied in the rendition of legendary animals in a tomb built probably in the late sixth century is South P'yŏng'an Province. The one–chambered sepulcher, the largest of a three–tomb group, hence called Taemyo or Great Tomb, has the granite walls of skilled masonry. The walls are regarded as four directions symbolized in accord with the five agent theory by four beasts, that is, a set of creation symbols : the Great Dragon of East, the White Tiger of West, the Scarlet Bird of South, the Black Tortoise of North, and the Yellow Dragon representing the dead in the center *(Plate 2)*.

The work is much more refined in both technique and total effect than a similar one done earlier in the Tomb of the Four Gods on the northern bank of the Amnok River. A portentous sense of strength and swift movement inherent in these fantastic beasts in dramatic pose are all animated by deceptively gentle, undulating lines. The elegant drawing of the figures and adept application of brushwork on every detail and in subtle coloration lend such realism to the work as to enhance the surrealism of the microcosm within the walls.

Although evidence shows that Koguryŏ was more advanced in many fields of art and technology than its neighbors to the south, little other than these sepulchral remains have survived to testify its former glory in its totality. And the dearth of Buddhist art works for the first adopter of Buddhism in the Peninsula can probably be explained in the completeness of devastation of Koguryŏ's cultural centers at the hands of the T'ang soldiery in 668. The same thing is more or less true with Paekche art.

Paekche Sculpture

In the case of Paekche's Buddhist art, however, we can have more than a glimpse of it, even though, of non-Buddhist art, nothing comparable with Koguryŏ's mural painting has survived. The religious art is represented by a number of sculptures, mostly religious images, and pagodas which disclose the Paekchean propensity in art. Interestingly enough, well-preserved Japanese Buddhist art of the Asuka period supplements what seems meager existing relics of Paekche art. Tracing its affinity in large measure to the art of the Six Dynasties of South China, the gentle, modest Paekche people created several distinct characteristics of their own.

The finest representation of Paekche Buddhist art is the late sixth century Paekche Kwanŭm or better known as Kudara Kannon in Japanese *(Plate 3)*. It has been and is kept in Japan at the Hōryūji near Nara. It was sent from Paekche, and the Hōryūji itself preserves features of Paekche temple architecture. The Kudara Kannon, standing nine feet tall and carved from a block of wood, has in a more refined form some partial features of the iconography favored in Six Dynasties South China. As a work of art, however, its aesthetic sublimity is radiant totally with Paekche spirituality. The mysterious peace and grace of the slender Goddess of Mercy are accentuated by the delicate lines of drapery. Its religious and artistic qualities, heightened by flowing lines of side drapery, lines that Koguryŏ artists were applying for a different effect, are indeed unsurpassed among the works of its kind in this period.

Equally important in Paekche sculpture is a seventh century work, the gilt bronze Bodhisattva Maitreya in a meditation pose in the Tŏksu Palace Museum of Fine Arts *(Plate 4).* * The seated Maitreya, with his right leg crossed over the left knee and fingertips of his right hand slightly touching the cheek, has been thought to be a Sillan work, but some of its salient character-

---

* As of this writing, there are two museums in the Tŏksu Palace : Tŏksu Palace Museum of Fine Arts and National Museum of Korea, to be soon merged into a national museum newly built in the Kyŏngbok Palace precinct. For both museums, the name National Museum of Korea is used hereafter in this book

istics are now regarded by some as closer to those of Paekche. † The most convincing basis for the reversed view is the fact that a few Japanese wooden statues were inspired directly by this particular work ; it is less likely that Silla influenced Japanese Buddhist art in this period. The artistic quality of the three foot tall, seated Maitreya, like the standing Bodhisattva, is heightened by soft drapery lines and linear grace emphasized by the slim nude torso and delicate bearing of the right hand fingers. Representing the last stage of Paekche sculpture, the figure stands for an artistic achievement of great magnitude.

The quality of peace and stability is further manifest in its architecture. Some excavated temple sites of Paekche and a few of the existing temples of Asuka Japan testify to the stately size of Buddhist temple as the religious and educational center of this period. A number of still standing stone pagodas that we see around the ruins of once magnificent temples also elegantly bespeak the architectural talent of Paekche. The seventh century Chŏngnimsa Pagoda in Puyŏ, a vast improvement over its prototype, the Mirŭksa Pagoda in North Chŏlla Province which in turn is a stone replica of wooden pagodas of earlier construction, is the most beautiful of the surviving Paekche towers *(Plate 5)*. The five-story pagoda, each story slightly smaller than one below with its gently raised eaves, has been standing in determined stability for more than a millennium.

Another artistic work attesting to the matured level of Paekche art is a piece of ornamental brick along with seven other similar pieces found at the site of a temple in Puyŏ *(Plate 6)*. The stamped design in relief on the one-square foot gray paste is a stylized landscape of Taoistic version, which is a refreshingly unique work in Korean art of this period. Rounded "three peak mountains," pine trees, clouds, and other components are all pleasantly arranged, and the work as a whole gives an impression of modern primitivistic production, if more sensitively rendered. As in Koguryŏ art, Paekche's artistic features, that are embodied in these scattered works, suggest divergent influences coming from Central Asia as well as South China. But it is worth noting that over these influences obviously triumphed the originality of Paekche artists, which made Paekchean characteristics quite different, though less in form but more in total impression, from those of the art of either Koguryŏ or Silla.

---

† The strong proponent of this theory is Professor Wŏn—yong Kim. See his book, *Han' guk misulsa* (*History of Korean Art*), p. 109.

Art in Silla

One large source for the art remains of Silla is its tumuli which, unlike those of Koguryŏ and Paekche, were of subterranean construction. Silla's method of tomb building was to place the chamber far below the ground level without entrance or murals and to cover it with and earthen mound of up 300 feet in diameter and sixty feet in height, to the dismay of would-be plunders. A relatively large number of items excavated from several of these mausoleums, ranging from vessels, weapons, and utensils to ceremonial and personal ornaments, are thought to have been produced before the official adoption of Buddhism because of a conspicuous lack of Buddhist elements in their artistic composition.

The best known of the pre-Buddhist articles are three gold crowns in the National Museum of Korea. The most noteworthy is the one discovered from Gold Crown Tomb, so named after its star piece, where 30,000 ornamental pieces of jade and other precious stones were also among the uncovered *(Plate 7)*. The crown consists of the inner and outer pieces. The feature of the inner cap, covered with designs in openwork, is marked by two horn-shaped projections extending somewhat backward. The outer band, making up the main part of the crown, has two long pendents suspending from, and five uprights attached to, itself. Of five uprights, three tree-shaped ones are standing on the front, and the two antler-shaped on the back ; the latter is regarded as of northern origin. The entire crown is covered with 133 round spangles and fifty-seven green *kog'ok* (*magadama* in Japanese), or comma-shaped jewels, which at slight movements of the crown sensitively vibrate, reflecting the light in all directions. The total effect of the crown, which seems to have been for ceremonial use, is splendid and must have genuinely solemnized the occasion.

Silla's dexterity at gold works has been amply displayed by many gold and gilt bronze appurtenances of high artistic quality, mostly preserved in the same museum. The gold belt and buckle, also from the Gold Crown Tomb, provide a particularly valuable study *(Plate 8)*. The sixty-four inch long belt is composed of the buckle, the plate, and the thirty-nine sections of the belt proper with round spangles. Each section, fastened on to the next, has two parts in floral and heart-shaped openwork, that is, the rectangular upper and the hear-shaped lower, also hinged together. In addition to small round pendents, suspended from the belt are seventeen elaborate pendents about nine inches long on the average, the longest being seventeen inches. Scholarly attention has been paid as to the origin of influence for the particular design of each pendent. More significant is the fact that the elaborateness of these components comes in sharp contrast with the startling simplicity of the buckle whose design is starkly functional. "Yet it remains in relation to it [the elaborate sections of the belt], since the heart-shaped point of the buckle—an excellent functional design—repeats the shape of the ring section of each plaque and also repeats the openwork pattern of the cutout." *

On the strength of such well developed artistic tradition, Silla, in the face of the sudden onrush of Buddhism after 527, could master all categories of Buddhist art with remarkable ease. The immediate pitch of temple constructions, which were, from an artistic point of view, a synthetic total of all artistic activities, attests to the fact of Silla's already high aesthetic attainment, even though Paekche technicians seem to have played a role in the early stage.

The Hwangnyongsa, Temple of Imperial Dragon, representing the early Buddhist architecture, was indeed a magnificent complex in Kyŏngju, which was, however, destroyed by the invading Mongols in 1238. After its original complex was finished in 553, the Hwangnyongsa was given new additions continually for nearly a century. Some of its well-known features were the main hall of more than 110 square feet in floor space, in which housed was a seventeen foot tall gilt bronze Buddha, and the nine-story wooden pagoda rising to a height of 230 feet. This magnificent pagoda, build under the supervision of a Paekche architect, might have served as the model for stone pagodas of later periods.

The Ch'ŏmsŏngdae, a non-Buddhist tower also in Kyŏngju, is a stone observatory, standing twenty-eight feet tall, built during the reign of Queen Sŏndŏk (632-646) *(Plate 9)*. The stamp-shaped structure today stands as a reminder of Silla's architectural diversity as well as cultural advancement.

Soon, in and around the United Silla capital, about sixty large temples came to grace the landscape, of which the Pulguksa represents the acme of Buddhist art of United Silla. The Pulguksa, built in 535, was during the reign of King Kyŏngdŏk (742-764) rebuilt and enlarged to a tremendous complex that embraced scores of stately buildings and a series of stone platforms, bridges, and stairs. The temple was burnt, along with other monuments in the area, this time, by invading Japanese in 1592 ; the reconstructed complex, now standing, is little more than two fifth of the original one. Of the stone structures that have survived, two pagodas, Sŏkkat'ap and Tabot'ap, are called the finest of the Silla pagodas ; their monumentality and potent vitality symbolize the serene dynamism of Silla life *(Plate 10, 11)*.

The Sŏkkat'ap or Pagoda of Sakyamuni, about twenty-five feet in height, is a monument of simplicity that comes in a most sharp contrast with the Tabot'ap right beside it. The single artistic preoccupation in its creation seems to have the use of as few stone slabs as possible. The general effect is one of austerity and restrained power contained in a series of straight lines in

---

* Evelyn McCune, *The Art of Korea*, p. 85.

parallel.

The Tabot'ap or Pagoda of Tabo Buddha is quite different in effect and appearance. On the unusually tall pedestal furnished with four staircases, the four conspicuously large corner shafts support the Pagoda's main unit composed of three octagonal stories and the finial making up a total height of about thirty-four feet. Each of three eight-sided tiers is all differently modeled after, and finely carved units such as supporting spokes, pales, and the rest, are casually thrown together to make up a monument which stands intact after fourteen centuries. The well balanced unity of the Pagoda as a whole, which completely absorbs its seemingly-ornate complexity, imparts a sense of serene confidence as well as religious devotion. It may be noted that the thematic combination of simplicity and complexity seen in the gold belt and buckle is repeated in this pair of pagodas.

The Sŏkkuram. In the Golden Hall of the Pulguksa sit two bronze Buddhas, Amitabha and Vairochana, dating from the early eighth century. While they may represent in many respects the sculptural works of seventh and eighth century Silla, we must look for better works to the Sŏkkuram grotto that houses, among others, a granite Sakyamuni, probably the best of the contemporary works of its kind anywhere.

The Sŏkkuram, built in the eighth century atop Mt. T'oham about a mile away from the Pulguksa, is not only a unique Silla temple of worship but also a veritable museum of sculptural masterpieces. Its plan, apparently based on the features of Chaitya and Vihara in India, includes about twenty-one by fifteen foot front chamber, the domed cave proper of about twenty-three feet in diameter and thirty-six feet in height, and a short vestibule connecting the two rooms. Honored in the center of the domed room is Sakyamuni flanked by major figures in the Mahayana pantheon, who are carved on the surrounding walls *(Plates 12, 13, 14)*.

After two centuries of experience in the religion and its art, the well proportioned granite Buddha, as the pinnacle of Silla's iconographic art, now completely wiped out that archaic smile which characterized early statues and grew to a startling realism. Indeed, the Buddha seems to have gone for a profound meditation in transcendental peace as signified by the gesture of the left hand. The surfaces of the voluminous body and the gestures are worked with utmost care to achieve sublime simplicity. To this end also, the draperies and the gestures of the hands are rendered disinterestedly inconspicuous.

The tones of sculptural rendition for two groups of figures, five Bodhisattvas and ten disciples, on the walls, each about seven feet in height, flare out in different directions again in sharp contrast. The five fragile-looking Bodhisattvas are carved in bas-relief with the same delicate care ; realism of fleshy body, swaying drapery, ornate jewelry, etc. has been said to rise far above the contemporary T'ang level in elastic quality. Against the feminine exquisiteness of the Bodhisattvas, the ten disciples are rendered muscular, humble, and ugly, but with no less artistic competence.

As increasing numbers of temples and monasteries were built in cities and in scenic mountains, especially around the mid-eighth century at the apogee of the Silla prosperity, so all manner of Buddhist arts came to be admired by a wider range of people. Understandably, the function of the temple as the religious and educational center enlightening the masses increased in importance, and at the same time the Sillans came to recognize the communicative as well as religious values of temple bells. The high enthusiasm in manufacture of great bells the Silla court showed during the eighth century was unusual. Of the five existing great bells, including the two now in Japan, the Pongdŏksa bell, cast in 771 in honor of King Sŏngdŏk (702-736) and placed now at the Kyŏngju National Museum, is the holder of several superlatives. It is one of the largest of its kind in the world : twelve and a half feet in height, seven and a half feet in diameter, nine inches in thickness, nearly 150,000 pounds in weight, and eighty miles in diameter of area that the bell's sound can cover, assuming the acoustic conditions of the weather to be favorable. The largest of the Silla bells, the Hwangnyongsa bell, completed in 754, was about four times as large as the Pongdŏksa bell. Later, it was recast into a half the original size and subsequently lost amid the destruction of that temple by the Mongols.

The most valuable aspects of a Silla bell are of course its surface decorations and sound. Decorations on the iron surface are delicately realistic as on wooden blocks. Of the motifs of decorations, most befitting the function of a temple bell are, as on the waist of the Pongdŏksa bell, the flying angels with musical instruments amid waving diaphonous draperies and clouds. * These exquisitely cast angels are obviously propagating the message of Buddha, flying to the undulating, endless waves of sounds that the bell strikes out. The vibration of sounds, depending on the quality of cast and the thickness and size of the bell, usually lasts from thirty to forty seconds.

---

* See illustration on page 73.

Part 4

Disintegration and Re-Centralization

詞薩羅喃三唵唎　眩那庾多設多素　槺坐婆盧迦俱　喃怛他揭多㙮伽　南謨納婆納伐辰　遍誦此陀羅尼曰　香花供養施遠七

1

Political and Economic Development

At least thirty-nine families in mid-eighth century Kyŏngju were possessors of tremendous wealth. Reportedly, some of them owned "three thousand slaves" in addition to land, pastures, and, probably villages of handicraftsmenserf in localities of their origin. Provincial aristocrats, too, if less powerful in national politics, certainly enjoyed social prestige and political power in their respective districts of influence. It is very likely that provincial as well as central aristocrats continued to maintain private armies of varying sizes.

As we have noted, the royal court felt it necessary in the early period of unification movement to curry favor with local and central power groups by dispensing Bone Ranks, land, and slaves and by discreet acquiescence in their local domination. The *sig'ŭp*, the most generous form of grant, went to a limited number of aristocrats, whereas the *nog'ŭp*. smaller in scale, were given to selected government officials. The Buddhist establishment proved to be not in the least undesirous of material wealth, inducing tax-free land and other gifts from the ruling class. The triumphant Silla court continued material distribution to maintain political consensus. But it was soon to face serious obstructions in the way of more effective centralization.

Of the centrifugal forces, the common people and slaves, that is, the source of labor supply, offered considerable problems for the central court. In fact, it was this group that led a series of rebellions in the late ninth century. A large segment of the lower class seems to have been the residents of the *hyang, so,* and *pugok* who were, as has been noted, formerly of conquered people and "traitors." The *hyang, so,* and *pugok,* some of which were very large in area, became in time regular administrative units, which continued to exist until the end of the Koryŏ dynasty.

These people, even though in some kind of bondage, were not slaves as domestic slaves were, but along with the domestic slaves, they were regarded as *ch'onmin* or the lowborn who constituted the bottom of the Silla society just below the *p'yŏngmin* or *yangmin*, both meaning common people. The class line between the *ch'ŏnmin* and the *yangmin*, however, was, as noted, not well defined in this period; during the later dynasties, especially in the late Yi period, it was more common for a *ch'ŏnmin* to become a *yangmin* rather than otherwise.

As the growth of the population and trade took place, which prompted the reorganization of production, coupled with the improved agricultural technique and the emergence of large landowners, the *ch'ŏnmin* classes' position tended to shift from the "depersonalized" labor force to the semi-independent farm workers or handicraftsmen who brought a greater efficiency in production than they had done under the former category. At the same time, the supposedly free farmers or peasants in a *sig'ŭp* or a *nog'ŭp*, who were tied together by tribal tradition, tended to become, inspite of themselves, semi-agricultural serf for the official recipients or formerly their patriarchal leaders. Such a reorientation of the lower classes in relation to landowners created the new productive and social pattern similar to that of the feudal lord-serf relations, which made the presence of the central administration less felf among the lower classes. On the other hand, as we have seen, there existed tightly organized administrative units on the village level that made up the bulk of the tax-paying, free farmers of United Silla.

The Royal Power

Monarchs of United Silla, eager to concentrate more power in themselves, naturally strove to undermine official-aristocrats' economic and political ties with the masses and to make them financially dependent upon the court. King Sinmun (681-691) discontinued granting the *nog'ŭp* with all its attached rights to recipients. Instead, he instituted a kind of salary system under which the officials were alloted certain amounts of land, according to their ranks, and given the tax grain yielded from the land they were assigned to as annual stipend. This system was also to strip the officials of their lordly power over the peasants living in *nog'ŭp*.

A more ambitious step in this direction was taken in 722 when King Sŏngdŏk (702-736) began to distribute land directly to free farmers between the ages of twenty and sixty, that is, those liable for military and *corvée* duties who had been dependent upon local patriarchs and central officials for arable land. But the conservative force against this centralization movement seems to have asserted itself, resulting, in 757, in restoration of the *nog'ǔp* system in place of the stipend system. With this reverse act, the distribution of land to the free farmers could have conceivably been stopped also.

This was a definite setback for King Kyŏngdŏk (742-764). But he won a political reform which was rather unobtrusive yet historically significant. In 757 King Kyŏngdŏk's court transliterated and mostly translated the place names into Chinese characters for official use, and in 759 he reorganized the government largely after the Chinese pattern, also including change of the tradition-soaked designations of offices to Chinese-style names. The overall result of this government reorganization was that, while administrative confusion was greatly eliminated and the status of the *Chipsabu* enhanced over all other ministries, the office of the Sangdaedǔng was left eclipsed. It is worth noting that the seemingly innocuous change of the offices and places in use since the tribal period seems to have been one important trick couched in this reform: it was to remove the anachronistic patriarchal aura from the government, thereby shearing the conservatives of some of their pretensions.

The scuffle between the royal authority and the aristocratic power, as seen in the above, was however, the beginning of decline of the former, which seemed rather an inevitable eventuality of the very political structure of the Silla society, as seen, for instance, in the Bone Rank system. The first serious sign of political disintegration occurred in 768 during the reign of King Hyegong (765-779). A free-for-all civil war, involving "ninety-six" conservative groups, broke out, lasting several years. In 776 the government reorganization of 759 was abrogated in favor of the pre-reform government structure, but only the geographical designations were kept as they were changed in 757. The eventual assassination in 779 of King Hyegong, the last of the T'aejong line, marked the reemergence of the Sangdaedǔng in power.

It is also important to note here that an attempt to recruit civil officials through government examination was made against such a background in 788. It was the most enterprising reform move ever made by the Silla court, which could have driven a wedge into the Bone Rank system, now the most conservative safeguard against progress, but again was frustrated by the conservative force. Although the Silla dynasty was to last still another century, the history of the Silla court during its last phase of existence was pockmarked by internecine struggles resulting from debilitated power of the royalty *vis-à-vis* the enlarged economic and military might of the aristocracy.

The Provincial Growth

The central court in chronic confusion and weakness became like the glue that lost adhesive power : things that were held together by it began to come apart. From the early ninth century on, patriarchs in the provinces, whose number was joined by central aristocrats routed from power struggles in the capital, gradually built up their personal following. Their large landholding was of course the basis of operations including maintenance of personal armies. Drifting peasants and absconding slaves were absorbed into these local powers. Even spirited village chiefs moved to consolidate and enlarge their personal power by bringing neighboring villages into their sphere of influence. Provincial and subsidiary capitals and military strongholds, which were usually castellated cities, offered the best conditions conducive to this pattern of development.

Kim Hŏn Ch'ang, a True Bone aristocrat who was eased out of the central political arena to the governorship of Ungju Province, the heartland of old Paekche, revolted in 822. The ill-fated rebellion was symptomatic in that he named his territory Chang'an, an independent kingdom. But these signs of political malaise, if they were indicative of internal contradictions and foreboding of evil times ahead, were in many respects a painful side of Silla's coming-of-age. Indeed, the eighth and ninth centuries saw many notable economic developments that stimulated regional advancement. Silla's artistic achievements discussed earlier may be seen in this context of economic growth.

The Foreign Trade

Silla's expansiveness in peacetime activities was most clearly evidenced in the maritime trade with the T'ang and Japan, which amply compensated for its failure in occupation of the whole Koguryŏ territory in war. Silla's command of sea necessitated by wartime contacts with the T'ang was now maintained for commercial and cultural exchanges with maritime neighbors. The population increase and various construction projects, coupled with the desire for luxury goods of the ruling class which was one of conspicuous social phenomena in eighth and ninth century Silla, invigorated domestic and foreign trades as well as agriculture and manual industries. The national energy released from the war efforts seems to have been channeled mostly into trade activities over the Northeast Asian sea.

Silla's foreign trade, for which the export of raw materials was about all there had been, rose, fifty years after the unification, to include a number of manufactured goods, of which textile fabrics and gold and silver products were the most popular items. Insam, a tonic medicine, also known as ginseng, was another popular and permanent item in Silla's foreign trade, for that matter, throughout the traditional period and today. The government-to-government trade by way of tribute missions was gradually overshadowed in value and importance by non-official commerce. The private trade between Silla and the T'ang, despite the ban imposed upon by the T'ang court in the 780's, began to flourish in the late eighth century and reached its peak in the ninth century when internal political disturbances in both countries weakened central administration.

There were three main trade routes: one was from the mouth of the Taedong River to Laichou on the Shantung coast; the second course was to navigate from Tŏkchŏk Island in the Gulf of Namnyang (Inch'ŏn), where ships from the west coast rendezvoused, to Tengchou also in the Shantung Peninsula; By far the heaviest traffic proceeded from Yŏng'am in South Chŏlla Province to ports of the Shantung-Kiangsu coasts and also Kyŭshŭ, Japan.

In some of these port cities, Silla traders established colonies with "extraterritorial" arrangements or special administrative setup exclusively for Korean residents under a Korean official called *taesa* (*ta-shih* in Chinese), the designation that is used for ambassador today. The most prominent Silla colony was in Tengchou in the Shantung Peninsula, the gateway to Ch'ang-an for official missions from Silla, Parhae, and Japan. The Silla community supported a Buddhist temple served by thirty monks and nuns, which attracted a usual congregation of 250 at a gathering. The well-known Japanese monk-diarist Ennin was a grateful guest at the temple in the 840's.

A heavy traffic in trade with Japan continued to flow. In Tsushima, Korean interpreters were posted to facilitate commercial transactions, which, though illegal, were overlooked or even encouraged by Japanese officials. The Japanese tribute missions to the T'ang in this period were often accomplished by the courtesy of Korean merchant ships or through employment of Korean mariners who manned their ships.

Chang Po Ko. Of the seafaring Sillans who thus played useful maritime role among these three countries, the most remarkable was Chang Po Ko, who has been credited with the establishment of the Buddhist temple in Tengchou. Chang Po Ko, while in military service to the T'ang court, witnessed rampant piratical attacks upon the coastal populace by the Chinese and Koreans and returned in 828 to Silla, purporting to police the sea. Authorized by King Hŭngdŏk (826-835), he set up the Ch'onghae chin on the island of Wando at the southwestern tip of South Chŏlla Province: a *chin* was a naval defense establishment that dotted along the coastal zones. Chang's contingent at the Ch'onghae chin eventually grew into a semi-private navy of

10,000 men, with which indeed he brought the piracy under control.

Chang Po Ko then proceeded to monopolize the lucrative international trade, periodically sending well-organized fleets of merchant ships to the T'ang and Japan. In 840 and 841 Chang sent even his personal emissaries to the Japanese court presumably to establish diplomatic relations with it. The Japanese court refused to consider such a presumptuous proposal made by a foreign individual; nevertheless, it allowed Chang's commercial activities in Japan. Understandably, the profits resulting from these commercial traffics were large and of two-way affair between Koreans and Japanese officials. Although he was embroiled and lost his life in 846 in one of those succession struggles, Chang was unquestionably an outstanding example of provincial power and wealth, which gradually hardened into political groups of various sizes independent of Kyŏngju in the late ninth century.

Chang-do Island(middle one) from the highest Sanghwang-bong peak in the Wan-do Island. Historic site of Admiral Chang Po Ko 'Ch'onghae Chin.'

2

The War of Dynastic Change

Despite the political debilitation of the central government, the economic prosperity, shrouded in a certain dilettante as well as decadent social climate that characterized the Silla society since the middle of the eighth century, continued into the ninth century. The life in the capital and probably other major cities seems to have been extravagant. The government issued a ban on the "life of luxury" in 806 and 834. Late ninth century Kyŏngju was described as a city of 178,936 households, containing not a single thatched house and full of song and music day and night. And they all used charcoal instead of firewood for fuel to prevent smoke, (a measure against air pollution from an aesthetic point of view). King Hŏn'gang (875-885) expressed his satisfaction with the well-being of the capital. But by then the internal political cleavage, long in the making, grew out of all proportions for the governmental ability to cement.

Intellectuals, mostly of the fallen True Bone and Six Head Quality origins, also became disenchanted with the central aristocracy and looked for employment with provincial powers. Prominent local leaders, by the late ninth century, came to call themselves generals or castellans because of castles they built or occupied and began cutting out their own territories of government. They owned vast areas of agricultural land and full-fledged private armies and imposed taxes upon the peasantry. Many of these generals carried on foreign trade independently. For a moment, Silla seemed to be heading for decentralized feudalism, even though generals had yet to completely subjugate powerful local families and to eliminate the presence of the central government from their respective territories.

Under such circumstances, the majority of peasants were hard put to pay taxes, more often than not, to the two storied government. The kinds and amounts of taxes became increasingly unpredictable. More and more peasants resorted to drifting or banditry. Still others found themselves in soldiery under those generals against the central government. The smouldering discontent erupted in 889 when Queen Chinsŏng (887-896) sent out officials to urge payment of the taxes.

When the dust settled after a period of a free-for-all scramble for supremacy, United Silla was disunited back to the three kingdoms, two other kingdoms being Later Paekche and Later Koguryŏ. During the period of next fifty years until 936 when the Koryŏ dynasty reunited the Peninsula, the unification drama this time was quite differently enacted.

Kyŏnhwŏn, a peasant-turned military officer serving in Chŏnju in modern North Chŏlla Province, called himself the King of Later Paekche in 892. Allegedly to take revenge for the demise of King Ŭija, the last King of Paekche, he claimed a wide support from the restless masses. By 910, the Later Paekche under King Kyŏnhwŏn covered all of modern North and South Chŏlla Provinces and the southern part of Ch'ungch'ŏng Province.

Another persona in this drama was Kung'ye, a Sillan of royal stock but with morbid hatred toward the Silla royalty, who consolidated local powers scattered in modern provinces of Kyŏnggi, Hwanghae, and Kangwŏn. In 901 he laid claim to reestablishment of Koguryŏ as the King of Later Koguryŏ. By 910, King Kung'ye, aided by his able general, Wang kŏn, was on the offensive mainly against the Later Paekche. Silla, now unable to cope with the situation, shrank to its original size or even smaller, depending on the aggressiveness of its neighbors at any given time. Thus, the major confrontation that would determine the final outcome was to between T'aebong, the name changed from Later Koguryŏ, and Later Paekche.

Although T'aebong and Later Paekche shared the border line of North and South Ch'ungch'ŏng Provinces, the major battles in the 910's were fought on the southwestern tip South Chŏlla Province. This strategy of disturbing the rear of the Later Paekche, engineered by General Wang Kŏn seems to have paid off handsomely for T'aebong. General Wang Kŏn occupied the island of Wando off the Southwestern coast of South Chŏlla Province, Naju, a major city in that province, and the area in between. T'aebong's firm control of this area effectively prevented the Later Paekche from conducting foreign trade. There were still about thirty to forty ports on the south and west coasts in active trade with the T'ang and Japan : it is conceivable that these ports were all now under Wang Kŏn's patronage. More important, Wang Kŏn's control of the Naju area kept the Later Paekche from absorbing small semi-independent local powers to the east, while making it possible for the T'aebong army under King Kung'ye, pushing southward, to gnaw away at strategic points around Silla.

Thus, the overall military situation was generally favorable to T'aebong, which now controlled the largest of the territories of the Later Three Kingdoms. But King Kung'ye, like other short-lived royalties, squandered treasury on construction of grand palaces and the capital city in modern Ch'ŏrwŏn in Kangwŏn Province, while proclaiming himself the Bodhisattva Maitreya whom the people were required to worship. Thus, he began to enjoy power and reverence rather in advance. Some of his later behaviors were clearly paranoiac, which eventually triggered an abdication movement climaxing in 918 in the installation of Wang Kŏn as the king. Although a series of small, ill-fated revolts followed, his ascension to the throne was generally received with much acclamation.

Wang Kŏn or T'aejo (Grand Progenitor), who proclaimed the Koryŏ dynasty, from which the name Korea was derived, proceeded extremely cautiously, paying particular attention to the matter of consensus. He was a man of modesty and prudence which characterized his campaigns against the two other kingdoms and his foundation work for the new dynasty. He first moved his capital from Ch'ŏrwŏn to Song'ak, the present city of Kaesŏng, which was his traditional power base. He made it known that his dynasty was the successor of Koguryŏ, as his dynastic name indicated, and northward expansion, therefore, constituted the most basic policy of his dynasty.

King T'aejo showed great interest in the rehabilitation of P'yŏngyang which had been laid in ruins. In 919 he rebuilt and peopled P'yŏngyang with well-to-do families under high-ranking resident officials. He named it western capital to which he expressly wished to move his capital, whenever feasible. The reason for his attachment to P'yŏngyang of such an importance, other than for his aspiration for northward expansion, was his profound belief in a geomantic theory that P'yŏngyang's physical feature still preserved certain supernatural energy which could support "ten thousand generations of prosperity."

T'aejo's more immediate concern, however, was the diplomatic problem of dealing with small semi-independent power groups, which he correctly estimated to have a direct bearing upon the inevitable showdown with the Later Paekche. No sooner had he acceded to the throne than he sent out personal envoys with "humble words and generous gifts" to local generals and castellans, especially those jammed between the Later Paekche and Silla, in order to woo them into his camp. When local mighties were acutely observing the military developments between the major contenders, this was apparently a shrewd move that was to greatly influence them in determining the course of action at the last minute.

Major battles between Koryŏ and the Later Paekche during the 920's were fought along the peripheral line of Silla as the two giants were trying to prevent each other from bagging the golden prize, Silla. In these campaigns

Koryŏ's T'aejo, with his diplomatic skill and many dedicated military subjects under him, clearly had the upper hand. He increased pressure against both the Later Paekche and Silla.

Silla, now lacking even the will to survive, relied squarely on the good-will of T'aejo for its very existence. What the Silla court could do was to ask him to pay a visit to Kyŏngju or to encourage him for a speedy conquest of the Later Paekche. But Silla's overt expression of love for Koryŏ seems to have stirred a devil in King Kyŏnhwŏn, who turned, in 927, to wanton destruction of the splendid city of Kyŏngju. Before Koryŏ's reinforcement arrived, on which Silla had pinned its only hope for its precarious defense, the Later Paekche army descended upon the hapless city. King Kyŏng'ae of Silla and his courtiers were amidst the usual banquet at the Abalone Pavilion, drowning their eschatological vision in the wine which flowed in that famous abalone-shaped canal in the Pavilion. Meanwhile, the Later Paekche soldiers sacked the city: King Kyŏnhwŏn was not far behind his men in destructive activities. Kyŏnhwŏn placed a new king on the Silla throne and carried off weapons, treasures, and hostages.

This offensive posture taken by the Later Paekche marked the begin-ning of another series of collisions between the two giants, in which the Later Paekche showed an increased aggressiveness. But in the battle of Andong in 930, the Later Paekche was frustrated in its intent to control the Taejae Pass (Chungnyŏng), a strategic point between Koryŏ and Silla, and it was forced to abandon what design it might have entertained over Silla. Only then, Koryŏ's T'aejo decided to honor his long standing invitation to Kyŏngju. His entourage consisted of a few ranking officials and no more than fifty guards. It was a conspicuously modest appearance for the king of a rising nation. His scrupulous discretion and humility, coupled with the impeccable discipline shown by his soldiers during his stay in Kyŏngju, in a sharp contrast with the nightmarish scene staged by Kyŏnhwŏn few years before, so much impressed the Silla court and people that T'aejo was compared to a "parent."

After Andong, the theatre of war moved to the western border in the Ch'ungch'ŏng area, and the fighting continued with the score in favor of Koryŏ. Koryŏ had been also favored by many local militaries who voluntarily chose to throw in their lot with T'aejo. Furthermore, in 935, King T'aejo unexpectedly reaped tremendous political fruits born of years of assiduously cultivated personal diplomacy and caution. Kyŏnhwŏn's eldest son, Sin'gŏm launched a coup d'état in which he confined his father to a temple and killed one of his brothers in whose favor King Kyŏnhwŏn wished to abdicate. Soon the incarcerated father escaped to Naju, Koryŏ's strategic stronghold, where he surrendered to Koryŏ. T'aejo sent forty ships to escort the deposed King to Song'ak, and he received his former foe, for whose ten-year seniority over him, with honor due to one's parents.

An even more spectacular part was performed by the Silla court in the same year. King Kyŏngsun of Silla, whom Kyŏnhwŏn installed when he invaded Kyŏngju in 927, saw no feasible alternative for his kingdom but a voluntary surrender to Koryŏ, if only to secure a peaceful demise for the dynasty that had gone through more than "nine" centuries of brilliant career. King Kyŏngsun summoned what amounted to the last Hwabaek conference on the question of surrender to Koryŏ. The crown prince gallantly opposed the proposal, but to no avail. When King Kŏyngsun led the procession from Kyŏngju toward Song'ak, followed by official families, ceremonial vehicles, and treasure–packed horses stretching more than thirty *ri*, people filled the road-side to witness the extraordinary event.

The final confrontation between Koryŏ and the Later Paekche occurred in 936 at Hwangsan, the very sport where Paekche General Kye Paek met the victorious Silla army under General Kim Yu Sin two and a half centuries before. The Later Paekche's internal unity had continued to deteriorate. General Pak Yŏng Kyu, Sin'gŏm's brother-in-law, secretly capitulated to Koryŏ. The showdown, which ended with the beheading of Nŭng Hwan, the mastermind of Sin'gŏm's *coup* in the previous year, was in actuality an anticli-max.

3

The Government of Early Koryŏ

The ideological and methodological basis for the organization of the new government was more of a reflection of T'aejo's personality than of any other circumstances. There was nothing much of a revolutionary change from the Silla type of government except doing away with the obsolete Bone Rank system. Never a high-handed conqueror, T'aejo wang Kŏn sought the solution of political problems through low–keyed compromise with due respect to the long established tradition and beliefs such as the geomantic theory of wind and water (p'ungsu) then in vogue.

T'aejo's mild or timid approach to government understandably resulted in strengthening local governments at the expense of the royal government. He never made any serious attempt at the total subjugation of local power groups. Instead, he allowed his military subjects and voluntarily submitted local generals and castellans to maintain their slaves, landholding, and private armies. In addition to these privileges, some of them, in the absence of central control, amassed personal wealth and unjustly enslaved people for private use even after the confusion of war. Thus, they acquired a surprising degree of local independency, and T'aejo organized local government on the basis of this political reality. He appointed actual strong men as heads of local governments, which more or less small replicas of the central government.

As a measure of ensuring local loyalty, T'aejo inaugurated the Kiin system under which the sons of local government heads were required to stay in the central capital as administrative liaison or "advisors." In Silla times, local leaders themselves were made to sojourn in Kyŏngju in the same capacity, that is, as a kind of hostages. Another device, of T'aejo's invention, to strengthen the ties between the central and local governments was the appointment of high-ranking central officials close to T'aejo himself as *Sasimgwan* who were required, in addition to their duties in the central government, to supervise the administration of their own home districts, where they could provide leadership on behalf of the central government.

King T'aejo's political style was clearly not conducive to creation of a strong centralized government. With the death of T'aejo in 943 and in the absence of a monarch of his stature, the problem of exacting loyalty from official-aristocrats, with large following in their home regions, rose immediately. Wang Kyu, who "presented" two daughters to T'aejo as his fifteenth and sixteenth queens and another daughter to Hyejong (944-945), T'aejo's successor, as his second queen, had entertained his own design on the matter of succession. Before materializing it, however, he was eliminated in 945 by Wang Sik Kyŏm, the garrison general of P'yŏngyang loyal to the King.

The establishment of the central government with more coercive administrative mechanism started with the ascension of Kwangjong (950-975). Kwangjong was the first monarch who made a substantial contribution toward the solidification of the royal authority. Of a series of policies implemented under him, the most outstanding were the review of the slave registers and the inauguration of civil examinations. The former was aimed at emancipation as tax-paying commoners of those unjustly enslaved by central and local aristocrats during and since the war of dynastic change. T'aejo is said to have lamented over irregularities in social status, but problem was already so deeply entwined with the entrenched aristocracy that he did nothing about it. The execution of the measure, which was sound morally and economically but difficult to enforce, took a few years from 956, accompanied by a great social upheaval in which slaves as well as owners came forth to dispute each other over the legality of their bondage. Kwangjong forced his will upon the vested interests, resorting to the imprisonment and purge of those recalcitrants, which seem to have been bloody indeed.

The more far-reaching was the establishment of a civil examination system in 958. More closely patterned after the Chinese model than the one tried by King Wŏnsŏng of United Silla, this system was perfected in time, ensuring recruitment of officials from a wider segment of the population. It also bore the royal intent of curbing the power and prestige of those aristocratic families who were militarily oriented but had manned key positions in the bureaucracy.

The Northern Policy. Another problem, to which the government of the young dynasty paid exceptional attention, was the defense and administration of the northern areas. T'aejo, as has been noted, went to great lengths to translate the express ideals of his dynasty as the successor of Koguryŏ into action. His rehabilitation and promotion of P'yŏngyang as the western Capital were followed by establishment of a series of fortified defense towns in the northwestern region, which pushed the northern border up to the Ch'ŏngch'ŏn River. It soon became clear, however, that Koryŏ's further advance beyond that line could not be anticipated at this juncture because of the rise of the Khitan Liao dynasty to the northwest.

Having risen to power in the Liao River valley during the period of the recent political division after the demise of the T'ang in China, the semi-nomadic, semi-agricultural Khitans, a branch of the Mongols, rapidly extended their control over a vast area of Inner and the southern arm of Outer Mongolia. Turning east, they destroyed Parhae (P'o-hai) in 926. Vigorous and strong, the Liao dynasty was destined to become in the early eleventh century a great empire that embraced several economic regions, including an agricultural area around Peking in North China. The destruction of the biracial kingdom of Parhae brought a continued flow of refugees of Koguryŏan descent into Koryŏ, whom T'aejo heartily welcomed. Prince Tae Kwang Hyŏn of Parhae, who came with several ten thousand followers in 934, was even granted the ryoal surname of Wang. At the same time, some Jürched, Tungusic tribes of Manchuria who had made up the lower layer of the Parhae society, moved to the northeastern Peninsula and began to encroach on Koryŏ from that direction.

The occupation of the former territory of Koguryŏ by the powerful Khitans bitterly frustrated T'aejo in his northbound ambition. He subsequently refused diplomatic relations with the Liao. He once proposed a pincers attack on Liao to the Later Chin, one of the Five Dynasties in North China in this period. After T'aejo, the government launched a vigorous defense program which called for organization of a 300,000 man army in 947 and fortification of twenty-three towns and cities in the northern frontier zone over a thirty year period starting from 947. In the face of the more urgent job of political ground leveling for the internal re-centralization, the government's vigorous northern management with a view to fulfilling one of its founding ideals was all the more enterprising, setting a tradition that was to influence the dynasty's basic policy for centuries to come.

4

Social and Intellectual Development

Social Changes

    War and political turmoil during the ninth and tenth centuries, as might be expected, produced significant social changes as well as dynastic change. Silla's Bone Rank system seems to have intended to prevent just such changes. As the central court of United Silla was weakened of internecine struggles, the provincial military and the Buddhist church, as has been noted, gradually rose with growing confidence in their own power and wealth, hastening the disintegration of United Silla.

    It may be noted, however, that the Bone Rank system had remained intact, though within Silla, until its demise; it disappeared only with the second unification by Wang Kŏn, who, probably of Six Head Quality family, represented a provincial power centering around Song'ak now Koryŏ's capital. Needless to say, he felt necessitated to substitute a new arrangement for the Bone Rank system into the backbone of his dynasty. As he was certainly not to destroy existing power groups in order to establish a new social order to his liking, T'aejo set about to make the royal family the strongest power group. To this end, he resorted to the traditional method of solidification based on regional and kinship relations. His transfer of the capital to Song'ak was the first of such moves. More socially important was his marriage to daughters of powerful families scattered all over the country. T'aejo's twenty-nine queens were all taken from political considerations; that is, the family of the lady in question needed to be the most influential one in the district or regions as his family was in the Song'ak area.

    The royal marriage seems to have often been consummated while

T'aejo was on a tour of the area where the would-be queen happened to reside. Queens did not necessarily reside in the royal palace in Song'ak; most of them seem to have stayed at their own home with children sired by T'aejo. Royal princesses were as a rule given the family name of the mother's, a fact that explains the notorious incestuous marriage within the royal family in later generations. Seen from a standpoint of the queens' families, the marriage to T'aejo was a short cut to a higher social standing and power. Indeed, these families formed the elite portion of the new ruling aristocracy. Thus the use of marriage as a means of ensuring loyalty and solidarity became the most feasible way to maintain status and enlarge wealth among the ruling class during the Koryŏ dynasty and also, to a lesser degree, in the Yi dynasty society.

In a society that had been dominated by the military, the emergence of a distinctly intellectual class was also a significant social phenomenon. Ninth century Silla saw such a phenomenon, though small but probably for the first time in Korean history, as a culmination of the combined efforts in education of individual scholars and the United Silla court. The intellectuals were largely of Six Head Quality families and some True Boners who sought to vent their political frustrations in intellectual activities. They delved in such fields as Confucianism, Sŏn Buddhism, and pseudo-sciences. It was their descendants who played an important role in political re-centralization in the tenth century.

Confucianism. The study of Confucianism among the general members of the ruling class, even though a great deal of government efforts were made for its development, remained on the utilitarian level; it rarely went beyond the attainment of reading and writing ability in Chinese as well as in *Idu.* The philosophical contents of Chinese classics were somewhat foreign to the Silla mind which was in many ways still moored in the tribal past.

The new dynasty, pressed by administrative needs, welcomed scholarly talents into its government. Kwangjong's inauguration of the full-fledged civil examination was unquestionably the most important event for the students of Confucianism, and its success, on the other hand, was indicative of the existence then of a sizable scholarly population, who also served to facilitate the adoption of the Chinese political system for re-centralization. Thus, in the wake of Wang Kŏn's victory which urgently called for a new political ideology, the ready-made Chinese political system based on Confucian ethics, as in the United Silla period, made itself attractive; this time, only more so, as the new dynasty more inclined toward its adoption. This advance of Confucianism in national life, politically necessitated, constituted an occasion of great significance in the social and intellectual history of Korea. Confucianism was to be placed on a par with Buddhism.

Sŏn Buddhism

As in China, Sŏn Buddhism came into vogue in the ninth century, teaching an entirely new approach to enlightenment, which Buddhist intellectuals explored with great *élan*. This coincided with Silla Buddhism's shifting from cities toward scenic verdure, as a corollary to the provincial growth in political and economic power. Sŏn Buddhism, with its meditation as the only path leading to the ultimate truth, was welcomed and patronized by local aristocrats with cultural aspiration.

Sŏn (Ch'an in Chinese; Zen in Japanese) or Meditation sect was the last phase of the sectarian Buddhism. What was new with the Sŏn sect was its employment of an intuitive method based on meditation and other related disciplines for enlightenment. Meditation as a means of immediate insight had been an integral part of all schools of Buddhism from birth, but the Sŏn sect relied solely on intuitive meditation as the one and only way to reach the Buddha reality. Sŏn found little help for attainment of Buddha-nature in scriptural expositions, religious rituals, or even performances of good works, which were in fact regarded as often clouding the insight into the ultimate truth. More emphatically than any other schools, Sŏn saw the Buddha-nature as inherent in human nature; therefore, it taught how to see through one's own heart to find the universal truth, that is, to experience a kind of intellectual enlightenment as against personalistic flight into that ecstatic emotional state called Nirvana.

To grasp the ultimate reality, Sŏn masters emphasized psychological purification of one's mind or mind's emancipation from all mundane concerns which hindered the mind in its penetration of the Buddha-nature. The basic method in this endeavor was called *chwasŏn* or sitting in meditation; this was done usually under the strict guidance of a master. The secondary techniques to help efficiency of meditation and cultivation of mind were many, and some of them seemed far-fetched in rationale. The practice in maintaining a proper posture and breathing, question-and-answer sessions between the master and disciples which laymen would be hard put to understand, beating, travelling among strangers in distant places, and self-incarceration in beauties of nature like a lone Taoist in quest for the secret of eternal life are a few interesting examples.

As may be apparent in these disciplinary programs, the Sŏn school did not have much room for book learning. Its anti-scholastic and iconoclastic attitudes were, however, balanced by its requirement for a high level of intellection. Sŏn also required complete submission to authoritarian discipline, a fact that might have been a contributing factor for its development into the most lasting of the Buddhist sects.

Ch'an (Sŏn) was introduced first into China by Bodhidharma, an early sixth century Indian monk. The Ch'an truth, which Bodhidharma perceived from his legendary nine-year long meditation, which had reputedly atrophied his legs, was transmitted from "mind to mind," that is, from a patriarch to disciples without theoretical formulation in written form. By the time it reached the Sixth Patriarch Hui-neng (638-713), Ch'an had grown into a distinct religious sect with increasing following. Ch'an entered Silla in about the middle of the seventh century, but its influence remained dormant until the ninth century when it became prominent in the sectarian movement.

During the period from the middle of the ninth to the early tenth century, there came into being the nine most influential Sŏn groups. Never having been laterally organized, these groups started its independent monastic existence each under a patriarch. The great patriarchs of Sŏn in this period, seven of whom had received *simin,* a kind of spiritual certificate, from Chinese Ch'an masters, were also the elite core of the intelligentsia of the time, around whom tens of thousands of Sŏn students gathered.

With support of local people, Sŏn groups founded their temples invariably in scenic mountain retreats where they advocated their own particular brand of Sŏn. With the rise of Sŏn, the traditional sects, based on the scriptural authority, came to be grouped under the term Kyo. Thus, Kyo-Sŏn came to mean Buddhism in Korea. But all Kyo sects began to lose their following and also theological distinctiveness from one another in the ninth century; the Sŏn sect became the main current of Buddhism in Koryŏ.

The Theory of Wind and Water

Of the pseudo-sciences that were practiced towards the end of United Silla, the geomantic thought gained a tremendous popularity. The *p'ungsu* (*feng-shun* in Chinese) or wind and water concept was originated from China and apparently much indebted to the *yin-yang* and the five agent schools in its theoretical contents. As the *yin-yang* forces interact in their creativity in the universe, according to the wind and water theory, they also fill and circulate under the surface of the earth like the blood running through arteries and veins. Just as damage to a blood vessel would result in sickness, the ill-treatment of certain vital spots on the land surface or, for instance, improper selection of a temple site, would disturb the subterranean circulation of the *yin-yang,* which might in turn disrupt the harmony of human society. Conversely, construction of a temple, a pagoda, or a house, or founding a town on an auspicious site was believed to revitalize the subterranean forces, just as skilled moxacautery would facilitate the blood circulation, and to prolong the prosperity of a dynasty or, on the lower level, of a family, clan, or a town.

Wind and water are regarded as carriers of the *yin–yang* forces issued from under the ground or from "arteries of the earth." Directions of movement of the two carriers are thought to have important relations with flows of the subterranean energy forces. The terrain features of a given area that might include a mountain chain or a zigzagging river, to be considered a good site for construction or burial, is supposed to contain flows of the *yin–yang* energies centripetal to the proposed site. When associated with the ten heavenly stems, the twelve earthly branches, and five agents, the metaphysical elaborations on the flows of the *yin–yang* forces in reference to the possible location of vital spots become as mfinite as the rugged topographic features of the Peninsula.

The vogue of this unusual idea, extending over the entire length of the traditional period, seems to have inseparable relations with the Koreans' love for the natural beauty of their land. It is worth noting, for instance, that the geomantic thought, together with the Koreans' strong attachment to "the embroidered tapestry of three thousand *ri*," ramified into their aesthetic concept, especially of architecture which, as we shall see later, regarded the surrounding terrain as an integral part of the unit as a whole. Nowhere was this concept more clearly manifest than in the layout and architecture of Song'ak, the capital whose "terrain power" was supposed to be sustaining the dynasty.

The greatest champion for this terrestrial, wind, and water theory was a Sŏn master, Tosŏn (826–898) who is reputed to have discovered all vital sites for temples throughout the land. King T'aejo made much use of Tosŏn's exposition of the theory. The ideological position of T'aejo as a representative intellectual of the time was embodied in his Ten Testamental Instructions, written shortly before his death in 943. Addressed to his posterity, the Instructions were ten political precepts embedded in the matrix of the religious and political ideologies of the period. Confucian, Buddhist, Shamanistic, and geomantic ideals were all duly mustered to support his economic and political injunctions, which were to strongly influence the political thinking of the subsequent generations.

5

Political Re-Centralization

Adaptation of the Chinese political system to the Korean reality had been on a piecemeal basis and that, as we have seen, only when institutional changes caused by the adoption of any Chinese system would not much affect the vested interests. In the fourth of his Ten Testamental Instructions, T'aejo enjoined:

> In the past, we the Easterners have admired the ways of the T'ang and patterned our institutions and social decorum after those of the T'ang. But we live in the land quite different from theirs; and the characters of the two peoples are different from each other. There is no reason, therefore, to copy too excessively the Chinese way.

But, since the beginning of the Three Kingdoms period, the royal power was always pitted against the central aristocracy which, under a weak reign, would gain the upper hand in government. In the recent case of Wang Kyu, the very existence of the Koryŏ royalty was seriously challenged. Naturally, the monarchs of peninsular dynasties strove for the establishment of a more strongly centralized government administered by a bureaucratic officialdom. In this quest for autocratic monarchal power, the Chinese political system which had been developed through more than a millennium of experience, had always rendered itself available for adoption in Korea. Despite T'aejo's warning above, the Koryŏ dynasty, from Kwangjong on, inextricably committed itself to the wholesale adaptation of the Chinese political institutions to the Koryŏ reality. Once the full scale centralization got under way, the Koryŏ court launched a series of governmental reorganization after the T'ang pattern during the period of roughly sixty years from Sŏngjong (982–997).

King Sŏngjong, the most Confucian of the early Koryŏ kings, assisted by the great scholar–official Ch'oe Sŭng No (927–989), plunged headlong into sinification of his government. A wide range of political, economic, and social institutions was modeled on those of the T'ang and the Han, even though unsuitability of some Chinese institutions to the Korean environ was obvious in the beginning. This span of sixty years is, therefore, one of the most significant periods in the Korean history.

Organs of the Central Government

The top policy-making bodies directly under the king were three *sŏng* : the *Chungsŏsŏng* or Royal Secretariat, the *Munhasŏng* or Royal Chancellery, and the *Sangsŏsŏng* or Secretariat of State Affairs. The Royal Secretariat served as the formulator of the government policies and the drafter of royal orders. Proclaiming these policies in the name of the king, the Royal Chancellery supervised the administration in general; in this capacity, the head of the Royal Chancellery was a virtual prime minister. The potent nature of this department was its working as a check on the royal authority through its right to review the royal orders before proclamation. In addition, it had the duty of remonstrating with the monarch on kingship in general which covered indeed many aspects of the royal life. Intriguingly enough, this risky job of reviewing and remonstrating was done by the junior officials of the Chancellery. The Secretariat of State Affairs was to execute the policies and the orders thus proclaimed; for this it had under its jurisdiction the Six Ministries : Personnel, Treasury, Rites, War, Justice, and Public Works.

Equally important as the three *sŏng*, the Privy Council (*ChungCh'uwŏn*) dealt with the military matters. But to decide on national policies of the highest order such as military expeditions or important new legislations, the heads of, and high–ranking officials in, the three *sŏng* and the Privy Council formed a council, an administrative tradition that under various names lasted until the end of the Yi dynasty. The members of the Privy Council were not necessarily military men; in fact, as time progressed, the Council was filled increasingly with civilian officials, who were also likely to be appointed even as field commanders of military expeditions.

Quite independent of these high departments, there was the Board of Censors (*Ŏsadae*) whose duty was to criticize and censure maladministration and irregularities in personnel appointments. The censors of the Board and the junior officials of the Royal Chancellery who had the similar job were men of high scholarship and impeccable personal conduct. Together, they had, in addition to their main duties of criticizing and remonstrating, the right to review personnel appointments made by the king.

The Finance Commission (*Samsa*) handled revenue, expenditure, and the storage of the tax grain. The Commission's importance in the management of the government finance seems to have been recognized as the national economy grew tremendously in the late tenth century; the Commissioners were soon allowed to participate in the highest council of the kingdom. There were also courts, directorates, and bureaus for the administration of minor areas in government and the management of the royal household affairs.

Provincial and Military Organizations

Local governments that were little meddled by the central government had enjoyed their semi-independent status until about the time of Sŏngjong. The organic relations between the central and local governments had been rather flimsily maintained by *Kiin* and *Sasimgwan* systems and by periodic dispatchments of tax officials from the capital. To reorganize these somewhat spoiled local governments and power groups that dominated them into the centralized system was reportedly a difficult task. The integration process was indeed gradual and forced.

The provincial reorganization, completed for the last time in 1018, divided the nation into five *to* (Provinces) and two *kye* (defense zones). Each *to*, governed by a civilian governor, was composed of a number of prefectures; the two *kye* covered the northwestern and northeastern frontier regions, respectively, and each had a military commander as governor, who was methodically remote-controlled from the central court. A number of *chin* or fortified towns and cities in the two *kye* five military centers strategically located in the nation made up the military network that tightened the defense and internal security of the kingdom.

The so-called Three Capitals, Song'ak, (also known as Kaegyŏng or, in modern times, Kaesŏng), P'yŏngyang the Western Capital, and Kyŏngju the Eastern capital which was later substituted with a new city site of modern Seoul as the Southern Capital, constituted political capitals, which were also regarded as geomantically important spots. The king was expected to stay for a period of time annually in P'yŏngyang and Kyŏngju. For more swift administrative and military communications, which were improved over those of the previous dynasty, was the network of postal stations along the main roads where official travelers were provided with room, board, and fresh horses according to their travel orders.

Consolidation of the military under the royal authority was also a tedious process. Early Koryŏ, the immediate inheritor of a highly militant society, was not much different in basic political orientation from its predecessor. The reorganization of the government based on the Confucian political system, which relegated the military below the civilian group, did not make early Koryŏ's military men succumb so easily to the civilian domination as the court would have hoped.

The ease with which Chŏngjong in 947 organized a national defense army of 300,000 against the Khitan meance is indicative of a profusion of local private armies. They seem to have simply been coordinated into such a large army under the royal authority. As late as 987 Sŏngjong moved to confiscate private weapons and recast them into agricultural implements, a double-edged measure that seems to have been aimed more directly at the disbandment of private armies, reflecting the die–hardism of the Koryŏ military.

Probably in 995 the organization of at least 45,000 man central army was completed, consisting of eight corps with duties in peacetime as the royal guard, police, and the *cortège*. There were also provincial armies, which seem to have been nationalized from local private armies. They were deployed in the provinces, especially in the two northern frontier zones, manning defense facilities and maintaining public peace.

The important feature of the Koryŏ military system is that the soldiers of the central army were "professionals" whose prescribed duties were hereditary. Supported by the government, land, they were recruited only from the *yangmin* or commoners, most of them being of peasant origin. Officers formed, according to their ranks, groups probably of political nature. The assembly of the Supreme Generals (commanders) and the Great Generals (deputy commanders) of each corps was called the *Chungbang*, obviously the highest council of the "professional" officers. In fact, the *Chungbang* served as the highest council the kingdom during the good part of the late Koryŏ period when the military was in power. Thus the central army of professionals was a solid, prestigious organization.

Economic Policies

The economic backbone of the dynasty was, needless to say, agricultural land and woodland for the production of fuel. They were now distributed much more widely than in previous periods. The principle involved in the distribution, especially among civil and military officials, throws an interesting sidelight upon the conscience of the Koryŏ dynasty. Understandably, recipients of larger amounts formed the nucleus of the new aristocracy close to the royal family. The first large-scale land distribution occurred in 940, which was based on the meritoriousness of service and loyalty to T'aejo, disregarding official ranks. In another comprehensive grant of land and woodland under Kyŏngjong (946–981) in 976, T'aejo's this basic principle was carried on in modified form.

Kyŏngjong divided the officials into four groups the same as the existing groups formed by rank and distinguished from one another by the color of uniforms as in the previous dynasties. Then, without regard to individual ranks, he assigned to the members of each group a number of grades in accordance with their *inp'ŭm* or literally the quality of personality, that is, loyalty to the royalty. In the above diagram, only the civilian recipients are shown.

Officials grouped by color in vertical order	Grades given for distribution:1st receives the largest amount	Amount of grant in arable land and woodland	Largest	Smallest
Purple	1st to 18th	Arable land	110 *Kyŏl*	32 *Kyŏl*
		Woodland	110 *Kyŏl*	25 *Kyŏl*
Red	1st to 10th	Arable land	65 *Kyŏl*	30 *Kyŏl*
		Woodland	55 *Kyŏl*	18 *Kyŏl*
Dark Red	1st to 8th	Arable land	55 *Kyŏl*	27 *Kyŏl*
		Woodland	40 *Kyŏl*	14 *Kyŏl*
Green	1st to 10th	Arable land	45 *Kyŏl*	21 *Kyŏl*
		Woodland	35 *Kyŏl*	10 *Kyŏl*

* Kyŏl, the name of a unit area, though used throughout th traditional period, seems to have denoted different sizes of area at different times. 1 kyŏl was equivalent to about 46 m^2 in this period.

The first grader of the purple group received 110 *kyŏl* of agricultural land and the equal area of woodland. And the first grader of the red group was granted 65 *kyŏl* of land far exceeding the square measure of the 18th grader of the purple group. The number of grades were not the same among the groups, even though the red and green groups had the equal number of division. Although this distribution system was apparently based on both rank and the *inp'um*, the latter consideration, that is, man's personality, ability, loyalty, etc. seems to have weighed more than his rank in the dispensation of land.

This system was readjusted in 998 in accord, this time, with the official rank, which had been previously divided into eighteen. The 998 revision, which was to have minor adjustments again in 1034 and 1076, covered not only civilian, military, and other branches of the government officials but also "professional" soldiers and ex-officials. Its salient feature was the slighted treatment of the military branch *vis-à-vis* the civilian wing, a partiality for which the court was to pay dearly later.

Such land distributions to the officials, however, were actually little more than the payment of salary in produce. In fact, they seem to received the payment in grain, that is, the equal amount of grain produced from same amount of land-area they were given. The recipients were required to return the land upon their resignation or dismissal. There was a category of land-grant with the attached right of free disposal by the grantee. This category was usually bestowed on those who rendered service especially pleasing to the monarch. T'aejo was particularly generous in giving out this category to his favorite subjects; some of them were later purged by Kwangjong. A 977 legislation, aiming at curbing the royal caprice involved in such a grant, stipulated that officials with the rank of the fifth grade or higher could qualify for this type of grant but of regulated amounts.

The governmental departments and institutions, down to a postal station inn, were also allocated varying amounts of land for maintenance purposes. Of these grantees of land, temples and monasteries, meritorious officials, and the royal household in time became large landowners of the kingdom. The government's administrative ability often failed to keep track of all the pieces of land parceled out. In the meantime, large land owners became even larger through illegal means of acquiring land, cutting directly into the government revenue, a phenomenon which usually occurred hand in hand with dynastic decline during the traditional period. In the undiversified traditional economy, it was thought to be as important as land itself to secure a constant level of labor force stabilized to land. The government policies on the *yangmin* and the *ch'ŏnmin*, especially those in *hyang, so,* and *pugok,* were formulated strictly to this end and also stringently implemented.

The majority of the common people, who were the descendants of hereditary slaves of Silla, gained the new status through service in the war of dynastic change under Wang Kŏn. They were given the right to take the government examination or to become soldiers; as farmers they were not only alloted but also provided with seed grain and plow oxen. But as the centralization reached its elaborate stage, they were gradually estranged through a series of legislations from what options they were originally allowed. They were subject to variant rules which were designed to fasten them to the land. In some cases, their costume, dwelling, marriage, etc. were regulated; they were prohibited from wearing swords, dealing in land, and above all moving out of the registered place of residence.

The *ch'ŏnmin* of *hyang, so,* and *pugok,* inherited from the previous dynasty, was another important segment of the labor force. As the producers of food, domestic articles, and weapons for the ruling class and the government, they were controlled, though not necessarily as slaves, by the government over their activities, including training in handicraftsmanship, choice of specialization, number of working days, and domicile.

An ancestval shrine sacred to the memory of Admiral Chang Po Ko in Jang-do Island(above). A foundation stone of gatepost encavation of 'Ch'onghae Chin.' relics.

Chang Po Ko portrait.

6

The Koryŏ-Liao Relations

With the establishment in 960 of the Sung dynasty which subsequently reunited China, the triangular Koryŏ-Liao-Sung relations began a delicate yet strenuous course. The fast rising Khitan empire, the most aggressive of the trio, was soon to administer a rather severe test to the responsive ability of the peninsular kingdom amid its internal reorganization. The Koryŏ dynasty, as has been noted, had steadily implemented policies for the development and defense of its northern frontier regions against the threat posed by the Liao. But the civilian control of the military affairs, Koryŏ's diehard martial spirit notwithstanding, may have placed the Koryŏ army on an amateurish footing.

KORYŎ
AROUND 1000A. D

Indeed, Koryŏ's subsequent response against Liao invasions lacked decisiveness on the strategic level.

Koryŏ's distrust of the Liao and the Sung's desire to recapture the sixteen prefectures around Peking which had been lost to the Liao brought together the two agricultural nations against the nomadic upstart. They were on the verge of a joint expedition proposed by the Sung, but the Liao acted first. In 985 Liao obliterated Chŏng'an'guk on the middle reaches of the Amnok River. Chŏng'an'guk, one of those small ephemeral states founded by the remnants of former Parhae-Koreans, had established relations with Koryŏ and the Sung. Then, in 986, Liao delivered a crippling blow to Sung T'ai Tsung in his attempt to recover the lost prefectures.

Having then brought under control the Jürched people in southern Manchuria close to Amnok River who had maintained ties with the Sung, Liao in 993 sent an expedition under Su Suen-ning into Koryŏ. The invasion that lacked a clear-cut purpose was more like a feeler exploring Koryŏ's terrains and attitudes toward the Liao. A stalemate in fighting was soon turned into a diplomatic conference. The Liao, as the occupier of the former Koguryŏ territory, insisted upon its territorial rights to the P'yŏngyang area. But Sŏ Hi, the Koryŏ envoy, more convincingly demonstrated the fact Koryŏ's very being the successor of Koguryŏ, as its name showed. As for the establishment of diplomatic relations with the Liao, an issue that seemed central to the purpose of the Liao intrusion, Sŏ Hi promised that Koryŏ would enter into relations with the Liao upon creation of the defense and administrative order in modern North P'yŏng'an Province. These arguments were reasonable enough to Su Suen-ning.

This North P'yŏng'an area, largely inhabited by the Jürched then, had been a kind of a twilight zone vaguely claimed by both Koryŏ and Liao. It was now established by Sŏ Hi's diplomatic sleight of hand that the area was a part of Koryŏ. In return for the withdrawal of the Liao army, Sŏ Hi offered that Koryŏ would use Liao's year period thereafter, instead of the Sung's, which meant, as translated into the current diplomatic terms, Koryŏs yielding to the status of a junior partner in state communication.

To make good Sŏ Hi's claim, Koryŏ immediately undertook construction of the so-called Six Fortifications East of the River (*Kangdong Yuksŏng*), that is, east of the Amnok river, thus pushing the frontier up to that natural border line for the first time. Liao, however, seems to have felt afterward that it was somehow coaxed into letting slip out of its hand the area most strategic in dealing with the Jürched. Liao belatedly re-claimed, and demanded the immediate return of, the region, which had by now become unnegotiable for Koryŏ, however. In 1010 Liao Sheng Tsung, who had just imposed upon the Sung the payment of annual tribute as the final settlement of a long series of conflicts, personally led an expeditionary force of 400,000 into Koryŏ.

Presumably, he was to look into a seemingly "disorderly affair" of the Koryǒ court, referring to the previous year's *coup d'état* in which Mokchong (998–1009) was assassinated.

Before embarkation, Liao Sheng Tsung notified Koryǒ of its impending invasion as if to give another chance for Koryǒ to return the said territory. In the meantime, the militarily weak Sung decided in advance to reject an imaginary request for help that might be coming from Koryǒ. By-passing P'yǒngyang that withstood the Liao attack, the invaders made their way south directly to Kaegyǒng and wrought havoc of the royal library and the city itself, sending the king in flight as far south as Naju. The destruction of the capital done, the nomads retreated as quickly as they had come.

The Liao repeated this meaningless exercise for the third time in 1018–1019, but Koryǒ was now well prepared for it. Its defense force of 200,000 was concentrated in the Six Fortfied Cities in North P'yǒng'an Province under Kang Kam Ch'an (948–1031), civilian official but better known as a general who met the Liao force of 100,000 under Su P'ai-ya, Su Suen-ning's brother who did most of the destruction of Kaegyǒng in the previous invasion. Su P'ai-ya, probably lured by the pleasure of another round of looting in the Koryǒ capital, rushed his army to Kaegyǒng, again avoiding the encounter with the main force of Kang, but they found the city and the surrounding area well defended. Kang's determined army was waiting for the retreating Khitans. At Kyuju, one of the Six Cities, General Kang Kam Ch'an let loose his army upon them and destroyed all but a few thousands. The Great Victory at Kyuju, so known in the Korean history, retrieved the national confidence that had badly sagged since the second invasion and made General Kang a national hero, comparable with General Ŭlchi Mundǒk of Koguryǒ.

Liao Sheng Tsung, though his imperial pride left rankled, came to terms with Koryǒ. The two countries resumed peace as if nothing had happened. But the devastation of the capital and other cities, especially during the second Khitan incursion, wrought a deep sense of national crisis into the official mind. The government, while stepping up its tedious process of centralization, inaugurated a series of defense and spiritual programs, of which the most notable were construcion of defense walls and carving of wood blocks for the Tripitaka publication.

The construction of the outer wall of the capital, that started in the early years of the Hyǒnjong reign (1010-1031), was completed in 1029 to the size of 29,000 "paces" in length and twenty-seven feet in height. In four years the construction of another wall began. The Long Wall, lining from the mouth of the Amnok River to the present city of Yǒnghǔng in south Hamgyǒng Province, was completed in 1044, and, with another short wall added later, it extended right to the eastern coast. This was the second such wall, the first being one built along the Liao River by Koguryǒ in the 640's which served as its main defense line against northern peoples. In the meantime, a great religious project was undertaken in 1021. This was the first of large scale Tripitaka publications by wood printing blocks to solicit for the protective power of Buddha, as we shall discuss later.

Portrait of an official on the wall of a Koryŏ tomb, 10th-13th century;seated stone Boddhisativa at Hansong-sa temple, Koryŏ dynasty(918-1392).

Part 5
Society and Culture Under Koryŏ

1

Confucian Moralism

If the Long Wall provided Koryŏ with a sense of security, it also symbolized Koryŏ's having come to the limit of its territorial expansion and coming-of-age as well. The methodical introduction of the Chinese government system seemed at first a mere superimposition of foreign institutions upon the ruins of Silla. But by the time that these Chinese institutions, as they were readjusted and indigenized, began to function in Korean reality during the eleventh and twelfth centuries, the Koryŏ dynasty found itself well on its way to prosperity.

The economic growth brought about by the astute management of the national economy, helped by technical advances, was of course the most encouraging factor for the prosperity of the new dynasty. It was in the context of this increasing productivity that the office of Finance Commission (*Samsa*) was elevated to the policy-making level in government. The surplus rice during the early twelfth century amounted to millions of bushels. Various textile fabrics, greatly improved in quality, were coveted items in foreign trade. It was also during this period of economic growth—or sometime in the twelfth century—that Koryŏ merchants devised the double entry system for commercial bookkeeping for the first time in history. *

In social reordering that went on in parallel with political recentralization, Confucian social ideals were naturally stressed as the goals to achieve. Notably the reign of Sŏngjong witnessed a series of social programs based on Confucian moralism seriously implemented as never before. Loyalty to the

---

* Korean merchants and bankers during the late nineteenth century found this traditional method of bookkeeping good enough to meet modern transactions.

sovereign and filial piety were reassured of being the highest of the social virtues. Possessors of these virtues were socially recognized by erection of permanent shrines and stone tablets in their honor. The court also rewarded "righteous husbands and faithful wives" and inspired respect for the old, upon whom, when they became eighty years of age, the court usually conferred honorary ranks.

Such institutionalization of Confucian social ideals, on the other hand, constituted a direct challenge to Buddhism. Occasionally, it produced political tensions at the court, as when kings or officials of Confucian persuasion proposed to discontinue a well-established Buddhist social institution or event. This was symptomatic of the discord between the two great ideological forces that erupted open towards the end of the dynasty. If compared to the *yin-yang* interaction, Buddhism remained undoubtedly the *yang* throughout the dynasty, however. Most of the official holidays, for instance, counting at one time 126 days a year, appear to have been Buddhistic.

Dry lacquer seated Buddha at Pusŏk temple.

2

The Nature of Koryŏ Aristocracy

In his twenty-eight article memorial on the current affairs to Sŏngjong in 982, the great scholar-official Ch'oe Sŭng No wrote that "the practice of Buddhism is for [one's] spiritual education, and the practice of Confucianism is for the government of a state. Spiritual education prepares one for the otherworld, and the government of the state is the business of today." This was a most succinct statement on the Buddhism-Confucianism relationship as generally cherished by Koryŏ aristocracy.

Koryŏ aristocracy, formed in this ideological matrix on a much wider segment of population than Silla's, comprised the descendants of T'aejo's close subjects who helped found the dynasty, great Buddhist monks, some of whose lineage could be traced back to Silla's Six Head Quality families, and Confucian scholar-officials employed and advanced in service through the government examination. Clannish provincial aristocrats, though they formed a peripheral portion of the ruling class, remained influential politically and socially, even after their traditional political strength was much stripped of.

In the formative process of the ruling class, the political marriage that T'aejo readily resorted to set the example for other families to follow. T'aejo's marriage to twenty-nine women, whose families were catapulted to nobility, was indeed a handy way of creating a sufficient power base for the royal family at short notice. And it was fashionable among aristocratic families to "present" to a king or kings in a row not just one or two daughters but, when possible, three daughters. As a result, the strong man of a queen's family not infrequently entertained the idea of throne for himself, a menace which, though never materialized, is indicative of the relative weakness of the Koryo royalty ; this never occurred in the Yi dynasty.

The Kim house of Ansan and the Yi house of Inju were the most powerful groups of this nature. The latter, which, like the Pak family of Silla, supplied queens to seven successive kings during a period of some eighty years from the 1040's, not merely monopolized all key government offices but actually ruled Koryŏ at the apogee of its power. Again, it is interesting to note that this domination of the government by filling important positions by the queen's family occurred in the Yi dynasty but only in the nineteenth century when political corruption had completely weakened that dynasty.

To perpetuate their status in the government and society, great families intermarried among themselves and, more often than not, within their own family without much qualm, despite the influence of Confucianism in whose view it was little less than an incestuous act. The incestuous union, which occurred more often in the royal family in the early period of the dynasty, seems to have been a legacy from the matrilineal past. These intermarrying and inbreeding ruling class meticulously maintained the family registers, which were written and kept in a form different from those of the common people. Through administrative devices and also Koryŏ's particular social climate, the class distinction was rather rigidly drawn in many ways.

As a result of adoption of the Chinese government system, the officialdom was divided into *tongban* or literally eastern section and *sŏban* or western section designating the civil and the military officials, respectively. Together they formed the *yangban* or two sections often denoting the ruling class. But the term *yangban*, which suggests the equality of the two sections, may be misleading, for the "professional" military was somehow excluded from the ruling machinery of government. Despite their glittering designations of ranks such as Supreme General or Great General, they were commanded by civilian offices. Koryŏ's unobtrusive relegation of the military to the limbo of government may have come more from the experience of the last one and a half centuries of the Silla dynasty, that witnessed constant internal warfares engendered by the unbridled power of military men.

---

* The cold problem in this connection is the one arising from the artificial division of the country. The deepening cultural gap between the democratic South and the Communist North may eventually become the stumbling block toward unification of the country.

3

Education and The Examination System

    As Confucianism was chosen as the ideological basis of government, the study of Confucian classics was assigned the first priority under the official educational system. The civil examination, which was based on the Chinese classics, gave their study an additional incentive. But the education in Confucianism that involved the mastery of reading Chinese through years of concentration plus heavy expenses became, as it turned out, unavailable to the lower class. For this reason, the civil examination, though theoretically open to all classes of people, came to serve as a protective screen for the upper class.

    Confucian education, though within this privileged class, came to flourish both at government schools and at private academies towards the middle of the eleventh century. But Koryŏ Confucianism, as in Silla, was yet an undifferentiated field of study ; in other words, its philosophical and literary aspects were not studied as separate fields until the fourteenth century, when Korean scholars seriously took up Neo-Confucianism as philosophy.

    Koryŏ's educational policies and institutions, however, grew out of that sense of impermanency which characterized those of Silla. The formal education, which was initiated by T'aejo, had been fully developed by the time of Sŏngjong (982-997). The Confucian-minded Sŏngjong was first concerned with the education of the local students who could not afford a lengthy sojourn in the capital to attend the government university. He sent out *paksa* (doctors) of Chinese classics and doctors of medicine to major provincial cities to teach in those fields. In 992 Sŏngjong expanded the national university in the capital, which he called *Kukchagam*. It consisted of three colleges and three departments. A college, with a capacity for three hundred students, was staffed by doctors and assistants who taught the Chinese classics.

Requirements for admission to these colleges were determined by the official rank of the candidate's family, even though the curriculum was the same at all three. At the three departments, the children of the lowest officials and the commoners were taught only professional subjects, law, arithmetic, and calligraphy, respectively.

Upon this basic educational arrangement, later kings, as they would intend, made new additions, physical or organizational, which might be then left disused during an uninspired reign. Yejong (1106-1122), the most education-minded King of the Koryŏ dynasty, further expanded the national university. He added a new complex of buildings and dormitory facilities and reinforced the administrative staff and the faculty. He made a curricular revision under which the classics studies were divided into six areas of specialization, each based on one particular classic, and a new military course was created, which seems to have been motivated by the Jürched menace looming up then in the northeastern area. Another important addition was the establishment in 1119 of the *yanghyŏn'go*, a fund to help the welfare of the students which, together with the library and the press established in 1101, became a standard fixture of the national university. For post graduate studies for established scholars, Yejong in 1116 erected within the precinct of the royal palace an academy composed of the lecture hall, study rooms, and the library that housed several ten thousand books.

Injong (1123-1146), in an effort to extend education, established in provincial and prefectural centers schools patterned after the central university. Technical training in such fields as astrological astronomy, geomantic geography, *yin-yang* theory, and medicine were conducted under the auspices of ministries concerned.

Mention may be made that the Buddhist church made its roomy temples and monasteries available to elementary education. It was also common to see at monasteries in quiet surroundings of nature Confucian scholars or Taoist masters meditate on metaphysical problems or the mystery of eternal life.

Private Education. The government often found it difficult to bear the educational cost, and at times students filed their protest in the form of memorial to the monarch on the governmental failure to maintain the established level of education. In parallel with the government-supported education or because of its lapse, the private institutes of learning sprang up and in time came to dominate the educational scene. In Kaegyŏng, retired scholar-officials founded schools where would-be candidates for the government examination received the tutorial treatment, which, the successful candidacy being an important purpose of learning, was indeed an attraction for students.

The best-known private school was the one founded by Ch'oe Ch'ung (984-1068), a great scholar-minister, after his retirement in 1055 from a colorful career in government service. Ch'oe Ch'ung was, above all, a Confucian scholar, who recognized the philosophical importance of the "Doctrine of the Mean," then only a chapter in the *Record of Rituals*, a half century before Sung Neo-Confucian philosophers did, and he commanded a large following of students. He organized them into nine groups, probably according to age, and taught the Five Classics, Chinese histories, poetry and essay writing which was the most important exercise in preparation for the examination.

Starting with Ch'oe's, twelve academies came into being by the late eleventh century. The students of each academy were collectively called *to* as in Hwarang *to* (group). Ch'oe Ch'ung's students were called Munhŏn'gong *to*, Munhŏn'gong being Ch'oe's posthumous title, and the student bodies of the twelve private schools the Twelve *to*. Each *to* was not just a group of class-mates or alumni, but it had certain internal hierarchic relations with the founder at its center. The proliferation of non-official institutes of learning also signified a wide spread of Confucian studies on a higher academic level.

The Kwagŏ. The young students, after a long period of concentration, were invariably expected to take the *Kwagŏ* or government examination, the gateway to personal success in life. The examination system, after a century of practical application from 958, became the most stable, well-functioning institu-tion. This was due partly to the constant encouragement of the *kwagŏ* by the court as a means of strengthening the royal authority, for officials thus pro-duced were expected to bear allegiance only to the king.

The *kwagŏ* system, as given a final touch by Injong (1123-1146), had three categories of examinations : *Chesulgwa* or literary test on the composi-tion of specified types of poetry and of essay on current political issues ; *Myŏnggyŏnggwa* or comprehensive test on understanding of the Confucian classics ; and *Chapkwa* or test on such "nondescript" subjects as medicine, law, arithmetic, geography, calligraphy, and so on. The literary test was the most popular category with more elaborate procedure, under which some 6,200 candidates passed during the entire length of the dynasty, whereas in the classics category only 450 were successful. The last category of test was the one given *yangmin* for recruitment of petty officials specialized in those fields.

The *Kwagŏ* was held every three years as a rule, but it was also con-ducted on happy occasions such as the birth of a royal prince. The acceptance of an application involved meticulous investigations of the candidate's social background by the Ministry of Rites. The number of successful candidates for the *kwagŏ* examination was preset at thirty for each of the first two categories of test. The *kwagŏ* consisted of three successive tests ; the last test decided individual standings among the thirty finalists selected from the second test.

The final examination was held at the royal palace, accompanied by a series of rituals involving many officials, of whom the most important was the Chigonggŏ. The Chigonggŏ was responsible for unsealing and grading the examination questions, and he had the pleasant duty of presenting the thirty or, sometimes, fewer triumphant candidates to the king. The king thereupon issued the certificates and gave a splendid banquet in their honor. This was followed by a street parade which at least in one instance lasted six days in a festive atmosphere. For their literary excellence, they were also rewarded with land and domestic hands.

One interesting social aspect of the *kwagŏ* was the relationship between the Chigonggŏ the examiner and the thirty successful scholars. The appointment of the Chigonggŏ usually went to a renowned scholar-official who accepted it as a great honor. The latter revered and obeyed him like a parent or a teacher who in turn helped them out throughout their official career. Maintaining lateral ties among themselves also, these scholars-alumni formed a tightly-knit group who in some cases presented a political block at the court, especially during the declining days of the dynasty. We shall see the kings of the Yi dynasty take over the Chigonggŏ's job themselves.

A 3-day celebration for a successful candidate for the highest degree.

4

The Development of Buddhism

The first of T'aejo's Ten Testamental Instructions begins with, "The successful outcome of the great enterprises of our state depends upon the aid and protection of Buddha." T'aejo's specific enhancement of Buddhism, even though it was only a reemphasis on the traditional belief in Buddhism as the spiritual guardian of the kingdom, set the developmental tone of Koryŏ Buddhism. The five Kyo sects and the nine Sŏn groups were all fairly treated by the government, while they readjusted themselves in institutional as well as doctrinal form to the need of the new dynasty.

A closer organic relationship between the government and the church was established during the reign of Kwangjong. Sometime after the inauguration of the civil examination, Kwangjong created a similar system for the ecclesiastical service for the monks of all Kyo-Sŏn sects. After passing the examination, monks had six ranks to advance to, and furthermore they were accorded the privileges to be appointed teachers and advisers to the monarch and the state with social prestige much higher than Confucian scholars'. Thus the examination system for the monks was by no means for controlling the church by the state. It was rather designed to perpetuate institutionalized coordination between the two. During the Yi dynasty, however, the device was used for the suppression of Buddhism.

It was under this organized ecclesiastical leadership, backed by the ungrudging royal support, that the church could undertake the large national projects hitherto unthought of in order to buttress the spiritual tenacity of the nation in time of emergency. The most notable and also of great cultural significance was a series of programs for block printing of the Tripitaka. The first publication was undertaken, along with the construction of the Long

Wall, right after the second Khitan invasion during the reign of Hyŏnjong (1010-1034). This first project consisted of carving wood printing blocks for 5,048 volumes of Buddhist literature, taking sixty years to complete.

The Unity Movement and Ŭich'ŏn

Scholastic Buddhism represented by the Kyo sect, probably challenged by Sŏn iconoclasm, reasserted itself, culminating in a movement which aimed at no other than a Kyo-Sŏn accord. It was also under Kwangjong's leadership that this was initiated. In parallel with his political and ecclesiastical centralization, as we have seen, Kwangjong was interested in ideological unification of the bickering sects. For this he advanced the Ch'ŏnt'ae doctrine as a rallying point which embraced the principles central to the sectarian bases of both Kyo and Sŏn. But Kwangjong's idea did not materialize in any substantial movement.

With the appearance of the great scholar-monk Ŭich'ŏn (1055-1101), Koryŏ Buddhism became firmly committed to the Kyo-Sŏn unity. Ŭich'ŏn, the fourth son of Munjong (1047-1083), represented Koryŏ Buddhism at its full prosperity. And the eleventh century saw the appearance of an impressive number of great monks of aristocratic origin in succession and the construction and repair of magnificent temples and monasteries in full swing.

On the lower level, Buddhist social events constantly basked the common masses in the grace of Buddha, of which the most important was *Yŏndŭnghoe*. Whereas the *P'algwanhoe* festival, inherited from Silla, was largely confined to the cities, the *Yŏndŭnghoe* was celebrated in worship of Buddha all over the country from Kaegyŏng to a remote hamlet during winter and, today, on the eighth day of April by the lunar calendar. In T'aejo's mind, the *P'algwanhoe* and the *Yŏndŭnghoe* were such important religious events that he enjoined not to make any modification to them in his Ten Testamental Instructions.

Amid the ostentatious affairs of construction and celebration, however, Ŭich'ŏn was keenly aware of a certain inner stagnation of Koryŏ Buddhism which now seemed to have reached an intellectual *cul-de-sac*. The rampant brawling that went on within the Kyo sects, for instance, seemed originated as much from the doctrinal meagerness as from economic interests in monasterial estates. His subsequent creation of the Ch'ŏnt'ae sect was an attempt to unite all Kyo-Sŏn sects under it, the most serious ecumenical move that came to characterize Koryŏ Buddhism. It is doubtful that he had acknowledged the earlier attempt made along this line by Kwangjong, but he emphatically professed that he was inspired by the great Silla monk, Wŏnhyo, and his *Treatise on the Harmonization of Ten Doctrines.*

The Ch'ŏnt'ae sect had not been included in the five Kyo sects, but certainly its thought was not new in Silla or even in sixth century Koguryŏ. The Ch'ŏnt'ae sect relied on the *Lotus of the Wonderful Law Sutra* as its scriptural basis which, in its all inclusiveness, could provide a theoretical common denominator needed for unity. Buddha, according to the Ch'ŏnt'ae doctrine, was thought to have revealed different levels of truths at the five progressive stages of his life. Indeed, this was a neat way of explaining obvious doctrinal contradictions which abound in the Hinayana and Mahayana *sutras*. The most synthetic truth taught at the final stage is contained in the *Lotus of the Wonderful Law*, hence the most important of all Mahayana *sutras*. Finding a rational basis in the *Lotus*, attempts had been made to unite the Three Vehicles into One Vehicle or to subsume the Hinayana and Mahayana doctrines under the idealism of the Middle Doctrine.

The Ch'ŏnt'ae synthesis starts from the principle of the Perfectly Harmonious Threefold Truth, that is, Emptiness, Temporariness, and the Mean which make up every realm and nature of existence in time and space. They are so thoroughly interpenetrated one another that three become one and one becomes three. "It follows that all beings have the Buddha-nature in them and can be saved." * Even at a thought moment, therefore, one may penetrate into the ultimate truth, since an element leading to that truth is regarded as immanent in any particular moment of thought.

The Ch'ŏnt'ae sect placed a great emphasis upon attainment of the ultimate truth through concentration and insight, which is none other than the very intuitive method for sudden enlightenment of Sŏn. In fact, it was to Ch'an (Sŏn) that the origin of the T'ien-t'ai (Ch'ŏnt'ae) sect in China could be traced. As the T'ien-t'ai sect grew away from the Ch'an matrix, shifting its emphasis to the rational, it came to embrace all major doctrinal contents of the traditional sects as the truth or relative truths. It encouraged study of the scriptures, guidance by teachers, and performance of rituals as well as meditation as methodologically valid for the ultimate enlightenment.

Thus in the Ch'ŏnt'ae doctrine, all Kyo-Sŏn sects could have a theological claim. When in 1086 Ŭich'ŏn assumed the office of the head priest of Kukch'ŏngsa which was made the central temple of the Ch'ŏnt'ae sect, Koryŏ Buddhism began the days of revival under the leadership of Ŭich'ŏn. Taking full advantage of the syncretic nature of the Ch'ŏnt'ae doctrine, he provided the basis for the Kyo-Sŏn reconciliation. He tried to make the Ch'ŏnt'ae truth palatable to all sects from the aristocratic, ritual-loving Hwaŏm sect on the right to the radical, individualistic Sŏn groups on the left.

During campaigns that ensued, the Ch'ŏnt'ae sect won a large number

---

* Wm. Theodore de Bary, *et al.*, *Sources of Chinese Tradition*, p. 351.

of followers, especially from the Sŏn groups, indicating that Ŭich'ŏn had pushed his doctrinal emphasis a little closer toward left. Against this Ch'ŏnt'ae inroad which, seen from the Sŏn groups' point of view, was little less than an incitement of apostasy from the Sŏn truth, the nine Sŏn groups resolved themselves into one organization under the sectarian name of Chogye and carried out doctrinal reinvigoration. Ŭich'ŏn seems to have also placed himself in a position to lead the Hwaŏm sect and urged it to concentrate more on the intuitive method for enlightenment. Ŭich'ŏn's success and influence in the ecclesiastical and doctrinal readjustment of Koryŏ Buddhism was no doubt helped by the availability to him of the royal authority : his three elder brothers successively reigned from 1083 to 1105, a fact that should be kept in mind when considering some of his other achievements.

By far the greatest of his scholastic achievements was his bibliographical collection and block printing. He made a list of all commentaries and expositions on the Tripitaka. The list, amounting to three volumes, contained 4,740 volumes existing then in Koryŏ authored by Korean, Chinese, and Liao scholastics. Then Ŭich'ŏn proceeded to block print them sometime between 1091 ad 1100, which he intended to be an extension of the first Tripitaka printed a half century earlier.

The Buddhist Economy. Ŭich'ŏn's range of interest was not confined to religious activities. In a noteworthy memorial to his brother, Sukchong (1096-1105), he in 1096 emphasized the feasibility of basing the economy on the circulation of a medium of exchange, specifically urging more improved minting and popular use of coins. Ŭich'ŏn's advanced economic view might have been a reflection of the church's extensive financing on the basis of the vast wealth which the church had accumulated.

The opulence of the Buddhist church was indeed of tremendous proportions. Its ever increasing, tax-free estates and other categories of properties, which sharpened the business acumen and diversified commercial ventures of the church, were, as has been noted, incompatible with the government's finance. This incompatibility was foreseen by T'aejo as in the first and second of his Instructions. His warning against the random construction of temples was not heeded by his successors, however.

The upshot of this was, for instance, the appearance of about seventy large temples in and around the capital alone by the eleventh century. The Hŭng'wangsa, or Temple or Royal Prosperity, probably the largest of the Koryŏ temples was completed in 1067, and its complex covered nearly 50,000 square feet in floor space, emulating the grandeur of the royal palace itself. These temples and monasteries all over the country, lording it over their vast possessions, material and human, contrived to enrich themselves further with ways and means more sophisticated and on a scale larger than anything known in the previous dynasty.

The most prevalent financial arrangements were the *po* and the *Changsaenggo*. A *po* was a fund, the interest of which was appropriated for a specified purpose such as carrying on relief works, providing scholarships for monks, or holding Buddhist festivals. A *Changsaenggo* was the capital in the form of estates intended to provide low-interest loans for the needy peasants or to pay a variety of costs that the church had to bear. The *Changsaenggo* was by far the largest unit capital in Buddhist finance, and *Changsaenggo* estates were among the largest in the country. With less noble purposes, Buddhists engaged at a brisk profit in various lucrative ventures also.

The labor force that carried on these secular activities consisted of monasterial serf and peasants who had voluntarily submitted to monasteries with what small holding they had in order to escape exploitation by local aristocrats. A more interesting category of workers was "monks" who were given the title but actually tightly organized and controlled work forces, including technicians and artists. They were specialized in tilling, architecture, sculpture, printing, painting, and pottery. There were also monksoldiers for the defense of the temples and monasteries against governmental interferences or of the kingdom against foreign invasions. In peace, like other monks, they conducted reading and prayer meetings and other fraternal activities, somewhat reminiscent of the Hwarang groups of Silla.

Besides Providing the spiritual leadership, Buddhism's most important function in society was making available recreational opportunities for the people. With various facilities and wealth, the Buddhist church could support its many social events that called for parades and festivals involving hundreds of thousands of bonzes and laymen, the *Yŏndŭnghoe* and the *P'algwanhoe* being the most splendid ones. And the church's extensive and permanent charity work in medical relief service should not be overlooked in evaluating Buddhism as a social institution. But for Koryŏ Buddhism in general, as it extended its interest in temporal business, and as it maintained too close a relation with the secular power, there was no denying the dilution or secularization of faith.

5

Geomantic Theories and Politics

In the second of his Ten Testamental Instructions, T'aejo enjoined :

All newly-founded temples and monasteries were built on the sites which had
been chosen by Monk Tosŏn in accord with the geomantic principles. Tosŏn said
that the indiscriminate construction of temples and monasteries upon the places
other than of his selection would damage and enervate the terrestrial force and
thus bring the dynastic decline···
Guard against this.

As has been noted, T'aejo's profounder concern couched in the above
injunction could have been even totally with economic waste that was likely
to result from "the indiscriminate construction of temples and monasteries."
On the other hand, T'aejo's such unequivocal expression of belief in geomancy made it an important element in official thinking on the business of
government.

Around the time that the sixty-year cycle cycled twice, starting from the
founding date of the dynasty, a geomantic speculation spread to the effect that
terrestrial force of the Kaegyŏng area, which had supported the monarchy,
was spent or sapped badly enough to warrant a transfer of the royal capital
elsewhere. Munjong (1047-1082) thereupon inaugurated a series of programs
in order to "prolong" the rule of the Wang line. He first appealed to the protective power of Buddha by building that mangificent Temple of Royal
Prosperity. Then he began to build a number of subsidiary palaces in propitious sites where the terrestrial force was supposed to be still fresh. The idea
was that, since it was not easy to transfer the capital, the reigning king would
go round and stay in these new palaces for a period of time as if to be

replenished with terrestrial force there. In actuality, it was more like a way of royal recreation or perhaps a Taoistic flight into nature.

The political conditions during the reign of Sukchong were even more conducive to the geomantic proliferation. Sukchong forced Hyŏnjong, his young nephew, to abdicate in his favor, after he had destroyed Yi Cha Ŭi of the powerful Yi family of Inju who had an eye on the throne for himself. Such bloody discord on the political scene prompted geomantic experts to argue for the reconstruction of the Southern Capital near the site of modern Seoul where the king was to spend the spring months. Eventually, large royal palaces were constructed there between 1101 and 1104. This, if anything, reduced the importance of the Eastern Capital Kyŏngju.

Yejong (1106-1122), however, paid his attention north to P'yŏngyang the Western Capital for which, despite the drainage in the treasury caused by Suckchong's costly management of the Southern Capital, he undertook an ambitious building program. Although no doubt he subscribed to T'aejo's asseveration of P'yŏngyang as a veritable dynastic center for its excellent geomantic location, Yejong exploited the city's geographic location for a military purpose in connection with the rise of the Jürched in the northeast. In parallel with the physical expansion of the Western Capital, Yejong enhanced its administrative status with upgraded organs of the city government which nearly emulated that of Kaegyŏng itself. Significantly, it was from this refurbished P'yŏngyang that in 1107 Yejong in person saw off a large expeditionary force to subjugate Jürched tribes in the northeastern region. At about this time, Yejong seems to have deeply felt a need for some fresh political and social movements, such as comparable with the Hwarang movement of Silla, against the international power configuration then being reshaped by the rise of the Jürched. His concentration on the northern management was of sound military necessity, for which he seems to advanced the familiar geomantic theory as a means of securing a political consensus.

6

Pattern of International Dealings

The military domination of the continent by non-Chinese empires, Liao (907-1125) and Chin (1115-1234), characterized the international relations of this period. This was an unprecedented blow to the Chinese' self-righteous concept of international order in which the Middle Kingdom was the center. The militarily weak Sung was forced to acknowledge the suzerainty of these "barbarian" empires with payment of annual tributes. Koryŏ, with realistic flexibility in diplomacy, kept itself ever alert to the vicissitudes of foreign development, acknowledging the nominal suzerainty of the strongest.

The waves of Khitan invasions starting from 993 had dampened Koryŏ's preoccupation with northward expansion. The ascendance of the Jürched people in the early twelfth century did not improve the situation for Koryŏ. Instead, Koryŏ was destined to go through several successive stages of diplomatic relationship with the Jürched, which bring the basic pattern of contemporary international dealings into a graphic clarity.

After the demise in 926 of Parhae, of which they had been part, the Jürched people, now under the Liao, were completely disintegrated into tribal units. Some of these Jürched hordes came into contact with Koryŏ along its northern defense wall. Koryŏ's northeastern border, facing the fertile Hamhŭng plain in modern South Hamgyŏng Province which attracted semi-agricultural tribes, was particularly vulnerable to their encroachments.

Koryŏ's Jürched policy in its first stage was largely of political manipulation. First, the official trade was encouraged so that foodstuff, cloth articles, agricultural implements, and other necessities could be peacefully supplied to them. Occasionally, the court moved to confer honorary ranks upon Jürched leaders, a move that also served to undermine the Liao-Jürched relations ;

some of conferees were punished because of their covert allegiance to the Liao. When some tribes, who had more agriculturally settled down, sought permanent protection, they were usually "naturalized." Koryŏ's success in the Jürched policy was indicated by the fact that the number of Jürched "naturalized" by Koryŏ, which they called "the parental country," steadily increased, counting by the thousands by the eleventh century.

But the spectacular rise of the Wenyen tribe in the upper basin of the Sungari River was soon not only to end the peaceful Koryŏ Jürched relations but to change the whole international balance in the Northeast Asia also. As might be expected, the Wenyen tribal leadership claimed the allegiance of those Jürched under Koryŏ's protection, and, in ensuing clashes in 1104, the Koryŏ army was dealt a resounding defeat. The Koryŏ government immediately organized a special force called *Pyŏlmuban* to deal with the Wenyen force. The *Pyŏlmuban* consisted of specially trained infantry units, including monk-soldiers, and cavalry units lack of which was blamed for the previous blow. The subsequent expeditionary force of 170,000 under Yun Kwan, which Yejong sent off from P'yŏngyang in 1107, attacked the Jürched from both land and sea and swept them out of the Hamhŭng plain.

Following the victorious campaigns, Yun Kwan fortified nine strategic towns in the gained territory northeast of the Long Wall. He peopled these towns with more Koreans and even built two Buddhist temples in one of them. These defense towns are the so-called Yun Kwan's Nine Fortifications which, like the Six Fortifications East of the River in the northwest, were scattered about in modern South Hamgyŏng Province, defending that area, including some Jürched tribes still residing there. After a year of defensive-offensive battles around these towns, however, Koryŏ, finding it difficult to permanently hold them, decided to yield to entreaties for the return of the area which the Jürched had repeatedly been making even while they were counterattacking, winning.

In 1114 A-ku-ta, the first great leader of the Jürched poeple, organized his tribesmen into an open rebellion against the Liao, and next year he declared himself the emperor of Chin (or Gold as probably against Iron, the Liao). In the war that followed, the Gold, as might be expected, was getting the upper hand of the Iron which was now clearly at the end of a "dynastic cycle." Meanwhile, Koryŏ, posing as a neutral, kept rejecting Liao's request for help. For this stand, the Chin rewarded Koryŏ by letting it take over in 1117 Liao's easternmost stronghold in modern Ŭiju that abuts on the Amnok River.

In the same year, Chin T'ai Tsu proposed a "brotherly relation" with Koryŏ as younger brother, while he still acknowledged the fact that the Jürched people formerly regarded Koryŏ as the "country of the parents." Chin's this generally-friendly communication was not answered by the Koryŏ court, which was somewhat upset by the proposal. In 1119 Chin T'ai Tsu, more confident of his military strength, addressed himself downright as the emperor in still another message to Koryŏ. Koryŏ, now thinking twice in deference to Chin's distended power, reciprocated the message in kind, but this time the Chin rejected Koryŏ's letter on the ground that among other things Koryŏ reminded the Chin of its "Korean origin." Thereupon, Koryŏ unobtrusively "heightened the Long Wall by three feet"

All this time, the Chin pressed hard upon the Liao. The Sung, on the other hand, saw in the war an opportunity to recover the sixteen border prefectures lost to the Liao two centuries before and, in spite of Koryŏ's advice to the contrary, formed a military alliance with the Chin. But the Sung, still no enemy of the Liao, could do nothing substantial to regain the lost territory, while the Chin pushed on victoriously southward, crossing the Great Wall at the Sung's request for help, until in 1125 the last Liao emperor was captured.

After a brief period of accord between the Chin and the Sung as elder uncle and nephew, the Chin the elder uncle swept southward over the northern half of China and sacked Kaifeng, the Sung's capital, in 1126. In the process, Hui Tsung, a great artist but an inept ruler, lamenting over the situation, abdicated in favor of his son, Ch'in Tsung. But soon they were both captured by the onrushing Chin thus ending the dynasty usually referred to as Northern Sung.

In 1127 another son of Hui Tsung, who escaped the capture, was proclaimed the new emperor known as Kao Tsung of the Southern Sung with Hangchou as his capital. And the Southern Sung was to enjoy another one and a half centuries of general prosperity until in 1279 the Mongols swept down. The Southern Sung carried on struggles for a decade but in 1141 concluded peace with the Chin. The peace treaty stipulated that among other things the Southern Sung was the vassal of Chin which it was to address as the lord in all state communications. Koryŏ succumbed to such an arrangement after Chin's destruction of Liao ; moreover, Koryŏ was forced to sever its official relations with the Chinese dynasty.

It is worth noting that throughout these developments political behaviors of each nation determined by its military strength and national interests, before which high-flown moral ideals and virtues each might profess to enhance seemed indeed flimsy. At the time of the second Liao invasion of Koryŏ in 1010, as we have seen, the Sung court, which had no extra soldiers to spare, refused beforehand a request for help that Koryŏ might make. Koryŏ was no less ready for extricating itself from international entanglement. In 1128 the Southern Sung asked Koryŏ to provide a byway for its attempt to rescue via the Yellow Sea and the Peninsula the two former emperors who were taken prisoner and moved to northern Manchuria by Chin. Koryŏ refused on the pretext of an unlikely possibility that Chin would make some such request and come to appreciate the conveniences of maritime traffic then, Southern Sung's coastal areas would be exposed to the Chin plunder. Koryŏ's real fear was of course a Chin invasion. Despite these occasional exchanges of transparent excuses and snobberies, however, the two agricultural neighbors kept right on asking each other's help when in need.

Cultural and Commercial Exchanges. Koryŏ's need for foreign goods and books were most constant, a factor which urged it on to international intercourse. With Chin, its northern neighbor, however, Koryŏ minimized official contact and prohibited private trade against which it quite hermetically sealed off its northern border. Koryŏ's foreign intercourse, therefore, was overwhelmingly with China as it had been during the Silla period, even though trade seemed now dominated by the Chinese merchants. Their mercantile activities were encouraged by the Southern Sung's favorable maritime policies and by the unfailing patronage of the Koryŏ court and aristocratic families, whether the official relations were severed or not. During the reign of Ŭijong (1147-1170), nearly 1,700 Sung merchants came to Koryŏ ; earlier, Arabian merchants made a few appearances, probably guided by the former. In the absence of official relations, the merchants sometimes served as liaison between Koryŏ and the Sung.

Although the two countries held different views of each other, the strong urge for these contacts between them was, in the last analysis, a desire for international amity as an expression of national well-being. Nowhere was this truly international amity more apparent than in exchange of embassies with elaborate rituals and welcome. The ambassador and the vice ambassador of both sides were expected to be men of impeccable decorum, great learning, and wit who could execute with facility literary and philosophical exchanges at the court or at unofficial gatherings.

The entourage of an ambassador, that counted fifty to 250, once landed in the host country, travelled and stayed at the expense of the host government. Su Shih (1036-1101), or better known as Su Tung P'o, one of the great poets of all time, persistently recommended against the large scale exchange of embassies with Koryŏ. To him it incurred too heavy a financial burden upon his government. As the Minister of Rites, he proposed a ban on Koryŏ's import of books and gold foils from the Sung. But Sung Che Tsung (1086-1100), under whom he served, asked a Koryŏ envoy to send 4,994 volumes of lost books and got many of them from Koryŏ. Despite Su Shih's illiberal attitude, which was an isolated case, Korean missions were generally well received. The Chinese entourage was even more elaborately received, and usually they returned with shipfuls of gifts.

Yesŏng, the port city at the mouth of the Yesŏng River, about ten miles west of Kaegyŏng, was one of the most splendid harbors in Northeast Asia in this period. Yesŏng was admired in poetry and painting indicating how prosperous it was in international commerce then. During the later part of the Southern Sung, Koryŏ merchants were allowed to pay duties at a reduced rate, a most favored nation treatment, at the ports along the Chinese coast. On the diplomatic level, the Sung court is said to have paid particular attention to giving literary excellence to the state papers bound for Koryŏ. Another measure of Koryŏ's cultural advancement may be discerned in the fact that, in sharp contrast with the previous dynasty, few students went to China for study ; instead, many Sung scholars came to serve at the Koryŏ court, and hundreds of Chinese lived in Kaegyŏng in the twelfth century.

A warrior of Chin Tribe.

7

Printing

The early literary society that invented printing, one of the most important events in history, has been thought to be T'ang China. The knowledge of stamping and rubbing, together with the existence of paper and ink, that led to this technical invention, had been long prevalent especially in China before the eighth century. In 1966 an excellent piece of a block-printed Buddhist *sutra* was found in the Sŏkka pagoda at the Pulguksa. The printed *sutra*, 5.3 cm., in height and 630 cm., in length, was verified as the oldest block-printed letters yet to be found anywhere. It was printed on the Silla-made paper sometime between 704 and 751. Some evidences show that block printing might have been well developed in United Silla around the early part of the first half of the eighth century or about the same time or even before it was in the T'ang.

In Korea as in some other religious countries in Asia, the development of printing had inseparable relations with Buddhist religion. The evidence shows that printing in Silla was solely for *sutra* publication, a tradition that was taken over by Koryŏ. As we have seen, the large-scale publications of the Tripitaka were undertaken under the auspices of the court during the Koryŏ period. It seems that the possession of the printed Tripitakas was regarded as a mark of cultural advancement in international context. There seems to have been certain jealousy and competition for Tripitaka printing among Koryŏ, the Sung, and the Liao. Su Shih's complaint about the outflow of too many books into Koryŏ was a representative instance of international cultural jealousy. But, on the other hand, each seemed to be only too glad to send its printed *sutras* and books to others as gifts.

The two great Tripitaka publications undertaken in 1021 and 1086, respectively, followed by another in 1236 which is extant today, can be also seen against this broader international background. In eleventh century Koryŏ however, printing was not confined to Buddhist literature. It came to cover Confucian classics and commentaries and medicine, and it was done not only under the royal auspices in the capital but, in fewer cases, also by inspired officials in provincial towns. It may be noted in this connection that the government allocated land to local governments as funds for the specific purpose of promoting the papermaking industry in their respective districts.

In parallel with block printing, printing by moveable metal types was introduced in the early thirteenth century. Although the concept of printing by moveable types was experimented with earthen types in the Sung earlier, it was in Koryŏ that the idea was realized into the modern metal type printing. The date for the invention of moveable metal types in Koryŏ has been recently fixed at 1232, but evidence shows that metal types had been already well in use by that time.

The cirumstances under which Koryŏ invented metal types, however, seem to have been not religious but of practical necessity. By foreign invasions and an attempt at a *coup* in 1126 which consecutively destroyed the capital, the Koryŏ court suffered, among others things, a loss of tens of thousands of books which, given the royal bibliophilic enthusiasm, might well have been traumatic. The technical foundation for development of printing had been well laid by the beginning of the twelfth century when in 1102 Koryŏ acquired the Sung method of minting. Koryŏ's coins were excellent in general shape and in evenness of letters, even though another category of casting, namely, of temple bells declined in technique and artistry, compared with the Silla period. Probably from this minting method, Koryŏ developed the technique of making molds for types, with greensand which withstood the temperature of up to 700℃.

This technique, as it was then practical enough, spread to the Sung and through which eventually, it can be assumed, to Europe. Probably because of the Mongol invasion of Koryŏ and the political instability that followed, Koryŏ, however, was unable to develop the technique further than would have been hoped for. The type printing, however, was fully developed and tremendously utilized by the literary Yi dynasty from the fifteenth century on. *

---

* This and preceding paragraphs are based mainly on Paw Key Sohn's "History of Printing," in *Han'gukmunhwasa taegye* Ⅲ : *Kwahak kisulsa (Outline of Korean Culture, Ⅲ : Histroy of Science and Technology)*, pp. 967-1061.

8

Literature

Although the existing literary works of the Koryŏ dynasty are far from vast, the resilient vitality of the Koryŏ people, coupled with their greatly increased economic productivity, made the Koryŏ dynasty one of the most interesting periods in the literary history of Korea. Attempts by the government to reinforce Confucian ideals in a predominantly-Buddhistic society inevitably produced social and ideological tensions which no doubt created an atmosphere conducive to literary production. Besides, the irresistible freedom of spirit and love and the optimism, that had characterized the peninsular people, remained intact. Now these combined with an earthier awareness of harmony and an adroiter sense of rhythm to produce in poetry and drama a refreshing variety of forms and contents. Also noteworthy is a greater mastery of the Chinese letters which undoubtedly enriched Koryŏ literature in variety and dimension.

Koryŏ's main literary current consisted mainly of lyric poems which tended to be much longer than those produced in previous periods. Inexplicably, Silla's *Saenaennorae (Hyangga)* dwindled in popularity ; probably, Monk Kyunyŏ was its last great author. Koryŏ's songs are generally called *changga* or long poem. The designation *changga*, which includes short as well as long poems, rather vaguely covers the vernacular songs as distinguished from those written in Chinese form. In general, the *changga* are full of rhythm and refrain conducive to group singing.

An unmistakable characteristic of the *changga* is a plethora of love ranging from a disfavored courtier's adoration of his liege lord to the erotic mirth between "good men" and "good women." The capacity for emotion was, to be sure, abundantly possessed by the Koreans of the adolescent Three kingdoms period, but their expressions, then, were more restrained and often shrouded in symbolic terms, as in Wonhyŏ's love song. But the Koryŏ people, matured in aesthetic outlook, seemed, regardless of social status, bound only to rhythm, lyrical humor, and worldly gratification through poetic enjoyment of the passion, often tending toward hedonic excessiveness. In such a setting, profound symbolism and religious devotion, in which the Silla poems abounded, were not to be expected but a kind of secularization of love as well as faith, which was indeed a literary consummation of the love possessed by the sturdy peopled.

The "Song of Ch'ŏyong." It is interesting to note that the portentous meaning of the "Song of Ch'ŏyong" was much exploited for Shamanistic rituals during the Koryŏ period, throwing an insight into the nature of Koryŏ literature. The powerful poetic drama of the "Song" was used for a sort of an opera for ceremonial use. The "Song of Ch'ŏyong" now became a forty-five line song as it was adapted for a stage performance calling for a series of elaborated stately dances, a little bit of acting, and singing in either *aria* or chorus accompanied by instruments. It was performed as part of the annual purification ceremony at the court. The idea was to invoke the spirit of Ch'ŏyong who, as we have seen earlier, with sheer magnanimity and courage, expelled the evil spirit from his bedroom. He was now expected to help clear the palaces of evil spirits and demons that might reside there.

The first six of the forty-five line "Song" serve as the prelude which ends with a sweeping statement on Ch'ŏyong's supernatural ability of warding off "three calamities and eight misfortunes." The next eighteen lines are devoted to a description of Ch'ŏyong's appearance from head to foot with high-flown objectives and phrases befitting a divine personality such as those we may see in Koryŏ painting. These verses are undoubtedly designed to cheer and also cajole Ch'ŏyong whose spirit might be reluctant to appear without them, a cajolery that intensifies into the next six line stanza ending with, " ·· ·· Twelve countries together created Ch'ŏyong. Who would dare make light of him ? "

Then, in the last phase of the drama consisting of fifteen lines sure enough, Ch'ŏyong appears and begins his incantation which is familiar with us, " ·· ·· Two have been mine ; whose are the other two ? " At this moment, that is, before he finishes his last two lines which are supposed to be, "Two had been mine ; no, no, they are taken," he is interrupted with a coddling verse, "Give Ch'ŏyong a thousand pieces of gold. Give Ch'ŏyong seven treasures." He is not allowed to finish his last two lines whose magnanimity, in fact, forces the evil spirit into the voluntary withdrawal in the original "Song of Ch'ŏyong."

It may be noted here that, because of his forgoing the most magnificent last two lines and of being coddled instead, Ch'ŏyong's personality becomes a shallow, give-and-take affair. Ch'ŏyong readily responds to the above pampering by saying quite candidly, "No need of a thousand pieces of gold or seven treasures. Only bring me pestilent demons," which is sung in the most solemn, climactic tone. This is it, of course. The message is more than delivered. All evil spirits and demons are frightened and disappear "beyond a thousand *ri*."

Hanmunhak. An unfailing emphasis on education in Confucianism by the government and individual families strongly motivated by the *kwagŏ* examinations produced a distinct class of literati. This literary class, still small in comparison with that of the Yi dynasty, contributed tremendously to the development of traditional Korean literature. The literature they wrote is usually referred to as *Hanmunhak* or Han literature. By the late eleventh century, some of Koryŏ *Hanmun* writers were compared favorably in literary merit with the best of the contemporary Chinese literati.

Kim Pu Sik (1075-1151) was the greatest of the Koryŏ prose stylists who was widely admired among the Sung writers. Yi Kyu Po (1168-1241), a poet and essayist, was a man of versatile creativity and erudition. For his peotry, he suffered little from comparison with Li Po (701-762) of the T'ang. A host of other brilliant writers and poets vied with one another to excel in all forms of this foreign literature.

The unique contribution to Korean literature made by the Confucian literatus group in this period, however, was the creation of a poetic form called *Kyŏnggich'e* or "How-about-that" style song. A *Kyŏnggich'e* poem is composed almost wholly of phrases written in Chinese which, however, are arranged so as to conform to the syntactic order of the Korean language and a basic rhythmic pattern of the *changga*. Its actual composition seems to have been of group production. On a one man-one canto basis, the group can go on, adding a canto after another, as long as the next poet is willing. Its recitation, with an undulating refrain, "How about that," at the end of every canto, seems to have required the participation of the entire gathering.

The Historical Writing. In the context of the literary development, the two most important historical works, that were written in this period and survive today, cannot be overlooked : The *Samguk sagi* or *History of the Three Kingdoms* and the *Samguk yusa* or *Memorabilia of the Three Kingdoms* are the unique sources of the historical knowledge of the early Korean life. The former was compiled in 1145 by Kim Pu Sik, *et al.* Patterned after Ssuma Ch'ien's *Historical Records*, the fifty-chapter history contains three "Basic Annals" for the Three Kingdoms, with Silla as the pivotal nation, and various essays on rites, ceremonies, music, costumes, vehicles, houses, geography, and the governmental tables of organization. The last part of the book is devoted to the biographies of important men and women. The *Samguk yusa*, written sometime between 1281 and 1283 by Monk Iryŏn (1206-1289), is a nine-chapter collection of stories, including some fantastic ones, on men and events of that period. Whereas the *Samguk sagi* is strewn with Confucian moralization at the expense of facts, the *Samguk yusa* is relatively free from such intentional ideological warping. It is in the *Samguk yusa* that we read the Tan'gun legend, fourteen *Saenaennorae* in *Idu*, and many other stories of historical and literary significance.

    Music. The traditional Korean music, as has been noted, was greatly developed under Silla, and the imported T'ang music was also employed at its court. In 1114 the orchestral music of the Sung was borrowed through the courtesy of Sung Hui Tsung, which the Koryŏ court used chiefly on ceremonial occasions. The full scale re-standardization of the Chinese music, that is, music of T'ang and Sung, as they had been used in Korea, occurred under the direction of Sejong during the early Yi dynasty. The traditional music that is taught under the name of *aak* (court music) or *kug'ak* (national music) at the National Academy of Traditional Music today is a blend of the traditional Korean and Chinese music.

Ch'ŏyong dance.

9

Art

Aesthetic creations of the Three Kingdoms and United Silla were, in general, those of a youthful enthusiast, which were characterized by purposefulness, straightforwardness, unmitigated symmetry, and consummated technique. Buddhism was the source of inspiration for the major categories of art, except for the pre-Buddhist Silla art, and the artistic works that it inspired were invariably of realistic interpretation.

The aesthetic current in Koryŏ, while it was largely a continuation from the previous period, markedly showed a different propensity, nourished by a profoundly-new outlook on life and religion. Sŏn Buddhism's single-minded efforts at the "sudden enlightenment," the geomantic belief in the terrestrial force, and a greater Taoistic longing for natural beauties unmistakably influenced Koryŏ art, countenancing an aesthetic point of view characterized by a more pronounced inclination toward nature, as against artificiality. The austere symmetry, the conscientious detail, the powerfulness, all hallmarks of the art of the previous period, were not emphasized. The works of Koryŏ art, which were of a mature artist nurtured by the above-mentioned ideological prompting, show a deepened concept of art that stressed a self-conscious, introspective refinement.

Nature as a Pervasive Theme in Art. Naturalism in Korean art, or even the general Korean attitude toward nature, seems to have become more clearly crystallized during the Koryŏ period. The Korean appreciation of nature is to be *in* nature. Unlike the Japanese who try to contain nature within the artificialities of the house with disciplined efforts, the Korean try to convert themselves to nature for enjoyment of the unbridled freedom that nature provides. This open-hearted attitude toward nature can be clearly seen in Koryŏ architecture, for instance.

In architectural arrangement, the relations of the location and surrounding terrain features of the planned structure to a larger geographical composition are considered to be of fundamental importance. The royal palaces in the Koryŏ capital were a perfect example in question. Their locations were no doubt determined by geomantic considerations, and the palace complexes were integrated into the rough terrain, rather than the other way around, with a series of flights of stone steps, waterfalls, and building foundations as high as fifty feet just to be level with adjacent structures. Thatched peasant houses are no exceptions in this question of harmony with nature, as indicated by their inclusion, as unit-components within the fence, of open yards, trees, possibly large rocks in corners which are actually part of the natural surroundings.

The main hall of the Pusŏksa in North Kyŏngsang Province, rebuilt in the 1370's, is by far the most beautiful of the about ten existing structures of the Koryŏ period. A glance at its interior would be sufficient to see stress laid on the artistic use of the inherent shape and texture of the material, mainly wood, with as little artificial treatment as possible. This preference for the original beauty of the material has been deeply rooted in Korean artistic mind, which we can see more clearly in the handiworks of the Yi dynasty.

Buddhist Art

All major categories of Buddhist art evolved, of course, from United Silla, showing fuller maturity in many instances, but, in others, along the path toward deterioration in artistic quality. Of the Buddhist statues, the giant stone Maitreya (Mirŭk) at the Kwanch'oksa near Nonsan in South Ch'ungch'ŏng Province is probably representative of Koryŏ idiosyncrasy in this category *(Plate 15)*. A product of unquestioned religious zeal but not of refined artistry, the sixty-foot tall figure looks like a physically and mentally retarded child, but placed in its environ with gnarled woods behind and a twenty-foot tall, well-carved stone lantern in front whose straight roof lines pleasantly echo those of his "double mortar-board" hat, the retarded child indeed radiates a certain charm from its very grotesqueness and size.

Stone lanterns became an important category of architectural sculpture during the Koryŏ period. The above mentioned lantern is one of the best products developed directly from Silla specimens *(Plate 16)*. The cylindrical plinth and four square pillars that make up the lantern proper are regarded as a major innovation in this field. Another best for the late Koryŏ period is standing about six feet in height at the Sillŭksa in Kyŏnggi Province, dating from 1379 *(Plate 17)*. Ornamental figures in relief around cuspidated arches, unpretentiously simplified execution of the roof in contrast with the usual ornate ones of other lanterns, and above all the overall feeling of stability make this work undoubtedly the foremost one among Koryŏ lanterns.

The most brilliant work of all surviving Koryŏ architectural sculptures, however, would be the Funerary Pagoda of Hongbŏp Kuksa (National Teacher Hongbŏp), formerly at the Chaengt'osa in North Chŏlla Province but now moved to the Kyŏngbok Palace precinct *(Plate 18)*. Slightly more than eight feet in height and dating from 1017, the marble Pagoda represents the most original of the works of this category in overall plan and rendition of individual parts. The center piece, a soft, simple ball, somewhat flattened from above and bound with graceful double bands, sets the whole tone of the structure. The pedestal portion, carved on the model of the conventional Buddha throne with embossed lotus flowers and dragons, has its octagonal aspects almost round. The top piece, also octagonal and larger in diameter, has scalloped eaves and down-curved ridges, all creating a series of gentle, curved lines which heighten the overall effect of the Pagoda's gentleness and serenity.

In sharp contrast in design and shape with the above ball-urn pagoda is another funerary pagoda dating from 1085. The Hyŏnmyot'ap (or funerary pagoda) of Chigwang Kuksa (National Teacher Chigwang), standing about twenty-one feet in height also at the Kyŏngbok Palace grounds, seems to have been built with an entirely different conceptual approach *(Plate 19)*. Its ornate furbelows and massive chunks contained by a series of heavy not so much a work of art as a funerary pagoda ; from this particular piece, certain characteristics of Korean traditional funerary art subsequently seems to have been developed.

A much larger specimen of pagoda is represented by an octagonal, nine-story structure at the Wŏlchŏngsa in Kang'wŏn Province *(Plate 20)*. Nearly fifty feet in height, the eleventh century Pagoda of exceptional beauty is placed upon a pedestal whose lowest plaque is covered with lotus flowers facing the ground-level foundation. This and the crown of upturned lotus flowers supporting the wrought-iron finial are only portions that have been cut in relief. The beauty of the otherwise unadorned Pagoda is achieved largely with the nine single slab roofs slightly upturned at the edge and arranged with each plaque a little smaller than one below in a pleasing proportion, as we have seen in Paekche and Silla pagodas.

In its total impression, however, it shows a sharp turn away from the previous period. An arrangement which was never seen previously is a superbly-done stone Bodhisattva of Medicine seated in prayer *facing* the pagoda, instead of being seated or engraved on the pagoda itself, as had been the usual case. This Wŏlchŏngsa example, one of a few such plans extant, might be of great significance, reflecting Koryŏ Buddhism's secularization. The Koryŏ people might have wanted to extricate themselves from too deep an involvement in matters of faith by, for instance, leaving behind their religious alter ego, so to speak, in the form of, in this case, a Bodhisattva of Medicine.

Ceramic Art

Since Kaya and Silla, Korean potters had had a long experience in their art, and, in the late eleventh or early twelfth century, the industry almost suddenly became a great creative field for the artistic talents of the Koryŏ potters. In fact, it was in ceramic art that the Korean artistic genius seemed to have fully realized. The initial technical stimulant, it is said, came from the Sung that developed the Chinese in some aspects, with technical and artistic inventions of their own.

A profounder impetus to the artistic excellence of Koryŏ ceramics seems to have been from Sŏn Buddhism and its related institutions such as ceremonial drinking of tea in the background of aristocratically-oriented, economic affluence. The Sŏn concept of Buddha-nature as pervading in every object and aspect of nature enhanced the spiritual value of the common objects as they were in their form, color, and relations to the universe.

They were now keenly observed by poets and artists as well as Sŏn intellectuals. Such social institutions as literary gatherings, tea ceremonies, and informal discussions on, and appreciations of, art and nature cultivated and sharpened an aesthetic taste for sophisticated refinement and simplicity and a bias for quiet detachment. Indeed, no works of art during the Koryŏ period excelled in these virtues more eminently than its ceramic master pieces, probably the finest of its kind the world has ever produced.

The ceramic works of Koryŏ display an amazing variety of types, colors, shapes, and decorations. Their types were classified largely by colors effected from the use of different glazes and methods of baking. The *paekcha* or white porcelain, the *ch'ŏngja* or celadon, the *ch'ŏnmok* (*tenmoku* in Japanese) or black ware, and the miscellaneous including vessels of lesser quality for common households are four major classifications.

Of these, the *ch'ŏngja*, literally blue porcelain, noted for its deep blue color more than anything else, is representative of Koryŏ ceramics. The *ch'ŏngja* glaze, of feldspathose minerals containing one to three percent of iron content the *pisaek*, that famous "secret" color, when its iron content was made ferrous oxide in reducing flames in the kiln, the technique that has been lost since, however.

The development of the Koryŏ celadon, after a short period of initial experiment, reached its full flowering in unprecedented splendor during the first half of the twelfth century. Its production, thought it tended to be crude in technique and appearance in the later period, continued more or less throughout the dynasty. Of Koryŏ's celadon masterpieces, a great many were taken, mostly illegally, to many parts of the world. Some, placed in art museums in Seoul, fortunately provide a cross-sectional view, though only impressionistic, of Koryŏ ceramic art.

The Duck-Shaped Water Dropper in the Kansong Museum of Fine Arts, dating from the early twelfth century, is a most brilliant example of artistic consummation in every aspect of pottery *(Plate 21)*. The pose in a graceful contour of the Duck is caught as it floats on the pond with a stalk of lotus flower in its mouth. The twisted stalk held in the mouth ends on the Duck's back where a modeled flower and a bud make the water hole and the lid. The wings and the feathers minutely incised, even the pupils of the eyes realistically done, and the glaze uniformly applied, resulting in the palest of the *ch'ŏngja* blue, all show a convincing hand at the execution of a delicate work.

Probably dating from the same period, the Openwork Posanghwa Wine Pot in the National Museum of Korea is an equally exquisite work *(Plate 22)*. The Wine Pot, less than five inches in diameter, is enclosed in a capsule of elaborately reticulated *posanghwa* (precious image flower) leaves and vines with seven children playing among them. The whole Pot is then placed in the protective bowl-holder covered with sixty-three incised lotus flower petals, some of which are warped backward as if in fading. The symmetry of the bowl-holder is, it may be noted, de-emphasized by a naturalism of warped petals.

The Koryŏ porcelain made another step forward with the invention of the *sanggambŏp*, an inlay method, in either the early or mid-twelfth century. The embellishment in design and drawing had been done by means of, as in the above two pieces, incising, modeling, openwork, or, hardly less often, relief or even stamping in the form of natural objects or geometric plans on the paste before glazing. The new inlay method was to simply fill in the engraved design or drawing with white or black slip. The piece was then baked without glaze and baked again this time with glaze applied.

It may be noted that the inlay method was used on non-plastic medium at about the same time or even earlier. On bronze vessels such as *kundika* (water sprinkler) and the incense burner used for Buddhist ceremonies, often inlaid were silver threads that depicted letters or scenery. As to the exact relationship between the inlay methods on the two mediums that then existed, it is yet to be made clear.

Of the inlaid celadons, the most splendid item is a *maebyŏng* or plum vase called Thousand Crane Vase in the Kansong Museum *(Plate 23)*.

Standing about sixteen inches in height and probably dating from the late twelfth century, the Vase, inlaid in white and black, is decorated, as its name shows, with cranes amid white clouds in the background of a most pleasing *ch'ŏngja* color. The black and white circlets, which encircle the cranes flying upward, and the black and white lotus petals which band around the base, are also prominent features of the embellishment, adding a sense of repose and shape. The shape of vases classified as *maebyŏng*, a creation of Koryŏ potters, is characterized by the exaggerated shoulders. The Thousand Crane Maebyŏng not only stands as the best of the Koryŏ works but also figures prominently among the best of the ceramic masterpieces of the world.

The Peony Jar in the National Museum of Korea, dating from the early thirteenth century, is adorned with sprays of peonys, not in linear design but in painting in black and white with slips spread out in the intagliated areas *(Plate 24)*. The celadon jar, slightly less than eight inches in diameter, is covered with an excellent grey-blue glaze with the fine crackles over the surface created by baking longer than usual, a means of decoration much used during the later period.

Roughly with the Mongol domination of the dynasty in the thirteenth century, the plastic art began to decline in that products generally became crude, compared with earlier refinement. About this time, another technical change was introduced : instead of reducing flames, oxidizing flames came to be applied with the result of turning wares rustic, brownish red. This change in the use of flames in the kiln constituted an important innovation, which was much appropriated by the Japanese later.

For decoration they changed from inlaying to painting in iron oxide under the glaze, a new method the Yi dynasty potters were to take over. If, assuming Koryŏ potters were under the pressure of the official demand, the underglaze painting was a way to get around the exacting workmanship of inlaying, it added a new freedom in decorating that in many cases produced delightful effects. In parallel with these new modes coming into vogue, the decorative trends understandably shifted from the earlier tendency of covering the entire space with delicate designs and refined lines in natural and geometric forms, as in the Thousand Crane Vase, toward, as in the Peony Jar, representation with as few lines as possible of unpretentious motifs from nature.

The Willow-Painted Water Bottle, standing about twelve inches tall in the National Museum of Korea, is a work produced by the new technical and decorative innovations mentioned above *(Plate 25)*. Against the background of brownish red stands a willow tree executed in black with carefree suddenness and absolute economy of line. The Sŏn concept of art is adeptly applied here, namely that a painting may be done within a moment of inspiration as man's salvation can be achieved through sudden enlightenment. The Water Bottle is no doubt one of the masterpieces of the late Koryŏ period. Even though somewhat coarse and melancholic in general impression, it can compare favorably in artistic quality even with the Thousand Crane Vase.

Another, probably the last, development in decorating, that occurred in the late thirteenth century, was painting with gold dust over the *ch'ŏngja* glaze preferably of splashy objects. This was to add more brilliance to the ornamental effect of a ware, supposedly heightening the exquisiteness of the *ch'ŏngja* blue, but not always to the enhancement of artistic values of the decadent taste of the old aristocracy. When one of these sumptuous works was presented to Yüan Shin Tsu, former Khubilai Khan, the austere Mongolian emperor offered an advice : to make no more.

As if to heed the blunt admonition, the Koryŏ potters began from the middle of the fourteenth century to lose interest not only in the production of gold dust vessels but also in carrying on the incomparable achievements of their predecessors. In short, the Koryŏ *ch'ŏngja* were no more produced. Among possible reasons, the most credible suggests that the rise in the fourteenth century of Confucianism in the place of Buddhism brought a distinctly different artistic taste to eminence within the ruling class that supported the art. Or it may be that, with the passing of celadon masters amid the political and social turmoil of the declining dynasty, the abstruse art of celadon production was also gone.

Various types of Koryŏ celadon (left to right) : bowl with inlaid design ; bowl inlaid with white and red celadon slips ; wine cup with stand, underglazed in copper.

Wooden blocks used to print 81.258 pages of the
Tripitaka Koreana, carved in 1237-1252.

Part 6

The Late Koryŏ Period

1

Internal Disturbances

Koryŏ's indigenization of the Chinese political system, accompanied by an unprecedented national prosperity, considered from a political point of view, was essentially a royal triumph in that it was all geared to the centralization of power. But the Koryŏ monarchs in general, circumscribed by the hands of tradition and pseudo-scientific beliefs and by their deference to the power and privileges of the aristocracy, remained relatively weak, while literary and artistic diversions of often decadent nature softened their fiber.

The *coup d'état* of 1170, the data that was usually set as the beginning of the late Koryŏ period, resulted, in the last analysis, from the royal inability to assert its power. Once the military's take-over of the country, with their characteristic way of government, made permanent, a reorientation in all major aspects of the dynastic life occurred, rendering the late Koryŏ society different, in some respects quite radically, from the pre-*coup* period.

The reign of Injong (1123-1146) saw two ill-fated attempts at the throne, which provide a graphic expose of the unseemly affairs of the court politics leading to the 1170 revolt. The first one was caused by Yi Cha Kyŏm, the representative figure of the powerful Yi clan of Inju. Yi Cha Kyŏm married one daughter to Yejong and two others to Injong. Together with his henchman, T'ak Chun Kyŏng, Yi eliminated key rival officials through a series of intrigues and accumulated wealth by means of graft and forceful seizure of estates of lesser officials. He seems to have established even a personal contact with the Southern Sung court to undermine the royal authority, an act that was risky but always open to a man of ill designs. Yi also forced the court to settle diplomatic relations with the Chin on the lord-vassal basis in

1126 in the face a strong opposition offered by Chŏng Chi Sang (ca. 1090–1135) representing at the court the officials of P'yŏngyang origin, who were understandably articulate exponents of the traditional northward expansion.

Injong had secretly ordered Yi's elimination but met with a counterattack led by T'ak Chun Kyŏng, which resulted in the complete burning of the royal palace in 1126. Soon, a quarrel broke out between domestic servants of the Yi and T'ak families, which eventually led to the severance of their masters' alliance.

A Yi servant had allegedly told a T'ak servant that T'ak should be condemned to death because of his monstrous act of burning the royal palace; the statement reportedly angered T'ak. The royal agent drove in the thin end of the wedge between the two men and won over T'ak who was then coaxed into disposal of Yi at a critical moment. In a year, T'ak Chun Kyŏng himself was banished by Chŏng Chi Sang's retroactive censure that branded T'ak's destruction of the palace as "the crime of ten thousand generations," as had been pointed out by the Yi servant.

Upon the settlement of the Yi–T'ak incident, Injong in 1127 promulgated a fifteen–article reform policy from P'yŏngyang, the Western Capital. This seemingly refreshing move was, however, a result of factional politics on the regional level. Like many previous kings, Injong subscribed to the familiar geomantic notion which viewed P'yŏngyang as a veritable site for the dynastic capital. This belief, in view of the fact that Kaegyŏng, the present capital, lay in ruins, whereas P'yŏngyang had been physically and administratively well established, now exerted more leverage on the royal sentiment.

Injong's sentiment was taken advantage of by a group of high-ranking central officials from P'yŏngyang. The mastermind of this group was Myŏch'ong, a monk of unquestioned courage, who Somehow ingratiated himself into the confidence of Injong with the help of Chŏng Chi Sang. Myoch'ŏng and his disciple Paek Su Han, the court astrologer who also seems to have been strongly influencing Injong's thinking, concocted a cryptic theory of Buddhist, geomantic, and *yin–yang* elements to abet the King in his aversion for Kaegyŏng. They succeeded in obtaining Injong's permission to build a royal palace complex in P'yŏngyang as preliminary toward the transfer of the capital to P'yŏngyang. The Taehwagung, or Great Flower Palace, was completed in a remarkably short period of four months in 1129, including a mysterious pantheon where the eight gods of Myoch'ŏng's creation were enshrined.

The actual transfer of the capital to P'yŏngyang, however, met with a strong opposition from a group of Confucian officials of the Kaegyŏng faction headed by Kim Pu Sik, the literary and political opponent of Chŏng Chi Sang. All considered, moving of the capital at this time was indeed well–nigh impossible; instead, Injong repaired P'yŏngyang several times at the solicitation of Myoch'ŏng. The monk urged the King to use his own year period, instead

Plate 17. Stone Lantern of Sillŭksa.
(p. 183). Height : 6 ft. Sillŭksa,
Kyŏnggi Province. Koryŏ late 14th
century.

Plate 18. Funerary Pagoda of
Hongbŏp Kuksa. (p. 183). Height :
8 ft. Koryŏ, 11th century. Kyŏngbok
Palace Pagoda Park.

Plate 19. Hyŏnmyot'ap (Funerary
Pagoda) of Chigwang Kuksa. (p. 183).
Height : 21 ft Koryŏ, 11th century.
Kyŏngbok Palace Pagoda Park.

Plate 21. Duck-Shaped Water Dropper. (p. 185) Celadon glaze. Height : about 3 in. Koryŏ, early 12th century. Kansong Museum of Fine Arts, Seoul.

Plate 22. Open-Work Posanghwa Wine Pot. (p. 185). Celadon glaze. Height : 7 in. ; diameter at base : $4^{1}/8$ in. ; Bowl-holder height : $3^{1}/2$ in. ; diameter at top ; $7^{3}/16$ in. Koryŏ, 12th century. National Museum of Korea.

Plate 20. Nine Story Pagoda of Wŏlchŏngsa (p. 183). Height : 49.5. ft. Wŏlchŏngsa, Kangwŏn Province. Koryŏ, 11th century.

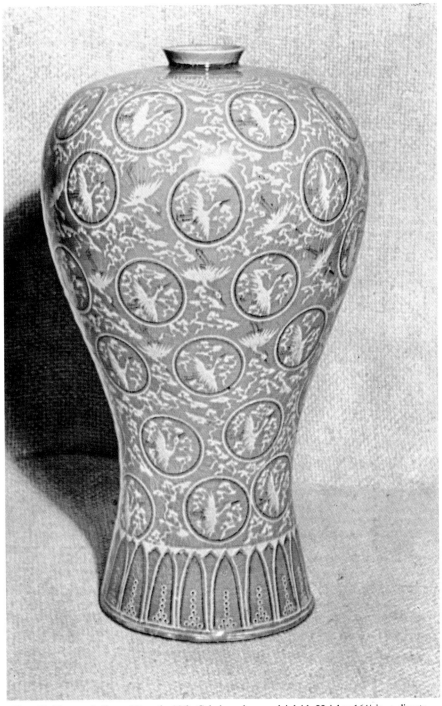

Plate 23. Thousand Crane Vase (p. 185). Celadon glaze and inlaid. Height : 16 1/4 in. ; diamteer at shoulder : 9 7/8 in. Koryŏ, late 12th century. Kansong Museum of Fine Arts, Seoul.

Plate 24.
Peony Jar. (p. 186).
Celadon glaze and
inlaid. Height : 7 7/8 in.;
diameter at base : 6 in.
Koryŏ, early 13th cen-
tury. National Museum
of Korea.

Plate 25.
Willow-Painted Water Bottle. (p. 186).
Celadon glaze and painted in under-
glaze iron. Height : 12 ft. : diameter at
base : 4 in. Koryŏ 12th-13th century.
National Museum of Korea.

Plate 26. Wine Bottle (p. 299). Punch'ŏng ware. Height : 6 in; diameter. 4 in. Yi dynasty, 16th century. National Museum of Korea.

Plate 27. Food Jar (p. 300). White porcelain. Height : 1 ft.; diameter : 6 ½ in Yi dynasty, 17th century. National Museum of Korea.

Plate 28. "Dreamy Vision of a Paradise" (p. 301). An Kyon. Horizontal scroll, ink and color on silk. Height : 1 ft ½ in ; length : 4½ in. Yi dynasty, 15th century. Collection of Mr. Junkichi Mayuyama (from Evelyn McCune, *The arts of Korea*).

Plate 29. "Looking at Water on a Leisurely Day." (p. 301). Kang Hŭi An. Album leaf, ink on paper. Height : 9 ½ in. ; width : 6 ¼ in. Yi dynasty, 15th century. National Museum of Korea.

Plate 30. "Viewing of the Spring Blossoms" (p. 301). Sim Sa Chŏng. Album left, ink and color on paper. Height : 10 $^{15}/_{16}$ in. ; width 6 $^{9}/_{16}$ in. Kansong Museum of Fine Arts, Seoul.

Plate 31. The Turtle Ship. For data and descritions, see pp. 308~309.

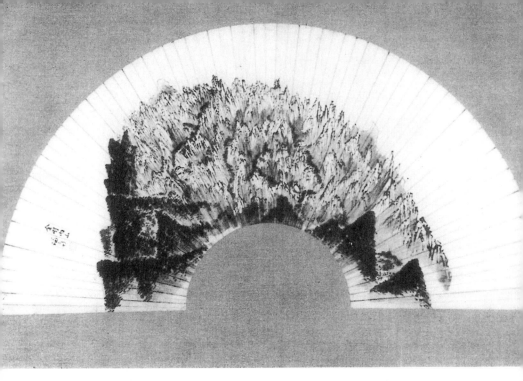

Plate 32. "The Diamond Mountains". (p. 343). Chǒng Sǒn. Fan painting, ink on paper. Height : 11 ¹/₆ in. ; width : 31¹/₁₀ in. Kansong Museum of Fine Arts, Seoul.

Plate 33. "Wrestling". (p. 343). Kim Hong To. Ink on paper. Kansong Museum of Fine Arts, Seoul.

Plate 34. "Ploughing". (p. 343). Kim Hong To. Album leat, ink on paper. Kansong Museum of Fine Arts, Seoul.

of Chin's, to call himself emperor, and to subjugate the Chin. These proposals were rejected by the Kim faction.

Meanwhile, the circumstances were militating against the P'yŏngyang group. During an unusually-long spell of inclement weather in 1134, an unmistakable sign of disharmony in *yin-yang* reaction manifested itself with thirty thunderbolts in succession making direct hits at the very Great Flower Palace itself. If the thunderbolts did not destroy the palace beyond repair, they most effectively aroused the public opinion that shattered Myoch'ŏng's scheme and Injong's enchantment with p'yŏngyang as well.

In 1135 Myŏch'ong, as if to prove his belief in the terrestrial energy of P'yŏngyang, created an "empire" himself with P'yŏngyang's well developed city government as its base and rose in rebellion against Kaegyŏng. His supporters at the court such as Chŏng Chi Sang were innocent of what was happening in P'yŏngyang. But they were summarily executed by Kim Pu Sik, the hurriedly appointed commander of the expeditionary army. Myoch'ŏng's tenacity was proved by the fact that the central forces took a whole year to subdue the rebellion. As might be expected, P'yŏngyang was sharply reduced in political importance thenceforth.

The victory of the royal army brought about another generation of political consensus with Kim Pu Sik as the leading spirit, though without any substantial increase in the royal power. It was in this period of political stability that a series of works of cultural significance were accomplished, including reconstruction of the royal palace and compilation of the *Samguk sagi*. But this period of relative peace was a deceptive one, for irregularities in government, especially in economic administration, such as private enlargement of estates through illegal means became rampant.

2

The Triumph of the Military in Government

The military seizure of power in 1170, or rather a vengeful explosion of the military against the civilian arrogance, was indeed a portentous event in the light of subsequent developments, a fact that cannot be overemphasized. Actually, it had been long in ferment. As the military's status as the western section of the *yangban* or ruling class made slightly lower than the civilian group (eastern section) in the beginning, as has been noted, the general institutional climate was set for gradual eclipse of the military in the council of the state.

Unscrupulous civilian officals could make and, more often than not, push through proposals that ate unfairly into the political and, above all, economic rights of the military. Formal education and the examination for candidates for military offices were not institutionalized throughout the dynasty. Both officers and men were appointed often from the lower class with qualifications no better than a strong physique, which added little to enhance the military's prestige. On the other hand, there had been always capable military officers, in many cases, of renowned lineage who reached the top echelon of the government, even though as civilian officials. Thus, men of military persuasion did continue to participate in government.

---

* The cold problem in this connection is the one arising from the artificial division of the country. The deepening cultural gap between the democratic South and the Communist North may eventually become the stumbling block toward unification of the country.

Succession of Coups d'État

There had been *coup* attempts before, to be sure, but the one led by Chŏng Chung Pu in 1170 was unprecedented in its vehemence and bloodiness as well as in its success. The immediate cause of the violence was the civilian misbehavior against the military, which in turn resulted from the mismanagement of the government under Ŭijong (1147–1170) and his favorite subject. Ŭijong or Sturdy Ancestor was actually a sensual mollycoddle and sturdy only in his persistence in merry-making, which lasted the entire length of his twenty-four year reign. He had 120-odd palaces, pavilions, and temples to hold feasts at and a coterie of sychophantic courtiers who pandered to the royal folly. When they were feasting, they were often bent on poking fun at officers on guard. These officers and men as royal guards, while thus subjected to petty insults thrown at constantly by civilian officials accompanying the King, sometimes went hungry on duty. In 1170, at Pohyŏnwŏn, one of royal pavilions, where nine guards were frozen to death in the previous winter, occurred an incident in which an old duty officer was slapped on the cheek by a young civilian official. Supreme General Chŏng Chung Pu (1106–1179), standing seven feet in height and with absolute loyalty to the King, decided with his colleagues, Yi Ŭi Pang and Yi Ko, that they had had enough and ordered his men to "kill all those who wear civilian headgears."

After the vengeful massacre that ensued and the inevitable deposition of Ŭijong in favor of his brother Myŏngjong (1171–1197), the Chŏng–Yi–Yi trio found themselves in the unaccustomed business of government. Their first order of business called for a complete replacement of the civilian officials with military men. The *Chungbang*, the assembly of the military officers with the ranks of Supreme General and Great General, as has been noted, was enhanced as the top organ of the military government. It was substantially expanded and moved to within the palace precinct in order to maintain closer communications with the monarch or rather more closely watch the royal movements.

But it soon became apparent that they were capable of no constructive government based on long-range policies. Vying with one another for wealth and honors, they instead engaged in power struggles in a tense, distrustful atmosphere which was to last for nearly thirty years.

First, Yi Ŭi Pang eliminated Yi Ko, followed by a large-scale slaughter in 1173 of civil officials who had survived the first massacre. This second purge resulted from an ill-fated expedition launched from the northeastern region to remove the *Chungbang* government. A logical casualty of this fail-

---

† A ri is about 1/3 mile.

ure was the deposed Ŭijong who had been banished to a southern island. He was assassinated by a Yi Ŭi Mun, an illiterate of extraordinary physique rising to a height of "eight" feet, who was then appointed general.

Another expedition against the military government was launched from P'yŏngyang in 1174; it lasted for two years, but without much result. During the turmoil, Yi Ŭi Pang was removed by Chŏng Chung Pu's son. The father-son team was in turn dislodged in 1179 by a twenty-six year old general named Kyŏng Tae Sŭng. General Kyŏng then proceeded as usual to liquidate rivals, entrusting his personal security to a death band of his creation, called *Tobang*. In 1183 he died of illness or probably of the tension too great for an inexperienced young man to bear, and the *Tobang* was disbanded.

To fill the *Chungbang*, as the current political mechanism required, Myŏngjong called upon Yi Ŭi Mun, the erstwhile assassin of Ŭijong, who had been lying low in his hometown, Kyŏngju, at the intimidation of Kyŏng Tae Sŭng. It was feared that with no one in the *Chungbang* in the capital Yi Ŭi Mun in Kyŏngju might rise in revolt, supported by the discontented peasants who were then in a continued state of uprising. His appointment to the *Chungbang* was calculated as a preventive move against possible peasant disturbances of more serious proportions. At any rate, Yi Ŭi Mun, a lowborn illiterate, proved, once given power, to be as good as any of his predecessors in amassing wealth and honors; in a few years, he entrenched himself firmly in the government. The next to top him was Ch'oe Ch'ung Hŏn (1149-1219) and his brother. The action seems to have been rather of spontaneous nature. The key to their victory was the organization of some units of the royal army into an anti-Yi force in a short time for a confrontation in the streets. This was neatly done at a lightning speed in 1196.

The Government of the Ch'oe Family

With the Ch'oe brothers' seizure of power, a generation of kaleidoscopic succession of *coups d'état* came to an end. In the beginning, they looked no different from their predecessors in the ruthless elimination of potential contenders for power. Soon, however, a pattern in their political conduct appeared, which set the Ch'oe Ch'ung Hŏn regime quite apart from the previous ones. Ch'oe's ten-article reform memorial, which was presented to the king upon his assumption of government, covered all major political and economic ills of the day. It was aimed at the removal of supernumerary officials, the return to peasants of the land illegally taken by powerful families, the reestablishment of impartial taxation, the prohibition of the construction of temples and the extravagant life of aristocratic, and so on. These became his basic policies.

It is doubtful whether he subsequently achieved all these aims, but his seriousness of purpose and strong-minded temperament were seen in his destruction of his own brother who, contrary to his advice, contrived, among other things, to marry his daughter to the crown prince. Ch'oe Ch'ung Hŏn was never interested associating himself with the royalty to enhance the prestige of his family but only in his personal ability and army, with which he in fact deposed two kings and enthroned four others during his life time. As no one had done before, he was able to put down peasant uprisings in the provinces and to cut off political and economic connections between the royal family and the church. On the strength of these achievements, he eventually created a hereditary government for his family.

The Ch'oe System of Government. Through more than a decade of evolution, the Ch'oe family government came to function in parallel with, or above, the royal government. At first, like his predecessors, Ch'oe yielded power as the head of the *Chungbang* where all major governmental policies were decided upon and administrative directives transmitted. It is interesting to note that the headship of the *Chungbang* did not necessarily require the highest rank, and Ch'oe took some ten years to be promoted by proper sequence to the highest rank in the regular government.

Then, in 1209, a *coup* attempt against Ch'oe was detected, and the *Kyojŏng Togam* or Office of Decision and Instruction was hurriedly established with the sole purpose of putting down the *coup*: it was a kind of field headquarters for Ch'oe. After the suppression of the *coup*, the *Kyojŏng Togam* continued its existence, only changing in function from the military to the administrative. It was in formality as the head of the *Kyojŏng Togam* that Ch'oe Ch'ung Hŏn ruled the kingdom. The *Kyojŏng Togam*, which became hereditary office, absorbed such important departmental works as personnel, censuring and part of revenue collection from the royal government, which in time atrophied into a kind of subordinate unit in the actual workings of the government. At the same time, significantly, the Ch'oe government began to employ civilian officials to deal with clerical matters. During the period of Ch'ung Hŏn's son, Ch'oe U (1219-1249), the second head of the *Kyojŏng Togam*, civilian officials, as their service became indispensable, were organized into a full-fledged department called *Chŏngbang* which chiefly handled personnel matters and communications with the royal government. It also lent itself to the permanency of the Ch'oe government.

The private army that served as the "claws and teeth" of the Ch'oe family was patterned after the *Tobang* that was first created by, and abolished upon the death of, Kyŏng Tae Sŭng. Ch'oe Ch'ung Hŏn's *Tobang* counted three thousand and later enlarged to a size about ten times that number. In addition to the duties of escorting and guarding the persons and private palaces of the Ch'oe family, it was during the Mongol invasion assigned to national defense, though occasionally. The military force with the sole purpose of national police and defense was organized by Ch'oe U. It was called *Sambyŏlch'o* or Three Special Units, which we shall see later. Ch'oe U also added a resplendently–equipped cavalry to the *Tobang* for ceremonial use. All this while, the royal army was active, of course, under Ch'oe's control, but it was surpassed in prowess, quality of arms, and, above all, pay by Ch'oe's private forces.

For the economic basis that supported his vast operations, Ch'oe Ch'ung Hŏn was assigned, in addition to the riches and estates already acquired, the Chinju area in modern South Kyŏngsang Province as his *sigŭp*. Chinju, where Ch'oe Ch'ung Hŏn seems to have served in some minor capacity before he seized power, was a substantially large administrative unit that embraced two counties (*kun*) and seven prefectures (*hyŏn*). And the taxes, which were collected by the agents of the *Kyojŏng Togam* but supposed to fill the national treasury, were often diverted to the Ch'oe family coffers, as when the Ch'oe were unable to pay the salaries of the family government officials.

The Ch'oe government came to be more fully developed in terms of organizational and administrative efficiency under Ch'oe U, as suggested above. Confident of his own power, Ch'oe U even condescended to return the properties his father confiscated by force to their former owners and to present the king with a variety of rare treasures. The officials of the royal government, a greater majority of whom were now Ch'oe appointees, had no recourse but to succumb to the Ch'oe power. Yet, interestingly enough, there is no evidence that usurpation of the throne was ever contemplated by the Ch'oe. Although the Ch'oe received a large number of exalted titles of nobility, the fact of their humble origin seemed simply unable to bear the charismatic veneration which the royalty now commanded of the people, probably including the Ch'oe themselves.

Social Unrest and Changes

Since Chŏng Chung Pu's overthrow of Ŭijong in 1170, more than a half century of the military management of the government brought in its wake a notable degree of changes in dynastic life; it resulted mainly from the reshuffle of wealth and social status. In the officialdom, the change was understandably sweeping and rigorous. All government posts, down to a local post station attendant's, were filled with military men. Civil officials who had somehow survived the consecutive purges voluntarily transferred to the military status to get new appointments. If thus the military became respectable again, a fact that constituted a major change in social climate, the increased number intensified rivalry among themselves, which required physical prowesses and quick maneuvers as prerequisite to survival and power. Mighty families came to rely on their family-maintained armies and, more often than not, put up naked fights for both political and economic gains.

As usual, wealth went with power. The use of such illegal means of concentrating wealth as usury and annexation through chicanery or by force of land owned by the weaker, which began to appear from the time of Yi Cha Kyŏm, became rampantly familiar during this period of naked force. The powerful military families, now great landowners, periodically let loose their private forces to "collect" arbitrarily-set taxes from peasants either in cooperation with government officials of in defiance of them. They seem to have generally picked their native districts as the base area from which to expand landholding. In the case of Chŏng Chung Pu, the base point was Haeju in modern Hwanghae Province, and his land expansion came into collision with that owned by Minister of Rites Yŏm Sin Yak. Subsequently, Minister Yŏm, who had the temerity to offer resistance, lost the job as well as the land. Lesser and provincial officials found it necessary to align with central mighties for survival. The peasants were a more unfortunate lot who found their produce carried off by two sources, while they were under the usual heavy loads of *corvée* service.

Hard-pressed peasants, as during previous periods of similar political and social unrest, rose in revolt, which characterized this period. Peasants, *ch'-ŏnmin*, and the lowest officials in revolt, sometimes, counted tens of thousands. Their slogans ranged from protest against the assassination of Ŭijong to revival of Silla or Paekche; their wrath, however, fell short of extending to those in the central government but upon their immediate tormentors around them. The military in power, including Ch'oe Ch'ung Hŏn who eventually terminated the endless series of uprisings, were generally conciliatory in dealing with the rebels. They often resorted to conferring honorary titles and ranks upon insurgent leaders or promoting recalcitrant villages or cities to a higher administrative unit—a *so,* a category of *ch'ŏnmin* villages, to a *hyŏn* (prefecture), for instance—as a means of settling the disturbances. Theirs were rather simple uprisings against corrupt local aristocrats, conniving magistrates, and lesser officials. It is worth noting that, as time progressed, the *ch'ŏnmin* class, mainly lowborn domestics and institutional slaves lashed out for their emancipation from hard labor and social stigma.

A classical *ch'ŏnmin* insurrection, though nipped in the bud, took place in 1198, which was led by one Manjŏk, a domestic slave of no other than the Ch'oe family. The portentous nature of the short-lived venture was indicated by the size of its force counting more than a few thousand slaves. Manjŏk rose before them at the clandestine initial gathering in a mountain north of Kaegyŏng and spoke:

> Since the wars of Kyŏng-kye [those of 1170 and 1173], the *ch'ŏnmin* class has turned out many noblemen of the state. No man is by birth a general or a minister. When time comes, any man can do the job. Why then should we put up with this physical toil under masters' cudgels?

They resolved to abolish the *ch'ŏnmin* class from the land by destroying their masters and burning the *ch'ŏnmin registers*. Upon this clean slate, they might do the jobs generals and ministers themselves. This was probably the most magnificent public speech on record of the Koryŏ dynasty. Unfortunately, the secret plan of action leaked out. For their temerity, Manjŏk and his cohorts were thrown into the river to drown.

Through these upheavals, however, they seem to have driven the point of protest home to the mind of the dynasty. A tremendous number of the *ch'ŏnmin* of all categories were appointed to governmental, that is, military, posts, if petty, on the basis of individual ability or some service well-rendered. This was one of the most conspicuous social phenomena in the late Koryŏ dynasty. It is significant to note that this upward social mobility, open to men of parts and ambition, regardless of social status, was frozen, as it were, by the foundation of the Yi dynasty with its own status system, but it was to reappear, if in a different mode, in the last half of the Yi dynasty when the ruling class spent its vitality.

In any case, the permanency of the Ch'oe government with a sufficient administrative mechanism and power *vis-à-vis* the shrunken royal authority, even though it was aberrant from the normal pattern, nevertheless prognosticated an interesting path the Koryŏ dynasty was to tread, which might have been a vigorous new Koryŏ with an elevated status of the military and a greater degree of social mobility. The possibility of such an idea, however, was nipped in the bud by invasions of the ferocious Mongols.

Mongol Invasions

By odd vicissitudes of the races, the nomadic hordes of North Asia, it now seemed, were given an empty stage, or indeed the whole world, to conquer and plunder. The Mongols, armed with the warlike mode of their existence on the open steppe, could yield and invincible power, provided that a strong leader could organize into the centralized system their disarrayed society plagued by chronic economic instability and intertribal rivalry. Temüjin, better known in history as Chinggis Khan (ca.1167-1227) was such a leader. With their number reaching not more than two and a half million then, the

Mongols under his leadership rose to rule most of the known world, the most spectacular performance which the world had ever witnessed.

With a penchant for organization and an unquenchable passion for conquest, Chinggis Khan by 1205 led his indomitable army of probably not more than 250,000 on his way to subjugate the world. The great Khan's well-trained personal cavalry, with fierce loyalty to him alone, could cover fifty to eighty miles a day, staying on horseback for an incredible length of time, probably up to ten days and nights at a stretch. During this period on the move, they lived on a meagre diet of animal milk and blood, probably lured by a vision of the next city where foods, riches, and women were theirs.

Probably a deeper secret, beside their incomparable skill and stamina in warfare, of their success in conquest and in maintaining the conquered territories was that they did not unreasonably insist on imposing their way of government upon the conquered peoples, but rather they let themselves be persuaded by local cultures. In short, the primitive nomads learned things quickly. In a short span of not more than twenty years, Chinggis Khan had done major conquests, enlisting services of the local political leaders, which constituted the groundwork for what was to become the largest empire in history.

By 1234 the Mongols in China wiped out the Chin and, after a decade of political uncertainty at Karakorum, the capital of all Mongols, they faced the Southern Sung. In 1231, before they completely extinguished the Chin, the Mongols invaded Koryŏ, the penultimate link to Japan, the eastern terminal for their conquest of North Asia.

The nomadic force under Salita met with strong resistance at such defense cities as Kyuju Chaju, and P'yŏngyang in the northwsest. The offensive-defensive battle at Kyuju, where General Kang Kam Ch'an annihilated the invading Khitans in 1019, was fought in the style of the Ansisŏng battle of 645, without success on the part of the attackers. Like the Khitans, Salita, leaving these impregnable cities behind, led his army directly to Kaegyŏng with a Korean named Hong Pok Wŏn as a guide who had voluntarily surrendered to the Mongols.

Some local magistrates in the face of the onrushing Mongols simply emptied their cities and towns, taking refugee into near-by islands with people under their responsibility, a move that proved extremely effective against the sea-shy nomads. The defense of the capital was a sorry affair; Ch'oe U, now in command, would not move a single squad of his well-fed army for national purpose. Instead, he let the royal government sue for peace before the Mongols hit the capital. Salita demanded an exorbitant amount of gifts, including 1,000 otters and 500 virgins preferably of aristocratic birth; this last item, though denied this time, became a standard fixture in the lists of Mongol demands thenceforth. With a satisfactory amount of gifts loaded, the Mongols withdrew, leaving behind "Daruhachi" or Mongol administrators in cities in the northwestern region.

Unlike such semi-sendentary nomads as Khitans and Jürched, the Mongols seemed impossible to be coaxed into a predictable pattern of behavior by the civilized diplomacy of the "humble words and generous gifts." They never even asked for a customary lord-vassal relation with Koryŏ but only for unlimited amount of gifts and occasions for looting. Thus, in anticipation of another mongol invasion, in 1232 Ch'oe U decided to evacuate the royal capital of about 500,000 to Kanghwa Island just off the mouth of the Han River, overriding some opposition. In this move, he was influenced by previous examples shown by local magistrates in the northwest. Ch'oe U also blandly ordered the whole people to take refugee into coastal islands or mountain strongholds. It was a determined move on the part of Ch'oe U, which seemed, however, more deeply motivated by his personal position. In international dealings, he might be hard put to persuade the Mongols to accept the anomaly of his family government; nor would he now be willing to tolerate even a nominal representation of the government by the monarch in dealing with the Mongols.

Soon after the evacuation of the capital to Kanghwa Island in 1232, Salit'a again pushed down southward. But indeed he was unable to do anything effective against the island capital, which lay, at the lowest ebb, not more than 100 yards away from the mainland coast. The Mongols demanded that the government move right back to where it was, while making plundering excursions where they would. On one of these trips, Salit'a was killed by an arrow shot by a monk. The leaderless invaders hurriedly withdrew from the country. Hong Pok Wŏn, the self-styled traitor, entrenching himself in P'yŏngyang, remained subservient to the Mongol influence. Eventually dislodged by the Ch'oe army, he fled to Liaotung where he was installed by the Mongols as an overseer of all Korean settlers in Manchuria. P'yŏngyang was emptied of people who were then forced to emigrate to islands.

The third invasion was coming in 1235, after the destruction of the Chin in the previous year. The invading hordes, this time, ignoring the Kanghwa government, carried on until 1239 the destruction in the best of Mongol-style that included not only looting and burning of cultural centers but also trampling under foot, and burning, of crops. Koryŏ was to receive four more such treatments until demise of the Ch'oe power in 1258.

It was a period of unbearable hardship and tragedy, especially for the common masses. In the 1254 invasion alone, more than 200,000 people were taken prisoner, beside the countless dead. Yet, it was the peasants and *ch'ŏnmin* who, if under capable leaders, fought the invaders off their cities and fortresses, while economically supporting the Kanghwa capital. The cultural loss was equally tragic; it was in this period that the splendor of Kyŏngju, the old capital of Silla, was really gone.

The Kanghwa Capital. Life in the temporary capital on the island went on seemingly undisturbed all this while. The layout and construction of the city, patterned in general scale and detail after Kaegyŏng, were carried out under a priority order. The defense system, by far the most important facilities, were first built more elaborately and solidly than those of Kaegyŏng. The national university, the royal ancestral shrine, *kujang* or "polo ground," and so on came into being at the end of a decade. Naval exercises around the island were occasionally seen. Cultural activities on the island were also held just as fully as before, a fact that the island's supply–economy was more than adequate. Some of the best celadon works were produced in this period.

Religious ceremonies and holidays were observed only more sumptuously or eagerly to win the help of Buddha and *Ch'ŏnji sinmyŏng*. To replace the first Tripitaka housed at the Puinsa near Taegu, which was carved during the Khitan invasion but had just been destroyed by the Mongols, the Kanghwa government started to cut in 1236, and finished in 1251, a much more comprehensive Tripitaka of 81,137 wood blocks engraved on both sides. Undoubtedly, the project was undertaken with a tenacious cultural pride as against nomadic barbarism. This so-called Great Eighty Thousand Tripitaka of Koryŏ, also known as the Tripitaka Koreana, indeed the greatest of its kind anywhere, is preserved intact at the Haeinsa in South Kyŏngsang Province, and its wood blocks are occasionally used for printing today.

The political situation at the Kanghwa court, as might be expected, was deteriorating into the polarization of views and opinions. With no military solution of the situation in sight, the civil officials became increasingly influential at the court. The attrition of the productive class the destructive presence of the Mongols in the mainland, which had sharply reduced agricultural yields, put the military on the defensive. The issue at stake was whether the war should be continued with the military in power or the civilian argument for capitulation to the Mongols and restoration of the royal authority should be followed. Time was on the latter's side. Thus, the assassination in 1258 of Ch'oe Ŭi, the last of the Ch'oe, engineered by the royalists, settled the matter for peace. The return of power to Kojong (1214–1259) followed immediately.

The Mongol troops were not in the country at this time. Their main forces under Khubilai, the ablest of Chinggis' grandsons, were fighting it out with the Southern Sung. To sue for peace, Kojong sent his crown prince to China where he met Khubilai. Khubilai was then on his way to Karakorum, after a hurriedly arranged truce with the Southern Sung, upon the death of Great Khan Mangu. Having defeated a brother who claimed the throne there, he simply assumed title of Great Khan in 1260. It was after this settlement that Khubilai Khan paid attention to the Korean affairs. At Khubilai's repeated request, Wŏnjong (1260–1274) paid a visit with him at his winter capital Peking in 1264, thus making himself the first reigning monarch who ever left the country in person on a diplomatic mission. Koryŏ had been forced to destroy the defense wall at Kangwha as a gesture of submission. The Mongolian Khan who knew, to his credit, of the historical fact of the Chinese failure in the conquest of Koguryŏ seven centuries before, did not conceal his pleasure at the Korean monarch's coming to him to surrender. Thereupon, he solved impending postwar questions generally in Koryŏ's favor.

The Revolt of the Sambyŏlch'o

Kanghwa's internal politics since the fall of the Ch'oe were far from set-tled, however. If the military as a whole acquiesced in the elimination of the inept Ch'oe Ŭi, that was because he failed in his leadership. The hard-core military never really came to terms with the idea of complete restoration of the royal authority, still less of the unconditional surrender to the Mongols. Soon they were on the offensive again.

Im Yŏn, representing the extreme right of the military, removed Kim Chun who went along with the peace group. In 1269 he moved to dethrone Wŏnjong who, in their view, seemed an ally of the Mongols, that he was. But Wŏnjong was reinstated in a few months by Khubilai's determined interven-tion on behalf of his protégé. This was the first occasion on which a Korean monarch was saved by a foreign power, a significant incident that influenced political thinking even after the period of Mongol domination. With Khubilai solidly behind him, Wŏngjong ordered the immediate return of the govern-ment and people to the mainland. But Im Yu Mu, now in command of the military after Im Yŏn, still stuck to anti-Mongolism, only to be overthrown by the royalists.

The general distrust of the Mongols, deepened through a generation of nomadic barbarism, was indicated by the reluctance with which the people obliged the royal order to return from the islands. And the Sambyŏlch'o (Three Special Units), which had become a kind of the cat's paw of the mili-tary group in the government, would not move from Kanghwa at all. As has been noted, they were organized during the era of Ch'oe U. To the two origi-nal units with the duties of policing and patrolling was added during the war the third which was organized solely with those who escaped from captivity under the Mongols. These special forces were in time turned into multi-pur-pose task forces specialized in defense of Kanghwa and guerrilla-like assaults upon the Mongol forces. They were also invariably used in the successive coups after the fall of the Ch'oe. Their ultimate loyalty, though paid by the royal government and patronized by those in power, seems to have been deternmined by their own fierce anti-Mongolism which had indeed justified their existence. Upon informed of their abolition by Wŏnjong, the Sambyŏlch'o men chose to revolt.

In 1270, having formed themselves into the semblance of a government, the Sambyŏlch'o under the leadership of General Pae Chung Son decided to try their fortune elsewhere. They forced the Kanghwa people who had not yet left the island into 1,000 odd ships with their properties and left for Chindo, near the erstwhile base island of Chang Po Ko of Silla, off the south-western tip of the Peninsula. There they immediately brought under control some thirty islands and some inland cities as well and threatened to build a Chang Po Ko–style empire.

In the eyes of Khubilai more than anyone else, this was a serious development. Khubilai, now Shih Tsu of Yüan, the dynastic name adopted by the Mongol amidst the campaigns against the Southern Sung, had kept his eye on the island of Cheju for its strategic importance with regard to the conquest of Japan as well as the Southern Sung. Naturally, the presence of the Sambyŏlch'o forces in the Chindo area was a threat that might interfere with his scheme. Yüan Shih Tsu's interest in Cheju seems to have been quite deep-seated, as we shall see.

An allied expeditionary force of Koryŏ and Yüan was ordered to dislodge the Chindo group. It seems that to Yüan Shih Tsu this expedition was not just for extinguishing a rebel force but the very departure for invasion of Japan and reinforcement of the forces in South China. Yüan had already forced Koryŏ to start building 1,000 ships which might be used either against Japan or for the war with the Southern Sung. And Yüan stationed some of its troops in cities near the capital and deployed others along the southern coast. Yüan did this on the basis of the *t'nn-t'ën*-style or self-supporting, permanent military colony, overriding Koryŏ's strong protest.

In the initial stage of the campaigns against the Chindo rebels, the allied forces found them well prepared. Their quick maneuvers and high morale did not allow the allied forces with superior strength and weapons—firearms—to launch a decisive attack. Only with the reinforcements under Kim Pang Kyŏng, one of the great generals of the late Koryŏ period, and his Mongol counterpart, Hsintu, who replaced a hydrophobic predecessor, could they destroy the Chindo stronghold but after two years of engagement. Still a substantial number of the Sambyŏlch'o rebels escaped to Cheju where they harassed the pursuing armies for another year until 1273 when the hard-core leaders killed themselves.

For all its persistence, anti-Mongolism of the Sambyŏlch'o was a lost cause from the start. But it represented the other side of the Korean mind which was stirred by the unspeakable savagery and barbarian ignorance of the Mongols into a quite distinct nationalism, as reflected in the carving of the Great Eighty Thousand Tripitaka and other historical and literary writings of

the period. It was also reflected, above all, in the heroic fighting and persever-
ence displayed by the common masses, of which the *Sambyŏlch'o* men were
a part.

The Mongols. A battle scene.

3

The Mongol Domination

One day, after the suppression of the *Sambyŏlch'o* rebellion, the two comrades-in-arms, Koryŏ General Kim Pang Kyŏng and Mongol General Hsintu enjoyed a moment together in Kaegyŏng. Presently, Hsintu caught a young sparrow, and, after playing with it awhile, he clubbed it to death. Then he asked Kim Pang Kyŏng what he thought of the performance. General Kim said: Hsintu's act would have been for the assuagement of farmers' distress caused by these birds that pecked at the grain. Nay, the Mongol said: the Koreans, like the Chinese, could read and believed in Buddha. They contemptuously looked down at the Mongols as barbarians who made a profession of killing, thinking that the Heaven would loathe them. But, he continued, the very Heaven bestowed it upon the Mongols; therefore, they simply accepted it, and the Heaven would not regard killing as sin. That was the reason why Koreans were now made to serve the Mongols.

The late Koryŏ people who were to be dominated by a people like this for a century were reportedly a hard lot. But Koryŏ had never been an easy enemy even for the Mongols. During a forty-year period of intermittent wars, the Mongols were forced to abandon the idea of terror-striking take-over of Koryŏ as they would have liked to. Of the Mongols who came to respect Koryŏ for its outrageously long and tenacious resistance, Khubilai was simply glad that Koryŏ capitulated at all. Even after the subjugation of Koryŏ, the knowledge of Koryŏ's military and cultural strength was a constant reference point in their formulation of Koryŏ policies, which were carefully developed with political experiences gained from ruling China. Koryŏ, on the other hand, having once let go of its will to resist, gradually failed to present a united front against the Mongol exploitation and subsequently mired itself in the political and cultural disarray caused by Mongol manipulation.

By the time of the official conclusion of peace with the Mongols, Koryŏ had found itself geographically much shrunken. In 1258 a group of rebels in the northeastern province (the southern half of modern South Hamgyŏng Province), taking advantage of a *coup* then in Kanghwa which ended the Ch'oe regime, killed the military commander of the region and surrendered to the invading Mongols. The Mongol government placed this region directly under its administrative control. In 1269 a similar incident occurred, this time, in the northwestern province. A rebel force, also availing themselves of a political crisis resulting from the dethronement of pro-Mongol Wŏnjong, surrendered to the Mongols after elimination of the key officials in the area. Thereupon, the Mongols in 1270 annexed this region roughly covering modern North and South P'yŏng'an Provinces. In 1273 the Mongols unilaterally annexed the island of Cheju, which was eventually turned into an open pasture, its potential strategic values having been sharply reduced by subsequent military developments. The latter two territories were returned in the 1290's at Koryŏ's protest, and the first one was taken back by the force of arms much later.

The Cheng-tung hsing-sheng. Yüan's immediate order of business with Koryŏ was on the matter of cooperation of the two countries for the subjugation of Japan. The Koryŏ court, weary of war, did its best to make both sides meet each other halfway. It urged the Hōjō family government of Japan to enter into friendly relations with the Yüan, while roundly suggesting to Yüan the danger of treacherous seas. The desire for more conquest of the Mongols and the parochial pride of the Japanese proved to be uncompromising, to Koryŏ's chagrin

The first expeditionary force of 25,000, to which Koryŏ was forced to contribute several thousand men and 900 ships, was dispatched from the port of modern Masan in South Kyŏngsang Province in 1274. In two weeks, the invading forces landed on Hakata Bay in North Kyūshū after wiping out the Japanese forces in the intervening islands of Tsushima and Iki. After the initial success in landing, the invaders were shaken up by what the Japanese call *kamikaze* or divine winds drowning nearly a half of them. The second invasion was postponed until after the complete conquest of the Southern Sung in 1279.

In 1280 Yüan Shih Tsu set up the *Cheng-tung hsing-sheng* (*Chŏngdong Haengsŏng* in Korean) or Forward Chancellery for Conquest of East in Kaegyŏng to deal with the Japanese matter and appointed Koryŏ King Ch'ungnyŏl (1275-1308) as its head. The second invasion in 1281 was of a much larger force of 140,000 with missile-flinging catapults as the star weapon. The expeditionary forces were launched both from China and from Korea. Given a six-year interval, the Japanese were prepared too. At Hakata Bay where they had built a defense wall, the individualistic Japanese warriors kept the invaders at bay for two months. Then, again, the *kamikaze* did the rest of the job for the islanders.

Yüan Shih Tsu made at least one more serious attempt at Japan but was dissuaded by domestic problems. But the *Cheng-tung hsing-sheng* remained unabolished; instead, it was transformed into a branch of the Yüan government in Koryŏ that came to exercise administrative power over the internal affairs of the Koryŏ government. It had its own subordinate offices that dealt with military and legal problems concerning Yüan personnel and interests in Koryŏ. The existence of such a powerful foreign agency, alongside the royal government, as might be expected, fostered a schism in the ruling class. With the protective backing of the *Hsing-sheng*, the pro-Yüan aristocrat–politicians did not hesitate to do business, whenever possible, directly with the Yüan court for personal gains.

Another Yüan-created agency, that further impaired the inner unity of Koryŏ, was the so-called Kingship of Shenyang, Shenyang being a strategic city in southern Manchuria. The Kingship of Shenyang was created in 1308 purportedly to look after the Koreans living in the Liaotung area. The Koreans there were of mixed categories ranging from permanent settlers to forced immigrants to those who drifted there during the war, numbering in time more than 100,000. Hong Pok Wŏn had been appointed their overseer. A prince or a former king of Koryŏ was now appointed king of Shenyang, as the Yüan appears to have intended, to impose a political check upon the king of Koryŏ. Indeed, the king of Shenyang, surrounded by politicians of doubtful sincerity, would make maneuvers, in collusion with interested officials at the Yüan court, causing at times serious embarrassments for Koryŏ.

The Disruptive Influence of the Mongols

One of the casualties of the Mongol presence was the royal family itself, whose demoralization caused by its marriage relations with the Khan family was a disheartening phenomenon of the period. It was at Wŏnjong's request that then Khubilai Khan, with considerable reluctance for several years, consented to the marriage of his daughter to the crown prince of Koryŏ; an arrangement through which Wŏnjong aimed to strengthen his authority at home somehow became the precedent for seven successive kings who occupied the throne during the period of Mongol domination. Khubilai's qualm over Wŏnjong's proposal might have been of the slighted pride of a conqueror who, if anyone, ought to take women of the conquered as wives of slaves. Instead, the Khan family required the married Koryŏ crown princes to stay with them until their ascension to the throne. In this period of sojourn at the Yüan court, they became little less sons-in-law of the Mongol imperial family than Koryŏ kings-to-be. Thus emasculated at the hands of conflicting duties and cultures, they became a passive, strangely inept products of the circumstances.

As kings, they were not allowed usual honorific and posthumous titles that had been on a parity with the Mongol emperors, and their government was reorganized on a smaller scale with the less elated designations of offices. Stripped of power and prestige and often harried by family troubles caused by their Mongol consorts, they found little authority to exercise for the formulation and implementation of national policies. King Ch'ungsŏn (1309–1313), the ablest monarch in this period with ambitious plans for political and economic reforms, found himself in every reform move blocked by aristocratic officials with vested interests and connections with the *Cheng-tung hsing-sheng* or even the Yüan court. Easing himself out of the throne, he returned to Peking where he engaged in the innocuous business of scholarly pursuit. His Man'gwŏndang or the Hall of Ten Thousand Volumes provided an intellectual forum for great scholars of Koryŏ and the Yüan.

The absence of *the* responsible authority at the top precipitated political and economic disintegration. The government's administrative ability, which had been deteriorating for more than a century could no longer maintain more than a skeleton of administrative mechanism. Especially, the complicated land administration had in all probability disappeared by the late thirteenth century. Most of the arable land was divided among the unscrupulous officials of aristocratic background with vested interests in the continuation of the dynasty. The royal family was by far the largest landowner who had 360 estates scattered over the country; kings created fellow estate owners, as it were, by randomly granting generous portions of the government land to their favorite subjects for real of fictitious services, thus fortifying the tenuous positions of their own. The borders of some of these estates, enlarged also through the means that we are now familiar with, are said to have been determined, by the middle of the fourteenth century, not by the measured lines of surveyors but by "mountains and rivers."

Most severely victimized by the blurred authority in government and the opportunism of aristocrat-officials were, needless to say, the common masses. They found themselves exploited by government officials, local estate owners, and Yüan agents. The Yüan court was notorious for its endless demands upon the Koryŏ court of various materials ranging from precious metals, insam, textile fabrics, grains, celadons, and falcons to eunuchs and nubile maids. The burden of meeting these demands, of course, fell upon the peasants; the collection of the last item, for instance, caused them tragic distress. The custom of early marriage might have originated from these crises.

One of the exceptions was Ki Cha O of Haeju whose daughter, upon being "presented" to Yüan Huei Tsung, somehow made her way to the position of the empress. The Ki family were showered titles of nobility and wealth by the Yüan and Koryŏ courts, and their impudence annoyed the royal family, with impunity.

Hard-pressed by demands for taxes and labor service from three sources and, more often than not, imposed upon in advance the "taxes" which they were supposed to pay for next few years, peasants fled. Most of these displaced farmers were absorbed into private estates which were, therefore, never short of labor force and could expand further. Many others, including local men of ambition to establish elsewhere, it is interesting to note, headed northward. Running the gauntlet of border magistrates with the Prohibitory law for border crossing, they moved to northern provinces now under the Yüan administration and to southern Manchuria where they were welcomed by the labor-short Yüan government. There, at least, they were guaranteed one government to which the tax might be paid. The founding house of the Yi dynasty was among these drifters who moved to the northeastern region.

Amid deteriorating affairs of the dynastic life, there was a new class of people emerging, beginning from the early fourteenth century. They were lesser bureaucrats newly entering government service through the civil examination. They were strongly Confucian-oriented and mostly of provincial origin. They made up the intellectual and economic middle class of sorts, even though some of them were without much inherited land. Since the government could no longer regularly pay salaries, they tended to be disinterested observers of the declining dynasty. In general, this new breed of officials were descendants of the local aristocracy of the early period who had so far kept themselves remote from the seat of power.

As we have seen, the Koryŏ court's basic approach toward the centralization in the beginning was to acknowledge, rather than to break up, the traditional political influence of old local families. They were appointed to the posts of local governments; although the court chipped off their power and privileges through a series of reorganizations of the local government system in past centuries, they still wielded substantial influence in their respective localities, especially when the central government became ineffective. Economically, they were by and large holders of modest of small areas of land which they had been able to protect from the outside encroachments. By the early fourteenth century, they aspired increasingly to participate in the government through the examination system. The emergence of this provincial class of intellectual-politicians, whose number was much larger than generally believed to be, was a most portentous political phenomenon of the late Koryŏ period, for they were circumstantially brought together to help disintegrate the dynasty.

4

The Development of Buddhism and Confucianism

Having been little adversely affected by the political and military turmoil of the past one and a half centuries, the two great religions, Buddhism and Confucianism, if the latter can be called a religion, with deeply-ramified roots in government and society at large, developed to an interesting contrast in the late Koryŏ period. Although Koryŏ Buddhism had steadily been reinforced in theological and ecclesiastical fields, it now began to decline as a religion. Confucianism, on the other hand, was rising with and exuberant vitality drawn from its new philosophical synthesis, known as Neo-Confucianism, consummated largely by Chu Hsi in the eleventh century. Like the *yang* element in the *yin-yang* interaction, it was soon to engulf Buddhism in temporal as well as spiritual leadership.

The Development of Sŏn Buddhism

Monk Ŭich'ŏn's attempt at sectarian unity in the late eleventh century was a success in that Wŏnhyo's philosophical advocation of sectarian harmony was carried into practice, a practice that became a tradition in major Buddhist movements thenceforth. One of the interesting movements in the Ŭich'ŏn-style was launched by Sŏn Monk Chinul (1157-1210). Whereas Ŭich'ŏn tried to unite major Kyo and Sŏn sects under the Ch'ŏnt'ae doctrine, one of the Kyo sects, Chinul attempted it from the Chogye, that is, Sŏn, point of view.

Chinul's emphasis was on sudden enlightenment into the Buddha mind, which is the source of all forms of life in the universe and, therefore, inherent in all human beings. Enlightenment is to "see" this Buddha-nature in one's self which, defying all specific descriptions, transcends into the realm of ultimate Emptiness. Chinul, also known as Pojo Kuksa (National Teacher Pojo), availing himself of the *Diamond Sutra* for his purpose, seems to have identified this Emptiness with what the Flower Garland (Hwaŏm) sect calls the Void or the realm of Principle, its actual aspect being the realm of Fact. Enlightenment, which is the intuitive ability to identify oneself with this Emptiness or Void, is by no means the achievement of buddhahood itself but only a beginning. One should also follow the path of gradual cultivation of religious life guided by Perfect Wisdom until death, an event which is becoming a Buddha. While on the path of gradual cultivation, one might engage, Chinul allowed, in addition to the Sŏn method of maintaining oneself in that Void of noumenon, also in scriptural or metaphysical studies and deliberations, thereby providing the basis for uniting the Kyo sects into the Sŏn or Chogye sect. He even regarded the concentration on *yŏmbul* (*nenbutsu* in Japanese) or invocation and repetition of Amita's name, which is the feature Pure Land salvationism, as helpful to the gradual cultivation for enlightenment.

Like Ŭich'ŏn, Chinul promoted the intersectarian studies through discourse and writing, if with an emphasis on the Chogye doctrine. In his movement, Chinul was strongly supported by the Ch'oe family probably with political reason that the Kyo sects, especially the Ch'ŏnt'ae and Hwaŏm sects, had been patronized by the royal and pre-*coup* aristocratic families in general. Iconoclastic Sŏn tenets, being "not founded on letters of theories," might have been palatable to the militarily-oriented men and period with less or no taste in Kyo metaphysics.

In any case, the Chogye sect after Chinul, with one foot always in some of the Kyo scriptures, became firmly established as the main support of Korean Buddhism. The original nine Sŏn groups, though lumped together under the name of Chogye, nevertheless remained more of less separate families. Sŏn Monk T'aego or Pou Kuksa (National Teacher Pou) (1301-1382) and one of his great contemporaries, Naong, endeavored to reinvigorate Chogyeism by lessening ecclesiastical differences among Sŏn groups. And, towards the end of the dynasty, there also arose several minor new sects which enjoyed existence even into the Yi dynasty period.

The Buddhist Economy

The status of the Buddhist church as the most privileged landowner had underscored its importance in society as the spiritual guardian of the dynasty. The church's economic power and privileges provided for an infinite possibility of secular activities, to which, as noted, the church had readily succumbed. Although the church under the leadership of many a scholastic monk had endeavored to strengthen divine economy as much, its wide–ranging investments in mundane economy, accompanied by flagrant abuses of its privileges, proved not only its own undoing but also a strong contributing factor to the demise of the dynasty itself.

Economically–astute monks managing monasterial estates and commercial activities were never behind their secular counterparts. Only they were in a more advantageous position, for people were always willing donators to the temples. Peasants with an intention of committing their small land to an estate to escape the taxes found the monasterial estates more congenial. There they were, as on any private estates, expected to officially reclassify themselves as serf or a similar category. But it is likely that they were less exploited there and plus assurance of salvation. Buddhists' profit–making ventures were also extremely enterprising; the major commercial undertaking, that further aggrandized the church's wealth, consisted of brewery, money lending, stock raising, horse breeding, apiculture, dealing in surplus grain and salt, and all this, inspite of government prohibition.

The list of clerical irregularities and excesses went longer. There were intersectarian squabbles in which a more influential sect might bring under its own ecclesiastical control monasteries and land belonging to another. Politically–inclined monks dabbled in the court intrigues. Others freely intermingled with laymen, ate meat, and enjoyed women. The Buddhist plethora of these extracurricular activities at times mounted to serious proportions, irreparably damaging the image of Buddha in the eyes of the society at large. Yet temples and monasteries were ever on the increase in number; so were ostentatious ceremonies and festivals at such frequent intervals that arrogantly attested to the church's affluence.

Great, majestic complexes of monasterial buildings spread themselves out in mountain valleys that included, in addition to the main halls, administrative offices, warehouses, and probably brewery facilities at corners guarded by the monk–soldiers. Indeed, these Buddhist establishments adumbrated the halls of certain secular power that ate right into the government revenue and social morality. To the newly–emerging class of Confucian intellectual–officials who were forced to do without even salaries, they had to go.

The Rise of Confucianism

Although, despite official policies for its dissemination, Confucianism had been less popularized than Buddhism throughout the Koryŏ dynasty, it was a surging force ever. With the import of Chinese political philosophy and institutions, Confucianism had firmly been assured of its future in Korea. The civil service examination, the national education system, and the private institutes of learning had steadily produced Confucianists, Confucianism-oriented bureaucrats, and intellectuals. Up until the end of the thirteenth century, however, one's Chinese learning was measured largely by the ability to compose essays and poems in Chinese as the occasion demanded. This was by no means exclusively a Confucian feat, for Buddhist monks might do better, all Buddhist literature being written in Chinese. Now the study of Confucian classics as philosophy began to be gradually encouraged by the government and a number of established scholar-officials during the period of the Mongol domination.

The period of the Mongol domination was also the period in which the cultural exchange between Korea and China was most actively carried out. As the Mongols opened China to the Western contact, Chinese cultural and technological achievements marked notable imprints on the West Asians and, through them, the Europeans. Arabian merchants, on the other hand, seem to have dominated the East-West traffic in commerce which was instrumental in the flow of cultural exchanges. Koryŏ was the easternmost beneficiary of this flow, with increased knowledge in astronomy, medicine, art, etc. of West Asian origin. The cotton cultivation and the gunpowder for firearms were also significant imports from the Yüan in this period.

In this cosmopoplitan background, Kŏryo's cultural emphasis was on learning and scholarship. A notable phenomenon in scholarship was an increase in historical writing, of which the aforementioned *Samguk yusa* by Monk Iryŏn and the *Chewang un'gi* or *Rhymed History of Kings* by Yi Sŭng Hyu (1224–1300), both extant, are the most important works. The interest in history-writing in this period is is of historical significance, as it seems to have been strongly motivated by Koryŏ's assertion of national dignity as against the Mongol barbarism. King Ch'ungnyŏl (1275–1308) reorganized the national university system. He added several new buildings and established the funds for scholarships for students and seven professorships in Chinese classics and history. He also set up the Institute of Teaching Classics and History for officials below the seventh grade. King Ch'ungsŏn's establishment of the Hall of Ten Thousand Volumes and the aforementioned upsurge of provincial scholarship may be seen in the context of this intellectual ferment. But one of the most important events in the Korean intellectual history occasioned in the late thirteenth century was the introduction of a newly-formalized Confucian philosophical system, known as Neo-Confucianism, and its far-reaching influence in the subsequent cultural development cannot be overemphasized.

Neo-Confucianism

The synthesis of traditional Chinese thoughts into Neo-Confucianism by the Southern Sung scholars during the eleventh and twelfth centuries was the intellectual achievement of the greatest magnitude in the Chinese history. This great scholastic accomplishment was initiated characteristically by scholar-officials with paramount interest in Confucian political philosophy. In their government service of scholarly endeavors, they had dedicated themselves to the re-creation of that idealized society of sage-kings. As Confucius and Mencius expounded, they believed that a just government was a moral institution with the governing principle based on the Confucian human relationships and virtues. Although the classics were much referred to, the scholar-officials drew more heavily upon the *Mencius* as the philosophical basis for political actions and reforms. As Mencius put an extraordinary emphasis on the monarch as moral leader with the responsibility for the economic well-being of the people, the problem of kingship had become an essential focus of their attention: debates on governmental and social innovations as such were often relegated to a level secondary to the clarification of the ways of ways of the sage-king, to which the historical scholarship, another aspect of the intellectual concern of the scholar-officials, was also unsparingly devoted. This was not to obscure the importance of other problems in Neo-Confucian thought, however. Political and economic reforms, social and ethical problems, and history compilations were handled with equal fervor within their philosophical perspective.

It is worthwhile to note that the resurgence of Confucian tradition during the Sung period was stimulated partly by a long domination in the ideological realm of Taoism and Buddhism, and, from them, some cosmological concepts and terminology were appropriated, as the discussions of the Confucian thought ventured into the final metaphysical synthesis. But Neo-Confucians believed in, and reaffirmed, the ultimate reality of Confucian humanism. Indeed, their movement was predicated upon the superiority of man-centered Confucian thought over its two ideological rivals.

Chu Hsi-ism. Neo-Confucian metaphysics, as developed by successive generations of the Sung and Ming scholars, were branched into two schools: the School of Principle or Reason and the School of Mind or Intuition. The latter, that placed emphasis on the promptness of mind or the consciousness in its perfect purity as its name suggests, reached its maturity in the early sixteenth century when it found the greatest champion in Wang Yang-ming (1472-1529). The former, the School of Principle, perfected by Chu Hsi in the late twelfth century, was made the Neo-Confucian orthodoxy. This idealistic philosophy has been also known as the School of *Li* (*I* in Korean, meaning reason) or of Ch'eng-Chu, because Ch'eng Yi of the celebrated Ch'eng brothers was thought to be a great proponent beside Chu Hsi, or simply Chu Hsi-ism or Chu-tzu-ism because Master Chu was regarded as the final synthesizer. It was this Chu Hsi-ism that made its way into Korea and Japan where it swayed the academic scene until the beginning of the nineteenth century.

Chu Hsi (1130-1200), a perfect Confucian both in private life and in public conduct, was a subtle, discriminating thinker. His greatness lies in the clarification, as from those of Taoism and Buddhism, of Neo-Confucian philosophical concepts which individual thinkers had developed and in their final organization into a vast, coherent system of thought. His scholarly erudition, combined with penetrating insight, resulted in a tremendous amount of literary and philosophical writings, giving new interpretations on almost all aspects of the Confucian classics. The *Chu-tzu-ch'uan-shu* or *Complete Works of Chu-tzu*, especially his commentaries on the Four Books in it which he thought to be the most important of his works, became the basic text of Neo-Confucianism.

As Chu Hsi examined the universe objectively, not subjectively as the School of Mind did later, many variant concepts of man and nature were better defined and arranged in their proper places in the Neo-Confucian metaphysical system. The basic cosmological concepts of Neo-Confucianism are rational principles, *li* or reason and *ch'i* (*ki* in Korean) or matter. The *li* exists in heaven, earth, and myriad things, determining the nature which makes what they ought to be. Objects like house of even abstract concepts like sovereign-subject relationship have their respective *li* which constitute their nature. These *li* in their cosmic operations partake of an all-embracing principle called *T'ai-chi* (*T'ae-gŭk* in Korean), usually translated the Great Ultimate. The Great Ultimate, being immanent in all things, is the *li* in its highest attribute and highest summation, transcending all particulars, a concept that bears a certain affinity to some of central doctrines of Taoism and Buddhism. Neo-Confucianists, for a broader use, named the *li* the *tao* (way), the character *tao* of Taoism.

What makes the *li* different from being either Buddhistic or Taoistic is its dynamic, creative activities with the *ch'i*. Things come into being as the *li* provides the *ch'i*, or matter, or physical principle with the plan of a thing in particular, or rather as the *ch'i* acts upon the *li*. In other words, the Great Ultimate "rides" on the physical principle to create an object, imparting itself to that object as its *il*. The question of priority of these two elements, that is, of which one of them "rides" on the other was a matter of controversy. Debates on this question constituted a great intellectual exercise among the Yi dynasty thinkers, as we shall see later.

As the *li* and the *ch'i* create things, the *yin* and the *yang* or the negative and positive forces within a thing interact and the five elements are created. Interrelation and interaction among these principles, forces, and elements are explained with highly subtle, elaborate metaphysical laws, which are worked out to a remarkable intellectual feat. But to the Neo–Confucian scholars, far more important than the mere philosophical explanation of the workings of the principles was the exposition in terms of metaphysical law of human nature, ethical and political problems, social relations, etc., that is, the practical, temporal matters that were uppermost in the Confucian mind.

As applied to the matters of the government as a moral institution under a moral leader, the theory of the *li* served its purpose well. The *li* (*tao*) of the government, as the *li* is pure and changeless, must have been there from eternity, whether rulers have practiced it or not. Since the Confucian belief that the ancient sage–kings practiced this *li* (*tao*) was the unquestioned premise, the government of sage–kings and the society under them must have been what they ought to be, hence necessarily good. The ideal government and society of ancient sage–kings can be re–created here and now if only the ruler and the subjects followed the *li* of government, of one's self, of social relations, and so on. Political reform, therefore, is an attempt to bring the government as close to its *li* as possible.

On the personal and religious level, the theory of *li* and *ch'i* smothered the realism of Hsün–tzu who held that human nature was evil. Although both Hsün–tzu and Mencius had faith in the perfectibility of human nature through self–cultivation and education, it was Mencius' view of human nature as innately good that was upheld. The *li* of humanity, of which individual man's *li* partakes, must be good, regardless of time and place. What makes a man different from another is because of his *ch'i*, (matter), or, in this case, his physical endowment which contains his *li*. A sage is the man who is endowed with a *ch'i* which is clear so that his *li.*, like a pearl, may shine as it should, whereas an evil man is the one whose *li*, having been endowed with a "murky" *ch'i*, is like a pearl lying in the murky water. There must be an infinite shades between the clearness of a sage's *ch'i* and the "murkiness" of an evil man's. As the muddy water can be cleared, so can an evil man be rehabilitated through education and selfcultivation.

The final goal of one's education and self–cultivation is to possess his *li* in its original state, thus to be one with the Principle that "rules all," the highest state of being, that is, one's harmonious awareness of the will of Heaven, which Confucius attained at the age of seventy, as we have seen. Chu Hsi, a consummate product of his own idealistic philosophy, emphasized, as a means of achieving that state, "the extension of knowledge through the investigation of things," which is the best known phrase in the *Great Learning*, one of the Four Books. The introspective meditation is another important method of self–cultivation, which was no less emphasized by all Neo–Confucianists. It is worth noting that Chu Hsi's Confucian moment of revelation seemed nothing other than a sudden enlightenment of Ch'an Buddhism itself, for he said, "When one has exerted oneself for a long time, finally one morning a complete understanding will open with a sudden flash before him..., every exercise of mind will be marked by complete enlightenment." * Yet Chu Hsi's enlightenment was not a mystical union with the ultimate Emptiness but a moral ecstasy excited by apprehending through the persistent exercise of mind the universal order and the harmony of things.

For the introduction into Koryŏ of Chu Hsi-ism, two scholar officials, An Hyang (1243–1306) and his contemporary, Paek I Chŏng, were traditionally given the credit. An Hyang also did much to revive the national education in Confucianism for the spread of Chu Hsi-ism through his official capacity, while Paek I Chŏng as a scholar introduced young promising scholars to Chu Hsi-ism. Although many great scholars in Neo-Confucianism appeared in the last days of the Koryŏ dynasty, Chu Hsi-ism's philosophical maturity and nation-wide practice came with the establishment of the Yi dynasty. In the meantime, Chu Hsi-ism provided the ideological grit for the inevitable reform movements which were geared, as it turned out, to reforming the dynasty out of existence.

Portrait of An Hyang, who introduced Neo-Confucianism to Korea.

---

* Yu-lan Fung, A *Short History of Chinese Philosophy*, p. 306.

5

The Reform Movement and Dynastic Change

The Koryŏ dynasty had long shown all signs of lost vitality. Necessary reforms, especially, if it was to survive, an economic reconstruction of the dynasty, were hopelessly overdue. As has been noted, King Ch'ungsŏn attempted at a sweeping reform, but he was frustrated by landed conservatives with the political backing of the Yüan court. But about the middle of the fourteenth century, the Mongol grip on Koryŏ or, for that matter, on China too, was fast loosening.

In China, it was the transitional period in which the Yüan gave way to the Ming. The solidarity of the Mongols as the ruling class in China actually began deteriorating after the death of Khubilai Khan in 1294. Corrupted by wealth and peace, the Mongols by the 1340's were no longer the world conquering nomads. They were torn by internal dissensions aroused chiefly by succession struggles. They were isolated from the Chinese people, who, hit by consecutive famines in the 1350's, now rose in revolt. The first revolt against their Mongol overlord was ignited by a secret religious sect known as White Lotus Society, which first appeared in modern Anhwei Province. Drawing its beliefs verbatim from Taoism and Buddhism, the group claimed to be able to communicate with the spirits, through which they allegedly did miracles such as curing the sick. They wore red bands in combat, hence the Red Band Rebels. Pursued by the Mongols, the Red Band Rebels ran into the Koryŏ territory in 1359 and again in 1361. On the latter occasion they even occupied Kaegyŏng for a while. In China there were many other groups claiming for the Mandate of Heaven. The Mongols in the 1360's were no longer a power to be reckoned with. The wars for supremacy were waged among the "group of heroes," that is, rebel leaders themselves, who, all of humble origin, had built their personal following in various regions.

King Kongmin (1352-1374), even though, like his predecessors, he was a Yüan-supported king, was to grasp this chance for reform, which meant, among other things, a direct defiance to the Yüan. The Koryŏ government could still muster, when determined, enough military strength with improved weapons to deal with internal and external threats. Probably because of having tolerated a greater measure of vertical social mobility, notably a rise of the *ch'ŏnmin* class, the late Koryŏ enjoyed an unusual degree of political stability resulting from the conspicuous absence of peasant disturbances that characterized the declining period of the previous dynasty. But the rigid conservative core of the ruling class failed to rally around King Kongmin in his attempt at the general reform and to take the initiative over the rising Confucian bureaucrats.

The Reforms of King Kongmin

King Kongmin was by all accounts a sensitive artist rather than an innovative ruler; nevertheless, he embarked on a rough course of remaking the dynasty. His first major actions were understandably political. He abolished the Yüan's *Cheng-tung hsing-sheng*, stronghold of the Mongol influence, and the *Chŏngbang*, a leftover from the Ch'oe government, while restoring the original administrative structure through four consecutive organizational revamping. The de-Mongolization of certain customs and the reinforcement of national education went hand in hand; at the same time, the Ki and other Mongol-tied families were destroyed.

King Kongmin's most determined move was the recovery by force of the northeastern territory in 1356 which had been still under Yüan control. In this military action, he was helped by Yi Cha Ch'un, the father of the Yi dynasty founder, who was then in military service to the Yüan in that territory. In 1360 the grateful King appointed him the regional commander responsible for the defense of that area. At the same time, he tightened military control over the northern regions south of the Amnok and Tuman Rivers, except for the northern half of modern North Hamgyŏng Province.

But the Mongol root that had ramified into the Koryŏ court for a century proved to be difficult to eradicate overnight. Through a series of intrigues, in 1362, remnants of the Mongol influence in collusion with the Yüan force in Liaotung, for instance, eliminated a number of prominent lieutenants of King Kongmin and moved against the person of the King himself.

But they were destroyed by General Ch'oe Yŏng, the loyalest general of late Koryŏ, and General Yi Sŏng Kye, the founder of the Yi dynasty.

Amid the turmoil, Kongmin's economic reform went on, though which was less enterprising. The death in 1365 of his resourceful queen, a former Mongol princess, who had been a constant inspiration to the gentle, introspective King, seems to have dealt him an emotional blow from which he never quite recovered. It was at this nadir of royal distress that Sin Ton, a Buddhist monk of doubtful discipline, somehow ingratiated himself with the King. King Kongmin entrusted the monk with all his authority. Sin Ton's only qualification for the extraordinary job of managing the state affairs was his obscurity itself, that is, the complete lack of vested interests in the government policies, thus ensuring impartiality in decision on reform matters.

After driving a few aristocrat–officials out of the government, Sin Ton set up the Office for Rectification of Land and Slave Ownership, proceeded to restore the forcibly–seized land either to the government or to lawful owners, and emancipated those slaves illegally held in bondage. This rectification business, the foremost in the reform list, had been attempted before without much tangible result because of the aristocratic sabotage. Sin Ton's drastic execution of the office, too, though with initial success, soon met with the united opposition of the entrenched aristocracy, which loomed too ominous for the monk to overcome. Sensing the hazardousness of his position, Sin Ton resorted to the esoteric art to keep the royal attention to himself, but he was soon put to death.

Kongmin's external move also came short of success. After two decades of inter–dynastic struggles for supremacy in China, Chu Yüan–chang (1328–1398) emerged the victor. A former novice monk and sometime beggar, Chu Yüan–chang, having crashed all major rebel groups, proclaimed himself the emperor of the Ming dynasty in 1368 and captured Peking in the same year. The remainder of the Mongols left for Mongolia where they established a regime known as Northern Yüan and lasted until 1391. Aiming to fill the power vacuum in Manchuria caused by the dynastic change, Koryŏ sent two expeditions into South Manchuria in 1369 and 1370, respectively. The Koryŏ forces under General Yi Sŏng Kye destroyed the remnants of the anti-Koryŏ Mongol power and captured the city of Liao-yang, the political center of Liaotung, in November of 1370. Thereupon, they re-claimed the South Manchurian territory east of the Liao River as having originally belonged to Korea; thus the long-standing policy of Koryŏ as the successor of Koguryŏ was accomplished at last. But logistic difficulties in the face of the inclement weather soon forced the troop withdrawal. Indeed, these decades were trying times for the declining dynasty. The Japanese pirates who were then pillaging the coastal areas were not the least trouble.

The Japanese Pirates

The japanese depredation was another serious problem for Koryŏ. Japanese piratical attacks on Korean coasts were seen as early as the Three Kingdoms period. But the rampancy of those that occurred in the fourteenth century amounted to a national scourge. The Japanese pirates, known as *Waegu* (*Wakō* in Japanese) or Dwarf Bandits, would land at any likely spots on the coastal zone for incendiarism as well as banditry before they carried off provisions and goods; some economically hard–pressed *ch'ŏnmin* took to piracy themselves. During the thirteen–year reign of King U (1375–1388), the Japanese raiders molested coastal districts 378 times. Their number varied from a few hundreds to, sometimes, tens of thousands, including horse–riding ones. Japan was, then, divided into the so–called North and South dynasties who fought each other for a half century from 1336 to 1392. The rapidly developing commercial class and assortments of lawless bands adept at the use of long swords, disillusioned by the barrenness of war–torn Japan, tended to look to Korea and China, both under governments without strong maritime defense, for livelihood. Those who aimed at the Korean coast would set out, as they had done from the Three Kingdoms period, from Tsushima Island, their base of operations, which lay only about twenty-five miles from Pusan and had been economically tied more closely with Korea than with Japan.

The Koryŏ government, whose sea–borne tax grains were often inter-cepted by the *Waegu*, first tried to bring "the" Japanese government, which was then virtually non–existent, to curb its own piracy, by dispatching four missions to Japan between 1366 and 1377, but to no avail. Meantime, the coastal people had to move to inland areas. The government, for its part, decided to build up sufficient naval defenses, while, in an unprecedented move, calling government officials into temporary military duties. About this time, Ch'oe Mu Sŏn (ca. 1335–1395), son of a minor official, succeeded in producing gunpowder and a variety of firearms through experiments he con-ducted for the express purpose of repelling the Japanese pirates. While head-ing the Office for Manufacture of Firearms, which the court set up at his rec-ommendation in 1377, Ch'oe Mu Sŏn also helped build ships that were capa-ble of carrying his firearms. For Koryŏ that knew of the gunpowder through a military alliance with the Yüan but had no knowledge of how to produce it, Ch'oe Mu Sŏn's service was timely and invaluable. Indeed, in 1380, the Koryŏ navy, with new weapons and Ch'oe as its deputy commander, destroyed no less than 500 Japanese ships around the mouth of the Kŭm River. This constituted the war's turning point in favor of Koryŏ culminating, after a series of resounding victories, in the expedition to Tsushima Island in 1389. With their lair wiped out, the Japanese pirates were subdued severely, if not completely.

Troubles with the Ming

The factional division between the entrenched aristocracy and the new breed of Confucian bureaucrats, which vaguely appeared as King Kongmin's reforms progressed, became clearly visible in the 1370's when Koryŏ established relations with the Ming. Naturally, the influential aristocrats in the government were interested in nothing more than maintenance of the *status quo*. The economic readjustment and anti-Mongolism that motivated the Kongmin reforms, on the other hand, were welcomed by the Confucian officials and also the new dynasty in China which still had the Northern Yüan to deal with. Ming T'ai Tzu's goodwill toward Koryŏ was readily seen in state communications, which also worked to consolidate the Confucian group at the Koryŏ court.

But the assassinations of King Kongmin in the aftermath of a homosexual scandal in 1374 and, three months later, of a Ming envoy began to deteriorate the relations between the two countries and intensified political disputes at the court. The government at this time was in the hands of the inept conservatives with their teen-age *Protégé*, King U (1375–1388), behind them. Soon after the above-mentioned incidents, the apprehensive conservatives in power, who might or might not be responsible for the assassination of the Ming emissary, reopened the diplomatic door ajar to the Northern Yüan. This policy, unnecessarily incurring the risk the Ming's anger, was particularly unrealistic in the eyes of the Confucian officials.

Led by Chŏng Mong Chu (1337–1392), dean of the national university and the most distinguished Neo-Confucian scholar, and Chŏng To Chŏn, an equally-distinguished Neo-Confucian intellectual and radical politician who later allied himself with Yi Sŏng Kye, the pro-Ming group kicked off another series of controversies. Chŏng To Chŏn, when appointed a reception officer for a Northern Yüan mission to Koryŏ in 1375, refused the office, an incident that triggered a fresh round of quarrels, ending in the expulsion of the pro-Ming group from the government. They were recalled a few years later in an effort to better the relations with the Ming.

The Ming, on the other hand, was now fast extending its military and administrative control toward Manchuria, and it became suspicious of, and increasingly hostile toward, Koryŏ. It was, however, of vital importance for Koryŏ at this time that it kept on at least speaking terms with its large neighbor under the aggressive Ming T'ai Tzu, lest some trivial misunderstanding should develop into an armed conflict, which Koryŏ would have been hard put to handle. The Ming, probably conscious of Koryŏ's vulnerability, assumed a bellicose attitude. It refused to recognize the enthronement of King U. Like the Mongols, demanding an impossible amount of precious metals, textile fabrics, and horses, it threatened Koryŏ with a military expedition, were it unable to meet the demands. Faced with these difficulties, which seem to have been imposed largely by the warped personality of Ming T'ai Tzu, Koryŏ frequently dispatched envoys to present its position. But the Koryŏ envoys were, sometimes, denied entrance into China at the border or even summarily banished by the Ming court. Chŏng Mong Chu, dispatched in 1384 and in 1386, did much to placate the devil in Ming T'ai Tzu. With his distinguished scholarship and dignified deportment, Chŏng Mong Chu tremendously impressed the Chinese monarch who immediately lifted his cross-grained demands.

But, again in 1387, the Ming refused to receive a Koryŏ envoy. Annoyed by these whimsical deflections in diplomacy, which accumulatively constituted nothing less than a national crisis for Koryŏ, the Koryŏ government, probably urged by General Ch'oe Yŏng, began to prepare itself for worse. It reinforced its army in the northern provinces and ordered the repair of defense fortifications and naval fleets, while strengthening the logistic system for possible military campaigns. And, in January of 1388, Ch'oe Yŏng in cooperation with Yi Sŏng Kye purged the corrupt conservatives out of government. In February of the same year, Koryŏ was informed by the Ming of, among other things, its intention of "recovering" Koryŏ's northeastern province on the pretext that the said territory was formerly in the Yüan's possession. To the straightforward General Ch'oe Yong, the Ming's claim seemed a nonsensical bickering beyond his patience. Approved by the twenty-four year old King U, who was now under his protection, Ch'oe Yŏng, in March, issued the mobilization order for an expedition against the Ming, more specifically for the re-occupation of Liao-yang in the Liaotung Peninsula now under Ming control, since, in the Ming plan, Koryŏ's northeastern territory was to be incorporated into the Liaotung Province.

The Troop Withdrawal from the Wihwa Island. In view of the existing social confusion caused by the Japanese piratical menace which was still real enough, the mobilization of a 40,000-man army against the fast-rising Ming was not necessarily the best move. Yet the evil that defeated this heroic venture was the enemy within, as represented by Yi Sŏng Kye. Ch'oe Yŏng, the supreme commander of the expeditionary forces, and Yi Sŏng Kye, one of his two deputies in this expedition, were the two great generals of this strenuous period. For the past thirty-five years, they had fought together many critical battles to successive victories, which had saved the dynasty so far. The similarity ends there, however. Ch'oe Yŏng, an austere military, was of a most illustrious family that traced its origin back to the very beginning of the dynasty. Literally heeding the parental instruction to avoid unjustifiable riches, he lived straight in poverty amidst the venal officials of his day. Even more virtuous was his impeccable loyalty to his sovereign, whether or not he was a bastard, that King U was.

YI Sŏng Kye's association with the Koryŏ monarchy, on the other hand, was only a generation old, starting with his father Yi Cha Ch'un's service to King Kongmin in the 1350's. Yi Sŏng Kye, a new face in the Koryŏ official-dom, fought his way through the top with his native ability and a well-disciplined private army of about 2,000. Thus, inspite of himself, he rendered himself politically practical as a rallying point around which the anti-conservative force might unite itself. In 1383 the ambitious and brilliant but unemployed Chŏng To Chŏn, for instance, was greatly impressed by the orderliness of Yi's private army and promptly enlisted himself into Yi's service. It is quite possible that Yi Sŏng Kye at once came under Chŏng's intellectual spell and more importantly reoriented his views of the Ming and the future toward a new vision which Chŏng, the architect of the Yi dynasty, might have entertained already then.

In any case, in 1388, after five years of acquaintance with Chŏng To Chŏn, Yi Sŏng Kye, a modest, cautious man, pitted himself against his superior. He was strongly opposed to the idea of an armed challenge to the Ming. Upon his appointment as a field commander of the expeditionary army, he registered his opposition, enumerating the famous "Four Wrongs:" first, it was wrong that the small country should defy the large one; secondly, that a military campaign should occur in summer months [which are a busy agricultural season]; thirdly, that the national mobilization for an invasion [of Liaotung] could be availed of for attacks on the real by the Japanese pirates ; the last "Wrong" was that the seasonal rain would thaw the glue of bows and cause epidemics among the troops. No doubt, these "Wrongs," thus pointed out, were reasonable in some respects, even though the first "Wrong" was a classic Confucian idea appropriated directly from the *Li Chi* (*Record of Rituals*). In view of subsequent developments, however, the memorialization of the "Four Wrongs" seems to have been more politically motivated than otherwise.

Strongly urged by General Ch'oe Yŏng, General Yi, in April of 1388, rather reluctantly led his army northward, along with another army under General Cho Min Su. The northward march soon ran into trouble, which was not predicted in the "Four Wrongs," however: the problems of desertion and food supply became acute. By the time the expeditionary forces reached the Wihwa Island located in the middle of the Amnok River, the troubles were seriously aggravated. Meanwhile, the unwilling Yi Sŏng Kye, who had requested Kaegyŏng for a permission to withdraw the forces in vain, was gradually hardened to the idea of troop withdrawal at any cost. Having persuaded General Cho Min Su, Yi ordered the troops "to turn the spearpoint back to Kaegyŏng."

Land Reform and the Dynastic Change

No sooner had the chips been down than reform-minded officials overtly threw their lot with Yi Sŏng Kye. Yi's most important lieutenants turned out to be, of course, Chŏng To Chŏn and Cho Chun, the foremost economist of his day. Yi, as might be expected, purged part of the opposition headed by Ch'oe Yŏng and deposed King U in favor of King Ch'ang. Cho Min Su, too, was soon eased out; with him went King Ch'ang, too, who was then replaced by King Kongyang (1390–1392). As for the Ming, probably realizing that it had pushed Koryŏ too far, it never again brought up the territorial question.

The first order of business for the new group in the government was again the land reform, which had been sporadically attempted even after King Kongmin. Having acquired an absolute majority behind him, General Yi Sŏng Kye was determined to give a chance to this long-overdue rehabilitation of the national economy as now proposed by Cho Chun. Yi's impetus to this undertaking sprang from his painful experience as a military commander who had been under constant apprehension over the shortage of provisions. The maintenance of his private army which was now substantially enlarged in number became a more pressing problem. Indeed, he had been an avid listener to Cho Chun's discourse on the necessity of a land reform. Even while heated debates on the Cho proposal were going on at the court, a land survey got under way. Cho Chun, by virtue of his capacity as the head of the censors, censured out of the government those who radically opposed the land reform, Cho Min Su being among them.

The salient features of the Cho proposal, purporting to restore the ideal of national, as against private, ownership of land for remuneration, were seen in the prohibition of private transactions of land other corrupt practices and in the regulations that aimed at reducing the taxes of actual tillers. It also stipulated that, for the assignment to government officials of land for remuneration, the land only in the newly-enlarged Kyŏnggi (Capital) Province should be made available. The other provincial land, except in the two northern provinces, was set aside to yield taxes for the government revenue, and the latter mainly for the defense expenditure there.

As finally approved after a long series of political maneuvers and debates, the land reform law contained such interesting provisions as: the land granted for the specially recognized service to the monarch should never be confiscated even when the grantee committed serious misdeeds, for which he would have been traditionally expected to lose his property or even his life. This provision, though not observed during the Yi dynasty, might have been a reflection of the official realization of how flimsy the nature of a misdeed or a crime under the traditional monarchical system was. And this article stipulating for land grant to meritorious subjects, as it was put in force in a modified form, was a virtual recognition of hereditary, hence private, ownership of land; it served as a loophole in the law safeguarding the national landownership, which eventuated in a downright legislation for land transaction a half century later.

Needless to say, the worst casualties of the land reform were the aristocratic estate owners and the majority of monasteries that had not been certified by the state. To them it meant the confiscation of their landed properties, when all land registers were burnt in 1390. But the final proclamation of the reform law in 1391 was acted out only after Yi Sŏng Kye was made the supreme commander of the newly organized army and Chŏng To Chŏn and Cho Chun his two deputy commanders.

By this time, the Yi supporters were fully aware of what they were doing. Almost concurrent with the debates of Cho's land reform proposal, the Yi force, led by Chŏng To Chŏn, now the fire-eating dean of the national university, opened its broadside on Buddhism. They attacked Buddhism not only as an institution harmful to the national economy but also as a conglomeration of superstitious doctrines harmful to the society. This was definitely a Neo-Confucian attack. Never before had there been such and assault upon Buddhism as a superstitious religion that "deluded the world and deceived the people." The Confucian aggressiveness and vehemence now became unbridled. Kim Ch'o a radical professor at the university, advocated the establishment of an ancestral shrine at every household and the return of Buddhist monks to secular life as tillers and soldiers. He also proposed that anyone who shaved his head to become a monk be beheaded. He even severely criticized King Kongyang for his faith in Buddhism. Against such Confucian onslaughts, Buddhists and Buddhist-sympathizers, whilst admitting the general corruptness of the Buddhist church, countered that the vicious language disgracing Buddhism was of wild Confucian radicalism oblivious of the founding ideals of the dynasty.

These exchanges were intensified after the new land system was promulgated in 1391. The Koryŏ court, which was to end its five century old history in a year, was now completely dominated by censor and polemic officials representing the Yi group, who had spearheaded the Confucian offensive in a series of political crises. But they appear to have had no concrete stratagem for administering the *coup de grâce* at this time, except for consolidation of their power that purposely kept the court in turmoil.

Chŏng Mong Chu, a man of gentle disposition and absolute loyalty to the dynasty, was a key persona in this anti-climactic stage of the dynasty. He came along with the Yi group as far as the land reform. In the controversy on Buddhism, however, he became suspicious of the Yi group in its maneuvers, and he strategically maintained a neutral stance. From this position, he successfully pushed through a political compromise which was designed to wind up polemical exchanges, thus holding the Yi force in check. But they were not to be harnessed for long in such a truce, which was at best tenuous from the beginning.

Yi Pang Wŏn, the ablest son of Yi Sŏng Kye, was apprehensive of political moves made by Chŏng Mong Chu, who now seemed in the eyes of the Yi faction a bulwark of the reactionary force. Yi Pang Wŏn, who wanted to know where Chŏng stood, stage-managed a banquet to which Chŏng Mong Chu was the guest of honor. Entreating Chŏng to a cup of wine, the anxious host sang in *Sijo* form, a poetic *genre* that had recently been developed.

> How about coming this side ?
> What about staying that side ?
> Entangled with the rank weeds
>   of Mansusan, how will you fare?
> We too, if we were thus entangled
>   we might dally a hundred years. *

The noble guest answered in kind :

> Though this frame should die and die,
>   though I die a hundred times,
> My bleached bones all turned to dust,
>   my very soul exist or not—
> What can change the undivided heart
>   that glows with faith toward my Lord? †

Their positions clarified, they returned to the game of political maneuvering, with enormous odds against the loyalist. Seizing upon Yi Sŏng Kye's temporary absence from Kaegyŏng, Chŏng Mong Chu successfully moved to have Yi's important lieutenants banished to remote places. Taken unawares, Yi Pang Wŏn resorted to violence. In 1392 his henchmen waylaid the former near the Sŏnjukkyo of Good Bamboo Bridge, where a trace of the blood spilt over the bridge's stone slabs from that "undivided heart" is said to be seen even today. With Chŏng gone, the situation became precipitately changed. All important offices of the government, both central and provincial,

---

* Translated by Richard Rutt in the *Transactions of the Korea Branch of the Royal Asiatic Society*, Vol. XXXIV, pp. 36-37.
† *Ibid.*, pp. 15-16.

were filled with the Yi men, and the formal enthronement of Yi Sŏng Kye became merely a procedural matter.

Another less known yet important figure at this juncture was a woman, a queen dowager who was usually given an extraordinary power for naming a succession at the end of the legitimate line caused by the absence of the male heir or by a *coup*. Upon the surviving Queen An of King Kongmin as the senior queen dowager fell the job of declaring the abdication of King Kongyang and "approving" the succession of Yi Sŏng Kye. What made her tragic was that she had to "approve" for the throne of a 475 year-old dynasty an upstart of a different name. When she succumbed to the pressure of the Yi group in 1392, three months after the death of Chŏng Mong Chu, was consummated a peaceful "revolution that only changed the name."

Portrait of Chŏng Mong-ju.

Part 7

Traditional Korea Under the Yi Dynasty

1

Political Maneuvers

The transition from Koryŏ to the Yi dynasty, as an outgrowth of the reform movement initiated by King Kongmin, was indeed a remarkable and unique process in many respects. The shrewd political maneuvers well executed through collusive action on the part of the jealous proponents of dynastic change and the overall peacefulness of the events characterized the historic transition. Since the ideals to which the reform movements were addressed were those of the early Koryŏ institutions, the new dynasty, created as it was through "a revolution that only changed the name," was not expected to bring about any radical change from the previous regime. But in little more than a half century from the founding date, the gradual cultural changes in a cumulative totality reached to revolutionary proportions, especially in terms of social changes and progress.

The guiding principle that motivated those changes and progress was, needless to say, Confucian ideals. As politically ramified, for instance, that principle became a bureaucrat-dominated government, whereas, in the previous dynasty whose ideological basis of life in general was Buddhistic, dominating the government were conservative aristocrats under a weaker royal authority. And it is to the credit of the Yi dynasty gentlemen that the government and the society they created lasted more than five centuries with only minor adjustments. The vitality and the brilliance with which they attended to dynasty building in the first century were indeed of unprecedented nature in the Korean history.

2

The Early Yi Kings and Officials

An immediately noticeable improvement over Koryŏ in the centralization of government under the new dynasty was the greatly strengthened royal authority flanked by the gentlemanly bureaucrats who rendered themselves tractable only to the Confucian ideals and virtues. The Yi bureaucrats contrasted clearly with the aristocrat-officials of the preceding era who were not necessarily subtle about assuming a defiant stance against the royal authority. The Yi dynasty government system and the bureaucratic officials who managed it, hence, one may say, the whole range of the national life, therefore, proved to be much more susceptible to the ability and personality of individual monarchs at least in the first half of the dynasty.

T'aejo and His Subjects

T'aejo or Grand Progenitor of the Yi dynasty was in many respects like the T'aejo of the Koryŏ dynasty. Beside being military geniuses and Buddhists, they were both cautious, modest, and politically shrewd, a personality that readily commanded loyalty from a wide variety of people. Yi T'aejo, like Koryŏ T'aejo, was elevated to the throne by his colleagues and tended to let himself be easily guided by his subjects, a tendency that was probably reinforced by his genealogical obscurity. His pliant disposition and uninspiring family background, pitted against the Confucian ardor for government of his former colleagues, seem to have had much to do with the subsequent development of the dynasty in an important way.

One of T'aejo's first acts, after he declared the laws and rituals of the preceding dynasty to be followed, was creation of the so called *Kongsin* or Merit Subjects, who rendered exceptionally meritorious service in the execution of critical maneuvers leading to his enthronement. His Merit Subjects, numbering thirty-nine, to whom he made generous grants of land, slaves, and special privileges, were made the political and bureaucratic basis of the royal authority, an important precedent that was followed by his successors usually after a succession crisis or the suppression of a treason. There were twenty-one occasions until 1728 which called for creation of the Merit Subjects, and those appointed in 1471 counted seventy-three. Although thus the practice was not always favorable to the government revenue, it widened the basis of the ruling elite much further than that under the previous dynasties.

Another measure to reinforce the royal authority was the establishment of a close relationship with the Ming court. Even after the establishment of the customary tributary relations with the Ming, Yi T'aejo went to great lengths to get on friendlier terms with it. Consequently, his overly low-posture diplomacy with the powerful neighbor, though obviously intended to share the imperial prestige of the Chinese ruling house for domestic consumption, in the long run, proved to be deleterious to the Yi sovereignty, as we shall see later.

Yi T'aejo's more likely move was the transfer of *sŏul* (capital) from Kaegyŏng to Hanyang, the site of modern Seoul, after a careful consultation with geomantic expertise. Upon rough completion of the Kyŏngbok Palace complex, he moved his court and government to Hanyang in 1394, while the city's civil and defense facilities were still under construction.

The dynasty's major policies that had a greater bearing upon the life of the country were decided by T'aejo's Merit Subjects who filled all the important offices, and T'aejo seems to have rubber-stamped his approval on them. The highest decision-making body was the Council of Ministers under the unanimity system, inherited from the previous regime. The various measures adopted by the Council during T'aejo's reign still sustained an aura of reform ; in other words, the dynastic ecdysis was to be gradual.

Understandably, the immediate administrative and political concern was centered around the elimination of inherited corruption and irregularities in administration and the encouragement of productivity in agriculture and sericulture. The profounder and more far-reaching policies, as was completely predictable, were directed towards the substitution of Confucianism for Buddhism as the ideological and religious foundation of the dynasty. Needless to say, education in Confucianism was reemphasized And Confucian ethics and rites were enforced through government decrees : every household from the commoner class up, for instance, was required to establish a family shrine for ancestor worship. At the same time, Buddhism was systematically demolished by means of taxation on monasterial properties and of ordination of monk-priests under a licence system. Anti-Buddhist measures were more and more stringently formulated and implemented by successive reigns.

The last years of T'aejo on the throne were marred by foreign and domestic troubles. In 1395 Ming T'ai Tzu again got warped over the wording in a state paper sent by the Yi court. Ming T'ai Tzu was notorious for his sensitivity to words suggestive of his lowly background. He demanded Yi T'aejo to sent to his court Chŏng To Chŏn who was reponsible for the drafting of the paper. Chŏng was the most meritorious of the Merit Subjects of T'aejo, whose scholarship and versatile talents had been instrumental in the formulation and execution of policies on such disparate fields as military, government, history, law, literature, religion, and music. Chŏng To Chŏn, who had defied the Koryŏ court in order to support the Ming, was now forced to lead the group who, exasperated at the Ming's high-handedness, came to advocate again an expedition into Liaotung. Chŏng placed all army units under a rigorous training program according to the drilling manuals of his own writing. But, upon the death of Ming T'ai Tzu in 1398, all diplomatic impasses were cleared.

Succession Squabbles and T'aejong

The crisis in the relations with the Ming was followed by bloody fracases among the royal brothers. The ambitious Yi Pang Wŏn, who had done a considerable service to his father, was not happy over the appointment of Pang Sŏk, one of his two half brothers, as the crown prince. Taking advantage of T'aejo's illness, in 1398 Pang Wŏn let loose his private army and destroyed the two half brothers and Chŏng To Chŏn whom T'aejo had entrusted with the task of education and protection of the crown prince. In the same year, T'aejo, profoundly shaken by the internecine feud, abdicated himself from the throne and retired to Buddhist monastery. The crown went to Pang Kwa, the eldest of the Yi brothers. Pang Kwa, now Chŏngjong or Settled Ancestor (1399–1400), was a man of well-rounded personality and had no ambition to hang on to the crown. For this reason, Pang Wŏn, now the master of political situation, gave a tacit consent to his uterine brother's accession.

Heeding the advice of the Office of Astrology, Chŏngjong, a kind of an interim king, moved the capital back to Kaegyŏng in 1399. But the next year occurred another armed clash, this time, between Pang Wŏn and Pang Kan, another of his uterine brothers who was equally ambitious for the throne. The latter was handily defeated, and the former's ascension followed almost immediately. In contrast with the comparable period of the Koryŏ dynasty, the succession struggles, it may be noted, were now strictly a family affair, with no outsiders aspiring to the throne ; this fact may be regarded as an indication of the strengthened royalty *vis-ŏ-vis* the politician-officials.

The situation, however, was far from the realization of an unbridled royal power. In fact, the Yi kings were to find themselves under the strong restraint drawn from the Confucian ideology. Their Confucian subjects who, after all, founded the dynasty were ever on their guard, lest too powerful a royal authority should impair their hard-won privileges and status. They would gently argue willful monarchs into straitjacket of Confucian *Wangdo* or Kingly Way, with the judgeship for interpreting Confucian government in general reserved to themselves.

Pang Wŏn as T'aejong or Grand Ancestor (1401–1418) did much to consolidate the dynastic foundation. Unlike T'aejo, T'aejong with his forceful personality was the prime mover of policy-making and implementation as well. He moved the court back to Hanyang which, in the next ten years, he built up as the permanent capital of the dynasty. Besides conventional features like palaces, defense walls, bell tower, etc., the city came to possess such modern facilities as the elaborate drainage system and fire prevention walls in the downtown area.

It was also T'aejong who set out to work for a serious readjustment of government organs and other important aspects of centralization in accord with the confucian standard. First, he understandbably prohibited the maintenance of private armies by royal princes and stripped the queen's family of its power potential. Then he abolished the Council of Ministers and the Secretariat-Chancellery of the preceding dynasty and established in their places the *Ŭijŏngbu* or Council of State made up of three councillors and the *Sŭngjŏng'wŏn* or Royal Secretariat. On a lower level, he inaugurated the *Hop'ae* system under which every male from sixteen years of age up, regardless of social status, was required to carry an identification tablet showing, among other things, age and domicile. The system seems to have been intended to mainly restrict the movement of the members of the productive class.

T'aejong's another pet project was typecasting and printing. The *Kyemi cha* or *Kyemi* types, that is, the copper types cast a his order in the third year of his reign (1403), the year of *Kyemi* or goat, counted several 100,000 which set in motion the dynasty's prolific activities of book printing. True to form, he high-handedly ordered those non-Confucian, apocryphal books burnt. His real destructive bent in policy matter, however, was directed toward those innocent sons born of concubines and remarried women. They were barred from taking the government examination, hence becoming officials. This injustice has been imputed by some to T'aejong's unfortunate experience with his half brothers. Buddhism suffered a further setback under T'aejong. All temples and Monasteries, except for 242 which were permitted to exist, were closed down, and the land and slaves that had belonged to them were confiscated by the government. At least, T'aejo had allowed all established temples and monasteries to remain in operation. Yet more blows were in store for Buddhism.

Great King Sejong and Chiphŏynjŏn Scholars

As Prince Yangnyŏng, T'aejong's crown prince with a propensity for self-indulgence, failed to measure up to the popular expectation, the studious and sagacious Prince Ch'ungnyŏng (later King Sejong) made a strong claim to the crown princeship. Tradition has it that the self-indulging crown prince, aware of T'aejong's diminishing confidence in him, simply accentuated his licentious activities to the extent of bordering on lunacy so as to make it easy for T'aejong to depose him as the crown prince. Any form of resistance to his father's wish might have meant a banishment or even death. If, on the other hand, he was unjustifiably jolted out of the crown princeship, that is, without a sound reason such as lunatic tendency, he might be then regarded, whether he was or not, as a menace to the new king. A royal brother or a royal uncle who happened to be in such an unfortunate position, as it developed later, was usually eliminated as a preventive measure. In this view, the Pang Wŏn-Pang Kan struggle was rather inevitable and the crown prince's pretended lunacy is understandable. Be that as it may, when T'aejong abdicated in favor of Prince Ch'ungnyŏng in 1418, T'aejong had just executed the most far-sighted political act he had ever done, for in Ch'ungnyŏng or Sejong was found that rare quality in a traditional ruler which combined intelligence, wisdom, firmness, and *demo*-centered considerateness. Indeed, the thirty-one year reign of Sejong (1419-1450) was the most brilliant period in the Korean history, and he is usually and fittingly referred to as Great King Sejong (Regenerating Ancestor).

There was virtually no aspect of the national life to which his concern and personal influence did not extend. He was not only a monarch but also a true innovator and inventor as well as a leading light in numerous policies and projects in government, humanities, and the sciences. Sejong's method of approach to the problems of many different natures, in none of which he was specialized as a king never was, was one of scientific inquiry combined with indefatigable pursuit of knowledge, which indeed he carried on until his death.

For his political and cultural endeavors, Sejong gathered around him a group of young, perspicacious scholars as his assistants, advisors, and researchers. They were placed and trained at the *Chiphyŏnjŏn* or Board of

Talented Scholars. The *Chiphyŏnjŏn* had been one of the governmental organs that managed the literary affairs–royal lectures, history compilation, drafting of state papers, etc.,–of the court and was organizationally expanded by Sejong. Twenty or so outstanding scholars selected from among young low-ranking officials were appointed as *Chiphyŏnjŏn* Scholars for a period of time. They were expected through their study and research to articulate Confucian ideals so that they could be properly implemented in actual government. Representing the intellectual elite of the ruling class, they were usually promoted to the positions of responsibility which constituted a bureaucratic backbone of the dynasty.

The greatness of Sejong as a ruler consisted in the practical application of that aspect of Confucianism which put a special emphasis on the welfare of the common masses. He has been said to be a "democratic" king. The most mass-centered work was, of course, the invention of the *Hunmin chŏng'ŭm*, better known today as *Han'gŭl*, or Korean writing system. The twenty-eight letters, which Sejong created in 1443 after years of study assisted by *Chiphyŏnjŏn* Scholars, have been claimed to be, as we shall see later, "the most scientific" system of writing in the world and certainly most easy to learn. Sejong's manifest purpose of official adoption of the *Han'gŭl* by a royal decree in 1446 was, above all, to provide the common people with a medium of expression, under whose circumstances the mastery of Chinese letters, being so expensive in time and money, was well-nigh impossible.

Even before the official adoption, Sejong launched the training program under which, for instance, a group of petty officials were instructed on Han'gŭl, who were in turn expected to teach others. The writing and composition of poems in praise of the royal family and the translation of Buddhist scriptures, Confucian classics, and agricultural books into *Han'gŭl* were immediately started, a court-sponsored program which, in a fifty year period from 1446, produced more than forty titles of books in translation alone. In the same period of time, the use of the *Han'gŭl* was widely extended among the common people. Indeed, nothing in the Korean history is more far-reaching in terms of cultural development and national identity than the invention and general use of the *Han'gŭl*. Yet, there was a number of Confucian scholar-officials even close to Sejong who were strongly opposed to the use of the *Han' gŭl* with no better reason than that one system of writing already in use, that is to say, the Chinese system sufficed. Some of the hardheaded ones like Ch'oe Man Li, when they persisted in opposition, were put in jail for a while by the annoyed Sejong.

Another outstanding work was a new legislation on land tax, affecting the life of the peasants and all others. Two *sŏk* or *sŏm* of unhulled rice per one *kyŏl*, a unit area where about twenty *sŏk* were supposed to be produced in this period, had uniformly been paid as land tax by the peasant-farmers. * But, in actuality, impartiality in taxation could be hardly achieved through such uniformity, the amount of the harvest being different year to year and district to district. The final form of the new law, as completed in 1444, called for the division of land into six grades according to its fertility and of year into nine grades from the worst to the best harvest which it brought. This tax system based on the fact of the varying degrees of fertility and the different amounts of yearly harvest became permanent with only some modifications later. Probably, a more significant aspect of it was that Sejong spent nearly fifteen years for study and experiment for which 160,000 experienced farmers and provincial officials were consulted.

In science, Sejong was chiefly concerned with astronomy and meteorology, the foremost areas of interest in traditional science, as they were closely related to the ideal of harmony between the ways of nature and human society and, more immediately, to agriculture. At the study of astronomy required, Sejong learnt mathmatics from one of *Chiphyŏnjŏn* Scholars, while sending some others to the Ming for further study. Like the director of a modern scientific institute, he assigned various projects to the selected groups of scholar-officials for completion. They were instructed, for instance, to edit a new calendar with consultation of the Yüan, Ming, and Arabian calendars, or "to measure the height of the north pole." The most talented technicians were Yi Ch'ŏn (1376–1451) and Chang Yŏn Sil who together made astronomical observation machines and sun and water clocks, which were then placed in palaces and other spots for the benefit of the capital citizens. Sejong was credited with the invention of a rain gauge made with iron in 1442, 197 years earlier than in the West. At a great moment of inspiration, he ordered the provincial governors to report, using rain guages, the rainfall in their respective provinces.

Sejong also reemphasized a nation-wide education in Confucianism and implemented policies that aimed at a wider practice of Confucian rites among the common people. At the same time, he dealt Buddhism another blow. He reorganized the major Kyo-Sŏn sects into two sects, that is, the Kyo and Son sects and allowed only thirty-six temples to function, disbanding all others. He banned Buddhist events and monks from the capital. It was also under Sejong that the entire Peninsula, namely, the whole territory immediately south of the natural borders of the Tuman and Amnok Rivers was put under firm administrative and military control.

In private life, Sejong was exceptionally loving and warmhearted. He fathered more than thirty offsprings. Of the children born of his first queen, the crown prince and the second son Prince Suyang, because of their categorical differences in ability and personality, seem to have stirred a certain anxiety

---

* A *sŏk* or *sŏm* is about 5.12 U.S. bushels.

in Sejong. The crown prince was a studious, intelligent but uninviting introvert who was easy to fluster in public and physically frail and fat, whereas Prince Suyang showed manliness and intelligence capable of executing highly difficult errands. At nineteen, Prince Suyang was allowed, on behalf of Sejong, to preside over a banquet given in honor of a Chinese ambassador. He actively participated in government and played a leading role in Sejong's cultural projects such as compiling and translating important books. Such inauspicious distribution of talents or constellation of personalities among the royal brothers boded ill. Sejong would bring his infant grandson (the crown prince's son) in his arm to the *Chiphyŏnjŏn* where he suggested to scholars around to protect and assist him in the future. Sŏng Sam Mun (1418–1456), Sin Suk Chu (1417–1475), and a few other young scholars were emphatically asked to take care of him.

In his old age, Sejong, suffering from palsy, became increasingly pessimistic of life, especially after the death of his queen followed by other family misfortunes. His Confucian learning profoundly failed to satisfy the spiritual need of this many dimensional man. He turned to Buddhism for personal salvation. He had gone much further than T'aejong for the suppression of Buddhism to become a good Confucian king. Now the old Sejong built a Buddhist temple within the very precinct of the royal palace and this in the face of a strong protest from virtually the entire body of the shocked Confucian officialdom. The *Chiphyŏnjŏn* Scholars and the university students went on strike. But Sejong did not budge an inch. He completed the resplendent temple in 1448 and died a devout Buddhist three years later.

Prince Suyang's Usurpation and Moral Crisis

What seemed another brilliant reign came to an abrupt end when Munjong (1451–1452), who succeeded Sejong, died after two years on the throne. His was an especially unfortunate death, for elevated to the throne after him was his teen-age son, Tanjong (1453–1455), that erstwhile infant in Sejong's arm. The young Tanjong came under the shadow of ambitious uncles who were not particularly imbued with Confucian virtues. Prince Suyang, who had been active in government, immediately set out to work for power. In seventeen months from Tanjong's accession, he seized political and military power after a bloody massacre of all key officials, including one of his own brothers and the loyal General Kim Chong Sŏ (1390–1453). The scenario of subsequent actions for usurpation was so thinly veiled that even the boy could see its true motif through. When in 1455 the fifteen-year-old Tanjong, fearful for his life, volunteered to hand over the royal seal, the symbol of power and authority, in person to Prince Suyang, the usurper, unprepared for this particular scene, wept impromptu tears.

This second power struggle, as it occurred after the Sejong period which was characterized by political stability and moral welfare, sharply focused public attention on its morality. As for Prince Suyang, now Sejo (Regenerating Progenitor) (1456–1468), he might have felt it necessary to strike forth if only to forestall his own downfall. The very officials who were now his own Merit Subjects, might have worked for his elimination, had he oscillated in moral scruples. But the inexcusable act of usurpation so nakedly committed failed even to grace itself with the benefit with the benefit of doubt. The shocking blow which it dealt to the country was a trauma to the public morality which seems to have caused a far-reaching complication in subsequent political developments.

The immediate outlet of this moral crisis was an ill-fated counter *coup* in 1456 for the restoration of Tanjong, masterminded by the six minor officials, Sŏng Sam Mun, Pak P'aeng Nyŏn (1417–1456), Yi Kae (1417–1456) and others ; they were mostly former *Chiphyŏnjŏn* scholars. Their interrogation by Sejo in person brought to light the interesting ways in which they solved the difficult moral situation. Sŏng Sam Mun, for instance, never consumed the salary rice which he received as an official under Sejo the usurper ; he simply piled up the rice in his house which he told the enraged Sejo to take back. In the case of Pak P'aeng Nyŏn, he never called himself a *sin* or 臣, meaning subject in his official reports to Sejo ; instead, he used the character 巨, meaning great, a character which looked like the character 臣 but meant nothing as written in official reports. The six men who were executed at the end of the interrogation represented those who lost their lives in the wake of the incident. As they were called *Sayuksin* or Six Dead Subject, there were the *Saengyuksin* or Six Live Subjects. Kim Si Sŭp (1435–1493), Cho Yŏ (1420–1489), and four other men who "lived" but, following a Confucian adage, "Never serve two sovereigns [the second being and illegitimate one]," left their official posts or abandoned the hope of entering the government service and retired to "the grass field" or even "the bamboo grove," that is, into obscurity. Numerous others followed their example.

The dynasty's first rebellion occurred in this period. In 1453, right after Prince Suyang's mass purge of high officials, Yi Tŭng Ok, the regional commander of the northeastern province, upon his dismissal because of his connection with General Kim Chong Sŏ, rose in rebellion at Chongsŏng on the northern tip of the Peninsula. He called himself the Emperor of the Great Chin in hopes of enlisting the help of the Jürched, but to no avail. In 1467 another uprising on a much larger scale in the same region was ignited by a Yi Si Ae, the magistrate of Hyeryŏng, arousing popular sentiment against governmental discrimination against that region in personnel appointment. The government had to dispatch an expeditionary force of 30,000 to suppress the disturbance.

Like T'aejong's, the reign of Sejo was marked by his forceful personality. In sharp contrast with Sejong whose government encompassed large segments of people participating, Sejo did not allow opposition and limited government council to his capable but morally obtuse Merit Subjects. He made the Six Ministries responsible directly to himself, instead of to the Council of State and sent out secret envoys (*amhyang ŏsa*) to the provinces with authority to fire corrupt or less cooperative officials on the spot. He proved extremely energetic and effective in the execution of governmental policies ranging from national defense to compiling and printing books of encyclopedic nature. One of his achievements of great significance was the codification in final form of the dynastic laws based on several codes of law compiled in previous reigns. The *Kyŏngguk taejŏn* or *Complete Library of the Laws for Government*, compiled under his personal supervision, was the most systematic and comprehensive work of its kind, and it was made the basic instrument of the dynastic administration and criminal justice. Its promulgation in 1474, after a series of revisions symbolized the completion of the dynastic centralization.

Interestingly enough, Sejo was the most actively-practicing Buddhist of the few Yi monarchs who truly understood Buddhism. Although, as a ruler, he did not go all out for the institutional revival of Buddhism, he, as an individual believer, never hesitated to render the royal support and prestige to the aspirations of individual temples and monasteries. He did much to undo restrictions previously imposed upon Buddhism. He built the magnificent Wŏn'gaksa at the site of the present Pagoda Park in Seoul and gave financial aids to the temples that needed repair, while establishing the Office for Publication of Sutras. Against such a moral dissipation indulged in by their sovereign, few Confucian officials raised a voice of protest as their predecessors had done in the last days of the Sejong reign.

During the reign Sejo, indeed much change was wrought into the nature of the Confucian officialdom. Sejo had elevated on three occasions a total of 199 men to the position of the Merit Subject, some of whom received the appointment twice. The Kyŏnggi land set aside by law for distribution to officials was already used up. In 1466 Sejo confined the land distribution only to the officials in active government service. Those former officials who were not blessed with the economic and social privileges of a Merit Subject were to find it gradually difficult to economically maintain themselves as members of the ruling class in the capital. This increased the dependency upon the government of those new and minor officials in service. More portentous were certain trends toward the polarization of wealth and moral outlook, therefore, of political opinions within the officialdom which clearly appeared toward the end of the Sejo period.

Sejo's belief in Buddhism was deepened as he suffered from the remorse for his earlier excesses of bloodshed. But, despite his devotion to Buddhism, he died a disturbed man. Yejong who succeeded Sejo at nineteen years of age was put under the regency of Queen Dowager Yun. Upon the death of Yejong in a year, Sŏngjong (1470–1494), his nephew, was enthroned at thirteen, who was also placed under the Queen Dowager's care for seven years. The regency of a queen dowager was descriptively called *suryŏm ch'-ŏngjŏng*, literally to listen to government behind screen. A woman was not to come out in the open in the Confucian world, even if she was a ruler. But this tradition of *suryŏm ch'ŏngjŏng* can be traced to the time of King T'aejo of Koguryŏ who acceded at the age of seven in 53 A.D. During the Silla dynasty, three queens were enthroned as legitimate heirs. The Confucian Yi dynasty, beginning from Queen Dowager Yun, was to resort to the queen dowager regency quite often, especially in its later period. In any case, like Sŏngjong of the Koryŏ dynasty, Sŏngjong, as he grew out of his grandmother's attention, proved to be conscientiously Confucian to the delight of the Confucian officials. Sŏngjong's was a period of general peace and stability. But, after him, again we shall see a series of bloodshed of quite different nature.

Statue of Sejong.

3

Institutional Development

Organs of the Government

The Chinese system of government, chiefly of the T'ang and Sung, when it was adopted by the early Koryŏ court, did not always fit the existing political reality, which was so much of Silla's. The rule for unanimity over a policy decision, a most persistent strain in Korean political tradition, was institutionalized during the Koryŏ dynasty in such organs as *Tobyŏngmasa* or *Top'yŏng' isasa* and, during the late Yi dynasty, *Pibyŏnsa*. These offices, which can be all called Council of Ministers, if shrouded in a strong military aura, were made the highest organ of the government. Through a series of readjustments, the four-century-old government system of basically Chinese origin, by the time of the foundation of the Yi dynasty, became perfectly indigenized. A significant change in the governmental structure effected by the new dynasty was the abolition of the above-mentioned Council of Ministers, a fact that was probably indicative of the increased monarchal power and the general political confidence, though only to reappear as the *Pibyŏnsa* in the late sixteenth century, the beginning of the dynasty's political decline.

The Yi dynasty upgraded the functions of the Six Ministries, which were, however, subordinated to the newly created *Ŭijŏngbu* or Council of State which was in turn responsible to the monarch. The Council of State, made up of three councillors, roughly equivalent to the Secretariat of State Affairs of Koryŏ managed the government, whereas the monarch, while being the chief executive, guarded the interests of the royal family and the court. Monarchs with aggressive dispositions like Sejo, as we have seen, tended to dispense with the recommendations of the Council of State, dealing directly

with the Six Ministries. The *Sŭngjŏng'wŏn* or Royal Secretariat as the trans-
mitter of royal directives exercised a strong influence over the royal decisions
and aspirations.

Offices that were made much more important than in the previous
regime were the *Samsa* or Three Offices. The *Samsa*, which was the name of
the Finance Commission in the Koryŏ government, came now to designate
the two boards of censors, *Sahŏnbu* and *Saganwŏn*, and the third,
Hongmungwan or Board of Literary Counsellors. The functions of the two
boards of censors, though similar to those of Koryŏ censors, became now
more articulate and disputatious.

The *Sahŏnbu* dealt with the dishonesty and irregularities in the government, whereas the *Saganwŏn* concentrated its polemics on the monarch himself. Especially junior officials of the *Saganwŏn* were known for the "straight
words" which they dutifully hurled at the king at a considerable risk of incurring the royal ire. The *Hongmungwan*, created in 1463 by Sejo in place of the
Chiphyŏnjŏn which he abolished for political reasons, was a selected group of
outstanding scholars who devoted themselves to academic and literary works
for the court. Their literary task consisted of compiling and redacting state
papers and royal enunciations. They also performed historical researches and
royal lectures ; the latter function was taken over by the *Kyŏngyŏnch'ŏng*, or
Office of the Royal Lectures later. The *Hongmungwan* scholars enjoyed the
privileges of daily contact with the monarch, and their counsels on government and rites rendered for the royal reference gradually took on the nature
of those of censors.

The Three Offices (*Samsa*) were indeed a governmental institution
unique to the Confucian dynasty, which served as the bastion of the
Confucian doctrine that severely limited the royal authority itself. The *Samsa*
officials were usually referred to as the *ŏngwan* or officers of words who were
equipped with the "straight words" of mouth, with engendered in many ways
far more political power and social prestige than the swords and physical
prowess of the late Koryŏ military officials had done.

The administration of justice was put in the hands of three unilateral
organs in the capital and of magisterial courts in the provinces. The Ministry
of Justice supervised the administration of justice in general and served as the
trial court chiefly for the commoners and the *ch'ŏnmin*. Grave crimes such as
treason and breach of the Confucian morals, especially of the five human
relations, were tried regardless of social status, at the *Ŭigŭmbu* or Court of
Righteousness and Prohibition by monarchal order or, more often than not,
by the monarch in person. The mayor of the capital city, in addition to the
administration and police of the city, was invested with the judicial power over
the inhabitants of the city in limited categories of litigations. A death sentence
required three trials, a judicial tradition that went back to 1047.

Various ministries, directorates, courts, etc., in the central government numbered about eighty during the T'aejo period, and certain lesser organs were added on later occasions. Although these government organs, except for a few, were administratively subordinated to the Six Ministries in accord with their respective functions, each office, however insignificant, was headed by an official sufficiently high-ranking as to link it directly with the monarch. It was also customary that the head of a high office concurrently headed a couple of other offices, a device that seems to have aimed to concentrate power in fewer hands than otherwise.

The Provincial and Local Administrative System. As was the case with the central one, the provincial system was basically an outgrowth of that of the Koryŏ dynasty. One of the revisions made by the Yi court was the division of the country into eight administrative provinces ; this division remained in use through out the Yi dynasty. A province, administered by a court-appointed governor, was divided into a number of smaller administrative units of different sizes nationally numbering about 200units. These units, *pu* (large city such as capitals of previous dynasties), *mok* (city), *kun* (country), and *hyŏn*(district) were administered by court-appointed magistrates supervised by the governor of their province. The governors and the local magistrates were prohibited by law from assignment to the region or district of their own birth and shifted around after a statutory term of office of one year for the former and five for the latter. Manning the magistracy, which was patterned after the Six Ministries of the central government, were a host of petty officials of commoner origin on hereditary basis and *without pay* ; understandably, they caused many financial irregularities in the provincial governments, especially in the late Yi period.

As representatives of the central authorities, the provincial and local magistrates were given, in addition to the administrative responsibility, the police and judicial power which even extended over the moral conduct of individuals. Against this magisterial power, the local gentry class came to form a certain forum where they discussed and criticized the magisterial administration. This political forum, known as *Hyangch'ŏng* or literally Country Court, developed into a self-governing body and came to function as a watchdog against the magisterial government, wielding tremendous influence over the political and social welfare of the district. The central government appears to have been rather forced to recognize its existence as part of the local government and appointed the officers of the *Hyangch'ŏng* by the recommendation of the *Kyŏngjaeso*, which may be rendered Office in the Capital. A *Kyŏngjaeso* was formed by a group of central officials from the same district, and it was asked to recommend likely individuals for the offices of the *Hyangch'ŏng* of that district; this was undoubtedly evolved from Koryŏ's *Sasimgwan* system.

The *Hyangch'ŏng*, which seems to have numbered about 360, far more than the number of local magistracies, presented at times a formidable centrifugal force, representing the local interests. Centralization-minded kings like T'aejong and Sejo moved to abolish the *Hyangch'ŏng* system only to be revived by their successors. During the late Yi period, however, the appointment of the *Hyangch'ŏng*, officers was taken over by local magistrates themselves ; this, of course, lessened the efficiency of the *Hyongch'ŏng* as a check against the magisterial authority.

The Military Organization

As given the final form in the 1450's, the military reorganization was effected with an emphasis on the deployment of forces in the strategic provinces to the national defense. The Capital Army consisted of five corps which were stationed in the five administrative districts of the capital, and the commander of each corps, which was called *wi*, supposedly assumed the command of one or more of designated provincial armies : this arrangement reminds us of the tribal tradition of Koguryŏ. The cadre of the five *wi* of the Capital Army were made up or men of the ruling class, and their chief function was guarding the royal palaces and the capital.

Although the provincial armies were in formality under the five *wi*, it is doubtful that there had been any strong command chain actually at work between them. In fact, the provincial forces were much more potent in defense capability. Each province maintained an army and a naval force and, in addition to these, in Hamgil (Hamgyŏng) and Kyŏngsang Provinces which were exposed to the Jürched and the Japanese encroachments were deployed another set of an army and a navy, and in Chŏlla Province only another navy was added. The governor of each province was automatically put in charge of an army force and, in many cases, concurrently held the commandership of other forces stationed in his province.

In addition to the officers of *yangban* origin who were commissioned through the military examination, there were those appointed simply because of some service rendered to the court by their ancestors. And there were two categories of soldiers, "professional" an recruit, both of *yangmin* origin. The former, selected through a simplified examination, manned the royal guards in the capital and units in important defense regions. The latter, comprising most of the national army, were conscript soldiers between the ages of sixteen and sixty who served in their assigned units for a stipulated period of time at regular intervals. The maintenance expenses needed for a conscript soldier during his period of active service, it is interesting to note, were paid by two others who were not on duty for that period. Because of administrative difficulties involved in carrying out such an arrangement which was prone to irregularities and because of the protracted peace which made the maintenance of large forces seem redundant, the government saw it feasible, later, to employ paid soldiers at least for the central army with taxes levied on men liable on military service.

The Yi dynasty navy had 45,000 men ; one third of them was on active duty, financially supported by the other two, and the individual ranks and duties were on a hereditary basis. Possessed of an advanced technique of shipbuilding and developed weaponry and, unlike the army, nearly always under "professional," (as distinguished from amateurish), commanders, the navy was a far more efficient affair than the land forces.

The Landownership and Economic Structure

Despite its purported intention to eliminate privately-owned estates and its stringent law to enforce it, the land reform of 1391 was, as it turned out, a partisan reform ; the private ownership of land for the new ruling class was soon legitimized. The traditional concept of land as belonging to the monarch, though still valid in official view, had been reduced to a fetish, which, since the thirteenth century, few had honored. The characteristics of the early Yi dynasty land policy were that it centered attention more on the enforcement of the tax law on land, along with the governmental encouragement of land reclamation, but less on adhesion to the traditional view of the monarchal ownership, which was usually accompanied by complicated laws to enforce it.

As has been noted, the Kyŏnggi Province, in which the *sŏul* (capital) was located, was sufficiently enlarged in 1391 so that it embraced enough land for assignment to the central officials and for royal grant to the Merit Subjects and others. This was in accord with a new stipulation of the 1391 land law that only the Kyŏnggi land was to be used for these purposes. The idea was that the central officials, even in retirement, were to remain in the Kyŏnggi Province to guard the royal family and the capital. The deeper motive may have been obviously to discourage the emergence of any land-based local powers. The provincial land was alloted in part to provincial government organs for their maintenance but mostly for cultivation by the peasants for government revenues.

The peasants or commoners, even though they were allowed to have their own land, if any, at the time of the land reform of 1391, were, however, excepted, unlike during the Koryŏ period, from land distribution. Most of the country's arable land was made government land comprising the above-mentioned provincial land, not for allocation for any individual support. The peasants, actual tillers of land, were thus denied landownership and became tenant farmers whose cultivation rights to land were protected only by an unwritten provision of the established tradition.

In the Yi dynasty land system, the problem, which in fact immediately arose, was the shortage of the Kyŏnggi land for allotment to newly-appointed officials. A piece of land, once alloted to an official who was required by law to return it upon his death, tended to remain in the hands of the family of that official, partly because he knew how to get around the law and partly because of the somewhat lukewarm enforcement of the law on the part of the government. This, of course, seriously cut into the limited acreage of the Kyŏnggi land available to new officials, while the generous land grant to Merit Subjects and other royal favorites was going on.

In 1466 the government of Sejo had to confine the land assignment to the officials in active service ; those in retirement were not provided for. In 1470 the land assignment system as a major means of remunerating the bureaucracy was altogether scrapped, never to be reinstated. The bureaucracy, thenceforth, was to receive only salary, that is, payment in kind, which they had been getting since the late Koryŏ times in parallel with the assigned land. Seen from the royal point of view, a sufficient number of the *yangban* had been given enough land to establish themselves as landowners who held the vested interests in the dynasty's future. Thus, from the sixteenth century on, it became increasingly difficult even for a *yangban* to get education and find his way into the central officialdom without a sufficient amount of ancestral land in his possession.

Wealth, as in the Koryŏ period, being mainly in the form of land, the emergence of private estates as the final form of individual economic success was an inevitable phenomenon. The appearance of private estates in the Yi dynasty, which were smaller in size, if larger in number, than those of Koryŏ occurred under circumstances somewhat different from any of the previous dynasties. Unlike the private estates of the late Koryŏ dynasty which were, to a large extent, the results of the military domination of the government under a weakened monarchy, the Yi dynasty estates were the direct consequences of the royal desire to cement the wider dynastic foundation in a short period of time. Elevation to the category of Merit Subjects of those close to the monarch was in economic reality an act of creating landowners, who then went about enlarging their holdings through, for instance, land reclamation.

A more productive policy which lent incentive to the appearance of large private estates was the governmental encouragement of land reclamation. The land reclamation as a government policy had been implemented usually at a dynastic beginning since the Three Kingdoms period. But it was the Yi dynasty that most vigorously pushed the reclamation policy through, which, in less than a century, brought under cultivation the total acreage nearly three times that of the late Koryŏ period.

The target areas for the government-sponsored reclamation were coastal districts and islands, and northern defense zones which had been abandoned to Jürched depredations during the closing days of the previous dynasty. For this and also defense purposes, the government, especially Sejo's, put into operation a policy for the systematically-forced immigration into the northern regions of peasant farmers from southern provinces. They were provided with houses, from southern provinces. They were provided with houses, foods, draft oxen, farm implements, and above all, the title to the land they were to reclaim. As the necessity of peopling the defense zones became more urgent, the government allocated tracts of land in the north to prominent families and royal siblings for reclamation with the right to use the immigrant labor force made available under the government program. Thus, by the middle of the fifteenth century, private land or estates which were, of course, taxed but placed at the disposal of individual owners for financial gains came into existence not just in Kyŏnggi Province but also in other regions at governmental sufferance. And also transactions for private gains of assigned land among officials, which were supposedly unlawful, became so prevalent that the official sanction was finally given in 1424, as has been noted.

This transfer of land into private hands, for the Yi dynasty in this period, needless to say, did not mean dynastic decline. In fact, the dynasty made significant improvements in the management of the national economy. The payment of tax for all land under cultivation, regardless of the status of owners, was rigorously enforced. In parallel with the collection of tax supervised under more articulate laws, the government made corresponding efforts to bring about impartial taxation as could be seen in the elaborate system completed by Sejong in 1444. The Yi dynasty government was less concerned with the administration of land titles. Even peasant farmers who cultivated a piece of the government land were generally allowed, as long as their tax payment was in order, to pass the right of cultivation down to their descendants, barring unexpected circumstances.

Other sources of the national revenue were salt production, fishery, manual industry, and merchandising, in which specialized groups of people were collectively engaged. Although they were not of the *hyang-so-pugok* category of Koryŏ, which was abolished under the new regime, their professions were virtually on a hereditary basis. Their production as tax sources figured large in the late Yi period when the management of the government finances became expanded and more sophisticated,

Thus, the government revenue of the peninsular kingdom, which was yet largely from the taxable land, was greatly increased, under the Yi dynasty. The expansion of cultivation over the reclaimed land, the general improvement of agricultural technology effected notably by Sejong and his scholar-assistants, and the continued cultivation of cotton, which was smuggled in from the Yüan in the 1360's, were, major factors in the economic expansion which the young dynasty had brought about.

The Human Sector of the Economy. The common masses who were the most important financial resources for the government, were also managed with a view to increasing the government revenue. The commoners' financial obligation to government in the form of *corvée* service and tribute materials was more articulately institutionalized than in the previous periods. At the same time, the number of labor-and tax-exempt *ch'ŏnmin* was drastically reduced as, for instance, the *ch'ŏnmin* of *hyang*, *so*, and *pugok* were reclassified as *yangmin* (commoners) at the beginning of the dynasty. Emancipation of slaves to the commoner status, whenever feasible, remained a dynastic policy throughout the Yi period, which was in keeping with the general social climate. Yet the *ch'ŏnmin* class embraced a substantial portion, probably a greater majority, of the population at least in the first half of the Yi period.

The *corvée* labor, which was mobilized under specific laws, covered a wide variety of the government's service demands. It was used, along with the army, for the construction and repair of the defense walls, roads, and irrigation dams and, sometimes, for transportation of materials such as tax grain and tribute stuff. It is interesting to note that the commoner inhabitants in the royal capital, even when compulsory labor service was needed for various projects within the city walls, were exempt from such services. A levied man usually paid his own expenses until the completion of the project for which he was summoned, and, when he wanted an exemption, he was required to pay the government a stipulated amount of usually textile fabrics (cotton).

The obligation to present special local products to the court and the government was another burden placed upon the commoner class. Tribute materials consisted in the main of textile fabrics, stationery, furniture, dye, medical plants, fuel, building materials, weapons, and local rare produce. These items, needed for the management of the royal household and governmental departments, were allocated for procurement to the local administrative districts where they were supposed to be rare produce or specialties. The customary presentation of laocl specialties to the monarch was of a millennium-old tradition originated undoubtedly from a simple act of offering the sovereign noted products as gifts on the part of local folks. The custom seems to have been gradually stiffened into a legal obligation since the Three Kingdoms period. Sejong reviewed the tribute matter with a view to lessening, if not abolishing, the burden of the people concerned. The tribute duty was nothing different from the payment of tax in kind, but actually it turned out to be, on all its aspects, the most burdensome duty for the common people.

Once allocated to a district, the item in question was hard to remove from the list, even if it was no longer the specialty of that district, a fact that was not infrequent occurrences. People in that district then would have to purchase it from other areas for the presentation. Some of these tribute items, being perishable produce, exacted extreme care for their transportation to the capital, which was also the responsibility of the people concerned.

These fixed encumbrances, namely, tax payment, labor supply, tribute presentation, of the common people were indeed heavy and difficult duties to fulfil. Irregularities that plagued the late Yi dynasty were, in many respects, not so much of political corruption or confusion in landownership, a familiarity at the time of a dynastic decline, as of complications stemming from the problems of exacting these financial duties from the masses.

The traditional concept of revenue and expenditure, despite occasional proposals to improve it, remained simply that "the amount that came in was made to go out," or to make do with whatever the amount that came in. It sounded simple enough, but the collection of the government revenue which was mostly in the form of products and produce put extraordinary strain upon the masses as they were also made responsible partly for transportation and storage. Although the government made notable efforts, the facilities for the circulation of goods were not improved sufficiently to cope with the extent to which the operational scale of the Yi government was enlarged. It is in this economic failure that the reasons for the political decline of the late Yi dynasty can be sought.

Education and the Examination System

The difference in education between Koryŏ and Yi dynasty is not institutional but one of emphasis and popularization. The formal educational system under the Yi dynasty was further expanded in facility and curriculum. More importantly, the administrative efficiency of the governors and the local magistrates was judged by the extent to which they promoted education in their respective areas of jurisdiction ; this device was one of the first administrative innovations which T'aejo put into practice for the improvement of education.

A new educational institution was private primary school called *sŏdang*, or literally hall of books. A *sŏdang* was to be eventually founded in every large village, supported either by individual families or by the entire village. The educational institutions and also the civil service examination, as in Koryŏ, were theoretically open to all classes of people but actually confined to the *yangban* class. Talented lower class children, however, seem to have, more often than not, been taught at the *sŏdang* level.

After the *sŏdang*, the children of the *yangban* moved on to government
schools, that is, in the provinces, the *hyanggyo* or local school, and, in the
capital, one of the *Sahak* or Four Schools. The *hyanggyo*, founded one in
each administrative district, admitted an age bracket of fourteen to twenty
numbering from thirty to ninety students, depending on the size of the district.
The daily curricular activities at a *hyanggyo* were duly reported to the governor. Its physical layout was patterned after the national university, including
the Confucian shrine, the lecture hall, and dormitories. The equivalent of the
hyanggyo in the capital was the Four Schools. Originally, the capital's five
administrative sections maintained one school each ; later the North section
was made to discontinue its maintenance, hence only Four Schools. The class-
room capacity was 100 students each, larger than that of the largest of the
hyanggyo, but had no Confucian shrine. The major function of both *hyanggyo*
and *Sahak* was preparation of the students for a degree examination, but not
necessarily for the preparatory work for entrance to the *Sŏnggyungwan* or
National University. The *Sahak's* graduates were in some cases given admission to the *Sŏnggyungwan*, however.

As the highest center of formal education in Confucianism, the
Sŏnggyunwan, which was called *Kukchagam* during the Kroyŏ dynasty, was
greatly expanded and managed with care. Its student body of 200 or more, all
lower degree holders, as we shall see, was required to go through a rigorous
curriculum under stringent rules for group living. Although an important goal
of study at the *Sŏnggyungwan* for the majority of students was a successful
candidacy for a higher degree, the students sometimes plunged into political
controversy against the court, often ending in a strike or a kind of sitdown
demonstration. In the latter case, they would sit down in front of the royal
palace until their demand was met ; the monarch usually gave in.

As the unique temple of Confucianism, the *Sŏnggyungwan* enshrined
the Chinese and Korean sage-gods of the past. It is most interesting to note
that Chŏng Mong Chu, that assassinated loyal subject of the Koryŏ dynasty
who was a formidable political enemy of the Yi Sŏng Kye faction, was apoth-
eosized at the pantheon in 1517.

The examination system, also the most effective way of preserving the
political and ethical ideals of Confucianism and of enlarging the basis of the
ruling elite, understandably increased its importance under the Yi dynasty.
Although mediocre children of officials with ranks of the senior third grade or
up could get appointments to government posts without taking the examination, a legacy from Koryŏ, the examination remained the principal gateway to
bureaucratic success for the *yangban*. It also served as the testing ground for
the intellectual elite of the ruling class. Understandably, the examination system was substantially reconstituted so as to ensure a more extensive participation in the government and a wider share of social prestige for the *yangban*

class. Included also in the system was the military service examination, a significant addition which was inaugurated in 1390, two years before the demise of the Koryŏ dynasty, when the Yi group fully entrenched themselves in the government. But the status of the military or western section of the *yangban* as such, even though thus institutionally recognized as important, was far short of being on a par in power and prestige with the eastern section or the civil officials.

Of the examinations, which were increased in kind and in frequency, the most prestigious was the triennial, five-stage examinations. The first two of the five stages constituted themselves a degree examination called *sogwa* or lower course, whereas the last three where known as *taegwa* or upper course for a higher degree. This was a noteworthy development from Koryŏ's three-stage examinations.

The *sogwa*, for which the graduates of the *hyanggyo* and the *Sahak* and other self-taught young scholars were qualified, consisted of preliminary and final examinations and also of two categories of degrees. And, for the *sogwa*, a quota of successful candidates was given to each province to ensure an arbitrarily-set geographical representation. Of the two categories of degrees, the *saengwŏn* degree or, as it can be best translated, new scholar, which was awarded through the examination on the comprehension of the Four Books and the Three Classics, was less popular than the *chinsa* or "presented scholar" degree, for which the candidates were tested for their ability of composition in prose and poetry. The preliminary test for these degrees was held at the provincial capitals under the governors presiding, which qualified successful candidates of 1,400, 700 from each category, the national quota which was later reduced to 1,080, to compete in the final examination. The final was given at the capital, which, under the auspices of the Ministry of Rites selected 200 successfuls. The degrees of *saengwŏn* and *chinsa* were conferred upon them according to their respective categories of candidacy. For most of the students, especially provincial ones, the *sogwa* degree was good enough. They could secure appointments to minor government posts, and they were also regarded as having proved their intellectual muscle as members of the ruling class, if not the ruling elite. The *sogwa* degree holders also qualified for admission to the *Sŏnggyungwan.*

For more ambitious scholars, there were the three-stage *taegwa* examinations. Qualified scholars for this upper course examination, namely, degree holders of *saengwŏn* or *chinsa* and *Sŏnggyungwan* students, first competed in the trial given at the provincial capitals ; for the latter category of candidates, at the *Sŏnggyungwan* itself. The 340, later, reduced to 223, successful participants were pared down to thirty-three through the second ordeal given at the capital and supervised directly by the Ministry of Rites. The final stage was performed at the royal palace where their relative standings among themselves were determined through yet another test. This was done withe the monarch as the examiner, whether theoretical or actual, a stratagem that dispensed with the *Chigonggŏ* in the Koryŏ system who, as noted, shared in the loyalty of the intellectual champions of the dynasty. But, as in Koryŏ the successfuls were showered upon with honors and coveted privileges, besides immediate appointments to strategic offices which usually led to the top.

Many other kinds of examinations for the degrees were held, in some cases, impromptu, on happy occasions such as the birth of the crown prince, a satisfactory conclusion of some diplomatic fracas with China, and so on. Successful candidates in these examinations seem to have been not always assured of official appointments. The court appears to have calculated that the larger the number of degree holders was, the wider the royal authority or grace extended. But the increase of degree holders, if it indeed did not diminish royal influences, fell on the debit side in its political and social consequences ; late Yi dynasty factional politics were a direct result from it, as we shall see later.

The military service examinations which were perfected by T'aejo and T'aejong who did not fail to see the importance of the military, Confucianism's onslaught in government notwithstanding, were equally elaborately conducted. The candidates were tested on Confucian and military classics and martial arts such as archery, horse riding, lancing, etc., through three levels of examinations. The twenty-eight finalists, rather than thirty-three, were tested, as in the *taegwa* (upper course) examination, by the monarch to determine their standings.

There were also examinations in the "professional" fields, namely, medicine, *yin-yang*, law, and foreign languages (Chinese, Mongolian, Japanese, and Jürched). Aspirants in these areas, who were mostly of *chung'in* origin, a class just below the *yangban*, were taught, trained, and given two-stage examinations under the auspices of respective government departments for whose work expertise in these subjects was essential.

4

The Nature of the Confucian Society

An important thing to examine with regard to the nature of the Yi society is the extent of ramification into every aspect of the dynastic life of the confucian political ideals and moral doctrines. In contrast with the Koryŏ period, the general social texture of the Yi dynasty, especially its official life which was rendered devoid of Buddhism's rightful role, was dyed monotonically with Confucian moralism. And the very name of the Confucianists, "the learned weaklings" or scholars, as against the men of the sword, suggests the nature of the Yi society most pungently.

The Philosophical Foundation

The Persuasive power of Confucian moralism, which was to leave an indelible mark on the Korean mind, was ultimately rooted in Neo-Confucian metaphysics of *Li* or Principle. This immutable Principle, as we have seen, constitutes the essence of all things in the universe, that is, the *Tao* (Way) of the universe. As man's mind partakes of this Principle, its power of reason enables man not only to know what all things are but also to understand how they ought to be and to work harmoniously. Human relations and conduct, too, therefore, are determined by the Principle or Reason that underlies all phenomena. Indeed, for this Principle, the Yi dynasty Confucians professed their willingness to die ; they were the soldiers of Confucian rationalism. It is surprising to note how great a power the Confucian ideology wielded in the Yi society. It was also this ideological power with which the ruling elite could contain the distensible monarchal power, if only to protect their own status and privileges as the co-founders of the dynasty.

As Confucian moralism was translated into practice, the five human relationships were most strongly stressed as the fundamental ethical standards of society. They were, as has been noted, relations between father and son with a greater emphasis on son's filial piety, monarch and subject on subject's loyalty, husband and wife on wife's obedience, elder brother and younger brother on the latter's respect, and friend and friend on mutual sincerity. Thus, the burden of proper conduct was squarely placed on the shoulders of the obedient inferior, except for the friend-friend relations. The authority, that is, the king in the country, the father in the family, and so on, was, of course, patriarchal one. Since the five human relations were the ethical manifestation in humanity of the metaphysical *Li* (Reason), the patriarchal authority was identifiable with the *Tao* (Way) of the universe. Hence, this authority, in political and social contexts, became absolute as in a Confucian adage : The parents do no wrong. Economically, it was equated with wealth, knowledge, and other human desiderata.

The Social Organization

The concept of authority and obedience in human relations could be applied to all political and social situations. In fact, this paternalistic nature of authority made the whole country or, at least theoretically, the world–in this case, with China or the Middle Kingdom as the center–great family. On top of the class structure, the *yangban* class, who swore lasting allegiances to the king as the head of the family, served as the bulwark of Confucianism and dealt paternally with the productive classes, the *yangmin* and the *Ch'ŏnmin*. The term *yangban*, namely, the civil and military groups that comprised the aristocrat–controlled Koryŏ government, as noted, was more prestigiously and widely used under the Yi dynasty as to embrace the whole class that enjoyed the exemption from draft and corvée labor and, above all, the privileges of candidacy for the government examinations.

The social realignment within the *yangban* class itself went on as the dynasty progressed, but most noteworthy was the way in which the *yangban* perpetuated themselves in the class. This was done fundamentally by emphasis on, and monopolization of, Confucian knowledge and education, in contrast with the late Koryŏ that put a high premium on the power of the naked sword. With faith in the moralizing influence of Confucianism, the Yi dynasty gentlemen, if anything, more firmly harnessed the people and themselves in the Confucian social status system based on the authority-obedience formula.

To maintain the status system and the social moralism in the Confucian preservative, they enforced by law the performance of family rites and ceremonies prescribed strictly by the Confucian moral code, that discriminated among the social classes. As we shall see later, the *yangban* scholars were to make an important field of learning out of historical study of the rites and ceremonies of the ancient Chinese society. The knowledge and ability of properly conducting them provided the *yangban* with an enormous source of authority. As the dynasty progressed, they strove for this sort of academic authority.

As a means of internal solidarity, the *yangban* placed a great emphasis on the importance of genealogy. Compilation of the genealogy, which clarified one's relative position in the family and the clan, was regarded as one of the most serious Confucian chores that distinguished the *yangban* from the other classes. The *yangban's* institutionalized clannishness, coupled with regionalism, became increasingly notorious ; it furnished a clan with internal cohesiveness and fostered the parochialism of the *yangban* class in general.

The Chung'in. Immediately below the *yangban* class was an interesting layer called *chung'in* or literally middle people–middle between the *yangban* and the *yangmin.* Not unlike the modern middle class, they were "professionals" specializing in such fields as medicine, language, accounting, meteorology, law, charity service, painting, etc., under the auspices of the government. They were also appointed, without promotive provisions, to that lower portion of the bureaucracy as clerks, messengers, guards, patrolmen, who made direct contact with the tax-paying *yangmin.* Their offices were made hereditary, a fact that produced painters who could not paint.

A more absurd element in the *chung'in* class was some *yangban* children born of concubines, who were not allowed to enter the government service and let sink to the middle people class. This inhospitable treatment was usually imputed to T'aejong, as has been touched upon. It is difficult, however, to draw a clear-cut class line as *chung'in* for the men of illegitimate birth. A great many of them, because of their talent and family standing in society, led the life of the *yangban,* if usually relegated to the limbo of that class. Since it was permissible for a *yangban* to have one or more concubines, these *yangban-chung'in* were ever on the increase in number. Given such a fatal handicap not of their own fault, they became a most discontented element in the Yi society throughout its existence.

The *chung'in* class as a whole, however, remained a very thin tier in social stratification. Probably, its *raison d'être* for the ruling class that created it lay in its role as a kind of buffer zone which absorbed those dropped out of the rank of the *yangban.* Or, more importantly, it took in those who somehow made their way upward from the commoner or *yangmin* class, thus protecting the *yangban* against a numerical encroachment from below. And, as evidence suggests, the *chungin* as a distinct class seems to have come into existence in the late sixteenth century.

About a half of the population was the *yangmin*, or literally good people, during the early part of the dynasty. Unlike the good people of Koryŏ the Yi dynasty's good people were not allocated land to till. The reason for this may have been that a great many *ch'ŏnmin* were at the dynastic beginning emancipated to the *yangmin* status, and their enlarged number made land distribution economically and administratively infeasible. But although they shouldered the heavy burden of economically supporting the *yangban* class, they were generally a contented lot under the care of Confucian paternalism, that never failed to see a heavenly volition in the will of the people and upheld the importance of agriculture as "the foundation of the society." Some of these *yangmin* were allowed to engage in commerce and industry, which were regarded as secondary or even tertiary to agriculture and kept effectively underdeveloped by heavy taxation and other deleterious policies. New market systems, for instance, were developed from time to time by commercially-oriented commoners but invariably made difficult to develop further or high-handedly abolished by the government. The pelagic fishery was prohibited outright by law. Profits that could be had by the common people from these ventures were thought to be improper and unwarranted.

At the bottom of the social scale were the *ch'ŏnmin*, people in bondage to whom "Confucian propriety did not reach ; " in other words, they were freed from the statutory performance of family rites and ceremonies. As in Koryŏ, the *ch'ŏnmin* of the slave category were owned by individual *yangban* families and various offices of central and provincial governments. They were used as items for gift, inheritance, tribute, and sale. The ch'ŏnmin's desire for emancipation constantly created conflicts between the owners and their slaves which usually ended in litigation, a fact that necessitated the Ministry of Justice to take custody of slave registers and other documents concerning their transactions, etc.

The law that stipulated for the children born of a slave parent to be slaves helped increase the *ch'ŏnmin* population, which seems to have slightly outnumbered the *yangmin* until the sixteenth century. The court generally showed an inclination to reduce slaves in number, taking concrete steps in that direction during the late Yi period, which effected, for instance, a large scale emancipation of royal household slaves in 1801. Entertainers such as singers and dancers, sorcerers, and butchers were also regarded as *ch'ŏnmin* ; especially, the latter, the spiritual descendants of the wicker-basket makers of Koryŏ, were looked down on as belonging to the bottom of the *ch'ŏnmin* class.

The Family

The nuclear unit in the Confucian social organization, down to the *yang-min* class, was, of course, the family. The importance of the family could be hardly overemphasized ; an individual as an individual, that is, apart from his family, was simply an unperson. Three of the five cardinal human relationships center around the family. Of them the most important was, needless to say, the father-son relations with a one-sided emphasis on the filial piety, a relationship on which not only the family life but also, it may as well be said, the national life itself devolved. The maintenance of the family solidarity, therefore, was a social ideal as well as a standing national policy that called for concentrated educational efforts to that end.

Filial piety, considered as an actual manifestation in the weightiest area of human conduct of humaneness, was the subject which was most actively discussed in all educational textbooks. The models of filial conduct in every possible live situation were described, for instance, in the *Book of Filial Piety (Hyogyŏng)* for emulation by the sons. Indictment in any form of one's parents for whatever reasons constituted the gravest crime second only to treason. A son was supposed to acquire some degree of medical knowledge because it was thought to be impious to leave a sick parent completely to the hands of the doctor. A son whose parent had just died regarded himself as a "sinner" who was expected "to wail until he fell into a swoon" and to barely live on gruel with vegetable and salt for three years. More pious son-"sinners" would usually build a small shed beside the parental graves "to wait on" for three years, which was a most sobering scene in a Confucian utopia.

A widely recited story from the *Book of Filial Piety* has that a dutiful son whose parents suggested the edibility of carps in winter went to the river to get them. Upon realizing the impossibility of catching the designated fish in the river which was completely sealed frozen, the filial son fell on his face and keened, inspite of himself. Unexpectedly, out of ice, several carps Jumped and laid themselves in front of the devoted son. The customary interpretation of this utopian incident was that the son's utmost sincerity in devotion to his pavents moved the Heaven. Comparable filial deeds were rewarded actually by the court and widely adored by the society.

Around this pivot of the father-son relationship, other relations between husband and wife, elder brother and younger brother, mother and daughter-in-law, etc., were formed with given status and duties to perform within the family. The ancestor worship, including the welfare of the living parents, and the birth and bringing-up of male children most constantly commanded the collective attention and service of the whole family. An important responsibility of the family in social context was passing the family name down to posterity in its original glory or, if possible, in a more illustrious state in terms of political and social influence based on wealth, scholarship, and the abundance of male children. To this end, the head of the family exercised an unquestioned authority. The branch or collateral families in turn were expected to make sacrifices for the good of the lineal family.

Understandably, the performance of the ceremonies and rituals exacted a tremendous amount of time and energy from the *yangban* family. The most important of these consisted of the so-called four ceremonies, namely, the doing-up of one's hair into a new hair style signifying his coming-of-age, the marriage, the funeral, and the sacrificial rite for the dead. These family rites and ceremonies were modeled mainly upon the *Rites and Ceremonies of the Chu Family* as conducted by the Chu Hsi family. A *yangban* and, in a much simplified form, a commoner, too, was destined to go through the four ceremonies. But the four ceremonies as such, it should be noted, did not necessarily constitute milestones as the marks of achievements in the course of realization of one's self, as in a competitive society, but rather as the marks of his familial and social status enhanced as he became older, which entailed new duties and obligations.

The group-forming tradition, as seen in such a productive and social organization as the *ture* of the tribal period and in a variety of other forms of grouping, seems to have manifested itself most strongly in the organization of family and clan. Confucianism as a philosophical rationale of the family and kinship organizations would have never been so thoroughly utilized and developed but for the Koreans' constitutional inclination for grouping.

A sociological cross section of the traditional family organization, as consummated in the Yi dynasty, shows that its fundamental substance was not universal love advocated by Mo-tzu (ca. 470-391 B.C.), but it was methodically-gradated love, an ingredient that actually yielded a stronger cohesiveness than otherwise for the Korean family. In no instance becomes the basic pattern of this gradated love more tangible than upon one's death. The mourning period for the death of the parents and the eldest son was twenty-seven months ; for the death of sons except the eldest, the grandparents, and brothers twelve months ; for the first cousins, daughters-in-law, etc., nine months ; for the second cousins, granduncles and aunts, etc., five months ; for the third cousins, etc., three months The sex of the dead, his birth, that is, whether born of legal wife or concubine, his marital status, or the relational situation in which the death occurred, for instance, the death of the eldest son when his parents were still living, effected some modifications to the mourning period but always meriting the one considered proper out of the five categories of mourning periods. Conditions and situations such as these, which spawned numerous complications, very often produced difficult problems of assigning a correct mourning period to all those with obligations of mourning.

The rules and regulations pertaining to the four ceremonies, as they were made part of a distinct field of scholarly concentration in the seventeenth century, as we shall see, were most elaborately established as to meet all complex situations.

Although the mourning did not extend beyond one's third cousins, various cooperative activities of economic and social nature among kinship groups bound them together spiritually, economically, and geographically. Promotion of the solidarity and welfare of the clan was indeed a most assiduously pursued business of the *yangban* class. Naturally, they tended to stick together, forming villages and towns with their own members. As late as 1933, villages made up of more than seventy families of the same clan counted some, 1,600 with heavier concentration in southern provinces.

Women. The Confucian Yi culture, with its singular concern about social decorum and order in harmony with its metaphysical universe, produced a type of individual characterized by resigned optimism born of a sense of social security and by willing submission to prescribed formalities and manners. On the other hand, it discouraged individual initiative and spontaneous activism. In this tradition-bound, family-centered society, an individual counted only as part of his family, clan, and district in which he was born and lived.

Unfairly treated by this Confucian regimentation of life were women. They had enjoyed a considerable degree of equality with men in social and sexual freedom. During the Silla times, they were allowed to be legitimate rulers, and during the Neolithic period, they were probably the very central authority in a matriarchal society as it is conjectured to have existed then. But, under the Confucian Yi dynasty, the decline in social status of women seemed complete, from which they suffered quite early in their life, or even from the moment of their birth.

A new-born baby girl was usually laid on the floor of the room, whereas a boy was served upon the bed ; thus the girl's life-long career of obedience got started. The entire social mechanism and education, allied with the restrictive legal setup, were geared to molding an obedient and faithful personality out of whatever native dispositions and abilities. In the family, she was expected to be a silent servant and producer of male children. In a larger society, she was made anonymous ; upon marriage, she was known in her husband's register only as the wife of so-and-so.

The hardest blow to the women, after T'aejong who, among other things, prohibited marriage for the third time for women, was given in 1477 when their second marriage was banned. "A woman must follow one man" became a sacred principle. A widow, even if she might die of starvation, should remain faithful to her dead husband, which was "the supremely important matter," could not be sacrificed for "the smallest matter." Young *yangban* widows more often chose death by drowning or hanging themselves, thus entering the ranks of that special species of dead women called *yŏllyŏ* or faithful women. Then, the government would give them a due recognition of the deed ; their clan would build monuments to their memory, which dot the countryside even today.

Yet, a wife might be high-handedly "sent back home," that is, divorced when found guilty of "seven sins." They were sterility, licentiousness, jealousy, "bad" disease, loquaciousness, stealing, and disrespect for parents-in-law. For many of the Yi dynasty women, life might have been rather hazardous until they became ensconced in that secure widowhood, or, in the case of the royal family, in the position of a queen dowager, surrounded by many sons and grandsons. But, generally, they were contented and made the best of them. Some of them went further by pouring their creative energy into literature and art to produce works of great magnitude.

Portrait of Yi T'aejo.

5

The Foreign Relations

The Sadae Diplomacy toward the Ming

As we have rather graphically seen in the development pattern of the international intercourse between Koryŏ and the Chin during the twelfth and thirteenth centuries, the traditional concept of diplomacy between any given two countries was based on the dynamics of their military strengths. Militarily weak countries ought to "serve" the militarily stronger country, a concept that was inherited from feudal Chou China. By the time the truth of this cold international reality was written by Tso Ch'iu-ming into his *Ch'unch'iu Tso chuan (Spring and Autumn Annals : Commentaries of Tso)* sometime between the late fourth and early second centuries B.C., it became nothing less than a most important Confucian virtue, *li (ye)*. *Ye* is, as we have seen, the rules of conduct which, when applied to human intercourse, are called etiquette, propriety, good manners, or proper rituals for the dead, and, when applied to international intercourse, *iso sadae* or the small should serve the large.

The "service" of a small country to a large one consisted in formality in the use of the "year period" of the latter or, in most cases, the Chinese empire and in the periodical dispatch to its court of tribute missions as a gesture of vassalage. These diplomatic formalities with China had been adopted since the tribal period, as has been touched upon in reference to Koryŏ's dealing with the Sung. What was really involved on the part of the peninsular governments, or for that matter, all "small" or "barbarian" nations maintaining diplomatic relations with China, was promotion of commercial profits resulting from the presenting of tribute materials for which the Chinese court usually returned far more in kind in the form of gift. Equally important in maintaining contacts with China, especially for Korea, was a need of cultural exchange, which was indeed pursued with zeal throughout the traditional period. We have seen Su Shih, Sung Minister of Rites, propose a measure prohibiting the Koryŏ embassies from buying up books during its sojourn in the Sung captial.

The tributary relations with China, as formed by the Yi dynasty, took on new dimensions. The genealogically-obscure Yi family wanted to share with the Chu family, the ruling house of the Ming, in the Chinese imperial prestige through a closer political relationship, if solely for domestic display. When Yi Sŏng Kye and his colleagues successfully wrested the throne from the highly aristocratic Koryŏ dynasty, in their hands were only military power and the political stability of country to their credit. What they suddenly found lacking was an aristocratic aura around the Yi family. No one was more keenly aware of this handicap than Yi T'aejo himself. He then seems to have moved to court the grace of the Chu family with which to butter up his own, as it were. The monk-beggar background of Chu Yüan-chang considered, the Chu family was also a *nouveau riche*, only more so than the Yi family, but that did not matter as long as it was the imperial house of China. Some of the missions that Yi T'aejo dispatched to the Ming court seem to have aimed specifically at purchasing a friendlier acceptance by the Chinese court of the Korean royal house. He even asked Ming T'ai Tzu to choose for him a new dynastic name out of the two, Chosŏn and Hwaryŏng ; Ming T'ai Tzu picked the former in 1392.

Such display of innocence and naivety in international dealing might certainly have looked like an act of "toadyism." But then the government of the very T'aejo was determined upon an armed resistance against the Ming, as intended and half-way executed by Ch'oe Yŏng of Koryŏ before, when the Ming tried to make a big issue out of some trivial matter in 1398. At any rate, the diplomatic aim and posture set by T'aejo, backed by the Confucian view of the *sadae* relations with the Ming as being morally correct, were soon translated, if unilaterally by Chosŏn, into a policy of "cementing the two families [Chu and Yi] into one," of which Sejong was an ardent advocate.

Another aspect, though less visible, of the *sadae* relations was of military significance for both countries. The Yi family's desire for a firm adherence to the Chinese ruling house, politically seen, meant the preclusion of scheming officials from approaching the Ming court individually, a threat which, however, seemed now far less real in comparison with Koryŏ times. Militarily, a close alliance of the two sedentary countries was indeed desirable against the ups and downs of nomadic and semi-nomadic peoples to the north. They needed each other for military coordination in dealing with them. We have seen in the Silla-T'ang alliance and Koryŏ–Sung-Chin relations complex factors at work always dominated by national interests. The Korean-Chinese relations were now so closely "cemented" by the national as well as ideological interests as never before. Indeed, they came to feel matter-of-factly obliged to help each other militarily in time of emergency. This was a diplomatic triumph for Chosŏn, but its over-reliance upon the Ming in international affairs, as we shall see, badly undermined its self-reliance.

The Friendship Diplomacy toward the Jürched and Japan

Whereas the Yi dynasty's *sadae* relations with the Ming were based on sincerity, its dealings with the Jürched and the Japanese who were regarded as "friends" were based on mutual trust. But this trust on the part of the Yi government was so often betrayed. Although there cropped up from time to time certain issues between Chosŏn and the Ming, of which solutions caused the former some distress, resulting at times in, in modern parlance, a compromise with sovereignty, its Chinese relations were generally smooth. The frequency of tribute missions, which was triennial, as proposed by the Ming, was gradually increased at Chosŏn's insistence to as many as four times annually plus occasional unscheduled missions with various purposes. Through these frequent dispatches of embassies, the dialogue and the transactions of goods between the two can be said to have been constat. In short, Chosŏn's Chinese policy was successful.

It was, however, in handling the Japanese and the Jürched that the Yi government could not come through. The principle of trust in diplomacy, as applied to these peoples without maintaining close contact to keep abreast with their internal political developments, proved to be disastrous, if still morally correct, as the Yi gentlemen would have said. This misplaced trust in the two neighbors eventuated in two great wars with them respectively in the last sixteenth and early seventeenth centuries.

With the fall of the Chin empire in 1234, the Jürched were again disintegrated into the various modes of tribal life. When, after the Mongol dynasty, the Ming took over Manchuria, it divided the Jürched country, in the beginning, into some twenty-odd military zones which were administered by the commander of the Chinese army occupying each zone. The Ming's tactic for subduing the Jürched was the traditional one of investing pliant tribal chiefs with honorary titles accompanied by privileges to trade with Chinese, thus keeping them divided. The Jürched tribes, on the other hand, especially those in regions remote from the political influence of the Ming or Chosŏn would become a military menace whenever under a strong leadership of their own, creating border nuisances for the two countries. It was because of these Jürched's marauding along the northern borders that the Yi government came to implement serious and flexible policies toward the Jürched.

An important development in this connection was a northward expansion of the territory up to the natural boundaries of the Tuman and Amnok Rivers. This territorial expansion, which actually began in the closing days of Koryŏ, reached its peak during the reign of Sejong when in 1433 General Kim Chong Sŏ started in earnest the management of the northeastern region. While wiping out Jürched tribal forces, he established the socalled *Rukchin* or Six Fortified Towns along the Tuman River. At almost the same time, a similar military and administrative undertaking in the northeastern region of modern North P'yŏng'an Province under another general got under way, culminating in the creation of *Sagun* or Four Counties in the area immediately south of the middle reaches of the Amnok River.

Chosŏn's Jürched problems rose in the wake of these determined efforts to bring the areas south of the two rivers under firm administrative control. Traditionally, the Jürched tribes living in the areas along the Tuman River had sought food and other supplies from Korean communities to the south either through peaceful exchange of goods or by armed attacks. As Korean boundaries were pushed northward, the conflicts between the Yi government and the provisions-hungry Jürched were natually intensified. The Yi government, occasionally limbering out of its usual defense posture, resorted to military expeditions into the Jürched territory even north of the Tuman River, sometimes, in cooperation with the Ming. Generally, however, the government pursued peaceful relations with the Jürched, that is, through the friendship diplomacy based on mutual trust.

The crux of success in this relationship lay in a minimum level of the flow of goods, mainly, foodstuff, textile fabrics, and agricultural implements into the hands of the Jürched. Chosŏn's main efforts were made toward an orderly transfer of materials as the basis of mutual trust. Like the Ming and Koryŏ before it, the Yi court encouraged peripheral tribes to place themselves in tributary relations with itself in order to be supplied with their necessities. Some tribal chiefs were permitted to stay in the capital or even to serve as royal attendants.

To render the Japanese trustable, the Yi government had to make more economic sacrifices and exercise more patience. With the Japanese, the trade on a larger scale was necessary to dissuade them from piratical itineracy along the coastal zones. Their piratical attacks, that plagued Koryŏ in its declining decades, were not completely subdued under the Yi government. The early Yi government urged Japan's Ashikaga shogunate to suppress the piracy, while building up naval defenses. T'aejo was characteristically cautious about handling the Japanese traders who were coming to Hanyang. He extended a kind of favored treatment under which they were even provided with the travel expenses for their way home. The Sō family of Tsushima, who had been in tributary relations with Korea since the late Koryŏ period, was given special favors in trade arrangements over other leading families of western Japan that traded with Chosŏn.

But Japanese piratical attacks upon Chosŏn and the Ming suddenly increased as a result of famines notably in Tsushima in the early fifteenth century. In 1419, at the order of the then abdicated T'aejong, an expeditionary force for the second time since the beginning of the Yi dynasty was dispatched to wipe out the piratical lairs in Tsushima. The next year the government ordered the island to be annexed to Kyŏngsang Province. At the repeated entreaties of the Sō family, Sejong softened the tough governmental stance and, a few years later, permitted the resumption of official trade.

What Sejong arranged for resumption was the opening of three harbors to Japanese traders and fishermen as ports of entry and call. Pusanp'o or modern Pusan, Naeip'o at the mouth of the Naktong River, and Yŏmp'o near modern Ulsan were officially designated harbor-cities where the Japanese might come and trade. Gradually in these cities, the Japanese came to illegally make permanent home, counting about 2,000 toward the end of the Sejong reign ; residence permits were eventually issued to sixty families. to stem the excessive outflow of grains, textile fabrics, and other materials, the Yi government in 1443 moved to impose drastic restrictions upon the trade, even with the most favored Sō family. The annual number of Japanese trade ships permitted to enter Korean ports were reduced to fifty ships, and they were required to carry certificates issued by the Sō family government. The amount of the annual grant of rice and beans to Tsushima was reduced to 200 *sŏk*. This new arrangement, which became a constant source of the Japanese complaint, lasted until 1510 when the resident Japanese in the said harbor-cities made serious disturbances at the instigation of the Sō.

In the meantime, the influx into Chosŏn of the Japanese was on the steady increase ; envoys from the shogunate and local mighties, traders in groups, individual adventurers with doubtful purposes, and downright pirates, too, made their way into the country. Together, they caused a tremendous outflow of goods and cultural items such as Buddhist scriptures, etc., from the country. Cotton cloth taken out by the Japanese during the 1480's, for instance, annually amounted to more than 200,000 bolts. Administration of rules and regulations on the reception of Japanese traders, transactions of goods, investiture, the length and place of stay and travel within the country, taxation, naturalization, and justice was another burden for the government to bear.

In general, the Yi government endeavored to satisfy the acquisitive desire of the often unwelcome people with a remarkable degree of patience and generosity. Indeed, the sincerity and trust that governed the friend-friend relationship in the Confucian society did motivate the conduct and attitudes of the Yi officials in dealing with them. They were, to the Yi officials, the "guests coming from far-off places." In the case of violation of laws by the "guests," which in the end became the rule rather than exception, the host officials were genuinely reluctant to use force and, in most cases, simply hoped that "guests" would come to behave in time.

The Japanese from Tsushima Island, who were familiar with the government system, the coastal defense setup, and local communities of the host country, proved to be most recalcitrant, inveterate law-breakers who might take to piracy at next turn. It was they who caused a series of uprisings along the southern coastal provinces in 1510, 1541, and 1555.

Japanese pirate.

6

Political Development

The Conservatives and the New Radicals

The reign of Sŏngjong (1470-1494) is usually regarded as the period in which the Confucian system of government and society came into full maturity. In politics, it marked the beginning of a new development after a century of dynastice growth. Those polemical Confucian radicals who wrung the throne from the Wang family and the spiritual leadership from Buddhism were one of the most interesting and ablest groups of politicians in the traditional period. As the founding fathers of a bureaucratic regime (as distingusihed from the aristocratic dynasty), they greatly widened the basis of the *yangban* class eligible for participation in government, with themselves as the core of that class. The successive generations of officials of this category ruled the country in the first century, during which they gradually grew conservative and even aristocratic.

As veterans of series of political crises and succession wars, they were a politically astute, worldly-wise, if morally blunt, lot. Mostly native sons of the metropolitan city of Hanyang, they were also urbane, administratively competent, and rich not only with higher salaries but also with the land granted as they were appointed Merit Subjects on eight occasions until the Sŏngjong reign. The latest appointment occurred in 1471 when, as noted, seventy-three officials were recognized for their meritorious service : they were supposed to have facilitated the accession of Sŏngjong by eliminating a powerful uncle.

As scholars they were not necessarily interested in the systematic exposition of Neo-Confucian metaphysics or in the production of original works as such. But instead they excelled in composing prose and poems and in compiling histories and other books necessary for the business of government based on their wide learning and research. It was their literary and practical scholarship that made possible the official publication in spate of a tremendous variety of works. In short, they were not philosophers but literati and, above all, politicians who, having spent their earlier revolutionary inspirations, were no longer interested in change.

This long-entrenched conservative group in the government had naturally created oppositions of various shades. On the surface, it was the moral issue that led to a political polarization within both the bureaucracy and the ruling class. Sejo's usurpation, for instance, caused clear, wide cleavages to appear among the vaguely opposing groups and never to be sealed. A large number of officials and their families separated themselves from those in power, seeking to peserve their moral integrity in the political obscurity of the "grass field" or "mountain and forest."

Some others indulged in cynical hedonism in the style of "Seven Sages of the Bamboo Grove." These Taoistic sages or recluses of the third century Western Chin was the most famous group in the so-called *ch'ing-t'an* movement then in vogue. The word *ch'ing-t'an* (*ch'ŏngdam* in Korean), meaning pure discussion presumably devoid of murky politics, was a sardonic characterization of the general disillusionment and cynicism of the day. Some disenchanted Yi intellectuals, while keeping themselves aloof from current social and political events, engaged in high-flown debates on arts and philosophy and nursed their pessimism through drinking in the beautiful surroundings of nature or in bamboo groves. This phenomenon also appeared in the Koryŏ period after the military take-over.

The foremost opponents who erected themselves to challenge the conservative group were a breed of scholars called the *Sallimp'a* or Mountain and Forest School. The Mountain and Forest scholars, mostly of the Kyŏngsang area remote from the seat of power, had lived in *ch'ŏngbin* or pure poverty, nurturing contemptuous attitudes toward the central officialdom for its moral turpitude. They had been immersed in Neo-Confucian metaphysics, in addition to the usual literary pursuit in prose and poetry. They were morally impeccable, therefore, outspoken and radical in their political outlook. The Mountain and Forest scholars, who might be said the spiritual descendants of the Koryŏ loyalists who refused to serve under the Yi dynasty, however, seemed ready by the Sŏngjong period to break out of their long political dormancy. Soon they plunged into the political arena to purify the bureaucracy with their radical view of politics and morals as the only weapon.

The initial introduction of this group to the court was made by Kim Chong Chik (1431–1492), the leading scholar of the Mountain and Forest persuasion. As a Neo-Confucian scholar and royal lecturer, Kim Chong Chik, through his close contact with Sŏngjong, was able to secure government posts for his disciples. Sŏngjong, who had been well indoctrinated in Confucian

kingship as a teen-age king, was ever receptive to the Neo-Confucian principles of Kingly Way and good government. Besides, he earnestly hoped to
refurbish the increasingly stagnant officialdom with more rigorous Neo-
Confucian learning. It was under Sŏngjong's patronage that Mountain and
Forest scholars made headway in the officialdom.

Scholarly and articulate in argument and criticism but shy of administrative detail, these idealistic gentlemen came to dominate the Board of Censors,
the Board of Literary Counsellors, the Office of Royal Lectures, and other
acdemic offices ; some of theses scholastic organs were substantially enlarged
under Sŏngjong. As the "officers of words," they never ceased to discourse
and criticize. Under the strong-willed Sejo, the "officers of words" were never
given a chance for their "straight words." Sŏngjong, however, countenanced
the full performance of their duties, which gave scope and opportunity for the
power potential of censuring organs.

Through successive years, the censors, with thus enlarged power, performed their duty well, making themselves the center of endless controversies
at the court. They would single out a hapless official for attacks which were
not always confined to his political view or public conduct but extended to his
private life ; then they would tongue-lash him out of office. Although arguments often hinged on moral questions, at issue were power struggles between
the old conservatives and the radical newcomers. As antagonism between
them were further intensified by differences in personality and wealth, they
seemed to be heading inevitably for a showdown.

The Sahwa and the Political Experiment

The term *sahwa* may be rendered misfortunes of scholars, misfortunes
being those inflicted upon as the result of a political purge. Great political
showdowns that occurred at least four times in the period of a half century
from 1498 usually ended in the large-scale purge of radicals. The first *sahwa*
took place in 1498 during the reign of the Yŏnsan'gun (1495-1506). The occasion was provided by the compilation of an official history. Kim Il Son (1464-
1498), an official historian, of the Mountain and Forest school, was a man
with a penchant for "straight pen" (or actually "straight brush" as they wrote
with brushes) and drafted on some misdeeds of certain conservative officials
with a view to including them in the proposed history. As a former disciple of
Kim Chong Chik, Kim Il Son also included in his draft one of his teacher's
essays accompanied by his own laudatory comment in juxtaposition with a
factual description of Sejo's usurpation. This audacity inflamed the whole
affair. The essay in question was a satrical story in which the author in his

dream mourned the death of I Ti of Ch'u (a Chinese kingdom : ca. 750–223 B.C.,) who was killed by Hsiang Yu, the famed opponent of Liu Pang, the first monarch of the Han dynasty, thus alluding to Sejo's disposal of his nephew, Tanjong.

Yi Kŭk Ton, a senior official whose misconduct was written into the historian's draft, decided to make an issue out of the essay as calumniating Sejo. The Yŏnsan'gun, the reigning monarch of completely different temparament from Sŏngjong's, had loathed the presumptuous meddling into his conduct of government by radicals of the Mountain and Forest style. Although he was not particularly fond of conservatives, the Yŏnsan'gun sided with them. The result was the purge of nearly forty officials, ironically including a few from the conservative group. The several executed and a still larger number banished were disciples and close associates of Kim Chong Chik. Kim Chong Chik, who had been dead six years, was branded as the arch-villain ; accordingly, his body was exhumed and "beheaded," an act that may be regarded as entirely befitting the Yi dynasty gentlemen who lived in an abstract world of Confucian idealism.

For the Yŏnsan'gun, the purge was elimination of a check to his authority rather than of a treasonous group who had the temerity to criticize Sejo. The Yŏnsan'gun was eventually given to debauchery, driven by his innate sensuality and inability to wipe out the system that restrained the despotic exercise of the royal power. His frustration and jealousy fed by the fact of certain past intrigues involving his mother's unhappy death, which was unexpectedly divulged to him, caused his reign to degenerate into an aberration of the lowest order unparalleled in the Korean history. He indulged in paranoiac sexual perversion and mass-execution of hapless officials, including two of his half-brothers, while destroying educational and religious institutions. Subsequently, in 1506, he was deposed through a lightning *coup d'état* tacitly approved by Queen Dowager Yun, the Yŏnsan'gun's stepmother.

Her son, Chungjong (1507–1544), succeeding the Yŏnsan'gun or Prince Yŏnsan who was, because of his infamous deeds, denied a usual posthumous title, ushered in another generation of cultural advancement. It was also the period that witnessed probably *the* most important political experiment through the entire Yi period, which, however, ended again in the misfortunes of scholars as a result of the clash between the young scholar-zealots of the Mountain and Forest style and the entrenched old-timers.

One of the first acts Chungjong, who bore much affinity in political view with Sŏngjong, was normalization of the functions of the *Samsa* (three censuring organs) ad educational institutions made defunct by the Yŏnsan'gun. While appointing as the Merit Subjects 103 officials who were supposed to have made his accession possible, Chungjong exerted genuine endeavors to restore the public morale and order through the encouragement of Neo-Confucian learning. This restored climate of learning again attracted to the court Mountain and Forest scholars who had been hiding low in the mountains and forests during the Yŏnsan'gun's reign of terror.

One of them was Cho Kwang Cho (1482–1519), an outstanding personality in the best of Mountain and Forest style. As a censor he distinguished himself by censuring senior censors out of office. As Chungjong fell under his spell, Cho vigorously pushed for the execution of his idealistic policies. Cho Kwang Cho seems to have had a religious faith in Neo-Confucianism as a social system. On the strength of it, he and his colleagues set out to create a Confucian utopia. Their political philosophy was that Neo-Confucianism should be put into practice as it was intended to be, a view which was not new, to be sure. What made the Cho group different from those radicals of the pre-Yŏnsan period was that, like other utopia-builders, they placed an emphasis on action. Although their actions seemed, in some cases, similar in concept to Taoistic non-action, little, or not even their reverence for the established tradition, was allowed to stand in the way of the actual implementation of their policies.

Three measures that were acted upon by the Cho group in 1518 throw a most significant light upon the nature of this political experiment, which was definitely a giant step forward in the logical development of the idealistic Confucian government. First, Cho Kwang Cho established a new simplified examination system, though which was more of political expediency. Prospective candidates, with the recommendation of a provincial governor, a local magistrate, or heads of the Six Ministries or the *Samsa*, were to take just one-stage examination on essay writing in the royal presence. Through this system, Cho recruited many like-minded young zealots in their twenties and thirties. They were also promoted with unprecedented rapidity.

The second measure was concerned with a military contingency plan. A surprise attack on a Jürched tribe, who had intruded into Hamgil (Hamgyŏng) Province, was decided upon at the court with the royal approval. All preparations, including the appointment of the commanding officer, were worked out by the Ministry of War. But Cho Kwang Cho, then a deputy counsellor of the *Hongmungwan*, demurred at the dispatchment of an expedition with the purpose of surprise attack. He argued that a surprise attack was not fair ; it was nothing less than a deception. Even the defense of the kingdom, however urgent, should first withstand the trial of truthfulness, or righteousness (*ŭi*). Chungjong agreed and the dispatch of expeditionary troops was cancelled.

The third action of the year was the abolition of an insignificant government office that administered annual sacrificial rites to Heaven required in accord with the Taoistic concept of the universe. However insignificant, it had been part of the Yi government since its formation ; for this reason,

Chungjong was adamant against Cho's proposal for its abolition. But Cho's assertion that only the Confucian concept of the universe should be made efficacious won the day. Buddhism by this time had sunken so low that no further suppressive measure was felt necessary.

The Hyangyak. By far the most important and nation-wide social program carried out by the Cho group was enforcement of the *hyangyak*, which can be best translated village charter. The village charter, agreed upon on a voluntary basis by all members of a village as a self-governing and cooperative community consisted of a series of articles dealing with the entire range of social and moral life of the community. A kind of social contract, of Sung origin, the *hyangyak*, as developed under the Yi dynasty, generally stipulated the mutual encouragement of virtuous deeds, the mutual solution of injuries, the mutual intercourse with social decorum and customs, and the mutual assistance in time of difficulties to be the basic precepts of the community. A *hyangyak* usually enumerated injunctive instances also : impiety, disrespect for teacher, maltreatment of legitimate wife, feud with neighbors, heterodoxical belief, drinking and gambling, contempt of law, neglect of productive work, etc.

The administration of the *hyangyak* was placed under the *Hyangch'ŏng* (Country Court). The administrative officers of the *hyangyak*, who were appointed by the head of the *Hyangch'ŏng*, were usually given a limited amount of judicial power for its enforcement. At the compulsory quarterly meeting of all members, the problems arising from the management of the *hyangyak* were discussed and disposed of, and rewards and punishments were meted out. There were minutely prescribed rules of procedure for the judicial disposition of various cases ; however, the *hyangyak* officers' judicial power seems to have put much restrictive pressure upon the peasantry.

The *hyangyak* and the *Hyangch'ŏng*, together constituting the local self-government, served to inculcate on the local people the sense of communal responsibility and voluntary conformity to the moral prescriptions of the society. A local magisterial government alone would have never been able to produce these results, especially the spirit of voluntary compliance with social authority, which, however, in a long run, ironically wrought into the Korean mind a certain indifference to the governmental laws.

In parallel with the general enforcement of the *hyangyak*, the Cho group also put into effect other social programs for enlightenment to, and refinement of, Confucian virtues. They ardently worked for the the exposure of superstitious beliefs. They printed books in *Han'gŭl* on agriculture, medicine and, above all, filial piety. The *Book of Filial Piety* became the most widely-read book in this period. The results of these social movements seemed to have been indeed remarkable. In a short span of a few years since Cho came to power, even the *ch'ŏnmin*, to whom, it should be noted, the

Confucian code of ethics was not applied in full, came "to mourn at the graves of their parents and dedicate memorial tablets to their ancestors." In a few more years, the Cho group's utopian goals would have been more firmly and popularly achieved.

Unfortunately, however, with characteristically youthful radicalism, in 1519, Cho Kwang Cho and his stalwarts, all in their thirties, turned to achieve at one stroke what was tantamount to a disintegration of the responsible conservative group in the government. Censors led by Cho Kwang Cho, now the senior censor at the *Sahŏnbu*, made a daring attack upon the irregularities supposeldy perpetrated in the appointment of the 103 Merit Subjects, many of whom, it was alleged, had been enrolled undeservedly. The Cho group insisted that this should be immediately rectified. At the threat of the mass resignation of the censors, Chungjong gave in to approve the abrogation of the titles of seventy-six out of the 103 Merit Subjects. To the conservatives, this was too intolerable a challenge. The economic stake involved in the struggle should be also noted : abrogation of the title meant, among other things, confiscation of the land. The all-out counterattack immediately launched by the Merit Subjects included shady intrigues and a specious pretext that the foundation of the Chungjong reign was undermined. Chungjong, who had felt somewhat weary of constant radical onslaughts, gave a tacit nod to the old-timers. The upshot was another mass purge.

The Growth of Confucian Culture

The Trials of Buddhism under the Yi Dynasty

As in other countries of Mahayana Buddhism, Buddhism in Korea owed its establishment and subsequent propagation to royal courts. Courts regarded the Buddhas as the spiritual guardians of the country and called upon them in time of emergency. Under the Yi dynasty, however, the court officially disowned Buddhism for the reasons which we have seen. Korean Buddhism fell on evil days. No sooner had the dynasty begun its career than the systematic demolition of Buddhist establishments got under way. The political enemy of Buddhism was, needless to say, the ruling Confucianists in and out of the government, for whom anti-Buddhism was a political require-ment. The monarchs as transcendental figures, however, it may be said, main-tained an option in religious devotion and a political understanding that the Buddhist church, too, paid its worldly allegiance to them.

Anti-Buddhist measures, as has been noted, comprised the confiscation of estates and labor force in possession of monasteries, the stringent regulation of the examination for monks and the tonsure for would-be bonzes, the pro-hibition of certain Buddhist rituals and social functions in the capital and other designated places, and so on. During the reigns of Sejong (except his last few years), Sŏngjong and Chungjong who were more Confucian in incli-nation than others, these measures were more strictly applied. But under the patronage notably of Sejo and Queen Dowager Yun (Munjŏng) who briefly ruled from 1546 to 1553 on behalf of her son, Myŏngjong (1546–1567), Buddhism, with some restrictions lifted, became respectable again, and the court-favored monks strove for Buddhism's revival. In an overall perspective, the pattern of such ups and downs occurred within the general trend of decline, which was inevitable as long as the Confucianists were in power.

Although, thus, Buddhism suffered from the immense loss of worldly wealth and social prestige as well as spiritual leadership, it would be a mistake to think that Buddhism was engulfed by Confucianism as completely as the Confucianists would have liked. On the contrary, a succession of highly reputable monks, remarkably devoid of any sense of bitterness toward their oppressors, carried on theological debates and religious disciplines. The main current of Yi dynasty Buddhism was of course Sŏn as it was made the dominating sect in the late Koryŏ period by Chinul, who attempted to unify sectarian movements with Sŏn as the ecumenical basis.

This ecumenical movement was carried into the Yi dynasty, and it seems to have been completed under Hyujŏng (1520–1604), probably the greatest of the Yi dynasty monks. His theological position was similar to that of Chinul, but his was more closely identified with Pou's (also known as T'aego), another great late Koryŏ monk. To achieve an intuitive insight into the Buddha-nature within one's heart, which was Sŏn's final goal, the scriptural knowledge should best be acquired first as preliminary to enlightenment, and Hyujŏng went further to stress the importance of *yŏmbul* or calling on the Buddha's name as an act of faith. Hyujŏng also asserted the oneness in the ultimate meaning of three religions, two others being Confucianism and Taoism. Although this was not untrue, it was, as interpreted from a political angle, a confession of weakness. The same thing was said in the Koryŏ period by Confucian scholars and writers.

Indeed, more and more Buddhist monks ventured into the intellectual domains of rival religions, thus taking the edge off their own. At the same time, the tendency was strengthened, namely that a variety of apocryphal cults freely called upon Buddhism to appropriate its doctrines. But, low as Buddhism's decline might have reached, its institutional influences were much felt even in the Yi dynasty culture. It is also worth noting that, during the Japanese invasion in the late sixteenth century, the monk forces of about 5,000 or more under Hyujŏng fought the island enemies.

Printing and Practical Scholarship

Although Koryŏ used histroy's first metal moveable types for bookprinting in 1232, or probably a decade or so earlier, the typecasting seems to have been rare in Koryŏ, reflecting the constant political turmoil of the period not conducive to such cultural undertaking. Besides, Koryŏ's main book-printing tradition was in block-printing of Buddhist literature for a small number of copies at a time. As the new dynsaty enlarged the basis of the ruling class with its footing in Confucianism, the demand for many kinds of books in a large number of copies suddenly increased.

The first typecasting under the Yi dynasty occurred in 1403 when T'aejong ordered "a few hundred thousand" copper types cast, setting off a new era of printing activities. Until 1580 were fourteen such court-sponsored typecasting undertaken, including the lead types of 1436 and the iron types of 1573 and 1580. Wood types, which, along with wood blocks, were usually used by provincial officials and families for private printing projects, were also carved at the court order for occasional use. Characteristically, Sejong introduced an improved method of typesetting which made possible printing of several ten to several hundred pages a day. By the early sixteenth century, the bookprinting was quite well popularized among the *yangban* class.

The other side of the printing activities was the equally-enterprising scholarly endeavors. The scholarly output in the early period of the dynasty was mostly on useful fields for the business of government, hence the term practical scholarship ; most of the works were also court-sponsored. Compilation of histories was an important area for concentration. The *Sillok* or *True Records*, the official dynastic history, was compiled customarily a few years after the end of each reign for the period of that reign, eventually comprising, 1,893 "volumes" (chapters) fort the five centuries of the dynastic career. The *True Records* of Koryŏ had been compiled in this fashion but either lost or destroyed. To ensure the factuality of the official history, the unprejudiced selection and protection from outside pressure of official historians were institutionally guraranteed. The official histories, as compiled one by one in four copies, were preserved in specially-built depositories scattered in four different places in the country. Interestingly enough, the monarchs were denied access to them. Even the despotic Yŏnsan'gun was refused their reading except for that portion in Historian Kim Il Son's draft which became the focus of the controversy.

The *Histroy of Koryŏ*, since most of the *True Records* of Koryŏ had been lost, was compiled based on the existing records in 139 chapters by Kim Chong Sŏ *et al.*, in 1451 ; a much shorter version of the same was written by Chŏng To Chŏn in 1395. In 1452 the *Condensed History of Koryŏ* was compiled in thirty-five chapters by the same team and in 1476 the *Condensed History of Three Kingdoms* by No Sa Chin. *et al.* The *Tongguk t'onggam* or *Comprehensive Mirror for the Eastern Kingdom*, a chronological presentation of the Korean history, patterned after Ssu-ma Kung's *Tzu-chih t'ungchien*, was completed by Sŏ Kŏ Chŏng, *et al.* in 1484 ; the book coverd the period from 57 B.C., to 1392 A.D., the year of Koryŏ's demise and was designed to be a mirror or a reference book for the ruler. Also for his daily reference, there were the *Kukcho pogam* or *Precious Mirror for the* [Ri] *Dynasty*, a chronological presentation condensed, if highly moralized, from the *True*

Records of each reign and the *Ch'ip'yŏng yoram* or *Outline of the History of Good Government* compiled based on Korean and Chinese histories from antiquity.

On a higher level, if physically, the true records of the Heaven were also meticulously recorded by the astronomical observatory under the supervision of the head of the *Ŭijŏngbu* (Council of State), whose duty was, besides the management of the government, "reasoning [or analysing] of the *yin-yang* principle [in action]." Astronomical and meteorological phenomena, which had a deep religious, metaphysical, and agricultural significance had been made one of the major intellectual concerns of the Korean government since its history. The Yi dynasty came to witness a tremendous advancement made in these scientific fields, as noted. Understandably, descriptions of the celestial occurrences and their preservation were equally important as for terrestrial events. The *P'ung'un ki* or *Records of Wind and Cloud*, which was the twenty-four-hours-a-day true records of the Heaven, was recorded for about four and a half centuries starting with the Sejong reign and has been preserved, except for those for the first and a half centuries destroyed in war. The *Chŏnbyŏn tŭngnok* or Copied Records of the Extraordinary Events in *Heaven*, sorted out from the *Records of Wind and Cloud* for ready reference was the heavenly equivalent of the *Precious Mirror for the [Ri] Dynasty.*

The *Nongsa chiksŏl* or *Direct Explanation of Farming*, completed in one volume under Sejong's direction in 1429, was an attempt at scientific farming. Its value today lies in its experimental scholarship, which has been touched upon. Another scientific scholarship that made tremendous headway during the Yi dynasty was cultural geography, which is also called descriptive geography. It was written in a manner of encyclopedic compilation, especially in the later period of the dynasty. A section on cultural geography, in a prototypal form, was included in the *True Records* of the Sejong reign. It describes physical geography, historical development, social characteristics, economic and military importance, road network, and fauna and flora of each locality under observation. And also an incipient cartographic development seems to have occurred during the Sejong reign.

In medical scholarship, too, the sound, scientific approach made the medicine, which had been largely Chinese, closer and more responsive to the Korean environ in terms of needs and materials available. The *Hyangyak chipsŏngbang* or *Library of the Folk Medicine* in eighty-five volumes was completed in 1433. The *Ŭibang yuch'wi* or *Classification of Pathologies* was edited in 266 volumes in 1445. Compilation of both, undertaken at Sejong's order, represents the apex of the early Yi dynasty scholarship in medicine. The latter, classifying the entire field into ninety-one categories of diseases with a pathological exposition on each, contains prescriptions for every possible case researched through 164 medical texts written since the Han dynasty of China. Compilation of the *Tong'i pogam* or *Precious Mirror for Eastern Medicine* was privately undertaken and completed by Hŏ Chun, the best known Yi dynasty doctor, in 1611. The twenty-five-volume book, regarded as *the* textbook for the doctors of the Yi period, consists of systematic discourses on five areas of medicine with clinical references then available : internal medicine, external medicine, miscellany, herb broth, and acupuncture and moxa-cautery. It is interesting to note that the medical books, especially Hŏ Chun's, were the most widely read of Korean books in China and Japan.

Codification of law commanded continued scholarly attention from the beginning of the dynasty. The *Chosŏn kyŏnggukchŏn* or *Laws for Administration of Chosŏn*, compiled by Chŏng To Chŏn in 139, was the first law code of the dynasty. In almost every reign, a law code was edited on the basis of the previous ones, as the promulgated decrees and edicts were increased, culminating in 1474 in the compilation of the most comprehensive *Kyŏngguk taejŏn (Complete Library of the Laws for Government)*. No less important than law in ruling a Confuican dynasty were rites, ceremonies, and music which, as instruments of securing social order and cultural stability, were articulately standardized. In parallel with the four rites and ceremonies of the family, the rites and ceremonies of the state consisted of five : sacrificial rites, ceremonies for auspicious events, ceremonies for honoring guests, military ceremonies, and rites for funeral and mourning. Compilation of the *Kukcho oyeŭi* or *Five Rites and Ceremonies of the [Ri] Dynasty* was completed in 1474.

Music, indispensable accompaniment to these rites and ceremonies, was comprehensively dealt with in the *Akhak kwebŏm* or *Rules and Patterns of Music* finalized in nine volumes in 1493. The *Akhak kwebŏm* classifies the existing music into *hyang'ak* or folk music, *Tang'ak*, another category of folk music of Chinese origin (T'ang), and *aak*, or court music taken over, with some modifications, from the Koryŏ court which, as we have seen, borrowed it from the Sung. While describing, in minute detail, music, musical instruments, musical attirements, accompanying dances, etc., the book also contains some folk songs and poems passed down from Koryŏ which make up part of the invaluable materials for the study of literature of that period.

Sejong as a Confucian Scholar. The practical-minded scholar officials, who under the royal order wrote and compiled a variety of great books of the dynasty, of which the above-mentioned were only a few, were in every respect a remarkable species of well-rounded amateurs, products of a literary age par excellence. Of these, Sejong provides a best model of practical scholarship as his scholarly interests ranged over a large number of fields. In Chinese classics, history, astronomy, music, arithmetic, law, agriculture, phonetics, literature, Sejong showed an insatiable intellectual drive and reached high attainments.

Like other scholars of his time, Sejong believed, without question, in the ideality of Chinese antiquity by which the present affairs could be measured. He regarded Chinese classics and histories as the fountainhead of knowledge as well as the training ground for mind. For the metaphysical study of classics, he confined himself to the *Hsing-li ta-ch'uan* (*Sŏngni taejŏn* in Korean), which was commentaries on classics and related subjects by Chu Hsi and others. He devoted a great deal of efforts to the mastery of Neo-Confucian philosophy on the theories of Great Ultimate, principle (*li*) and material force (*ch'i*), workings of *yin-yang* and five elements, human nature and mind, and so on. His mind bent toward utilitarian goals of knowledge, Sejong, however, seems to have kept philosophy at a distance when the could help it.

He put a greater emphasis on the understanding of history as a "mirror" for the Cutivation of one's mind as well as for the management of the family and the country. His erudite scholarship in this field academically placed him in a presiding position at royal lectures which he often turned into a kind of seminar meeting. At times, he seems to have keenly felt an insufficiency in historical knowledge of his officials. In order to improve this situation, he appointed officials prominent in historical scholarship as special advisors to the *Chiphyŏnjŏn*. He urged his scholars to familiarize themselves with the good men (wise rulers, loyal subjects, great scholars, etc.) and the bad men (tyrants, traitors, crafty courtiers, etc.) of history in order to gain moral lessons from the past. He wrote short surveys of important histories, accompanied by songs rhyming their essentials which he composed to help memorize histories. In these attempts at the promotion of historical studies for the practical purpose of good government and moral edification, Korean histories seemed less important. In fact, T'aejo's usurpation of the Koryŏ throne and unsavory wars of succession involved, any discussion of the dynasty's, hence Korea's, own past, considered from a covert nook, would have best been avoided.

All told, Sejong was a Confucian scholar of the highest order in a strict sense of that term. Through his extensive scholarship and native intelligence, he could take full advantage of Confucianism at its best as a way of government and life. As a good Confucian, Sejong enforced with utmost sincerity the Confucian rites and ceremonies of the family and the state as the behavioral standards for men of all classes. But, encumbered by the relentless rationalism of Neo-Confucian Principle, Sejong suffered from a certain emotional wasteland in his closing years, as indicated by his devotion to Buddhism. Yet this was not a defeat of confucianism in him but rather a maturer realization of himself as a man. *

---

* These paragraphs are helped by Dr. Sung Nyŏng Lee's original study on Sejong in *Taedong munhwa* (no. 3 ; 1968) issued by Sŏnggyungwan University.

The Sǒwǒn

The intrinsic urge in a Confucianist to participate in government had received rude setbacks resulting from the series of unwarrantably large-scale purges at the central court. Especially, a decade of misrule by the Yǒnsan'gun rendered havoc of the inveterate aspirations for bureaucratic carrer of the *yangban* in general. The sense of frustration and alienation that pervaded among the greater majority of the people tended to turn disinterested *yangban* scholars inward to metaphysical study and meditation and also to the "mountains and forests" in the provinces where, surrounded by members of the same clan and close academic followers, scholar-notables established themselves as local sages. Now they were there to stay, forming strong political and social groups on the basis of common ancestral wealth and influence, a phenomenon that had been long in process from the early sixteenth century.

While, sometimes, presenting portentous political opposition to the central authority, they also made their locality a center of learning, of which a *sǒwǒn* or private academy was the major institution. The *sǒwǒn* was roughly patterned after *shu-yuan* of the Sung, and, once brought into existence in Yi Korea, the *sǒwǒn* was established in rapid succession all over the country from about the middle of the sixteenth century. This was indeed a conspicuous phenomenon in the development of Confucian culture. The decline of official education, seems to have been also a contributory factor in the proliferation of *sǒwǒn*.

The private institution of learning had been existent along with government schools since the early middle of the Koryǒ period. Under the new dynasty with its stronger emphasis on learning, founders of the well-run, if, sometimes ephemeral, private schools were invariably commended for the court's recognition. The social conditions that called for the establishment in provinces of college-level educational institution were felt quite early at the court as well as locally. And the first *sǒwǒn* established as a local college in 1542 was court-sponsored.

The organization and regulations of a *sǒwǒn* were similar to those of the Sǒnggyungwan (national university). It consisted of a lecture hall, dormitories, a library, and a shrine where one or more well-known sages were enshrined. The dean of *sǒwǒn* was selected from among distinguished scholars, with at least a lower degree, by the consensus of all scholars of the district concerned, and his appointment was subject to the approval of the court. Customarily about thirty students, strictly from that district concerned, and his appointment was subject to the trict, who had passed at least the first provincial examination for a lower degree, were admitted. More than twenty such *sǒwǒn* were founded during the reign of Myǒngjong (1546-1567) and 124 during that of Sŏnjo (1568-1608). Increasing steadily, its number, by the middle of the nineteenth century, reached more than 650, of which 264 were endowed with land and slaves by the court.

The *sŏwŏn* in addition to its primary function of education, in time came to serve also as the center of political and religious activities for the local *yangban*. A *sŏwŏn* if not endowed by the court, was financially supported by prominent families of the district who were more likely the descendants of the scholar enshrined there. It provided a kind of public forum for discussions on current political and metaphysical problems for the *yangban* intellectuals. They might or might not entertain the idea of careers in the central government ; yet having been once enmeshed in politics at the court, they held a lasting interest in the political vicissitudes and academic debates going on in the capital and provincial centers. And, tightly formed on the basis of consanguinity and teacher-disciple relations, they came to exercise certain extralegal powers in their respective districts. While regarding those in power with contemptuously-critical eyes, they in a few instances during the late Yi period could even rescind, in the name of their *sŏwŏn* deities, were they powerful enough, the government edict itself.

The distended authority of deified *sŏwŏn* sages, which sustained such political audacity, was periodically solemnized through seasonal sacrificial rites dedicated to them. The *sŏwŏn* as a religious temple containing only the portrait of its sage-god looked indeed shabby in comparison with the temple of Buddha, and the religious contents of Neo-Confucian metaphysics of Principle (or Reason) were even shabbier, compared with those of Buddhism. Nevertheless, the Confucianists most painstakingly performed the elaborate rituals which called for long periods of preparation and proselytizing zeal. Thus the *sŏwŏn* the highest fane for the collective performance of these religious rituals, provided cathartic occasions for the Confucian rationalists.

Philosophical Development

With the general intellectual climate leaning toward creative writing, history, ethics, and other *practical* fields, the metaphysical aspect of Neo-Confucianism attracted less scholarly attention than one might think. The Yi dynasty scholars, however, were more or less all philosophers, that is, philosophers of things in general. Among them was a thin but steady line of notable philosophers who kept systematic metaphysical thinking alive. By the middle of the sixteenth century, the philosophical study of Neo-Confucianism came into full bloom, and what aspects the Korean thinkers were interested in was brought into relief. The ontological exposition of man and universe and the cultivation of oneself as a moral and psychological being in conformity with the universal principle proved to be central to the metaphysical concerns of the Yi dynasty philosophers.

Sŏ Kyŏng Tŏk (1489–1546), who refused to step into a bureaucratic career, lived a life of speculative thinking and writing in the strictest sense of that term. His philosophical position was in line with that of Chang Tsai (1021–1077) of the Sung. He postulated the *ki* (*ch'i*) or material force, rather than the *i* (*li*), to be the basic substance that makes up the universe. To Sŏ Kyŏng Tŏk, the *yin* and *yang* forces themselves were nothing but the attributes of the *ki*. Through the operations of *yin-yang* forces, that is, integration and disintegration of the *ki*, the myriad things of the universe, including man himself, were created. The Great Ultimate, which Sŏ identified with the material force, was itself only an undifferentiated or disintegrated state of the matter. Sŏ went further in his materialistic view of the universe to posit man's senses and mentality as nothing other than attributes of the *ki* and to cap his philosophical system with the indestructibility of material, the logical extreme of the *ki*-only philosophy, of which he was the unique champion. he relegated the *i* (*li*) or principle to almost a nonentity, dismissing it as an expedient designation for an operational function of the *ki* (*ch'i*). ——

Thus, with Sŏ Kyŏng Tŏk, probably the first serious, not peripatetic, philosopher of the Yi dynasty, started in earnest exercises in Neo-Confucian metaphysics. Wider and more intensive metaphysical discussions came to the peak with the appearance of the two great philosophers, Yi Hwang (1501–1570) of Kyŏngsang Province and Yi I (1536–1584) of Kangwŏn Province. Yi Hwang, better known as T'oegye, the finest product of Korean Confucianism, has been often referred to as Chu Hsi of the East. Although his official rank reached far above the ministerial level, he was never a politician or even a statesman. He longed for a life of learning, meditation, and writing based on his motto : "Sincerity and Reverence." He had them for most of his life in the beautiful surroundings of his native Tosan ; he often declined royal invitations to government service. He emphasized the inseparability of knowledge and conduct. He believed the progress of one's life to be the best source of learning. His metaphysical position was very much the same as Chu Hsi's, but he was thorougher in viewing the interaction of *i* and *ki* as dualistic ; yet he accorded an unmistakable priority to the *i*.

Opposing this view, Yi I, also known as Yulgok, said that, although all things were created by the two cosmic forces of *i* (*li*) and *ki* (*ch'i*), the *i* as an immaterial and immutable principle did not participate in creation through action as such. It is the *ki* alone that creates through its ability to change and act. It is the *ki* alone that creates through its ability to change and act. A much more dynamic personality, Yi I was not only a brilliant scholar but also a far-sighted statesman and active social experimentalist. It is fitting that he

upheld the preeminence of the instrumental *ki* over the static *i*. But his
Confucian learning and belief simply disappeared when he was once in his
youth broken down under the weight of the grief at the death of his mother,
a great feminine painter and poet known as Sin Saimdang, his shattered soul
gathered itself after a year of his excursion into the healing grace of Buddha
at temples in the Diamond Mountains.

   The Four-Seven Debates. In the 1550's took place a philosophical debate
between Yi Hwang and his disciple-friend Ki Tae Sŭng (1527-1572), of Chŏlla
Province, which lasted through correspondence for eight years. Much later, Yi
I came to comment on the issue involved in the debate, generally siding with
Ki Tae Sŭng. Probably because of its being initiated by the greatest scholars
of the day in a gentlemanly fashion, the debate continued and engaged a
tremendous number of earnest scholars all over the country, lasting, if sporadically, for the next two centuries.

   The debate, which also helped popularize the metaphysics, centered
around the so-called "four beginnings" and "seven emotions." The "four
beginnings," as discussed in the *Mencius*, are the most basic attributes of the
human nature : to commiserate with fellow men in misfortune, to feel
ashamed of one's own wrong-doing, to be courteous to others, and to distin-
guish right from wrong. These human capacities are regarded as "beginnings"
of the virtues of human-heartedness, righteousness, propriety, and wisdom,
respectively ; together, they are thought to constitute human nature.
Happiness, anger, sorrow, fear, love, wickedness, and desire are the "seven
emotions" or activities of the mind, as seen in the *Book of Rites* and the
Doctrine of the Mean. In Chu Hsi-ism, the nature and the mind of man are
two different things : man's nature, that particular part of *li* or *i* (principle), as
it is inherent in the human body, is of pure, good, and unsullied entity,
whereas the mind is dominated by the *ch'i* or *ki* (material) capable of mental
activities such as thinking feeling, etc., which are not always good and pure.

   Yi Hwang, closely following Chu Hsi, said that in the "four beginnings"
of the human nature the *i* "rises" and the *ki* (the material force) "follows"
the *i* ; in other words, the "four beginnings," which are by nature good, are
originated by the *i*. In the "seven emotions" of the human mind, he continued, the *ki* "rises" and the *i* "rides" on the *ki*. The *ki* being capable of origi-
nating bad as well as good activities of the mind and the *i* incapable of bad,
it is the *ki* that makes the conduct of individuals different from one another.

   After Yi Hwang and Ki Tae Sŭng gone, Yi I, arguing with one of Yi
Hwang's disciples, Sŏng Hon (1535-1598), insisted that in the "four
beginnings" and the "seven emotions" *alike* the *ki* "rises" and the *i* "rides" on
it. He further said that everything that occurs in the universe is initiated by
the material force. Even the "four beginnings" that is, human-heartedness,
righteousness, etc., are nothing but the mental activities of the mind as when,

for instance, one commiserates with a child who is about to fall into a well. The principle is omnipresent in the universe, but it is the material force that particularizes.

So went on the four-seven debates through successive generations, in the end, with certain geopolitical complications. Scholars of the central provinces and Chŏlla Province generally followed Yulgok's theory, whereas T'oegye influenced those in Kyŏngsang Province. And the latter also greatly influenced Neo-Confucianism in Japan. The overall contributions of the Yi Chosŏn philosophers to the metaphysical development of Neo-Confucianism, despite a tremendous amount of their philosophical output, were only adding consummative touches here and there. Their real failure, however, lies in their inability to grow out of the confines of Neo-Confucian School of Principle and to achieve a breakthrough toward a broader philosophical conception before the eighteenth century was over.

The Yehak. Another field for scholarly endeavors, that began to make headway in the early sixteenth century, was *Yehak.* The *Yehak* or Learning of *Ye* (rites and ceremonies) as such was anything but new. But an increasing importance that came to be attached to *ye* in this period made the *Yehak* school a prestigious group. Including in its field a whole range of *ye*, the "four rites and ceremonies" being the most important area of attention, the *Yehak* scholars examined what seemed to be confusion in the rites and regulations for human conduct and advocated its rectification through research into the historical precedents in Confucian ethics. Kim Chang Saeng (1548-1631) is usually regarded as *the* authority in this field.

The emergence of the *Yehak* as the "objective ethics" with an emphasis on form and regulation, while it became an important area for intellectual exercises, can be regarded in historical perspective as a logical development oh Hsün-tzu's doctrine of human nature as innately bad. Although Hsün-tzu was dismissed as heterodox by Confucian scholastics because of his view contradictory to Mencius' concept of man's inborn goodness, his beliefs in rituals and ceremonies, rigidly hierarchic social order, stringent discipline in government, etc., as correctives for evil man and his society were gradually, perhaps unconsciously, incorporated into the main stream of Neo-Confucian rationalism in Yi Korea.

Confucian Triumph? Neo-Confucian rationalism, as it became the main intellectual current in Korea, had mustered a peculiarly tenacious intellectual vigor since the closing decades of Koryŏ. It is worth noting that such vigor and tenacity were directed, as we have seen, against Buddhism which had dominated the intellectual scene for so long ; indeed, Confucianists' was a politically motivated intellectual movement. In parallel with the political development climaxing in Yi Sŏng Kye's take-over of the Koryŏ throne, the Korean Neo-Confucianists, equipped with rationalism with which they, too, had built up a metaphysical system, now confidently seized from the Buddhists the Western Paradise which the Neo-Confucianists reconstructed into a heavenly or rather earthly utopia of their own with up-to-date Confucian materials.

While ridiculing the "superstitiousness" of the Buddhist theology, the Neo-Confucianists blandly appropriated some important metaphysical concepts from Buddhism. They also placed a heavy emphasis upon meditation as a means of obtaining none other than a sudden enlightenment, the very method and the goal which Sŏn Buddhism had perfected and strove to attain. While proscribing Buddhist rituals and services, they most ardently endeavored for a widespread practice of elaborate Confucian rites and ceremonies. To make Confucian literature more widely available, they, too, plunged into the enterprising business of printing, a tradition that Buddhists had long established. While drastically reducing the number of Buddhist temples and monasteries and confiscating their estates and slave labor, they built hundreds of shrine-centered *sŏwŏn* supported by a vast amount of land and slave labor. Thus, the utopia they built, though plausible and even durable, yet as it was supported by the rationalistic props of the metaphysics of Principle, was indeed barren and fragile at best, as partly evidenced by permanent or brief flights into the embrace of Buddhism of Confucian kings and scholars. Understandably, the emotion-dry Neo-Confucian rationalists all took to occasional dipping into the romantic world of literature and art.

Tosan Sŏwon built in 1574 at Andong.

8

Literature and Art

Nature-bound freedom and spontaneity in literature and art, which were inherited from the previous periods, now took on a special significance as the dynastic life became more rigidly regimented by Confucian ethics and moralism. Confucian scholar-officials, who were condemned to the study of Chinese, a most difficult foreign literature, and the set pattern of thinking, tended to seek emotional release in free play of passion under the guise of art or through songs of nature. With the invention of the *Han'gŭl*, which was unquestionably the most significant event in the Korean cultural history, the common people, too, came to possess a means of literary expression. Indeed, the Yi dynasty, especially in its later period, witnessed creative activities in art and literature flourishing as never before.

Hunmin Chŏng'ŭm

Although there were writing devices such as the Silla vintage *Idu* for vernacular expression, writing as art had been confined to a small group within the ruling class of each dynasty. And, with the *Idu* system of writing, which itself required a high degree of mastery of Chinese ideograms, literary activity on a popular level could hardly be expected. Chinese being so completely different from Korean in all its linguistic aspects, and its ideographic symbols being so intractable to the Korean use, any phonetic system developed from them were bound to be less than satisfactory. The Japanese *Kana*, meaning false letters as they have been developed from Chinese letters, which are presumably "real" letters, have nothing to do with the ideographic contents of Chinese characters and are phonetically incomplete at best, if not "false."

The Kyŏnggich'e ("How-about-that" style) poems, which were popular for group singing among Confucian scholars of Koryŏ, were an interesting, yet peculiar product of this predicament of not having a vernacular writing system. A *Kyŏnggich'e* poem, as we have seen, consisted entirely of Chinese phrases which were arranged so as to suit that rhythmic pattern intrinsic to the Korean language. Sejong's invention in 1443 of a phonetic system for writing Korean remedied all this and, as might be expected, ushered in a new era in Korean literature.

The *Hunmin chŏng'ŭm*, as Sejong named his creation, literally Correct Sounds for Instruction of the People or popularly known today as *Han'gŭl*, meaning the great or unique letters, is often regarded as the most scientific and easiest of the writing systems now in use anywhere. To have a glimpse of these superlative features of the *Han'gŭl*, the descriptions of its twenty-eight symbols, that is, seventeen consonants and eleven vowels may suffice :

Velar consonants :

1) ㄱ(*k*) ·····This symbol is patterned after, as Sejong explanins in the *Hunmin chŏg'ŭm (as the book), the glossal base and the* vocal cord when the former touches the velum to block the passage of the breath just before producing the *k* (or actually *g*) sound as in *god.*

2) ㅋ(*k'*) ·····A horizontal stroke is added to indicate the passage (often frictional) fo the breath stronger than needed for the ㄱ, that is, an aspirated voiceless velar stop. It is pronounced *k* as in *king.*

Lingual consonants :

3) ㄴ(*n*) ·····This symbol is patterned after the glossal tip touching the front third of the palate as when making a dental nasal, or the *n* sound.

4) ㄷ(*t*) ·····A horizontal bar is added to indicate the push of air (through the mouth) stronger than needed for the ㄴ; it is pronounced as a lax dental stop. This is actually the *d* sound as in *do.*

5) ㅌ(*t'*) ·····Another horizontal stroke is added to indicate an aspiration +ㄷ, actually, an aspirated voiceless dental stop. It is pronounced *t* as in *table.*

Labial consonants :

  6) ㅁ(*m*) ······This square is modeled upon the appearance of the
     mouth when it produces the *m* sound.

  7) ㅂ(*p*)······The two vertical lines of the ㅁ are heightened to sig-
     nify the push of air (through the month) more power-
     ful than required for the ㅁ. It is a bilabial stop and
     pronounced *p* (or actually *b*) as in *ball*.

  8) ㅍ(*p'*)······This symbol is the form of ㅂ with its two vertical lines
     lengthened downward, as in ㅍ, to show an aspiration
     + ㅂ, or an aspirated voiceless labial stop, but it was
     rolled over to become ㅍ. The actual sound is *p* as in
     pace.

Dental consonants :

  9) ㅅ(*s*) ······This symbol is modeled upon the shape of a tooth. The
     tip of the tongue is brought near the upper alveolar
     ridge to make a vioceless dental grooved fricative, or
     the *s* sound as in *song*.

  10)ㅈ(*ch*)······A horizontal bar is attached to show a push of air
     coarser than for the ㅅ. This symbol is usually pro-
     nounced as a lax prepalatal affricate, or *j* as in *jazz*.

  11)ㅊ(*ch'*)······A dot is placed on the bar to signify an aspiration + ㅈ,
     but actually a voiceless prepalatal affricate. The sound
     is *ch* as in *chair*.

Guttural consonants :

  12)ㅇ(*ng*)······This circle, symbolizing a horizontal section of the vocal
     cord, has no sound as such. But placed at the end of
     an orthographic syllable, it produces the velar nasal, or
     the *ng* sound as in *sounding*.

  13)ㆁ ······These two sounds are similar to ㅇ but now
  14)ㆆ out of use.

  15)ㅎ(*h*)······A dot is added on the bar of ㆆ. This is an aspiration
     of the following vowel and often pronounced as a velar
     fricative (*x*).

"Semi-dental" or lateral consonant :

  16)ㄹ(*l*) ······This sign symbolizes the flapping of the tongue in pro-
     ducing the *l* sound (a flapped lateral).

"Semi-dental" consonants :

17)△(z) ······The triangle is made by adding a bar to the bottom of ㅅ(s). This sound is now retired, but it might as well be recalled into use to better transcribe such foreign words as *jazz, design, quiz,* etc., which are now in daily use.

Vowels :

1) ㅏ(a)   2) ㅑ(ya)   3) ㅓ(ŏ)   4) ㅕ(yŏ)   5) ㅗ(o)
6) ㅛ(yo)   7) ㅜ(u)   8) ㅠ(yu)   9) ㅡ(ŭ)   10) ㅣ(i)
11) ·(a)

These signs of vowels are made of three basic elements, ·, ㅡ, and ㅣ, which symbolize heaven, earth, and man, respectively. In the actual combination of consonants and vowels, one should note that one syllable makes one unit-letter. For instance, *Han'gŭl* spells 한글, that is, in two unit-letters. The ways in which these symbols may be combined are nearly infinite : a set of two consonants and a set of two or three vowels can be combined to make up one-syllable letter. 쒱, for instance, is the combination of ㅅ+ㅅ+ㅗ+ㅏ+ㅣ+ㅇ, and it represents the sound one hears from a jet plane flying away closely overhead. The · sound (11), being so slightly different from that of ㅏ(1), is now out of use.

The nature of each sound, the dialectical relationship between symbols in combination, etc. are all extensively dealt with in the book. *Hunmin chŏng'ŭm (Correct for Instruction of the People)* in Confucian cosmological and metaphysical terms based on theories of the *yin-yang* and five elements as well as in terms of phonetic science. The complicated metaphysical exposition of the alphabet, whilst interesting, is of no use in the practical application of it.

용비어천가

해동 육농이 나르시어
  일마다 천복이시니
    고성이 동부 하시네.

뿌리 깊은 나무는
  바람에 아니 흔들리니,
    꽃 좋고 열매 많이 여느니,

샘이 깊은 물은
가믐에 아니 마르므로,
내가 되여 바다로 흐르도다.

The first three cantos of the Songs of the Dragons Flying to Heaven
(Yŏngbi ŏch'ŏn ka) *above are written in the* Han'gŭl *as they are written today
(see the next page). Below is an English translation by James Hoyt in his book
of the same title (see Bibliography), followed by a transcription into English
alphabet.*

The Six Dragons of Haedong fly;
Their works all have the favor of Heaven;
Their auspices are the same as the worthies of old.

A tree with deep roots,
Because the wind sways it not,
Blossoms abundantly and bears fruit.

The water from a deep spring.
Because a draught dries it not
Becomes a stream and flows to the sea.

haedong yungnyong'i narŭsiŏ
　ilmada ch'ŏnbog'i sini,
　　kosŏng'i tongbu hasine.

ppuri kip'un namunŭn
　parame ani hŭndullini,
　　kkotchok'o yŏlmae manhi yŏnŭni,

saemi kip'ŭn murŭn
　kamŭme ani marŭmŭro,
　　naega toeyŭ padaro hŭrŭdoda.

With all *Han'gŭl* symbols representing just one sound each all the time with
only a few exceptions, and with four sybolsa, ㅇ, ㆆ, △, and ·, now being
obsolete, a beginner may find a few hours of concentration sufficient to
enable him to pronounce any sentence written in *Han'gŭl*

As we have seen, Sejong, even before the proclamation of the *Hunmin
chŏng'ŭm* in 1446, set in motion a flurry of programs for writing, teaching,
and extensive use of, and translation of books in Chinese into, the *Han'gŭl*.
The first group of books written in *Han'gŭl*, the most significant in Korean
literature, includes the *Yongbi ŏch'ŏn ka* (1445), the *Sŏkpo sangjŏl* (1447), and

the *Wŏrin ch'ŏn'gangji kok* (ca. 1448). The *Yongbi ŏch'ŏn ka* or S*ongs of the Dragons Flying to Heaven*, co-authored by those *Chiphyŏnjŏn* scholar who helped create the Han'gŭl, contains 125 two-line cantos in praise of Sejong's six immediate ancestors. The *Sŏkpo sangjŏl*, which can be renamed A *Literary Biography of Sakyamuni*, was written by Prince Suyang at the order Sejong. The twenty-five volumes that it comprises, now partly lost, were dedicated to the memory of Sejong's Queen Sim (Sohŏn) who died in 1446. On the basis of this biography of Buddha, Sejong himself composed about 580 two-line cantos extolling Buddha which he called the *Wŏrin chŏn'gangji kok* or *Songs of the Moon Shining over the Thousand Streams*. The *Songs*, now also partly lost, shows Sejong's already unswerving commitment to Buddhism ; the moon as Buddha incarnate lightens thousand streams of the world which in turn reflect the thousand moons, glorifying the virtues of Buddha.

These works constituted an auspicious and healthy beginning for Han'gŭl literature. Their high literary quality and uninhibited themes are particularly refreshing. Buddhism, if under political tribulation, seemed now safe in literature ; in fact, it was to make a recurrent motif especially for romance. And those Confucian official-literati in authoring the *Songs of the Dragons Flying to Heaven* set out to glean poetic words used daily among the common folks. Thus, the *Hunmin chŏng'ŭm* was already spawning a new experience in creative activity which they had never had before. It also created a new field scholarly concentration for Korean phonetics, as we shall see.

Poetry : the Sijo

With the appearance of the *Han'gŏl*, the *Kyŏnggich'e* style song disappeared, which is understandable. But the *Sijo*, which was also inherited from Koryŏ, became almost suddenly popularized; it could be now recorded in *Han'gŏl*. Besides, in the *Sijo* seemed deposited all the essential ingredients of the traditional poetry developed since the Three Kingdoms period. Indeed, with the *Sijo* with its rhythmic pattern and singable quality, the Koreans found a poetic form most congenial to their language. Several thousand *Sijo* produced during the ups and downs of the Yi dynasty, to say nothing of those gone unrecorded, bespeak of its popularity among all classes of people.

The subject matter of the *Sijo* covered every aspect of dynastic life : loyalty to sovereign, filial piety, love, drinking, patriotism, righteous indignation, self-pity, and, above all, beauty of nature. The nature-boundness is, as might be expected, the most pronounced of all thematic characterstics of the *Sijo*. Even though Korean traditional literature and art or, for that matter, Northeast Asian arts are highly nature-nourished, the *Sijo* is particularly so. It is difficult to find a *Sijo* which is completely deviod of the imagery of nature. If the prevalence of the geomantic theory of wind and water were of a certain reverence to the mysterious, subterranean force of nature, the feast of nature in the *Sijo* would have been the manifestation of an acute, if somewhat inveterate, love of its surface beauty. The Koreans are a nature-addicted people.

Sŏng Sam Mun, one of the Six Dead Subjects, once sang his intense loyalty to his sovereign in a *Sijo* :

> When this frame is dead and gone
> What will then become of me?
> On the peak of Mt. Pongnae
> I shall become a spreading pine.
> When white snow fills heaven and earth
> I shall stand, lone and green. *

The man's loyalty, reminiscent of Chŏng Mong Chu's, and the popularity of this particular poem are actually sustained by the imagery of nature–the dramatic juxtaposition of a gigantic green pine at a summit of the Diamond Mountains and a thick pall of white snow that covers it.

To some, the scene might make a scroll of classic oriental painting, but nature in this poem is too profoundly involved. The consequence of his extraordinary loyalty, that provoked a devil in Sejo who executed him in a cruelest manner, is presaged by the white snow. The white snow, whilst its whiteness looks pure and beautiful, but when excessive, becomes the cold evil that smothers life beneath. But in the metaphysical world of the *yin-yang* interaction, there is nothing moral or immoral, or good or evil but inexorable circular change. Humanity's role is to conform to the workings of the universe, that is the higher reality. When the author decided for the greenness of a pine against the whiteness of snow that "filled heaven and earth," therefore, he willed his own destruction. Sŏng Sam Mun had a deeper motive in a microcosm of humanity where the concepts of good and evil become relevant. He had resolved to pit himself against the Sejo force personifying the evilness of the white snow, just as Captain Ahab in Herman Melville's *Moby Dick or the Whale* saw through the whiteness of the whale something evil or, probably evil principle itself and turned against it. Ahab wanted to know what is hidden in the "heartless voids" covered by "the sinister and universal whiteness," and Sŏng Sam Mun, on his part, refused to be snowed under. The defiance at the whiteness of both the snow and the whale ended in a complete tragedy.

---

* From the *Transactions of the Korea Branch of the Royal Asiatic Society,* Vol. XXXIV, p. 16.

It is difficult to comtain the *Sijo* in a strict mertrical form. In general, the dominant metrical patten in the three verses that comprise a *Sijo* is 3:4 or 4:4 in syllable grouping. The *Sijo* had about four variant forms, of which the following is the most popular one:

First line	3	4	4	4/3
Second line	3	4	4	4/3
Third line	3	5	4	4 *

The cardinal numbers indicate the number of syllables; each line had four syllable groups. Change in form usually occurs in the first and second lines, which can a little extended by adding a few more syllable groups, that is, words or phrases, but not in the last line. The last verse, being the line for concluding the theme stated in the first and elaborated in the second line, has a slightly different metrical pattern which is necessary for making a dramatic turn from, or a sharp contrast with, the thematic and rhythmic contents of the previous two lines.

Although there other poetic devices to add to the charm of a *Sijo*, craftsmanship and intellectualism are less admired virtues. The *Sijo* is generally disposed toward the free, pervasive mood, and that mood, even when the theme is on sadness or self-pity, betrays the man's inner security and freedom. The key to understanding of the *Sijo* is an impressionistic grasp of that mood.

The following song, undoubtedly a masterpiece with a philosophical depth, is authored by Song Si Yŏl (1607-1689), one of the great Sijo writers as well as of the notorious partisan politicians of the late Yi dynasty.

> Green mountains gently gently,
>   Blue waters gently gently
> Hills gently gently, streams gently gently,
>   And between them I, too, gently gently,
> In the midst gently gnetly, this body growing older,
>   Gently gently shall it be. *

This is a rare moment of ecstasy one attains only through harmonious union whith nature, a state of religious exaltation to which Taoism, Buddhism, and Confucianism, all endeavor to attain. The poem is certainly a literary consummation of the ultimate goals of the three religions–indeed through evocation of a mood.

---

* From "Introduction to the *Sijo* : the Epigram" by Peter H. Lee in *East and West,* VII, no. 1, Rome, April 1956, pp. 61–67.
* From the *transactions of the Korea Branch of the Royal Asiatic Society,* Vol. XXXIV, p. 44.

The *kasach'e* verse, a longer form, also inherited from Koryŏ, is quite different from the *Sijo*. With syllable groups of 3:4 and/or 4:4 as the dominant pattern, a *kasach'e* song can go on almost indefinitely like prose; hence, it is also called *changga* or long song. Apparently, the *Sijo* belongs to the *tan'ga* or short song. Characeteristics of *kasach'e* songs are more spontaneous and descriptive and usually at their best when dexcribing, in high-flown and somewhat satirical diction, natural beauties blended with the salty cynicism of life.

Fiction writing in the early period of the dynasty was still in an incipient stage. The *Kŭmo sinhwa* or *New Tales of the Golden Turtle* Modeled on a Chinese prototype and written in Chinese by Kim Si Sŭp (1435–1493), one of the Six Live Subjects, has been thought by some to be the beginning of the modern fiction in Korean literature. But, actually, it was a collection of fantasies likeness of which had appeared already in the Koryŏ period. It was from the seventeenth century that novels almost suddenly began to dominate the literary scene.

Meanwhile, works in Chinese continued, needless to say, if only by a larger group of writers than in the previous dynasty. The appearance in 1478 of the *Tongmun sŏn* or *Selections from Eastern Literature*, an anthology of literary writings in Chinese collected from Silla times on, was a notable event in the history of Korean literature in Chinese(*Hanmunhak*). The *Tongmun Sŏn*, compiled by Sŏ Kŏ Chŏng (1420–1488), *et at.*, at the roya command, contains 1,415 works in verse and prose and provided a model for logies of this kind.

No less significant was the appearance of feminine writers in Chinese in the sixteenth century. The emergence of women as poets and artists sporting pen names, considering the social pressure applied against them for such extracurricular activities as learning and writing, was like certain spring plants coming out into full bloom through rocky soil after many seasons. Sin Saimdang (1504–1551), the versatile artist mother of Yi I, Hwang Chin I (ca. the middle of sixteenth century), the famed *kisaeng* or professional entertainer of Songdo (Kaegyŏng), and Hŏ Nansŏlhŏn (1563–1589), the daughter of that illustrious literary family, are the first prominent feminine figures known in Korean literature. Their literary contributions, mainly in poetry, are considered precious gems embedded in the Yi dynasty literature, signifying the dynasty's cultural maturity also.

Ceramic Art

Nowhere is the difference in artistic taste between Koryŏ and Yi Chosŏn more evident than in the field of pottery. Koryŏ's ceramic art was characterized, as we have seen, by that deep, lustrous "secret color," a rich variety of shapes and decorations, and a remarkable freedom from libidinal inhibition. The aesthetic sensitivity in ceramic art of the Yi dynasty gentlemen, on the other hand, was generally restrained in terms of color, decorative design, and execution. Indeed, restraints were deep-seated trends in the official Confucian culture in general. The greatness of the Yi dynasty potter-artists lies in the re-creation of spontaneous freedom, as in literature, and refinement within those limited conditions, they achieved them with simple, unpretentious contours executed in a sudden flash of inspiration and an economy of color. In fact, the aesthetic concept from Sŏn philosophy of sudden enlightenment, oddly enough, seems more apparent in Yi ceramics than in Koryŏ's. But, in the last analysis, the enduring quality of the Yi dynasty pottery is its being functional, rather than ornamental as was the case of its predecessors.

The *punch'ŏng*, a variant of celadon, and the *paekcha* or white porcelain are the two predominant categories of the Yi pottery. The transition from the crude earlier types to these two seems to have coincided with the dynastic change. By the middle of the fifteenth century, they were produced at 321 kilns, probably government-operated and scattered over the whole country. The *punch'ŏng*, actually the designation of a new technique which called for brushing white slip over parts or, sometimes, the entire surface area of a piece, is apparently a development of the Koryŏ celadon. It uses the same or a similar method of decorating and the same celadon clay but achieves decidedly inferior effects in refinement.

One of the wine bottles at the National Museum of Korea, dating from the sixteenth century, displays conspicuous features of *punch'ŏng* wares *(Plate 26)*. Its shape, one of the popular types of the Yi wares, looks like a Koryŏ *maebyŏng* (vase) upside down. An archaic bird, meshed with the brush lines which seem to have been applied to blur the defectiveness of the bird, is in a pose which we are not told whether for running or for swimming. But the bottle's functional soundness and rustic simplicity in decoraton achieved with coarse, unsullied lines are indeed the very quality for which *punch'ŏng* works are admired.

The *paekcha*, generally more elegant than the *punch'ŏng* wares of course originated from the Koryŏ white porcelain, and, naturally, it was favored by the aesthetic palate of Confucian intellectuals. It was mainly for ceremonial use; probably because of this reason, *paekcha* wares were produced throughtout the dynastic period, whereas the production of the *punch'ŏng*, more or less popular wares, somehow discontinued after the end of the sixteenth century. Like *punch'ŏng* wares, the *paekcha* (white porcelains) have the general characteristics of simplicity and unpretentious utilitarianism, and more refinement although the coarseness can be readily detected in many cases of the *paekcha*, it came to attain to perfection its inherent later period of the dynasty when the technique was much improved under the steady government support. Delicate grace and austere elegance are the two most distinctive traits of the *paekcha* wares, and they are, as in many works, blended into poetic simplicity, which is the very essence of the Yi dynasty white porcelain.

The virtue of white color, which might be in art considered colorless, seems to have been, intriguingly enough, accorded a special place in the aesthetic spectrum of Confucian moral symbolism. Confucianists' suppression of emotions and aversion to gaudiness seem to have been translated into whiteness. For the internal decoration of Korean houses and also Korean traditional clothing, it was the white color that was predominant; indeed, the Koreans call themselves "the white clad people." The subtle tonal differences in the porcelain white ranging over pure white, milky white, greyish white, bluish white, and a diffused combination of all these are consciously appreciated. The grudging use in general of decorative designs painted in cobalt, iron, or copper under the glaze, which contrasts sharply with some of Koryŏ *ch'ŏngja* pieces whose surface is crowded with figures and sings, serves only to heighten the whiteness of *paekcha* works.

A food jar at the National Museum of Korea, probably dating from the seventeenth century, is a rare piece of stunning beauty-rare because the white space that usually covers most of a ware's surface in preponderant cases of the white porcelains, is here pushed into serving as a background that contains a splashy picture *(Plate 27)*. The grape vines and leaves and the clusters of fruits that nestle among them, painted in underglaze blue and iron, take up a goodly portion of the creamy background.

Painting

For the dearth of extant works of Koryŏ painting, we are fairly well compensated with the remains of the Yi dynasty painting. Painting of Chinese characters as art also flourished during this period. As a certain degree of skill in calligraphic art was an imperative requirement for a gentleman, a large number of the *yangban* achieved mastership in styles of their own or in style that masters of the past had created. Painting of pictures, however, were done by more select groups. The court painters who did royal portaits, wall painting, etc., constituted the "professional" group, that is, hereditary artists of *chung'in* origin. They were expected to follow prescribed styles and generally were less competent artists. A few of them under the royal patronage, however, produced some of the great masterpieces of the Yi dynasty. The gentlemen painter group consisted of talented *yangban* amateurs who painted as they would. From the seventeenth century on, many of this group were "professionalized" and accountable for a notable development of painting in terms of technique and subject matter during the late Yi dynasty.

The predominant motif in painting is also man and nature, as in the *Sijo*. The *Sansuhwa* or Mountain and Water Painting, the main current in the early period of Yi painting, is invariably an idealization of universal harmony : man is always treated as part of, and being in, nature but as never against it. The development in the treatment of this theme on landscape, as in other aspects of the Yi dynasty culture, reflects a cross section of the dynastic development itself. The early paintings show that quality which is vital, deathless, and fantastic, and they seem to have been technically guided by the Sung painting. But from the beginning of the seventeenth century, which is usually regarded as a dividing line between the early and late Yi dynasty, the romantic characterstics gradually gave way to the depiction of tangible realities immediate to life; this was effected by the assertion of individualities of, and the technical innovations by, a surprisingly-large number of inspired artists, which also resulted in thematic diversity.

The "Dreamy Vision of the Paradise" reproduced here was painted in color by An Kyŏn, a fifteenth century court painter *(Plate 28)*. Mountains, dales, blooming peach trees, and cottages are all harmonized into a fantasty with such ease and deftness. Similarly unreal is a black and white piece, "Looking at Water on a Leisurely day," by Kang Hŭi An (1417-1464), one of those scholar-amateurs who were equally adept at calligraphy, verse-making, and scholarly compilation at the court *(Plate 29)*. A series of calligraphic strokes sweepingly employed delineates an old contented sage amidst rocks, water, and foliage which together convey the pristine, timeless ideality of a "dreamy vision." The old man is perfectly fit in the rock, as if in communion with nature.

The same motif was carried into an eighteenth century work in color. The "Viewing of the Spring Blossoms," kept at the Kansong Museum of Fine arts, was done by Sim Sa Chŏng (1707-1769), son of an illustrious family in Kyŏngsang Province who pursued his art until his death *(Plate 30)*. Several elderly village gentlemen are enjoying the arrival of spring, and, in the stream, half-naked youths are exerting themselves to net fish. In sharp contrast with the exaggeration and dreaminess of earlier works, everything in this scene is so real that it is almost banal. But beneath that banality lies the same motif as that in the "Looking at Water." One feels overwhemed by a compelling awareness of spiritual harmony between man and nature as they are astir with the renewal of life.

Construction of a turtle ship. By having turtle ships built during the Japanese invasion in 1592, Admiral Yi Sun-sin.

Part 8

The Late Yi Dynasty : Toward Modern Era

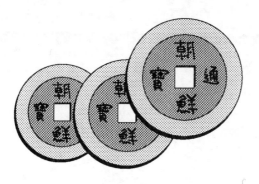

1

Political Decline

The institutional relevancy and the political dynamism which the Confucian ruling class had shown in founding the dynasty seem to have been spent by the time of Sŏnjo's reign (1568-1608). The two centuries of cultural stability and peaceful relations with China, during which the Confucians unremittedly nurtured themselves with Chinese antiquarianism, had rendered them inflexible in thought and action for readjustment. The Mountain and Forest scholar-bureaucrats, who, whether conservative or radical, now dominated the court, were singularly unable to face, with other than high-flown words of mouth, the political reality which became replete with internal contradictions and external dangers.

The examination system, for instance, clearly needed revamping. A variety of examinations, through which degree holders, that is, candidates for government posts, were produced in a disproportionately large number to that of offices available. Under such circumstances, the best thing the unemployed, degree holders, who were utterly useless in terms of economic productivity, could do was to put themselves under the patronage of wealthy, high-ranking officials as their "family guests." Or, they might move to the *sŏwŏn* where they would languish, talking fiercely-partisan politics. Indeed, the factionalism was the most deleterious political problem that came to plague the country from the late sixteenth century on. But the ruling elite lethargically eschewed its correction and the political reforms in general presumably in deference to the sacredness of the ancestral institutions.

The economic disorder, which went hand in hand with the official demoralization, was even more serious. Landholding and labor systems were deteriorated into the familiar pattern which we have seen in the closing decades of the Koryŏ dynasty. The productive capacity of the peasant class as financial resources for the support of the government and the ruling class was taken undue advantage of by local magistrates and petty officials. The petty local officials, who were bent on compensating for their unpaid, hereditary service by whatever means they could contrive either at the government's or the peasants' expense, were the single most notorious group for the exploitation of the peasantry. Usually, in alliance with conniving higher officials and local *yangban*, they lined their pockets through extortion by unlawful impositions upon their victims of taxes, tribute assessments, and labor service. Such irregularities, which were to eventually trigger peasant revolts later, were allowed to go on.

Factionalism

The *Yangban* class's intellectual inability, despite a proliferation of sŏwŏn, to grow out of Chu Hsi-ism was a profounder sign of the dynastic decline. The emergence of the *Yehak*, with which Confucianists attempted to shore up the government and social morality, was in a deeper sense a confession of governmental impotence for action. The reform problems now looming so large, no one seemed able to squarely face the enormity of undertaking long-range reforms except for piecemeal readjustments. Politicians of the Mountain and Forest persuasion, men of abstract principle utterly devoid of pragmatic bent, were hardly expected to bring about a reform on any appreciable scale, as it meant correcting the tradition, much less a revolution. Inevitably, the stagnant climate of lethargy and volatility set in, and sequacious politicians crowded together around powerful leaders, gradually forming rival parties not necessarily of policy but of man.

The initial occasion for political division was provided by the personal animosity between Sim Ŭi Kyŏm, a high-ranking conservative, and Kim Hyo Wŏn, holding the office of the *Chŏngnang* in the Ministry of Personnel, a relatively low-ranking but powerful office where all new official appointments were initiated. Kim Hyo Wŏn, whose appointment to the post of the *Chŏngnang* earlier was delayed by the obstruction presented by Sim Ŭi Kyŏm, now rejected the recommendation to the *Chŏngnang*-ship of Sim's brother. It was in 1575 when the resultant controversy divided the court. Those who rallied around Kim were called the Tong'in or Easterners because Kim lived in the eastern part of the capital, and the opposition the Sŏin or Westerners with Sim living in western Hanyang (Seoul)

But actually Sim and Kim had no control over the situation. Even after they were relegated to provincial posts, taking the blame for the factional fission, partisan politics went right on, splitting existing parties into more factions. By 1589, the Easterners who had dominated the court were divided into the Namin or Southerners and the Pug'in or Northerners, and in a decade the Northerners, when they got the upper hand of the Southerners, became separated into the Taebuk or Great Northerners and the Sobuk of Small Northerners. The Westerners, after a period of political ups and downs, were also splintered into the Noron or Old Doctrine and the Soron or Young Doctrine in 1683. These were four parties known as *Sasaek* or Four Colors, that is, the Old Doctrine, the Young Doctrine, the Southerners, and the (Small) Northerners, who, then without further division, worked out a certain power balance among themselves.

Major considerations in these party affiliations were generally made on the basis of consanguineous and teacher–disciple relations and personal friendship. Loyalty became an esteemed virtue, which came to be identified with ŭi (righteousness). Characteristically, a black–and–white moralism that rejected any compromising shades in between, as shown in the subsequent power struggles, was advanced for the destruction of enemies which was usually in the form of purge from the government or, in a few cases, even death.

The Japanese Invasion

While thus the internal political consensus at the court was being torn asunder, more ominous threats were rapidly mounting from without. Both the Japanese and the Jürched had never been centralized states for long in the same sense that Korea and China were. Under strong leadership, however, each of them, consolidating itself from decentralized localism into an effective nationalism, was capable of generating tremendous military power. The 1580's witnessed the unsettling rises of Hideyoshi (1536–1598) in Japan and of Nurhachi (1559–1626) in Manchuria who were to shatter the long peninsular complacency into two humiliating defeats in a row.

No sooner, by 1590, had Toyotomi Hideyoshi united Japan under his sway, thus terminating more than two centuries of incessant local wars, than he began contacting the Korean court in an attempt, as he did not know better, to conquer China through an alliance with Korea. Hideyoshi's subsequent invasion of the Peninsula has been variously attributed to his megalomaniac desire for conquest, psychological blow dealt by the untimely death of his infant son, desire for the expansion of trade toward the Asia mainland or to his scheme to spend abroad the military and economic strengths of his vassals in order to maintain his own military supremacy at home.

At any rate, the problem that faced the Yi government form the beginning was to what extent the country should be prepared against a possible invasion. To this question, the Yi government's attitudes were one of ambivalent indecision resulting partly from the inordinate presumption of continued peace, an inertia hardened by two centuries of "morning calm" and partly from the fractured unanimity caused by partisan politics. The reports of the two envoys on the same mission sent in 1590 to the Hideyoshi court, purporting to find out Hideyoshi's real intention, presented conflicting views because of their different party affiliations.

Earlier, in 1583, Yi I, the philosopher-statesman, then the Minister of War, proposed that 100,000 troops be trained and maintained for an emergency, which was to him a distinct possibility in view of international developments. The majority of officials led by Yu Sŏng Nyong (1542-1607), then a senior censor, who advanced the theory, in line with Cho Kwang Cho's Taoistic political philosophy, that the "maintenance of an army in peace time is like maintaining a misfortune," talked Yi I's insightful proposal out of existence. Indeed, the government had by then long discontinued, in spite of itself, to maintain what could be called an army for national defense. Alarmed by some serious signs of an impending emergency, the government, only in the early 1591, reluctantly stirred itself to conduct a series of defense preparations which were, however, rather late or lukewarm at best.

The Turtle Ship. One of the belated defense measures, recommended by Yu Sŏng Nyong, now Left State Councillor, proved to be the most opportune, namely, the promotion of Yi Sun Sin (1545-1598), Yu's boyhood friend, from the magistracy of the Chŏng'ŭp district to the Left Admiralship of Chŏlla Navy. Admiral Yi Sun Sin immediately set out to revamp the coastal defense under his responsibility. While putting his navy under intensive training, he proceeded to construct armored warships, usually referred to as the turtle ship because of their turtle-like shape (*Plate* 31). The prototype for the turtle ship which Admiral Yi built seems to have existed from the time of T'aejong, but it became now armored for the first time in history. A turtle ship was similar in size to that of a smaller warship of the day with a length of about 100 feet or less and had eight to ten oars and six loopholes on each side. Under the turtle's head and its tail was also a loophole each. Through the opened mouth of the turtle, the sulfurous smoke could be shot out. The turtle's back was covered with awl-shaped nails, except in a narrow path on the back in the pattern of a cross, to prevent enemies from climbing aboard. The ship, manned by a force of about 160, could charge deeply into the enemy fleet and knock against the nearest ship, while shooting firearms and cannons from all sides and jetting out the sulfurous smoke from the mouth to scare the wits out of the enemy. * These dauntless sea monsters which were on duty in the

---

* The early nineteenth century turtle ship was manned by 277 men and officers.

Yi fleet, however, seem to have counted not more than five, contrary to those fleets consisting entirely of turtle ships shown in some of the later pictures of Yi's naval engagements. The first turtle ship was launched on March 27, 1592. With its variety of cannons and maneuvering capacity tested, it was ready for combat on April 12, just two days before the invasion from Japan.

From Pusan, which fell in ten hours, the invasion force of about 160,000 led by Hideyoshi's trusted generals thrust northward in a three-pronged fork. Konish Yukinaga's army advanced along the central route connecting Pusan, Taegu, Ch'ungju, and Seoul; Katŏ Kyomasa's force marched along the eastern, Pusan-Kyŏngju-Ch'ungju-Seoul course; and Kuroda Nagamasa's the western course that went through Sŏngju, Chirye, Ch'ŏngju, and Chuksan before reaching Seoul. Thus started the *Imjin Waeran* or Dwarf War of the Year of Dragon (that is, 1592)

These "Dwarf" armies mainly from western Japan, battle-hardened through domestic wars and Dwarf Banditries (*Waegu; Wakō* in Japanese) abroad and equipped with long swords and, above all, modernistic Portuguese arquebuses, found little resistance in their northward dash. The Yi Chosŏn force of little more than several thousand cavalrymen was hastily organized under General Sin Ip (1546-1592) against the 160,000 invaders. General Sin Ip, who impressed the court by repelling a small-scale Jürched invasion nine years before, deployed his troops around a strategic position near Ch'ungju "with a river in the back." As might be expected, his small unit of cavalrymen only with short swords was resoundingly crushed in the initial contact, the news that sent Sŏnjo and his courtiers taking refuge northward to P'yŏngyang. The *ch'ŏnmin* in the capital who had been long exploited and alienated, rose in

AD. YI SUN SIN S
OPERATIONAL WATERS

EASTERN SEA

YELLOW SEA

NAK TONG River

CHŎNJU
TAEGU KYŎNGJU

NAMWŎN
ULSAN
(YŎMPO)

KWANGJU
KIMHAE
CHINHAE
CHINJU
PUSAN
NAEIPO

NAJU
SUNCHŎN
KŎJE

YŎSU HANSANDO

CHINDO
KOGŬMDO
WANDO

TSUSHIMA

MYŎNGNYANG
STRAIT

CHEJU

rebellion, setting fire first upon Ministry of Justice and *Changnyewŏn* offices that kept their registers. On May 2, the Japanese walked into the almost deserted capital. From there, Konish led his troops P'yŏngyang which he took on June 13. Sŏnjo, who left the city two days before for Ŭiju, a border town abutting on the Amnok River, was forced to request help from the Ming. Katō, Konishi's fierce rival, marched his army northeast, overrunning Hamgyŏng Province where in Hyeryŏng he captured two royal princes, and he even sent a detachment further north across the Tuman River.

Yi Sun Sin and Naval Operations

The Right Navy of Kyŏngsang under Admiral Wŏn Kyun, rather a scheming politician than a naval officer, and also the Province's Left Navy, the two naval forces which received the first impact of the war, collapsed in ten days. With characteristic cautiousness, Admiral Yi Sun Sin did not rush to Wŏn Kyun's aid. On May 4, with the court's sanction to operate in Kyŏngsang waters, he moved out of his Yŏsu headquarters a ninety ship fleet with twenty-four warships as its mainstay. During the two-day period from May 7, Yi destroyed forty-two enemy ships in three battles around Kŏje Island off the Chinhae Bay where the modern naval headquarters are situated. The second operation covered from May 29 to June 10, the period in which Konishi's army was rapidly approaching P'yŏngyang. Thus, it was strategically important for the Japanese navy to seize control of the southern and western coastal seas, a fact that helps explain the precipitate pressure the Japanese navy was applying westward, despite its previous defeat, and that Yi's sailing out for the second time much earlier than planned. This time it was combined operation with turtle ships participating probably for the first time. Under Admiral Yi, a fleet of fifty-one ships, joined by Admiral Yi Ŏk Ki's Right Navy of Chŏlla and Wŏn Kyun's remaining force, went through four bitterly fought battles in which seventy-one Japanese ships were sunken. It was probably because of these Korean victories at sea that the triumphant Konishi was reduced to sue for peace twice, while he was reaching P'yŏngyang, winning.

The Japanese navy, badly mangled by repeated blows, were reinforced by three separate naval forces of Wakiida Yasuji and two others dispatched by the direct order of Hideyoshi. Admiral Yi, again in cooperation with Admirals Yi Ŏk Ki and Wŏn Kyun, set out with a total of about fifty-five ships for the third operation, which took about a week from July 5. In two engagements fought out during this maneuver from Yŏsu to An'golp'o in the mouth of the Naktong River, the Korean navy claimed eighty-nine out of a combined Japanese naval force of 115 ships that participated in the fighting. Of the two, the Battle of Hansando, waged around an islet west of Kŏje Island, was the most decisive action of the war. With his favorite tactics of inducement maneuver and concentrated fire power in full use, Yi destroyed forty-seven and captured twelve out of Wakiida's seventy-three ship fleet. It also played havoc with Hideyoshi's strategy for the control of the sea and the Japanese morale on the land as well.

From then on, the Japanese navy preferred, whenever possible, to stay closer to land, protecting their vessels moored along the coastline by shooting from the hills behind. The Yi fleet on the fourth maneuver in search of the enemy was thus frustrated in encountering any sizable enemy fleets. It was on September 1, the last day of Yi's week-long search, that the Battle of Pusanp'o (Pusan) occurred. It was not as strategically important as the previous one but a more spectacular one in terms of the number of ships claimed. In the day's climactic fight, the Yi fleet of 166 ships descended upon more than 470 Japanese ships, mostly transport vessels, anchored in Pusan Harbor with the enemy shooting from hillocks encircling it. Under heavy volleys of fire from fortified positions on the surrounding hills, the Koreans burnt down at least 100 ships, upping the day's total to 130. Not the least remarkable feat was the fact that, throughout these four periods of his major operations, Admiral Yi Sun Sin lost not a single vessel under his command.

The Counterattacks

With the armies spread thin and the control of the sea ever remote, the Japanese were more and more inclined toward peace, with Konishi Yukinaga as its proponent. The Koreans, on the other hand, just recovering from the initial setback, turned with a vengence to their island foe whose piratical predecessors had implanted a deep feeling of animosity in their mind.

The Ŭibyŏng. As if to retrieve the misplaced confidence in the government, privately-organized armies, known as *ŭibyŏng* or righteous army, sprang up. A *ŭibyŏng*, variously of several hundred to several thousand men, was usually commanded by a former official or a local *yangban* with a strong sense of moral obligation to the nation and the financial means for arming his men. Men who volunteered for *ŭibyŏng* were exceptionally determined groups including *yangmin* or even *ch'ŏnmin* of the same localities as *yangban* organizers'. Originated mostly in Kyŏngsang and Chŏlla Provinces, *ŭibyŏng* groups, some of which came into being as early as late April or 1592, began harassing the enemy's rear guard in coordination with the hastily reorganized government army or, sometimes, in defiance of it. The *ŭibyŏng* phenomenon reappeared in an even more serious national emergency in the early twentieth century against modern Japan. But far less expected was a simultaneous appearance of the righteous army of Buddhist monks. Monk Hyujŏng, now seventy-two years old, organized and commanded a combat force of 5,000 monks. Some of these monk-soldiers participated in the most bitterly contested battles of the war, together with their Confucian colleagues-in-arms.

In the meantime, the Ming, at the request of Sŏnjo, decided to dispatch its army, that arrived in the field toward the middle of July, 1592. Upon their unsuccessful attempt at routing Konishi's army out of P'yŏngyang, the Chinese immediately entered a peace parley with the Japanese, despite the Koreans' urging otherwise. While this peace negotiation was going on, the Japanese, as noted, made a determined attempt to establish a supply route over the sea for Konishi's army, only to be frustrated by Admiral Yi. Then they concentrated on occupying the whole Chŏlla Province, the area in which now major encounters occurred. During July, at about the same time that Admiral Yi successfully concluded his third operation, a Japanese thrust toward Chŏlla was beaten back at Kŭmsan by Kwŏn Nyul (1537–1599), a magistrate–turned general. In October, another Japanese force of about 30,000 marched toward Chŏlla from the Pusan area. This Japanese drive was blocked at Chinju, a western Kyŏngsang city garrisoned under General Kim Si Min (1544–1592). The Battle of Chinju, in which the Japanese lost most of their number and the garrison force its general, was regarded as the most important victory since the Battle of Hansando.

Reversing the previous peace stance, the Ming now reinforced its army under Li Ju–sung. The Chinese army under General Li Ju–sung, in coordination with Korean forces, retook P'yŏngyang in the early January 1593 and pursued the enemy southward. But Li Ju–sung's army was dealt a blow at Pyŏkchegwan north of Seoul. The victorious Japanese then turned southwest to Haengju, a mountain fortress, where General Kwŏn Nyul and his assorted forces—government, *ŭibyŏng*, and monk troops—of about 10,000 strength had been ready for and assault into Seoul which was still in the hands of the invaders. In the fighting that followed, the Koreans, though outnumbered three to one, defended the fortress to a third great victory of the war in mid-February. The so-called Three Great Victories of the *Imjin Waeran* are those at the Hansando sea, Chinju, and Haengju.

The armies of Konishi, Katŏ, and other lesser generals in the north, much plagued by supply shortages and guerrilla harassments, began withdrawing to Seoul and further south with the resumption in April of peace talks between the Chinese and the Japanese. Meanwhile, the Japanese took up defense positions of rather settled down, under a long–term proposition, along the coastal zones of Kyŏngsang Province. They built fortifications in Japanese style and took to farming.

To these Japanese forces, the stronghold of Chinju, eighty miles west of Pusan, that held out the Japanese onslaught a year before, was a menace. But, more from his piqued pride, Hideyoshi ordered another attempt at the city. In June, an expeditionary force of about 60,000, made up of detachments from the armies of Katŏ, Konishi, and others, laid siege to the city of Chinju defended by government and ŭibyŏng armies of slightly more than 10,000 plus several ten thousands of its citizens. The pitched battle that ensued for a week witnessed every improvised weapon and trick of an offensive-defensive war. This second battle of Chinju represented the grimmest account of the Japanese atrocities committed against the defenders. But the final triumph went to a *kisaeng* named Non'gae. Non'gae was an entertainer of *ch'ŏnmin* origin who belonged to the city-magistracy of Chinju. While entertaining elated Japanese generals on the rocky bank of the Nam River right after the fall of the city, she jumped into the river with one of the drunken Japanese in the tight clutch of her arms and drowned together.

The Second Japanese Invasion and Yi Sun Sin

While the peace negotiation between the two foreign armies were in progress and the Japanese main force was unobstrusively withdrawing home, the Yi government gathered itself together and proceeded to reestablish its military system. Notably, in 1594, it established the *Hullyŏn Togam* or Office of Training, under which the *Samsu* units, or literally Three Hands, that is, firearmsmen, bowmen, and lancemen, were newly organized and trained. Another addition was the post of the Supreme Commandership of the Navies of Three Provinces, namely, Kyŏngsang, Chŏlla, and Ch'ungch'ŏng, to which Admiral Yi was appointed. During this lull, the Japanese, too, substantially improved their navies by building more useful warships which were equipped with firearms and even partially armored. And they were ready for a second invasion a few months after the peace talks were broken off.

About 140,000 troops under Katŏ, Konishi, and other familiar names, which, at careful intervals, landed at Pusan in the early 1597, spread to their previous strongholds along the coastal zones, instead of making, as in the first invasion, a northward dash immediately. This uncharacteristic cautiousness of the Japanese seems to have stemmed not from Hideyoshi's order but from his field commanders' fear of the Korean navy. The now better-prepared Korean army and the more promptly-responded Chinese reinforcements, by June, took up their positions in strategic cities in the south to meet the Japanese.

In this critical period, all of a sudden, Admiral Yi was relieved of his

command to be tried at the court for his cautious refusal to execute an operational order which seemed, to his judgement, to be based on an unfounded
information. * As his successor was appointed Admiral Wŏn Kyun for whom,
however, the job was clearly above his ability. He drank heavily, unaware of
an inevitable confrontation with the tremendously improved Japanese navy
close at hand. In the middle of July, the Japanese were indeed coming with a
strength of at least 300 ships. In the ensuing clash, Wŏn Kyun lost the entire
navy of more than 200 ships manned by men and officers who had been battle-hardened under Admiral Yi. The Japanese lost only eight ships. In the
meantime, Admiral Yi, whose life had been barely spared from execution,
was demoted to a kind a rankless officer and put in the service of General
Kwŏn Nyul, now the Supreme Commander of the Army and the Navy.

      With the Korean navy gone, the Japanese marched northward, this time,
via Chŏlla Province simply because it had escaped destruction in the previous
invasion. In the middle of August, they routed the allied forces of Koreans
and Chinese out of Namwŏn and Chŏnju, two major cities in that province.
But at Chiksan Sosa area, fifty miles southwest of Seoul, the Japanese were
resoundingly defeated.

      Meanwhile, the government, bewildered at the naval loss, reinstated
Admiral Yi in his former post. Although he was deeply mortified at the
plight of his invincible fleet, Yi proceeded to undertake the impossible job of
naval reconstruction. While, in August, looking for his former officers and
men who might have survived along the Chŏlla coast, more than 100 miles
west of his erstwhile theatre of war, he found twelve warships that somehow
got away from the fateful battle a month before. Around this time, the court,
mindful of the naval demoralization at its nadir, ordered Yi to abandon his
rehabilitation efforts and to join forces with the army. He again refused to follow the instruction, saying that he still had the twelve ships, but, this time,
with impunity.

      The Admiral was not allowed time, however, to strengthen his minus-
cule navy, for in a week he began contacting the enemy. After their army's
defeat at Chiksan, the Japanese navy seemed again all out for an attempt at
the establishment of a seaway along the west coast. They were pushing westward in pursuit of the remainder of the Korean navy. The twelve-ship
Korean fleet was retreating, though maintaining contact with the enemy, as far
as the Myŏngnyang Strait which was Yi's choice for battle. The Myŏngyang
Strait was a narrow seaway between a small peninsula at the southwestern tip

---

* A Japanese named Yoshira, an emissary of Konish Yukinaga, informed a Korean general of
  the date of Kagŏ Kyomasa's arrival, suggesting that Admiral Yi might waylay him at sea. The
  personal rivalry between Konish and Katŏ considered, the informant might have told the truth.
  The court order was based on this information, but Admiral Yi refused to rely on it. Indeed,
  the Katŏ army did arrive on the alleged date.

of South Chŏlla Province and the island of Chindo. The speed of the current in this particular strait, which at flood tide reaches up to 11.5 knots, could be exploited against the enemy, if only at the right time.

As expected, a Japanese fleet of 133 ships was fast approaching the strait, as the twelve were waiting. For some time, the flagship alone kept the enemy fleet at bay, while the awe-striken eleven ships kept themselves several hundred yards behind their commander and seemed ready to flee. The Admiral overawed them into action for an hour's battle, which claimed thirty-three enemy ship with the calculated help from the tide. As usual, the admiral lost not a single ship.

Yi's victory at the Myŏngnyang Strait forced the Japanese armies into their semi-permanent positions along the 100-mile coastal zone from Ulsan to Sunch'ŏn. The Korean and Chinese armies, which had been by the early 1598 reinforced to strength of 140,000, attempted to dislodge the Japanese from those positions, but the Japanese refused to budge. The most determined allied attacks, which turned out to be the last also, occurred in the month of September, 1598, without much results. The Japanese had a secret withdrawal order issued by the dying Hideyoshi in the previous month. The Japanese' problem, therefore, was how to find a loophole on the sea and to escape homeward with as little loss as possible.

Since the Myŏngnyang, the Korean fleet was vastly improved in number and facility, and admiral Yi moved his headquarters to Kogŭmdo, an island about eighty miles west of Sunch'ŏn. The Korean navy was soon joined by a larger Ming fleet under Admiral Ch'en Lin, a querulous Chinese military who was not at all serious about this last phase of the war. The maintenance of discipline among allied navies, which now embraced more than 500 ships, was a grave problem. While generously attributing campaign results to the Chinese, Admiral Yi worked the recalcitrant Ch'en and his men into a functioning ally virtually under his command. The immediate objective for the allied navies was Konishi's army stationed in Sunch'ŏn, which was to be brought under a pincers attack in coordination with the army.

For two months from the last part of September, Konishi desperately sought an escape path, and he finally decided to bribe his way through. The gift-laden Chinese army commander on the other side of the pincers already lifted the siege for the Japanese to go. But Admiral Yi firmly reasoned the also heavily-bribed Ch'en Lin into action and set out for what was to be the last naval battle on November 18: the 500 enemy ships that were coming to the aid of the Konishi army were to be destroyed. In this well-balanced engagement, in which the enemy was taken unawares in the dark of night somewhere between Noryang and Namhae Island, the allied navies obliterated more than 200 enemy vessels. But, the next morning, they found the great naval commander and man of noble character killed in action already a few hours. *

Thus ended the seven years of prolonged conflicts. In a historical perspective, the Japanese attacks on the Peninsula was the culmination of a long
turbulent period in the Japanese history which was characterized by
internecine wars among local powers and by predatory activities abroad. The
Japanese' meaningless yet systematic destruction of life and cultural centers
and their depriving the country of imponderable national treasures, scholars,
and artisans, even though they appropriated those material and human
resources for their cultural improvements, were indeed little more than piratical exercises on a larger scale. The Japanese, at unguarded moments, call
their invasions of 1592 and 1597 the War of Celadon and Printing Type, the
two important cultural items which they carried off most, along with tens of
thousands of noses and ears cut off from killed Koreans.

The Manchu Invasions

The country was destined to go thru another foreign invasion, this time,
from the north before the painful experience with the Japanese was quite
healed. Unlike the invasion from the south, the Manchu invasions of 1627
and 1636 were not inevitable clashes between the two countries on any irrec-
oncilable interests. They were rather an outgrowth of mismanaged diplomacy
on the part of the Yi government, which in turn was a consequence of political factionalism at the court.

Like A-ku-ta, the founder of the Chin dynasty (1122-1234), Nurhachi
emerged as a great leader who was able to consolidate the Jürched tribes into
a centralized state, taking advantage of the declining Ming. He established
various government institutions and devised a writing system which tremendously facilitated administrative efficiency and general cultural improvement as
well. The most important of his creation was the "banner" system which was
at once a military and administrative system. To the nucleus of original eight
"banners" made up of Manchus were later added eight Chinese and eight
Mongol "banners". And the number of 300-man companies that comprised
"banners" was also increased, reaching, by 1644, a total of 563 companies. On
the strength of the effectiveness of this "banners" system, he in 1616 proclaimed himself the emperor of the Later Chin dynasty, indicating his preparedness for territorial expansion. His aim was the conquest of China. By

---

* Paragraphs on Yi Sun Sin and his naval operations are based mainly on In Pok Cho, *Yi Sun
  Sin chōnsa Yōn'gu* (study *on Yi Sun Sin's Naval Operations*)

1625, after a series of decisive battles with the Ming force, he moved his capital to Shen-yang (Mukden) which commanded the vast agricultural Liaotung area.

Against this new development in the north, the Yi government took up the traditional position, that is, cautious two-directional dealings with the Later Chin and the Ming, while augmenting the defense system at home. In 1618, for instance, when the Kwanghaegun (1608-1623), then the reigning monarch, dispatched a reinforcement at the request of the Ming in its confrontation with the Later Chin, he secretly instructed Kang Hong Nip, its commander, to act as the situation demanded. Accordingly, General Kang surrendered to the Later Chin when it got the upper hand of the campaign, a move which seemed to have removed the Manchus' misgivings toward Chosŏn.

The continued sensitivity to the portentous convulsions of the continent in travail, though yet in an incipient stage, was imperative on the Yi court. But that sensitivity became blunted by the factional disputes which were intensified after the Japanese invasions. The Great Northerners, then the dominant faction which had been instrumental in enthroning the Kwanghaegun after a succession trouble, now importuned their *protégé* to eliminate his rival brothers and even the queen dowager. The immorality eventually perpetrated bt the Great Northerners and the Kwanghaegun's inability to prevent it provoked a palace *coup* masterminded and executed by the Westerners in 1623. The Kwanghaegun, as in the case of the Yŏnsan'gun, was consequently denied a customary posthumous title. The newly-installed Injo (1623-1649) and the Westerner-dominated court, as might be expected, abandoned what had seemed a shrewd foreign policy of the Kwanghaegun, discontinuing diplomatic exchanges with the Later Chin in favor of the Ming.

Later Chin T'ai Tsung (1627-1643), the eighth son of Nurhachi now on the throne, regarded the Westerners' overthrow of the Kwanghaegun and subsequent reversal of his Later Chin policy as hostile toward the Later Chin. He was also offended by the presence in the Korean territory of a Ming force which fled from Liao-yang upon the fall of that city into the hands of the Manchus in 1621. The runaway Chinese stationed themselves in Tando, an island off the coast of North P'yŏng'an Province, from which they harassed the Later Chin in the coastal areas of Liaotung. In 1627 Later Chin T'ai Tsung sent an expeditionary force of 30,000 into the Peninsula. The Yi court immediately took refuge in the temporary capital on Kanghwa Island. Badgered on its rear by *ŭibyŏng* guerrillas, they stopped short of seizing Seoul and sued for peace. The Kanghwa court responded to this overture, which resulted in a tentative peace. The treaty arranged then was that Yi Chosŏn and the Later Chin were brothers and the former would stand neutral in the future between the latter and the Ming.

In 1632, as it felt sufficiently strong, the Later Chin demanded that the two countries enter a lord–vassal relationship with Yi Chosŏn as vassal and that the vassal shoulder a substantial burden of material contributions to the Later Chin for its showdown with the Ming. Unlike their Koryŏ counterparts who were flexible enough to accommodate themselves to the demand of the then rising Chin, the seventeenth century Yi dynasty gentlemen politicians, however, failed to measure the Later Chin expansion that nothing could stop. They rebuffed what seemed to them only a contumelious proposal.

The 1630's saw the furious extension of the Manchu power in all directions under T'ai Tsung. In 1636 he declared the use of the name Ch'ing dynasty to supersede Later Chin; he had previously adopted the name Manchu for all Jŭrched tribes. In the same year he personally led an expeditionary force of 100,000 again into the Peninsula. Like tempestuous "barbarians" before them, by–passing fortified strongholds that they could not fell on the way, the Manchus were closing in on Seoul in two weeks' time. Taken unawares, the hapless Injo and his court, who were not even allowed sufficient time to take customary refuge in the Kanghwa sanctuary, ran south behind the walls of the Namhan Sansŏng, a mountain stronghold about thirty miles south of Seoul. The invaders laid siege to the fortress on a long time basis, which all government and *ŭibyŏng* forces could not break from outside. In the meantime, Kanghwa city, where the royal family was protected, fell under the Manchu attacks, delivering the crown prince into the hands of the Manchus. Under the added pressure from the shortage of provisions, Injo, at the end of the forty–day defense, surrendered to Ch'ing T'ai Tsung as a vassal.

Factionalism Continues

The defeat dealt the Injo court a humiliating blow, which was further aggravated by the traditional assumption that the Manchus were the "barbarians," sinking the national self–esteem to a traumatic depth. Hyojong (1650–1659), Injo's second son who succeeded the throne, set out in earnest for preparation for a northern expedition in revenge of that defeat; the war preparations immediately recouped the national morale. Hyojong, who spent eight years at the Ch'ing court with his elder brother, then the crown prince, as hostages, was determined to push his military program to a successful end. The war preparations, that largely consisted of reorganization and vigorous training of the army and procurement of weapons and provisions, were secretly undertaken under his personal supervision. In this venture, Hyojong commanded a solid consensus of not only the officialdom but also highly motivated *yangban* gentlemen who individually readied themselves for military service. All these activities, however, came to an abrupt end upon the untimely death of Hyojong in 1659. The satisfactory outcome of the intended military action, had it been ever launched, against the vigorously expanding Ch'ing, which was destined by 1662 to rule all China, would have been at best doubtful. The demise of Hyojong's purposeful leadership was extremely unfortunate, however. It brought factional struggles out in the open again.

One of the bitterest partisan disputes was occasioned by the very death of Hyojong. The bone of contention, this time, was of *Yehak* complication: how long Queen Dowager Cho should mourn for the death of Hyojong, her stepson. The Westerners, then the party in power, led by Song Si Yŏl, that redoubtable partisan politician who, as a disciple of Kim Chang saeng, was also regarded as an authority on the *Yehak*, recommended a twelve month mourning period for the Queen Dowager. Their recommendation was based on the *Rites and Ceremonies of the Chu Family* and other classical texts which, as noted, laid down a twelve month mourning for the parents for the death of the sons except the eldest. And Injo and Queen Dowager Cho, then as the Queen, mourned "three years" (twenty-seven months) for the death of the original crown prince, Hyojong's elder brother, as the parents should for their first son. Besides, the *Five Rites and Ceremonies of the Dynasty* (*Kukcho oyeŭi*) flatly stipulated for a twelve month parental mourning for all sons including the eldest. The Westerners' recommendation, therefore, was considered reasonable and accepted by Hyŏnjong (1660–1674), Hyojong's son.

The Southerners, whose main force had been long out of power, presented against the Hyŏnjong-approved court decision on the mourning period an argument which warped what was essentially a *Yehak* question into political wrangling. Spearheaded by Yun Hyu (1617–1680) and Hŏ Mok (1595–1682), both well-known scholars of the day, the Southerners insisted that the Queen Dowager's mourning period should be twenty-seven months; of course, this could be also supported with quotations from the classics. If Hyojong as the legitimate successor to the royal line was accorded the rites for the second son of a family, then, the Southerners maintained, would it not be that he only represented the royal line, while the deceased crown prince was regarded as continuing the family line? This was absurd. In a few years, 1,400 Confucianists in Kyŏngsang Province and some *Sŏnggyungwan* students sympathetic with the Southerners jointly memorialized for the rectification of this absurd administration of rites. But Hyŏnjong, who stuck to the provision of the *Kukcho oyeŭi*, overruled their demand.

In 1674 when Hyojong's Queen, that is, Hyŏnjong's mother, died, again arose the question of how long the surviving Queen Dowager Cho's mourning period for her stepdaughter-in-law should be. The Westerner-controlled government recommended a nine-month period. The Southerners, led by To

Sim Ching, an obscure Confucianist in Kyŏngsang Province, argued for a twelve-month period. The *Kukcho oyeŭi*, which set a parental mourning period of twelve months for the death of all sons, also stipulated the same mourning period for the eldest daughter-in-law and a nine-month period for other daughters-in-law. To the Southerners, the Westerners' proposal showed that they still viewed Hyojong as the second son, that they did. Then the Southerners contended, would it not be that Hyonjong, the present sovereign, could not be allowed to mourn as the lineal grandson but only as a collateral one, when Queen Dowager Cho died? This reasoning, which was extremely shrewd and also based on the *Kukcho oyeŭi*, seems to have touched the responsive chord in Hyŏnjong's heart. The result was the purge of the Westerners, with the Southerners returning to power.

In 1680, after six years in power, the Southerners were knocked out of the government by the Westerners, who thereupon split into the Old Doctrine (Noron) and the Young Doctrine (Soron). From then on, major political squabbles were performed between these two parties, reaching their factional peak during the long, mediocre reign of Sukchong (1675-1720). Then, Yŏngjo (1725-1776), an able monarch, came up with the *T'angp'yŏng Ch'aek* or Impartial and Leveling Policy, purporting to bring an end to factionalism. The impartial and leveling Policy was designed, among other things, for an "impartial" distribution of government posts so as to secure a balance of power among four major parties (*Sasaek*). Yŏngjo's policy, carried on by his capable grandson Chŏngjo (1777-1800), while it also served to make the royal authority stronger than it had been with the government dominated by one party, did check factional controversies to a great extent. The sound and fury of the Four Color factionalism, however, even though they were thus considerably muffled, kept on well into the nineteenth century.

Developed from these protracted partisan bickerings were some political devices which look extremely modern today, but the debit side of these basically power-for-power's-sake struggles were slowly sapping away the political energy of the country, which was solely needed for the national reconstruction after the two devastating wars. In the meantime, the governmental decline continued. Indeed, the gravity of the political debilitation of the late Yi dynasty has since provoked a series of scholarly investigations, especially into the possible causes of the factionalism as its main factor. One of the most insightful observations was made by Yi Ik (1681-1763), a great eighteenth-century scholar. He saw evil in the government examination system as it was conducted in the last half the Yi dynasty. A large number of degree holders or candidates for official posts almost annually produced by so many kinds of examinations, as has been noted, far outnumbered the government offices actually available to them. These brilliant yet unemployed *yangban* men were the most volatile elements in the factional struggles, which were in turn deeply motivated by the widespread economic malaise of the *yangban*. Basing his view solidly on this economic premise, Yi Ik wryly observed in his *Trivial Essays of Sŏngho:*

> Suppose there are ten hungry men thrown together for meal for one. Before they finished it, a quarrel or two are likely to occur among them. They might accuse one another of impolite words or impudent attitudes. People, not familiar with the situation, might think of quarrels as caused by mismanaged words or manners, but the real cause lies in the [availability of] meals···If the ten men were given ten meals, would they not eat their meals in a happier atmostphere?

A painting of the scene of Korean soldiers defending Pusan during the 1592-1597 war.

2

Economic Readjustment and Social Growth

As the constant political discord at the court loosened its administrative grip of the various centralized systems, new changes were wrought into the economic, social, and intellectual complexions of the dynastic life. They were in essence similar to ones that characterized the late Koryŏ dynasty but on a much larger scale in breadth as well as depth. For the weakened central government whose prime concern amid institutional deteriorations and changes was now the question of economic survival, the first order of business was to bring about an increase to the prewar level of the governmental revenue. To this end, the government implemented, taking rather a long time, a series of tax reforms of far-reaching significance.

The most important phenomenon in this period, however, was the social advancement of the common people. As we shall see, they came to acquire hitherto-unthought-of economic confidence and freedom of physical movement. It was this common mass that supplied the leadership for that great revolutionary movement which occurred during the nineteenth century. Indeed, the politically-failed late Yi dynasty would have found its salvation in the emergence of the lower class, had the mass-inspired revolution been allowed to finish its natural course without foreign interferences.

The New Pattern of Landholding

Concentration of land in the private hand, as the government approved, if not encouraged, the practice of land transaction since 1424, was the general trend in landownership before fifteenth century was over. The two foreign wars, especially the seven–year war the Japanese, precipitated this trend. Death and dispersion of peasant farmers and shortage of food and agricultural implements resulted in the adandonment of arable land; moreover, loss of land registers added further confusion to the already chaotic state of land administration. This was a sort of an ideal situation in which individual aspirants for wealth such as ranking officials, local mighties, and now enterprising small farmers could scramble for land; in fact, they did so with whatever means available.

The party which was in the most difficult position in the matter of land was the government itself. The taxable land, as of 1611, was only about one third of that of the prewar period. To retrieve the lost tax resources, the government began a land survey, if languorously, and made the new land registers. While resettling the displaced farmers, the government distributed to various governmental departments land lying in waste to defray the maintenance costs. The government, however, was unable to prevent or even substantially lessen the diversion of public land into private possession.

As in the late Koryŏ period, the largest landholders, by the middle of the seventeenth century, turned out to be the royal and collateral families. As the law that stipulated for land grant to the royal siblings became obsolete, because of the shortage of land set aside for official distribution, they received usual grants considerably less. Sŏnjo, for instance, had twenty–three princes and princesses to marry, which meant endowments of land, and he bestowed on them salt ponds, woodland, or wasteland for reclamation instead of land. They then steadily expanded these motley pieces of realty into estates of which boundaries became marked again by "rivers and mountains." The governmental departments that were given wasteland, woodland, or land formerly owned by "traitors," that is, victims of the partisan power plays also became landholders of great proportions.

As these categories of estate owners who were also legitimately exempt from taxation presented a stiff competition in landamassing for the landholders of bureaucratic category, the latter in 1729 brought up the question of taxation and argued the collateral members of the royal family into paying taxes on land and fisheries which were not originally granted by law. And since the Sukchong period (1675-1720), a great number of local *yangban* and small farmers of humble origin made tremendous headway in land acquisition, thus providing themselves with a capital backbone for the commercial activities, which made a distinct mark in the agricultural Yi dynasty history during the eighteenth and nineteenth centuries.

But all this, of course, did not mean any substantial increase in the government revenue. In 1719 the land under cultivation amounted to 1,220,366 *kyŏl* of which only 830,508 kyŏl yielded tax for the government, whereas, in 1769, of a total of 1,411,948 *kyŏl* under cultivation, which represented an increase of nearly 200,000 *kyŏl* in fifty years, the tax-yielding area was only 800,843 *kyŏl*, a decrease of 30,000 *kyŏl* in the same period, which must have somehow gone into the tax-evading private hands.

Tax Reform : the Taedong Law

The reform which the decidedly reform-shy but financially hard-pressed Confucian government undertook first was that of the tribute system. The tribute system, which was collecting local specialties presented as gifts to the sovereign, as has been noted, was an integral part of the governmental financial structure. This time-honored system of tax in kind, however, entailed a number of difficulties in collecting, of which the transportation and perishability of the tribute goods were the most serious. To obviate these difficulties presumably for the local people who were also required to transport them, the merchant-middlemen came into being, whose job was to deliver the goods to the government at the required time and to receive remuneration from the people of the district responsible for the goods delivered. But this middleman system in time became a source of glaring exploitation of the common people. The middlemen, whose chicanery was usually backed up by conniving officials, assessed upon the people concerned the service costs several times what was actually spent.

The necessity of streamlining the tribute system, therefore, was most urgently felt even before the Japanese invasion. The government responded with the *Taedong pŏp* or the Law of Uniformity, a legislation which, transferring the burden to the landowners, called for delivery or rather payment in rice of the tribute materials uniformly to the amount of twelve *tu* or about eighteen liters per *kyŏl* annually. With this *Taedong* rice, as it came to be called, as the funds, the government was expected to procure whatever goods at the time of need. Starting from Kyŏnggi Province first on a tentative basis in 1608, the implementation of the new law was slowly extended, over a period of 100 years, to all other provinces. The office in charge of administration of the *Taedong* law, which was euphemistically called *Sŏnhyech'ŏng* or Office for Spreading Benefit, was established and put under the direction of three state councillors and three ministers. Soon it became the largest and virtually most important department in the government as it absorbed other minor offices which had been handing financial matters.

In this context, mention might be made of the grain loan system which had been fully developed, capitalizing the government grain stored in each district. The original purpose of the establishment of storehouses for tax grains on the district level was, from the Three Kingdoms period, to provide the peasants with food and seed grains in spring time and to collect them back in harvest season without interests. And the locally stored tax grain, which was, needless to say, used in time of national emergency such as famine and war, was also used for price–controlling. To make up the decrement resulting from taking the grains in and out of the warehouses, the government came to charge a small amount of fees in kind. This practice the government, after the Manchu invasion, converted officially into one of interest–charging, which became another source of official corruption, as we shall see. In 1687 the *Sŏnhyech'ŏng* took over the management of the grain loan system and turned it into an enterprising business which came to produce by the late seventeenth century the annual interest grain of about 700,000 *sŏk* for the government.

Tax Reform : the Kyunyŏk Law

Another major tax reform was concerned with national defense. The regular national army, after a century and a half from is its inception, was left to degenerate into well–nigh naught even before the Japanese war. The *Samsu* force, hastily organized with volunteers during that war, became an elite corps of the foot soldiers. After the two wars, the government continued efforts to strengthen the regular army, and until 1682 four army corps came into being, each with specific purposes and duties. This reorganized army was financially supported by a special military tax levied from those eligibles who wanted to stay out of active service. The military tax of this sort was actually devised and levied long before the sixteenth century was over.

They were required to pay two bolts of cotton cloth annually, a bolt measuring about forty feet. As the majority of able-bodied men found the army life harsh, a fact that resulted more from the lack of official discipline and the administrative corruption, those who preferred the payment of cotton cloth to the active duty counted 300,000 during the reign of Sukchong and were ever on the increase. The government, which might have never felt a need of draftees as many, filled the decrease of draftees with paid volunteers. As, again, peace lessened the necessity of maintaining an army, the governmental relapse into the state of military neglect followed. But the military tax, namely, payment of cotton cloth, remained in force, if only more strongly. This was partly because of local officials who took advantage of this law as a means of lining their own pockets; in many cases, they collected the military tax from the already dead or boys far below the draft age. Such blatant abuse of the common people worsened as time progressed.

Legislation to ameliorate the lot of the common people under a heavy burden of taxes without jeopardizing the financial resources of defense had been debated and attempted at occasionally from late seventeenth century, finally resulting in a tax reform in 1750. The *Kyunyŏk pŏp* or Law of Equalizing Service stipulated for the annual payment of one bolt of cotton cloth for all able-bodied men, regardless of the social status, while assessing upon the landowners two *tu* of rice per *kyŏl*, except those in P'yŏng'an and Hamgyŏng Provinces. The law, whose legislation was proposed and strongly urged by Yŏngjo (1725-1776), was first opposed by the *yangban*-bureaucrats who, long unencumbered by the military duty, considered the royal proposal an encroachment upon their privileges. Eventually, they agreed to the taxation only on the condition that all collateral branches of the royal family, too, should be made liable to it.

These *Taedong* and *Kyunyŏk* laws are of great historical significance, for the two laws, especially the latter, provided more than anything else specific occasions for the subjection for the first time to new substantive, uniform taxation of the ruling class long addicted to the financial privileges *vis-à-vis* the service duties of the lower classes.

Commerce and Industry

The readjusted financial structure, including the new government procurement system which greatly encouraged the circulation of goods, came to stimulate commerce and industry. It opened up new vistas of productive activities for the common people who were now being released, to a great extent, from the slackened clutches of the status system as a result of the administratively enfeebled government and the change of the general social climate.

Agriculture, the basis of the economy, had been tremendously improved through technical advances made in the seventeenth century. The wide-spread practice of raising semi-annual crops, coupled with the increased capacity of irrigation facilities repaired or newly constructed after the wars, nearly doubled agricultural production. A great many independent peasant-farmers, a new category of people that came into existence, began to diversify their crops with a view to a commercial end. Tobacco plant, Insam (ginseng), cotton fruits, etc., were highly favored products with ready markets.

The increased agricultural production provided the most needed underpinning for the development of non-agricultural sectors of the economy. The amount of the tax rice collected under the *Taedong* and *Kyunyŏk* laws, in addition to the conventional land tax, rose three times that of the prewar period. In strategic places where the grain traffic converged sprang up new cities like Samnangjin in Kyŏngsang province and Wŏnsan in Hamgyŏng Province. The *Taedong* rice, the largest portion of the tax grain, turned out to be also the mainstay of the commercial activities. With the *Taedong* rice as procurement funds, the government contracted merchants, known as *kong'in* or tribute men to deliver the commodities needed by the court and the central and provincial governments. The *kong'in* soon established a nationwide network of business transactions; this was an important commercial development which served to disrupt the existing system of commercial exchanges into a new order.

A special group of merchants of the capital under the government patronage had enjoyed the monopoly of designated goods which they were licenced to sell in return for obligatory supply, though remunerated, of goods for the royal household and the government. They had been the government's procurement agents from the very beginning of the dynasty; now with the emergence of the *Kong'in*, their monopoly rights and status as the government-favored merchants became precarious. But local markets and hostels where various goods were sold, catering to travellers and also the organized peddlers were enormously benefited from dealing with the *kong'in*. The more enterprising of the *kong'in*, whose business network contributed to a wider use of currency and credit, seem to have by the middle of the eighteenth century accumulated enough capital for commercial investment.

Despite the government's occasional suppression of commerce as undesirable, since its uncontrolled activities were thought to be diminishing the importance of agriculture as "the foundation of the society," there were sophisticated groups of merchants, the elite core of commerce who from the early period of the dynasty had steadily developed their respective territories and methods for commercial ventures. The *Kyŏngsang* or merchants of the capital, the *Songsang* or merchants of Songdo (Kaegyŏng), and the *Mansang* or merchants of Ŭiju were well known for their business acumen. In the seventeenth century, three large markets were extablished in Seoul, the home base of the *Kyŏngsang*, where the articles from the provinces, China, and Japan were daily merchandised. The *Songsang*, descendants of the inventors of the double-entry bookkeeping and probably the most penny-pinching of the three groups, maintained semi-nationwide business branches, netting more substantial profits from the provinces, while the *Mansang*, with the geographical advantage of Ŭiju facing the Amnok River in North P'yŏng'an Province, specialized in the lucrative trade with the Ch'ing.

The most interesting group, however, was the peddling merchants called *pobusang*, as their name showed, carried on their back a variety of goods wrapped in cloth, personal appurtenances, textile fabrics, and household necessities. They belonged to tightly-knit guilds with well-defined routes and territories for each guild, collectively covering more than 1,000 local markets and still more villages in the country. The *pobusang*, whose origin seems to hark back three Kingdoms period, were unfairly slighted and loathed by the general populace for some obscure reasons, inspite of their services. Yet they paid taxes and were fiercely loyal to the king and the government. In fact, their patriotic service far exceeded what they would have normally been expected of, as, for instance, in the Battle of Haengju when *pobusang's* indefatigable action was one of the critical factors that led to the victory.

The manufacturing economy, embracing 130-odd kinds of productions, had also so far been strictly controlled by, and meeting the need of, the government, a fact that had kept this sector of the economy deplorably backward in scale and organization. Pottery, minting, casting, and paper manufacturing, which comprised the major government industries, had maintained a consistent level of output, but no more. For manufacturing of other items, the government by the early eighteenth century saw no reason to employ as many artisans as it had, as its procurement system changed. As many of these artisans were released from the government service, they directly put their wares on the market, which they found bringing in more profit. Occasional conflicts in getting raw materials between individual artisans and merchants tended to appear, which was also a new phenomenon. Despite the development of market system and the division of labor, the industry as a whole remained on the basis of small-scale operations or on the "cottage" level until the end of the dynasty.

Social Changes

In parallel with the economic readjustment and growth, social readjustment, for which also the government played an important role, occurred, especially in the status system, as a result of the prolonged dissension within the *yangban* class and the social advancement of the lower classes. The social climate inevitably created by these changes was decidedly different from that of the early period of the dynasty.

As the factional cleavages within the officialdom were irretrievably widened, the partisan political alignments, which were the sum total of political differences and consanguineous and regional divisions, gradually hardened into hereditary discord. They refused in many cases to intermarry or even mingle socially and made built-in identities in raiment. In the course of these developments, a large number of *yangban*, renouncing the bureaucratic careers or aspirations, turned to scholarly pursuits with a critical view of the dynastic norm. Still others, unable to cope with the economic rigor of being a *yangban*, lost themselves among the ranks of the common mass; they came to be called *chanban* or *yangban* residues.

The social advancement of the lower classes, interestingly enough, was initially spurred by the financially hard-pressed government during the Japanese war. To help finance the war, the government came up with the idea of selling official ranks for grain or money. The ranks for sale were limited to those below the senior third grade, which were displayed, as it were, with the price tag of up to 100 *sŏk* of rice or the money equivalent. Although they were only honorary ranks without actual offices, the customers, ranging from those low officials who wished to be promoted if nominally, to those half-*yangban* born of concubines to men of *yangmin* or even *ch'ŏnmin* origin, all with extra grain or money to spare, eagerly responded to the offer. Accordingly, the government, from 1593 on, made numerous sales.

Since the possession of an official title meant elevation to the *yangban* status, many of the *yangmin* and the *ch'ŏnmin* with sufficient means could throw off the bonds in which they had been unfairly shackled. Their late Koryŏ predecessors achieved the similar *tour de force* with physical prowess and excellence in martial arts, but now money was the stuff to have. Naturally, in such a social climate, the pristine concept of *yangban* was fast eroded.

It was also during the Japanese war that the government started to enlist into provincial armies the *ch'ŏnmin* who had so far not been accorded the honor of military service. This also proved a popular move. The 110,000 men during the reign of Injo (1623-1649) and 200,000 during Sukchong's reign (1675-1720) of *ch'ŏnmin* origin reclassified themselves out of the stigma-laden class through military service, with their tax payments duly made to the government, (not to the former masters.) Probably with a view to increasing tax-paying commoners, a new decree was effected in 1669 that the *ch'ŏnmin* born of *yangmin* mother be thenceforth made a commoner. In 1801 the slave-service within the royal household was abolished, and slavery as an institution was to be nullified in 1894.

Although the majority of the *ch'ŏnmin* class remained in bondage to the traditional status and duties, their chances for social mobility were open, which indeed many of them anxiously took advantage of. "Money is *yangban*," the popular saying which correctly characterized the social climate of the late Yi dynasty, began to undermine the Confucian doctrine of social stratification as natural law. Now *yangban* families in need of money came to rely increasingly on lowborn but rich merchants, who were ready to lend money advice and suggest solutions for financial problems. It is doubtful, however, that these social changes, which were in many respects a cultural diffusion downward which the Yi dynasty people did not experience much before, were as widespread in tne rural communities as in the cities.

3

Intellectual Development

The Neo-Confucian orthodoxy that had straitjacketed creative energies of the Yi gentlemen for two centuries could no longer contain religious and intellectual discontents which had been long in ferment. The time of profound reflection on the sterility of abstract rationalism of Neo-Confucian Chu Hsi set in among serious Yi thinkers as soon as they attained the mastery of its metaphysical contents in the late sixteenth century. Moreover, they were disillusioned at the ineffectiveness of the *Yehak* movement, which only seemed to bring more political confusion and even bloodshed, as we have seen. From the beginning of the seventeenth century on, those scholar-officials who were more inclined toward intellectual activity or who were victimized by factional power struggles and those enlightened intellectuals who held no abiding interest in politics turned to a wide range of scholarly pursuits, sidestepping, if not openly repudiating, Neo-Confucianism.

No less important than these internal factors in this trend were stimuli from abroad. The Neo-Confucian School of Mind with its idealistic emphasis on intuition and subjectivity of thought, long declared heterodox in Yi Chosŏn yet unofficially studied, clandestinely undermined the authority of the School of Principle. Another subversive influence over the official thinking was rendered by the inductive method of research which the Ch'ing scholars successfully applied to the so-called "empirical research" mainly in the fields of philology and etymology. Refusing to blindly follow the Neo-Confucian orthodox path in seeking after knowledge, the Ch'ing scholars exhausted all available sources to formulate hypotheses to test against an evidence or a particular question under investigation. Then there occurred the discovery, around

1600, of the West with its science and religion, a culture which provided a refreshingly new perspective for the Yi thinkers.

The Sirhak and Its Stars

The intellectual movement that appeared in the late Yi dynasty period under these internal circumstances, coupled with the timely external stimuli, is usually referred to as *Sirhak* or Practical Learning. The practical scholarship had been a long established tradition in Confucian learning, as we have seen in the phenomenal creative upsurge in a variety of scholarly fields, especially during the reigns of Sejong and Sejo. But what made the *Sirhak* movement, which reached its peak in the eighteenth and first half of the nineteenth centuries, different from earlier scholarship was that the movement was primarily individual scholar–inspired, not government–sponsored, and its subjects were much more inclusive. It included, in addition to traditional fields such as history, government, etc., commerce, technology, natural science, custom, or even the study of surnames; the list is much longer. More importantly, the methods and attitudes encompassed in the *Sirhak* scholarship in this period were definitely directed toward the specific examination and solution of the immediate; in short, they were scientific and modern. But the *Sirhak* movement, of course, was not a sudden breakaway from tradition but a development of it.

One of the first *Sirhak* scholars, whose academic interest rather sharply deflected from the scholasticism of Mountain and Forest or *Yehak* formalists, was Yi Su Kwang (1563–1628). Of his voluminous works, the most important, which characterized him as a *Sirhak* scholar, is the *Chibong yusŏl* or *Collected Essays of Chibong* compiled in 1614. The *Chibong yusŏl*, consisting of twenty chapters on such disparate subjects as astronomy, nations, government posts, poetry, raiments, plants and birds, etc., contains 3,435 essays, referring to 348 previous scholars on the subjects. His "encyclopedic scholarship" covered some western nations such as England, France, their firearms, and Catholicism; knowledge of these subjects was made available largely by Yi diplomats returning from Peking. His descriptive essays, that comprise the major portion of the book, are characterized by a conspicuous absence of moralistic tone, as in one on the *T'ien-chu shih-i* (*Ch'ŏnju sirŭi* in Korean) or A *True Disputation about the Lord of Heaven* written by Mateo Ricci (1552–1610), the greatest of the Jesuit pioneers in China. They are unmistakably modern in tone and disinterested attitude. Yi Su Kwang's lead in "encyclopedic scholarship" was followed by Yu Hyŏng Wŏn (1622–1673), the author of the *Pan' gye surok* or *Occasional Writings of Pan'gye*, and successive generations of scholars.

The field of Korean history made a favorite subject for the *Sirhak* scholars, indicative of a new consciousness of the nation as having trodden a unique historical path. Yi Ik (1681-1763), who wrote that poignant analysis on factionalism, is well known for his scholarship of the Yi Su Kwang tradition. His representative work is the *Sǒngho sasǒl* or *Trivial Essays of Sǒngho* made up of 3,057 items compiled around 1720. Yi Ik's treatise on history in the *Sǒngho sasǒl* shows a crucial departure from the conceptual approach of the Confucian moralists. He first wrote in terms of the traditional concept of history as an interaction of good and evil or of the "genuineness and falseness" of a dynastic line, but in the end, it seemed to him an old intellectual skeleton only to be stashed away in the family closet. One of his central concerns was the problem of establishing historicity. He stressed the empirical method, calling for gleaning as many evidences as possible with which to produce a hypothesis and bringing that hypothesis against the historicity of the alleged fact under investigation to bear. He came to view history not as succession of "success and failure of fortune and misfortune" but as happenings of things of their own accord, according to time and place; to him, history was an autonomous realm divorced from the vicissitudes of anthropomorphic volitions of Heaven. In the process, the Tan'gun myth was debunked out of history for the first time.

Based on this view of history was the *Tongsa Kangmok* or *Outline and Explanation of the Eastern History* written by An Chǒng Pok (1712-1791), a friend and disciple of Yi Ik. Completed around 1756, the twenty-chapter *Outline*, with its objectivity and geopolitical interpretation of historical development, marks a new era in Korean historical writing. The *Yǒllyǒsil kisul* or *Accounts of Yǒllyosil*, a fifty-nine solid chapter Yi dynasty history written around or before 1778 by Yi Kǔng Ik (1736-1806) and the *Haedong yǒksa or History of Ses-East* (Korea), an eighty-five chapter history written around 1810 by Han Ch'i Yun (1765-1814), its last fifteen chapters on geography being finished by his nephew, Han Chin Sǒ later, are also outstand additions to Korean historiography produced in this period.

Geography, as noted, commanded an unmitigated fascination for the traditional Koreans, with which they had created apocryphal and seasoned art, and now they finally rounded out a scientific field from it. The theory of wind and water, an eleventh century brand of geographical study, as we have seen viewed any given terrain as containing, or being sustained by, a certain cosmic force at work under it like blood flowing through arteries in human body. The propitious sites for temples, houses, burial refuge, etc., where the subterranean force was thought to work for human fortune, could be found by careful examinations of terrestrial features. This site-selecting based on the wind and water theory had since been a most persistent field activity or an outdoor sport for scholars and would-be esoterics.

These activities of field investigation had long been developed into a useful area of learning usually referred to as human or descriptive geography. Descriptive geography was greatly enhanced in comprehensiveness and scientificness when the *T'aengni chi* or *Notations for Selection of Livable Villages* was written probably in the 1730's by Yi Chung Hwan (1690–c.1750). What seemed a promising career in government having been nipped by factional machinations, Yi Chung Hwan made a "grand tour of the eight provinces," that is, of the whole country, taking notes of every city, town, and village he passed through. The first of the two volumes, dealing with history, geography, climate, produce, and populace, etc. of each locality, is little different in substance from earlier works in this field, which were mostly compiled at royal orders as administrative references in previous centuries. But the second volume, the main feature of the *T'aengni chi*, sets forth the standards with which to judge the "livableness" of any given place. The set standards include, of course, those physical features of mountains, plains, and rivers from which the wind and water theorizers usually infer their esoteric doctrines, but Yi's theorizing, though based on the same geographical components, always points toward common sense conclusions. His investigations of the fertility of soil, the transportation and circulation of commercial goods, the general characteristics of regional populaces, etc., together with other useful observations, are indeed of tremendously practical value and make refreshing reading today.

Other scholars of descriptive geography described the well known mountains, rivers, and the road network. Chŏng Sang Ki (1678–1752) transferred them on maps drawn in color on a reduced scale. About a century later, the indefatigable Kim Chŏng Ho (c.1800–1864), the greatest of all private and government map-makers of the traditional period, made the comprehensive *Ch'ŏnggu to* or *Map of Blue Hills* (Korea) with a graphic method on a reduced scale in 1834 and the *Taedong yŏjido* or *Map of Great East* (Korea), a more practical and detailed version of the former, in 1861. In 1864 he published the *Taedong chiji* or *Geographical Notations on Great East*, a thirty-two chapter book on Korean geography, to be read with the a two maps supplementing one another.

The rural economy and life, whose deterioration in many localities worsened by the late eighteenth century to tragic proportions, as we shall see later, as a result of administrative corruptions of provincial and local governments, naturally drew much scholarly attention. But, on the other hand, the general increase in agricultural productivity was made by technical advances and, more significantly, by scholarly writings for improvement of the rural economy.

The *Sallim Kyŏngje* or *Management of Rural Economy* Written by Hong Man Sŏn (1643–1715) is typical of writings of this category. Hong Man Sŏn, a former local magistrate, deals in his book with sixteen different subjects that cover almost every aspect of the rural life. Besides those the management of agriculture, horticulture, and animal husbandry, the book includes discourses on house-building, longevity, food processing, household medicine, and prized possessions such as scrolls, musical instruments, and porcelainous vessels. When Sŏ Yu Ku (1764-1845) wrote his *Management of Rural Economy,* also known as *Sixteen Discourses on Rural Economy,* in his later years, he seems to have been inspired by Hong's hand-copied book. Sŏ Yu Ku extended his views to 113 chapters referring to 900-odd books. The great agriculturalist, of an illustrious family politically belonging to the Old Doctrine party, reached a ministerial rank at the peak of his long government career and greatly enlightened the court on the rural economy and life in general.

Sŏ's contemporary, Chŏng Yak Yŏng (1762-1836), whose main scholarly attention also centered around the agricultural economy and the rural administration, is regarded by some as the greatest of the *Sirhak* scholars. In contrast with Sŏ, Chŏng Yak Yong advocated an all-out economic and governmental reform with a special emphasis on the disciplinary measures against the corrupt officials. His reform ideas are contained in 2,469-odd poems and some 314 manuscript chapters, of which the most important works are a trilogy, *Kyŏngse yup'yo* or *Discourses on Government Memorialized, Mongmin simsŏ* or *Guidance for the Pastor of the People,* and *Hŭmhŭm sinsŏ* or *Discreet Administration of Criminal Justice,* on the reform of the government, the rural administration and economy, and criminal justice, respectively. It was a noble attempt to recapture the original vitality of the dynasty by reforming and the officials, thus reinvigorating the traditional economy.

Although his thought was deeply imbued with Confucian learning, he readily absorbed Western scientific knowledge and Catholicism. Because of an alleged complicity in a movement to spread the practice of Catholicism, which resulted in a mass purge of Southerners in 1801 right after Chŏngjo's death, Chŏng Yak Yong, a Southerner and Chŏngjo's trusted subject, was banished for eighteen years; his two brothers, both Catholic believers, were also victimized in the purge, one losing his life. It was during this period of exile, which proved intellectually productive for Chŏng, that most of his works were done. The merit of his works lies not in the originality of his reform ideas but in his thorough and systematic expose of the bureaucratic failures of the government. It was a serious indictment of corrupt officials, his political enemies, if not of the dynasty itself. In some of his poems, we see him nursing a certain demoniac urge to destroy them, as when he secretly craves a peasant revolt, which was indeed coming soon.

The Court Sponsored Learning. The scholastic activities sponsored by the court were also a distinct phenomenon most notable in eighteenth century. The government now being financially better off through the two tax reforms, and the factional disputes at the court considerably subdued under the *T'angp'yŏng Ch'aek* (Impartial and Leveling Policy) earnestly pursued by

Yŏngjo and Chŏngjo, the Yi dynasty in the eighteenth century seemed to renew its old vitality. The dynastic renewal was most fully realized scholastically of which the current *Sirhak* movement was a part. The intellectual energies of the scholar–bureaucrats released by the relative absence of factional bickerings were understandably channeled into compiling, editing, and writing books under the royal auspices. They also re–edited and supplemented existing books on law, diplomacy, government, economy, and rites and ceremonies as governmental and institutional changes necessitated their revision. Chŏngjo was the leading light in these scholarly performances and other programs for the reinvigoration of Confucian learning. He established the *Kyujanggak*, a royal academy similar to Sejong's *Chiphyŏnjŏn*, which functioned as a kind of intellectual forum on learning, government, and official discipline.

As an ideology of dynastic rejuvenation, the *Sirhak* takes on a decidedly modern outlook when it is referred to a group of socioeconomic and reform–minded intellectuals. They are usually called *Pukhakp'a* or School of Northern Learning. Besides their excellence in verse and prose, they had a number of interesting common denominators. They were all youthful, urbane, erudite, and born, many of them, of concubinage; yet they were unprecedentedly under the royal patronage accorded by Chŏngjo. They were held together by the modernity of their reform ideas, and they maintained negative attitudes toward Neo–Confucianism and the government examination. Above all, they were all inspired in their thinking by intellectual and social advancements made by the Ch'ing, hence School of Northern Learning, north being in this case Ch'ing China. They contended that the animosity against the Manchus should be forgotten and, in fact, Yi Chosŏn should learn from them for its own good.

Of their writings that characterized the Northern Learning, the most important works are the *Tamhŏn sŏlch'ong* or *Views of Tamhŏn* by Hong Tae Yong (1731–1783), the *Yŏlha ilgi* or *Jehol Diary* by Pak Chi Wŏn (1737–1805), and the *Pukhak ŭi* or *Discourse on Northern Learning* by Pak Che Ka (1750–1815). These were written as the results of the authors' critical observations on the economic advancements of Ch'ing China, while they made a brief sojourn in the Chinese capital as members of Korean missions there.

By far the modernest of the advocates of Northern Learning was Pak Che Ka. He was a friend and disciple of Pak Chi Wŏn and served under Chŏngjo as a librarian at the *Kyujanggak*. In the *Discourse on Northern Learning*, which he wrote in 1779 to enlighten Chŏngjo, Pak Che Ka sought the cause of political stagnation and social backwardness in the government's suppression of commercial activities. He said that wealth was like a well which, if drawn, would be refilled with fresh water and become stagnant when not in use. Wealth or goods should be consumed so that production might be encouraged; conversely, the Confucianists' favorite economic policy of enforcing frugality to discourage consumption of luxurious goods would only stagnate the economy. And he blandly proposed that the unemployed *yangban*, who were not supposed to work physically, should be allowed or even forced to engage in all lines of productive work and commerce with the government's financial support. In order to facilitate production and circulation of goods, he asserted, technical advancements, especially in the manufacture of agricultural implements, should be made, roads constructed, and the use of vehicles, ships, and the currency more popularized as in China.

While encouraging overseas trade, he advocated the training in Western technology of young aspirants under Western missionaries who would be glad to come, were they invited. He pointed out that both Catholicism and Buddhism were the same in their ultimate doctrines of paradise and hell, but Buddhism had no science to offer for utilitarian purposes. Why, then, should the former be prohibited when the latter was allowed? And he related to national defense the country's economic strength, including public facilities such as transportation network; these could be in turn better built by the practical application of science. Pak Che Ka's explicit equation of national defense with the national economy was to be appreciated only a century later, however.

Among the scientists produced by the *Sirhak* movement, Chŏng Yak Chŏn (1758-1816) the naturalist and Yi Kyu Kyŏng (1788-?) the experimentalist figure prominently. Chŏng Yak Chŏn, like his brother Yak Yong, was exiled, because of his professed Catholicism, to Hŭksan Island off the Chŏlla coast until his death there. His *Chasan ŏbo* or *Fish of Chasan*, (Chasan being another name of the Island), was produced during that exile. The book describes the geographical distributions, morphologies, and habits of seventy-three kinds of scaled fish, forty-two kinds of non-scaled fish and crustaceans, and forty miscellaneous marine lives that inhabit the southwestern sea. Not the least interesting is that the one-volume work was co-authored by Chang Ch'ang Tae, a native scholar-naturalist of the Island; probably, this was the first recorded instance of scientific achievement through teamwork in the Korean history, except under the royal order.

Yi Kyu Kyŏng's representative work, *Oju sŏjongbangmul kobyŏn* or *Study of Practical Science by Oju* (Oju being his pen name), completed in 1839, deals with precious and base metals, their alloys, precious stones, quicksilver, firearms, naval vessels, their strategic use, and hundred other subjects; the properties, production process, and maintenance of these items were meticulously described. The real merit of the book lies not in the description, however minute, but in the fact that those descriptions were the author's experimental and experiential reports, which were accumulated through a long period of time. The *Oju yŏnmunjangjŏn san'go* or *Long, Discursive Manuscripts of Oju*, completed somewhat later, is an "encyclopedic" account in sixty manuscript volumes of studies on a variety of subjects in the Yi Su Kwang tradition.

As the *Sirhak's* intellectual contents became diversified and philosophical attitudes reoriented, the Neo-Confucian metaphysical system inevitably underwent an overhauling. The foremost in metaphysical reexamination was Ch'oe Han Ki (1803-1879), whose pioneering works not only in philosophy but also in science and political thought seem to link the *Sirhak* movement directly with the arts and sciences of modern times. His philosophy is solidly based on an empiricism, claiming that all knowledge comes from experience. In establishing his system of thought, as it is contained in his books reportedly counting hundreds, he seems to have been influenced by Western science and philosophy via China. *

The metaphysical question with which the Yi thinkers mainly concerned themselves after the middle of the sixteenth century was, as we have seen, whether man's experience of emotions and virtues was caused by the *i* (*li* in Chinese: principle) or by the *ki* (*ch'i* in Chinese: ether or matter). Although Ch'oe Han Ki did not deny the existence of the *i*, in accord with which the nature operates, he effectively discarded the *i* from the human mind.

The Neo-Confucian *i,* which was the fundamental principle of form ramifying into all phenomenal existences, was, to Ch'oe, merely the product of the reasoning power of the human mind.

Like Sŏ Kyŏng Tŏk and Yi I, Ch'oe Han Ki found the *ki* (*ch'i*) more useful in his metaphysical deliberation. In Ch'oe's philosophical system, however, the *ki* was made another substance called *sin-ki* which was thought to be the foundation of perception. The *sin*, an "immaterial" or "divine" force or energy, is the essence of the *ki*, while the *ki* is its substance two are inseparable, and one cannot exist without the other, as they are immanent in the universe. For man it is the *sin-ki* in himself that perceives things, but only through his sense organs. The principles of the things abroad come in, or even the human emotions are created, through the ear, the eye, the nose, the mouth, and the skin which "contact," or "dye," the *sin-ki* in oneself; indeed, the *sin-ki* is perception itself.

Each piece of knowledge thus received, infinite in kind and chaotic in order, is schematically memorized and rearranged as to be utilized according to its own channel of availability. The utilization of ideas calls for the mind's full function which Ch'oe called *ch'uch'ŭk*. The term *ch'uch'ŭk*, as used today, means surmise conjecture, but Ch'oe meant it to be the mind itself in the act of estimating and measuring the unknown with the knowledge already acquired as the foundation.

---

* Paragraphs on Ch'oe Han Ki's philosophy are based on *Han'guk ŭ sasangjŏk Panghyang (Ideological Direction of Korea)* by Chong Hong Park.

An important aspect of Ch'oe's philosophical thought is the use of mathematics. Through application of mathematics, things, Ch'oe said, could be exactly measured and estimated for their "largeness and smallness in number and size, farness and nearness, thickness and thinness, and concentration and dispersion." He further elaborated that even the abstract principles of things could be also mathematically measured for their goodness and badness, truthfulness and falseness. Finally, these measurements and judgments, to be correct, must be tested against, and verified by, the realities of practicalities of things.

Ch'oe's fundamental break with Neo–Confucian metaphysics, which is revolutionary, to say the least, is presented in his argument that the mind's perception of ideas, that is, the *sin–ki* in action, is possible strictly via the sense organs as the agents of transmitting the external happenings, which are, to him, the only source of knowledge. His thoroughly empirical theory of knowledge, which he repeatedly emphasizes, set to naught Neo–Confucian moralism based on innate goodness of man. When one sees a child about to fall into a well, he instantly feels pity because, as Mencius said, man's nature is innately good and because, as Yi Hwang said, the *i* in the man is aroused. But nay, Ch'oe Han Ki says, one feels pity because he has heard of, or seen, children who actually fell and drowned in wells. If the idea of children's drowning in wells has not "dyed" his *sin–ki,* his mind would have remained blank on this score. Conversely, as there is no such thing as innate idea, the mind that has been "dyed" with an idea can be also blanched, even though it will never be quite the same.

Trends in Literature and Art

If the Practical Learning was the domain of the *yangban* intellectuals, it was in literature that more or less all classes of people participated. The advent to a certain level of literacy of the common mass and womenfolks as reading public, together with the economic improvement of the former, represents the most important literary development in the late Yi period. The primary reason for this was a wider use of the *Han'gŭl,* needless to say. The *Han'gŭl* provided the common people with a means of cultural advancement, and for a number of *Sirhak* scholars in linguistics who had had a shock of recognition, the *Han'gŭl* became a field for life–long concentration. Yu Hŭi (1773-1837), the author of the *ŏnmun chi* or *Study of Vernacular Letters,* was one of the eminent champions of the *Han'gŭl.* The most confucian of the *yangban* of Ch'oe Man Li style came to recognize its merit and now generally used the *Han'gŭl* for private communications or composition of poems such as *Sijo*.

The *Sijo* was still the prevailing mode of poetic expression and of singing as well. And a new form of *Sijo* called *Sasŏl sijo*, (*sasŏl* meaning narration), came into vogue. The *Sasŏl sijo* is much longer and irregular, therefore, freer in form than the standard *Sijo*, which has already manifested a marked degree of indifference to formalism. Although of course it retains the normal structure consisting of three verses, each verse of the *Sasŏl sijo*, especially the middle verse, could be elongated with a greater number of words, hence *sasŏl*. Needless to say, this "formlessness" of the *Sasŏl sijo* is attributable to the genetic origin of the *Sijo* as a lyric for recitation rather than versification for intellectual enjoyment, a reason that made the *Sijo* popular and durable.

The *Sijo* was no longer an avocation of the *yangban* literati only. The two greatest name in *Sijo*, in fact, were men of humble origin. Kim Ch'ŏn T'aek (who lived in the early eighteenth century) and Kim Su Chang (1690–c.1770), both former petty officials belonging to the *chung'in* class, were prolific *Sijo* writers as well as great anthologies. The *Ch'ŏnggu yŏng'ŏn* or *Eternal Words of Blue Hills*, a collection of nearly 1,000 *Sijo*, completed by Kim Ch'ŏn T'aek in 1728 and the *Haedong kayo* or *Songs of Sea-East* (Korea) containing 638 *Sijo* compiled by Kim Su Chang in 1763, the two oldest anthologies of *Sijo* extant, constitute the most precious legacy of korean poetry.

Far more eminently representing the reading trends of the late yi period was fiction. The long and short stories, whose development was marked out by a sharp departure in motif and setting from the supranatural, fairy tales of the previous periods, came to dominate the literary scene rather abruptly from the beginning of the seventeenth century. Some 300 novels are known to have been written during the late Yi period. They cover variant themes from love, heroism, family tragedy to social injustice and satire, unfurling a delightful Saturnalia of romanticism steeped in Buddhism, Taoism, and Confucianism.

The best known, and also the first, novel with modern trappings to appear in this period in Korean literature, for that matter, is the *Hong Kil Tong Chŏn* or *Story of Hong Kil Tong*, a social protest novel, written by the brilliant prose stylist Hŏ Kyun (1569–1618) sometime between 1608 and 1613. Hŏ Kyun, a brother of Hŏ Nansŏlhŏn, was too intellectually perceptive and politically reckless to prosaically follow the path to official glory as the members of his family were expected to, even though he eventually reached a ministerial rank in government. As a man of literature and social thought, he was particularly sensitive to social injustice done to men of illegitimate birth, a sensitivity that resulted in the creation of the S*tory of Hong Kil Tong*. Eventually, he lost his life in the vortex of factional disputes that involved his complicity in a *coup* attempt masterminded by "seven illegitimate sons."

The *Story of Hong Kil Tong* tells how Hong Kil Tong, born of a high-ranking *yangban*-official and his slave-maid, leaves home because of intolerable discrimination; he was not even allowed to call his father father. He becomes the leader of "righteous outlaws" who take delight in harassing corrupt officials. A master of a certain occult art with whch he can make himself invisible to the mortal eyes, Hong Kil Tong and his company cause a series of disturbances to the administration of the kingdom. Kil Tong's private war against the comes to an end upon his appointment as the minister of war and the abolition of the unjust law. Having no intention of overturning the kingdom itself, much less of taking the job, he leaves for a utopia which he has built in one of the present-day Ryŭkyŭ Islands.

Kim Man Chung (1637-1692) was another minister who wrote popular novels. He was particularly aware of the rhythmic beauty and power of the vernacular language as spoken among the rural people. He consciously tried to capture them in his stories, while condemning Chinese poems written by Koreans as a parrot's imitation. Kim Man Chung is also known for his filial piety. He is said to have written his *Ku unmong,* Known as *Cloud Dreams of Nine,* "overnight" during his political exile in order to please his mother.

Of the nine protagonists of *The Cloud Dreams of Nine,* eight fairies incarnate eight beautiful, obedient women whose statuses range from princess and female entertainer to chamber-maid, and one discipline-weary Buddhist monk transforms himself into a young man named Yang. These nine people weave back and forth in a colorful tapestry of "dreams" in Chinese setting. As a young man of a good family, Yang marries the eight women one by one as the story progresses; as a government official, he also conquers the barbarian rebels. When thus his personal happiness and social glory reach a saturation point, he realizes that life is an evanescent spring dream. Accordingly, he returns to the monastic discipline. In Kim Man Chung's another romance, *Sassi namjŏng ki* or *Story of Lady Sa,* which also occurs in China, Lady Sa, a paragon of virtue but a sterile wife, urges her scholar-husband, Yu, to take a concubine to beget a son. The concubine turns out to be the other extreme of Lady Sa in personality. Because of the second wife's slanderous intrigues, Lady Sa is forced out of the family into a period of crucible. But, as might be expected, the intrigues are exposed, the Lady is restored, and the Yu family prospers ever after.

The Chinese setting which Kim Man Chung chose for his novels seems to have been designed to avoid possible political inconveniences that might occur by coincidence; nevertheless, the recourse to the Chinese environ as the stage for the actions of his narratives became a tradition for many of later works mainly catering to upper class readers, including the royal family.

Probably, the greatest of the traditional popular stories would be the *Ch'unhyang chŏn* or *Story of Ch'unhyang* produced in the early eighteenth century, which saw the peak of fiction–writing. The *Ch'unhyang chŏn* is one of twelve such works which were written by unknown writers and later added and developed by successive *kwangdae*–writers; a *kwangdae* was a falsetto singer, a kind of minstrel–actor whose long–drawn, dramatic singing blended with occasional narrating, called *P'ansori*, dominated the popular entertainment of the eighteenth and nineteenth centuries.

The *Ch'unhyang chŏn*, which has a great variety of versions preferred by different *P'ansori* singers, is a story of love at first sight, which develops into a tragicomedy, between Yi Mong Nyong, the sagacious son of a local magistrate and Ch'unhyang, the fair daughter of a *kisaeng* in Namwŏn in South Chŏlla Province. The formal union being unthinkable because of the status lacuna, they enter into secret matrimony. The corrupt, greedy new magistrate, who replaced Mong Nyong's father, immediately sends for Ch'unhyang. Ch'unhyang's refusal to submit to his wish brings unbearable tribulations upon her for a prolonged period of time. In the meantime, Yi Mong Nyong passes the government examination with the highest distinction and is appointed an *amhaeng ŏsa* or secret royal envoy. A secret royal envoy was usually commissioned to secretly investigate local administrations and magistrates for alleged malfeasances. They were given minutely outlined guidelines for action as well as the authority to punish wrongdoers on the spot. This institution was much in use understandably in the late Yi period.

The young *Amhaeng ŏsa* Yi Mong Nyong makes his appearance in the middle of a gala feast held by the bad magistrate on the very day of Ch'unhyang's scheduled execution, and after a pandemonium of mass arrests, he rescues Ch'unhyang just a moment before her beheadal. Their eventual marriage is consummated with the royal blessing, and they are also divinely blessed with three sons and two daughters, an ideal set of off springs.

The broad moral of the story has been said to be an indictment of the flagrant misconduct of the official class and an affirmation of the dignity of the suffering common folks. Against a background of tragic social conflicts bred in the status system, a burgeoning consciousness of individual worth, which is indeed the ethos of this *P'ansori* drama, is seen in the dramatic juxtapositions of events in a delightfully–earthy realism which relentlessly exploits the underside of the society.

Belonging to the same category as *Ch'unhyang chŏn*, that is, those written originally for the *P'ansori*, more or less equally popular are the *Sim Ch'ŏng chŏn* or *Story of Sim Ch'ŏng* which tells the unbelievable career of a filial daughter, Sim Ch'ŏng, and the *Hŭngbu chon* or *Story of Hŭngbu* in which not only good is rewarded but also bad is converted to good.

The theme of the fiction which was trained more closely to the current social changes was the satirical treatment of the *yangban* class. In fact, the satire and the humor in late Yi dynasty fiction seem to have been subsisted only on poking fun at, or making a mockery of, the *yangban* who clung still fast to the traditional values and manners in a changing world around him. In stories such as *Yangban chŏn* or *Story of a Yangban* and *Hŏ Saeng chŏn* or *Story of Hŏ Saeng* by Pak Chi Wŏn, that noted Northern Learning scholar satirical and humorous treatments of the *yangban* were transformed into the downright castigation of his incompetence.

Understandably, the *yangban* women were spared such treatment in these social novels. In Pak Chi Wŏn's another story, *Yŏllyŏ Hamyang Pakssi chŏn* or *Lady Pak of Hamyang the Faithful Widow*, Pak Chi Wŏn describes long, anguished nights of the widow in an inverted sort of first person narration, which is intended to prick the guilty conscience of the *yangban* men. In the *Yi Ch'un P'ung chŏn* or *Story of Yi Ch'un P'ung*, probably around the middle of the nineteenth century by an unknown author, we see a *yangban* wife playing the role of a responsible *yangban* man, whereas her husband, Yi Ch'un P'ung, as his name Ch'un P'ung or spring Wind implies, is made incorrigibly flippant. He squanders his fortune on a *kisaeng* in P'yŏngyang. Ch'un P'ung's wife erects herself to save the family from disgrace. Ingratiating herself with the governor of P'yŏng'an Province, she persuades the governor to accept her as his deputy, and she in the deputy's attire tries both Ch'un P'ung and the *kisaeng* on an alleged misdemeanor and recovers the lost money. Later, Ch'un P'ung, who had believed in his luck, was to shamefacedly accept the truth.

The development in painting extending into this period has been briefly discussed in the previous chapter. It is worth noting that the longitudinal survey of the trend in painting closely parallels the historical development of the Yi dynasty in terms of the ideological perspective and the sophistication of the dynastic life and value. The unreal, visionary quality of the early paintings was superseded in the seventeenth and eighteenth centuries by that of the immediate and the tangible. This transition was effected partially through a careful study of spontaneous paintings of the Southern Sung; the early pieces showed the influence of Sung painting. If this constituted a cultural lag in art, the Korean painting soon trod its own path into the eighteenth century which saw an artistic flowering of distinctly Korean synthesis.

Of the impressive number of painters who contributed to this flowering, many achieved unique positions in the late Yi painting on the basis of individual propensity and technique. Chŏng Sŏn (1676–1759), a court painter, was probably the first one who grew out of the Chinese–influenced, conventional concept of painting and developed the refreshingly–new skill and taste of his own. Like Yi Chung Hwan, the descriptive geographer who explored every nook of the country, Chŏng Sŏn, better known as Kyŏmjae, went around scenic spots of pristine beauty, which he sublimated into his art on paper. His "The Diamond Mountains" was produced during one of these itineracies

(*Plate* 32). Chŏng Sŏn's intention was to contain the "twelve thousand peaks" of the Diamond Mountains in a circular solidarity in one picture. The fantastic and indeed bony formations of the All Bone Mountain, (another name for the Diamond Mountains), are represented by a multiplicity of vertical strokes and lines, and trees that cover the left foreground and valleys in the right half seem to unify the piece as a whole. Such composition under the bird's-eye view had rarely been experimented in the long history of landscape painting.

Chŏng sŏn's experiment in methodology and his interest in depicting from direct observations, not from imagination as had been usually the case, were followed by many painters of younger generations. Sin Yun Pok (Hyewŏn: 1758–c.1820) showed an insatiable delight in the portrayal of men and women in a dramatic moment of action. There were also Kim Tŭk Sin (Kŭngjae: 1754–1822) and others; but, in Kim Hong To (Tanwŏn: 1760–c.1820), the new artistic synthesis, that is, individualization and popularization of art initiated by Chŏng Sŏn, seems to have been most fully attained. His dynamic style, augmented by a dexterous command of brushwork, combined with inhibition-free thematic exploration, served to enhance the vital human spirit as seen in the local subjects. He displayed versatile talents for all styles of painting, but he found a profounder inspiration in depicting intimate scenes from daily life. With such spontaniety, relish, and care, he caught the essential stuff of life in living moments in, for instance, wrestling youths, people in a ferry boat, village school, ironsmith in action, house building, the plowing farmer, etc., all from everyday encounters of men, events, and nature in the life of the common folks, the personae hitherto unthought of being honored in pictures (*Plates* 33,34).

For painting in the form of calligraphy, Kim Chŏng Hŭi (1786–1856) occupies a unique place in its history. Kim Chŏng Hŭi, who was also a brilliant *Sirhak* scholar in epigraphy, developed a style, usually referred to as *Ch'usa ch'e* or Ch'usa style after his pen name Ch'usa, which is favorably compared with the best of Chinese calligraphy. *Han'gŭl* calligraphy also came into vogue with several distinct style developed by womenfolks. This was due largely to an increase in demand for the popular novels which was partially met by hand-written copies.

The Panggak Pon. It is not in the least significant that, falling into the general pattern of the cultural renaissance in the eighteenth and early nineteenth centuries, printing, an important underpinning of the literary Yi Chosŏn civilization, was further extended downward, as it were, for appreciation by the common people. It was popularized out of the hands of the court, *yangban* scholars, and Buddhist monasteries. To meet the demand for books of less well-heeled, non-*yangban* readers, commercially-motivated printing shops began to be established in major provincial cities as well as in the capital from the seventeenth century. First, they produced textbooks in Chinese and

Han'gŭl such as basic Chinese classics and histories and their translations. And, from the nineteenth century on, these small private printing shops were turning out popular novels which came to be called *panggak pon* or locally-printed novels. These locally-printed novels, so far found, count 130 titles, making possible the conjecture that most of the popular stories written in the late Yi period were locally printed. Understandably, they used, instead of meta types, wood and, sometimes, earth blocks carved in relief for the *panggak* enterprise.

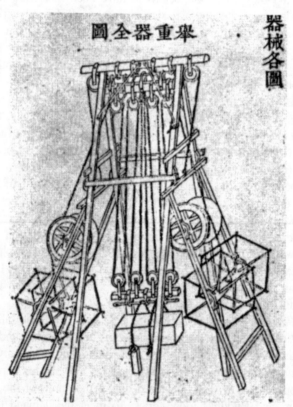

A crane created by Tasan Chŏng Yak-yong.

4

Religious Development : Western and Eastern Learning

Confucianism as a religion had tried to satisfy the spiritual life of the people with heavy doses of ancestor worship and with occasional sacrificial rites to the Heaven. The myriad spirits of ancestors and the Heaven, however, were never to issue any adequate otherworldly promises but only to be pampered. Confucian rationalism had engaged, with great success, in regimentation and control of the mind of the people through the doctrine of graduated love with miser-like precision and of the social institutions through the policies of social stratification and economic exploitation. But like other philosophies, Confucianism as religious and social philosophy, as long left unmatched by renewed political and social programs, became now reduced to a dead letter in that, although the greater majority of the people rather tenaciously stuck to it as the unique standard of moral and social conduct, it could no longer inspire its believers for new social action.

Indeed, the common people covertly but undoubtedly hoped for the end of the Confucianism-based dynasty. This desire manifested itself most notably in a wide circulation of the apocryphal *Chŏng Kam nok* or *Prophetic Notations if Chŏng Kam*. The *Chŏng Kam nok*, written sometime in the early eighteenth century by an unknown author, deals with the coming of a new dynasty, suggesting a variety of eschatological promises and preparations for the near future, which were avidly read especially by the common people.

By the middle of the eighteenth century, after centuries of patience and submission, the people came to long openly for a certain transcendental assurance for spiritual salvation beyond the world of present reality as well as for social freedom here and now. Both Catholicism and native Ch'ŏndoism that made appearance in this period were expected, if they were to viable as religions, to meet these double needs, spiritual and social. Buddhism, a political loser to Confucianism, had long lost its attraction, especially at a time when strenuous and even bloody campaigns were foreseen in achieving the double-edged goal.

The Coming of Catholic Christianity

The historical pattern of influence which had usually flowed from Northeast Asia toward the west was reversed in the late sixteenth century by the maritime expansion of Europe led by the Portuguese. Of whatever complex motives couched behind this expansion, which was unprecedented in zeal and scope, the commercial and religious ones were undoubtedly the most compelling. It was the latter that extended Catholicism and some general knowledge of the West to Korea. Stated more accurately, the diplomatic officials of the Yi court brought them to Korea, beginning around 1600, from Peking where they eagerly sought contact with the "blue-eyed" westerners, namely, Jesuit priests, a determined group of men in the service of their faith. Catholicism and Western studies, including Western technology, which came to be called *Sŏhak* or western Learning, were greeted avidly by *Sirhak* scholars with irresistible intellectual curiosity.

Yi Su Kwang, in his *Chibong yusŏl (Collected Essays of Chibong)*, writes about the *T'ien-chu shih-i* (*Ch'ŏnju sirui* in Korean : *A True Disputation about the Lord of Heaven*) by Matteo Ricci:

Europe is also called Great West. A man named Li Ma-tou [Matteo Ricci's Chinese name], after eight years of sea travel over eighty thousand *ri* of winds and waves, reached Canton where he resided for ten years. In the two volumes of the *Ch'ŏnju sirŭl* which resided for ten years. In the two volumes of the *Ch'ŏnju sirŭl* which he wrote, he first discusses how God created the Heaven and the earth and he governs them in peace. Then he discusses how the immortality of the soul of man him different from birds and beasts. And he extends his discussions to subjects of how the Buddhist doctrine of the transmigration of souls through the six worlds is wrong and also of the paradise, the hell, and the law of recompensations for good and evil. Lastly, he reasons that man's nature is innately good; therfore, he muspect and serve God. According to their custom, the king is caed Pope who does not marry, hence no heir. The successor is chosen from among the wise. And they set value on friendship and do not accumulate private wealth. He [Ricci] also wrote the *Discourse on Friendship* .Chiao Hung [a Ming scholar] says that the wise kings of the West regard their friends as the second self. but this sounds very strange [to me]···

This was the beginning of Catholicism's career in Korea, which was indeed an unobtrusive one.

Books on Western Learning, of which catholicism was an aspect, were steadily imported from Peking, and they soon became as familiar as those of the Hundred Schools, Taoism, and Buddhism in the studies of prominent *yangban*. By the 1720's, Catholicism, having attracted a great deal of religious as well as intellectual interests, came to be advocated as a worthy religion by some young *yangban* literati. But conventional scholars like An Chŏng Pok, whose historical scholarship was not as conservative, opposed such advocation on the ground that Catholicism, laying too much emphasis on the "superstitious" theories of the hellfire and the heavenly city, tended to take a warped view of this world and, worst of all, catholicism undermined one's relations with the parents and the sovereign. Needless to say, this was a fundamental difference that divided the Confucian society and the Catholic world built upon universal love. This hiatus, more than the controversies resulting form the papal claim of spiritual superiority, proved to be unfortunate. It caused a head-on clash between Catholicism and the court later.

In the meantime, Catholicism caught on at surprising rapidity and with a devastating effect on the traditional family and status structure. The populace, except those of the static northern provinces and the rigidly Confucian Kyŏngsang Province, seems to have been quite receptive to this iconoclastic influence of the Western religion. Evidence shows that, by the 1750's, the essentials of Catholicism composed in the style of folk rhyme were widely popularized among the common people. In 1758 many commoners in Hwanghae Province were reported to have forgone ancestral sacrifices as recommended by their newly-adopted religion. By the 1790's many commoners in the provinces of Kyŏnggi, Ch'ungch'ong, and Chŏlla came under Catholic influence. Kyŏngsang Province needed a generation longer to be receptive. Once embraced by the new religion, people of *yangmin* and *ch'ŏnmin* origin and women, including girls (who attended services usually in disguise as married women), generally stuck to their faith, whereas *yangban* and *chung'in* believers readily showed amenability to the external pressures such as governmental prohibition, which took on an increasingly ominous substance as the Catholic enthusiasm mounted.

The Catholic Movement

In the 1780's an organized movement for the establishment of a Catholic congregation was started by a closely-knit group of self-styled Catholics led by young intellectuals of the Southerner party then long out of power. Yi Sŭng Hun (1756-1801), a brilliant Southerner-intellectual, who had accompanied his father, the secretary to a Chosŏn embassy to the Peking court, was baptized a Captized a Catholic there in 1784. Upon his return, the first church-sanctioned Catholic moved to administer baptism to the leading members of the group, Yi Pyŏk (1754-1786), Kwŏn Il Sin (1736-1801), and others. Their followers numbered a few scores in several months, including such *Sirhak* scholars as the Chŏng Yak Yong brothers. In 1785, however, their clandestine congregation was detected and disbanded by the government, which then took to burning, and putting a ban on the import of, books on the "evil religion."

    After a brief apostatic period, the leaders met in Seoul in 1787 and, this time, moved to organize the church itself. The meeting appointed Kwŏn Il Sin the "bishop" and Yi Sŭng Hun, Ch'oe Ch'ang Hyŏn (1759-1801), and a few others "priests" with the full right to administer sacramental rites. The church, in the eyes of Rome, was of illicit birth. They believed, however, that their establishment of such a church came under the provisions of the ecclesiastical laws of Rome. Soon stranded on the rock of doctrinal doubts and inexperience, in 1789, they sent secret emissaries to the Bishop of the Peking Diocese with inquiries as to the legitimacy of their church, the possibility of sending missionaries to Korea, and the relevancy of performance of ancestral rites. Since the Korean church was established by ordained clergymen with the papal approval, the official answer said, the Korean church should not function beyond the administration of baptismal rites; however, it promised the appointment of ordained priests to Korea. As to the ancestral rites, the believers were enjoined in such unequivocal terms to have nothing to do with the "pagan" rites.

    The period of Confucianism-Catholicism accommodation had long passed in China, and a century (ca. 1640-1742) of the so-called "Rites Controversy" that followed failed to bring any compromise but had only widened the difference between them. The injunction against the last question on the ancestral rites delivered a profound shock especially to *yangban* believers, many of whom, including Yi Sŭng Hun and the Chŏng brothers, chose to disown their faith either permanently or temporarily

    In 1791 occurred what seemed a serious scandal in which two young catholic believers in Chŏlla Province renounced their ancestral rites by burning the ancestral tablets. What made this incident different from the similar case committed, for example, by the commoners of Hwanghae Province in 1758 was that the two iconoclast were impeccable *yangban,* a fact that the court could not possibly overlook. The ensuing controversy resulted in their execution; needless to say, it was an unfortunate precedent which was followed by a series of bloodier ones.

    The first large-scale persecution of Catholics as a heterodox sect occurred in 1801, a year after Chŏngjo's death which signified a resurgence of factional politics after four score years of relative dormancy under the Impartial and Leveling Policy. Queen Dowager Kim who, as the regent, took over the government of the boy king, Sunjo (1801-1834), was immediately enmeshed in the factional strife, in spite of herself. She and her Old Doctrine party picked the suppression of the heterodox religion as an excuse for promotion of their cause, many of their political enemies being catholic-Southerners. The great persecution of 1801 brought the death of more than 300 Catholic believers, including some female members of the royal family, Yi Sŭng Hun, and one Hwang sa Yŏng.

Hwang sa Yŏng, a devout Catholic who had worked with Father Chou Wen-mo, a Chinese priest who was sent from Peking in 1795, struck upon a plausible idea amidst the persecution. He wrote a 13,000-word letter addressed to the Bishop of the Peking Diocese, requesting, among other things, the dispatchment of a naval force to intimidate the Yi government into allowing religious freedom for the Catholics. But the Hwang Sa Yŏng silk Letter, so called as it was written on a roll of silk, was intercepted by the government and used for justification of the governmental prejudice against Catholic evangelism. Hwang's idea was only successfully employed for the opening of Japan by Americans a half century later.

To be a Catholic now became an extremely dangerous business. The spread of Catholicism, however, though greatly hampered, was never completely obstructed. At the persistent request to the Bishop of the Peking Diocese and the direct appeals to the Pope by native believers, the Korean Diocese was established in 1831 under the responsibility of the French Society for Foreign Missions; assignment to Korea of French priests, training of Korean priests, and other related programs soon followed. Thus, Korean Catholicism was firmly established, though against an uncertain future, by 1850 the number of known Catholics reached 11,000, and in fifteen years that number more than doubled. In the meantime, the Korean Catholics were further tried by the crucible of constant persecution and occasional massacres of their number until 1873. Today, Korean Catholic Christianity takes pride in its own initiative and efforts which alone made the establishment of the christian church in Korea possible.

The Birth of Ch'ŏndoism

While the government was hotly engaged in the suppression of the foreign religion, there was a new religion in the making on the native soil, which was one of the most extraordinary events in the Korean history. Like other religions, Ch'ŏndoism or Teaching of the Heavenly way, also known as the *Tonghak* or Eastern Learning, as against the Western Learning, was a product of the social circumstances in which it occurred. What makes it historically significant is that Ch'ŏndoism germinated and grew on the grass-roots level of the Korean culture. Even thought it jealously claimed to be of Korean originality, Ch'ŏndoism enfolded in its dogmas all major religious and apocryphal beliefs then in vogue, including wind and water theories and Christian and some downright superstitious doctrines. A religion of such unabashed syncretism, Ch'ŏndoism was thoroughly oriented in social and political interests toward the common masses of the nineteenth century Yi society, who embraced it instantly, as in love at first sight.

Ch'oe Che U (1824-1864), the founder of Ch'ŏndoism, was born of an obscure *yangban* father and a widowed peddler-woman, therefore, with little promise for the future. Neither a career in government nor a happy social life as a *yangban* in his home town, Kyŏngju, was a sure possibility. In direct proportions to his well-endowed intelligence, burning ambition, and handsome look, his frustrations at the social injustice and the political corruption, if which he was a victim, were indeed profound. A man of deep thought and insight, he first sought the universal truth in books, probably to transcend the unpleasant present.

At the age of twenty, he burnt all Confucian books which he had been perusing and set out in quest for certainty. Through a life of wandering and observation for the next ten years, he became convinced of the "nearness of the end of the world." His new vision consisted in the fast-decaying Yi dynasty engulfing itself in the mire of foreign influences *vis-à-vis* the rise of the common people taking over national leadership. Ch'oe Che U was keenly aware of political developments in China and Japan and of the aggressiveness of Western powers, whose "black ships" were then making frequenter appearances in Korean waters.

Upon his return home, he sat, for a prolonged period at a time, in meditation and prayer in caves in the beautiful surroundings of mountains, as did the Silla Hwarang, in an attempt to "perceive a way," during one of these sittings in 1855, he received "a heavenly revelation" that he would serve as the surrogate of *Ch'ŏnju* or the Lord of Heaven. As he persisted in his efforts to organize an agglomeration of thoughts and mystical experiences and feelings into a doctrinal system, he fell into a trance at the end of a usual fast and contemplation period at the at the Yongdam Pavilion near Kyŏngju in 1860. He felt an ecstatic, probably Shamanistic, communion with the Lord of Heaven and was given a divine approval with which to found a new religion.

The basic tenet of Ch'ŏndoism thus created was: "Man and Heaven are one and the same." The Heaven here is not the Confucian Heaven but the one identifiable with the *Ch'ŏnji sinmyŏng* or, more popularly, *Hananim*, the native anthropomorphic God who is usually enhanced far above the Shamanistic gods. Ch'oe called his Lord of Heaven *Hananim*. Man's inner union with the Heaven is achieved by the influx into him of *Hananim's* spirit and, at the same time, by his awareness externally of, and contact with, the *Chi-ki*. The *Chi* of *Chi-ki* is the Ultimate Force, while its *Ki* is the same as Ch'oe Han. *Ki's ki* of *sin-ki* and the Neo-Confucian *ki (ch'i)*, that is, matter or ether. The *Chi-ki* of Ch'ondoism is the Ultimate Force of the universe which creates and changes with its own principle and yet had no attributes that can be discerned by human senses. Ch'oe Che U made *Hananim* the one and only God in the universe who administered the workings of the universal elements and forces, *but only through the human mind.* He stripped all other Shamanistic gods, good or evil, of their anthropomorphic disposing of their ghostly phenomena as the discordant interaction of *yin-yang* forces. But he appropriated much of rituals strewn with talisman and incantation from Shamanism and other apocryphal religious practices which taken such deep roots in the life of the common people.

Ch'ondoism's social teachings, which are historically more important than its religious contents, are based on the equality of man, with an emphasis on such Confucian virtues as sincerity, respect, and trustworthiness in interpersonal relations. Since everyone has the spirit of *Hananim* residing in himself, or rather everyone "serves the Lord of Heaven within himself," he should regard everyone else as the Lord of Heaven and treat him accordingly. Although the Ch'ondoists did not propose any radical action to do away with the unjust status system then, it was understood that the doctrine of the sameness of man and Heaven rendered the status system null and void. Ch'oe Che U adopted one of his two female slaves as a daughter and made the other a daughter-in-law. The Ch'ondoist concept of equality of man is more clearly, if not philosophically, couched in such an adage as, "All men are sages and princes." It was enhancing of the common masses to the level of the highest status of the traditional society rather than the other way around.

Theirs was a utopian society on earth people by virtuous sages and princes or individuals saved, that is, everyone. Ideally, it was a kind of utopia where the Taoist doctrine of "achieving everything by doing nothing" might be hoped to prevail. And they believed that the Lord of Heaven had already abandoned his support of this obsolete world and turned to the creation of a new one, which was calculated to begin its career in 1884.

There was also in Ch'ondoism a militant aspect. They drilled themselves in a sword dance accompanied by incantatory yet aggressive songs, preferably in mountain glades in the dead of night. The sword dance and songs, which were created by Ch'oe Che U himself, was a means of cultivating the expansive soul which had just been emancipated from the spiritual and social fetters of the old. Combination of the religous promise with the military discipline was strictly in line with the Hwarang tradition. As in the Hwarang movement which was at once religious and military as it prepared the youths for the unification of the Peninsula, the Ch'ŏndoists' inclusion of the martial art in their curriculum seems to have been from their keen awareness of a certain portentous national crisis looming on the horizon, which they had to overcome before the advent of the new world. Undoubtedly, this aspect of Ch'ŏndoism developed into a revolutionary movement led by the *Tonghak* army in the late nineteenth century.

The Ch'ŏndoist Evangelism

Convinced by the divine disclosure of 1860 that he was chosen to lead the people along the righteous path in the chaotic world, Ch'oe Che U, who was later called *Taesinsa* or Great Godly Teacher, immediately plunged headlong into the propagation of his religion, *Tonghak* or Eastern Learning, Ch'ŏndoism being its later name given by Ch'oe's successor in 1905. For this purpose, he wrote a series of religious treaties and songs of literary merit which were later collected in Ch'ŏndoism's two bibles, *Tongyŏng taejŏn* or *Great Eastern Classic*, written in Chinese, and *Yongdam yusa* or *Bequeathed Songs from the Yongdam Pavilion* in *Han'gŭl*. And he embarked on the organization of an ecclesiastical body which first called for appointment of *chŏpchu* in major cities and towns, starting from Kyŏngsang Province. The *chŏpchu* was an evangelist–administrator who managed the local church. In three years, the number of localities that hosted a *Tonghak* church counted fourteen, and Kyŏngsang Province came quite thoroughly under *Tonghak* influence. An official report of 1863 describes, "One can hardly pass a day without hearing about the *Tonghak* doctrine [in Kyŏngsang Province]···Even women of village stores and children of mountain valleys all recite it."

The government, which was again shaken up by this heterodoxical challenge,as might be expected, moved to suppress the *Tonghak* movement along with the current Catholic practice. The government officials who investigated the *Tonghak* doctrine resoundingly identified the *Tonghak* Lord of Heaven with the Catholic Lord of Heaven and were more alarmed by the former because of the *Tonghak's* growing organizational strength shrouded in a militaristic aura. Foreseeing his arrest by the government, Ch'oe Che U handed down leadership to Ch'oe Si Hyŏng (1827-18), the most eminent of his followers, and in 1864 he was executed for his "deluding the world and deceiving the people."

The martyrdom of Ch'oe Che U simply marked the beginning of the second phase in the development of Ch'ŏndoism. The new leader, Ch'oe Si

Hyŏng, uneducated thought he might be in traditional learning. cautiously and dauntlessly worked for the spread of his religion. While putting out the bibles at the printing shops set up in houses of believers, he greatly strengthened the church doctrine, and the ecclesiastical organization which was soon extended to the three provinces of Kyŏnggi Ch'ungcgh'ŏng, and Chŏlla. No less important developments in the second phase of Ch'ŏndoism were the crystallization of political demands and the budding of modern Korean nationalism on the grass-roots level, which were the natural corollaries of the *Tonghak* teachings.

They demanded, among other things, the redress of the unjust execution of the Great Godly Teacher, the emancipation of women and slaves, and the elimination of other social injustices and corrupt officials, while repeatedly warning against international skulduggeries going on in neighboring countries. These were the basic goals of the *Tonghak* as a secular movement which climaxed in the short-lived military action in the 1893-to-1894 war. And the movement subsequently provided much of the enlightened political leadership in modern times.

Execution of the Catholics, including some French priests.

5

Government Under the Taewŏn'gun : The Last Attempt

Despite notable advances made in other areas of the dynastic life, the political deterioration which set in before the seventeenth century almost suddenly worsened with the beginning of the nineteenth century. The debilitated officialdom simply lacked the will to reinvigorate itself. There had been, for instance, the proposal for remuneration of petty clerks of provincial and district governments in order to eliminate clerical chicaneries, but the central government somehow failed to get around to implement the much needed measure. Meanwhile, the exploitation of the masses, in direct proportions to worsening irregularities in the central administration, was fast reaching the point where even the in ponderable reservoir of patience of the peasantry might run out. Moreover, foreign pressures on the government, the kind of which had never been experienced before, were steadily mounting. By the 1860's Western powers, who had devastated the traditional order in China and Japan, were zeroing in on Korea, so to speak. Thus, because of the inability of the bankrupt group in power, the political situation had entangled itself into a kind of Gordian knot, which the reform-minded Taewŏn'gun or Grand Prince, who took over the government in 1864, tried in an Alexandrian spirit to cut at a singles stroke, but within the traditional framework of government and morality. It was the last and most serious governmental attempt at dynastic revitalization before the end of traditional Korea.

The Clan Government

The recrudescence of the political illness as a result of the open resumption of factional struggles immediately after the death of Chŏngjo in 1800 took the form of monopolization of all important offices by one clan who came into power by virtue of having provided the reigning monarch with the first queen. The four successive kings who reigned during the nineteenth century, all, besides their being typically mediocre, acceded to the throne in their teens or younger, which meant the regentship of queen dowagers. Queen dowager–regents usually delegated their power to the members of their own families who were then geared only to perpetuate themselves in power. The similar form of this one clan government occurred in the Koryŏ dynasty when, for instance, the Yi clan of Inju in the early twelfth century completely controlled the government with Yi Cha Kyŏm as its leading figure. He became so powerful that he nearly usurped the throne. The Kim clan of Andong, its dynasty counterpart, dared not so much as cast a furtive glance at the throne itself, but they managed to stay in power from 1801 to 1863, except for a brief interlude in the 1840's when the Cho clan of P'ungyang enjoyed its own one–clan government.

In the absence of responsible authorities in the central government, provincial and district governments were largely controlled by those officials who bribed their way through to their present positions; they squeezed out of people, namely, the peasants not merely the sum of money invested but many times more. Indeed, the hardship of the peasantry under the one–clan government was beyond description. The *sŏwŏn,* now heavily parasitized by *yangban*–riffraff, also lorded it over the masses. And those small-time, low-class cheats who purchased high–priced petty clerkships in alliance with magistrates became the most notorious tormentors of the common masses. They imposed the land tax on the land that never was and the military tax upon infants or dead men. They mixed a half bushel of unhulled tax rice with a half bushel of chaff to make one. These were only a few, widely practiced methods for extortion of extralegal fees and tribute from the peasantry and defrauding the government of its revenue. Moreover, the peasants were subjected to a great variety of tax as assessments unilaterally and frequently levied by various departments of the central and provincial governments to allegedly disburse their maintenance costs.

The Peasant Uprising. The first serious outbreak against the one-clan government, which was inevitable under the circumstances, occurred in P'yong'an Province in 1811, when one Hong Kyŏng Nae and his followers rose in rebellion, pretexting the rectification of the government's discrimination in personnel appointment against the northern provinces. Hong Kyŏng Nae seems to have wandered, like Ch'oe Che U later, for an extensive period of time after his failure in the government examination, but to rally like-minded persons for a rebellion. Even after its suppression, for which the government force took five months, remnants of the Hong rebels continued to make troubles with an unsettling influence over other provinces. Brigandism, famine, epidemics, floods, all catastrophic upshots of misgovernment or traditional signs of a dynastic end, hit the nation with unusual frequency in the early nineteenth century, causing profound disaffection among the people.

Then, in 1862, a more serious and peasant–inspired uprising swept the southern provinces like a prairie fire, which was ignited at Chinju and lasted a few months. Although a general spread from Kyŏngsang to Chŏlla and then to Ch'ungch'ŏng Provinces of the revolt was discernible, they were nearly simultaneous and spontaneous. "The grapes of wrath" were exploded, as usual, toward corrupt officials and wealthy individuals in disrepute.

In parallel with the social unrest, peasants' hegira from farm villages was another serious but familiar problem which the government could do nothing about. Their destinations were mainly the *sŏwŏn* and the residences of high–ranking officials in the capital where they served as handymen of henchmen, languishing most of the time. * Nowhere is popular demoraliza-tion more graphically shown than in demographic statistics. The total number of households in P'yŏng'an Province before the Hong Kyŏng Nae rebellion was 302,844, which, however, were reduced to 192,867 immediately after it. The nation's population stood at 7,561,403 in 1807 but that number dwindled to 6,755,280 in 1837, a decrease of some 800,000 in thirty years.

Foreign Pressures. The international situations, created by the inroads of European powers into Asia, were even more confusing and fast changing at a disturbing velocity. With attitudes born of arrogance and jingoism, Britain, tak-ing advantage of the military weakness of Ch'ing China, provoked the Opium War (1840–1842) through which it forced the Ch'ing into signing the Treaty of Nanking. In order to enforce the provision of the Treaty, the British in alliance with the French picked yet another quarrel with the Ch'ing in 1860 and took Peking, sending the Manchu emperor beyond the great Wall to Jehol. In the same year, Russia wrung a territorial concession from the con-fused Ch'ing of the maritime region of Manchuria, its ancestral homeland. This was a successful climax of Russian expansion in Northeast Asia, which made Russia conterminous with Korea along the lower reaches of the Tuman

---

* In his *The Tragely of Korea*, F. A. McKenzie states: "In Seoul, in particular, great armies of hangers-on attached to the nobles and the Court gave an impression of laziness, of dirt, and of worthlessness···" This description of Seoul of the 1910's, when the political situation of the country was at its worst, may be applicable to Seoul of this period also. The "hanger-on" were actually smart and lucky ones, having escaped from local aristocratic exploitation.

River. Meanwhile, in 1854 as United states naval force under Commodore Matthew Perry threatened Tokugawa Japan with the cannon fire into opening up its door to the West, plunging Japan into period, if relatively brief, of political and social convulsions. The West's self-righteous play of naked force in the neighboring countries of Korea certainly boded ill for the Static Yi government.

While these foreign developments were not merely "fires on the other shore," the more immediate predicaments that beset Korea were the precariousness of intellectual and political positions of the ruling group. It was a misfortune of tragic proportions that those in power failed to keep abreast with the current *Sirhak* and social developments which were still vigorously going on. And it is an absurd yet undeniable commentary on this period, one or the most crucial times in the Korean history, that the power elite that comprised the one-clan government was less informed of, than the catholics, and less concerned with, than the Ch'ŏndoists, the aggressive Western incursions which were shaking the entire Asian civilization at the very root.

Only in domestic politics, that is, in personnel administration and suppression of the religious and social unrest, the one-clan government was alert, bold, and decisive. Needless to say, this decisiveness was from the fundamental weakness or precariousness of its power, which was dependent upon the marriage arrangement for the future monarch as well as the longevity fo the present one.

The Taewŏn'gun's Domestic Reforms

Since the longevity of the reigning monarch was not always predictable, the political fortunes of the Kim of andong came to an abrupt end in 1863, when it became Queen Dowager Cho's authority to name a new king. It was also through Queen Dowager Cho that the Cho clan of P'ungyang briefly controlled the government in the 1840's. Now as the senior queen dowager, she, in a brilliantly executed maneuver, crowned a collateral prince, the Taewŏn'gun's twelve-year-old son to be Kojong (1864-1907) and made the Taewŏn'gun (Grand Prince) the virtual regent. The Taewŏn'gun, who had masterminded all this, which was the climactic stage of long, sedulous planning and intriguing, was a man of indomitable will and master of traditional politics and orchid-painting. With deep resentment, he had witnessed, and suffered from, the one family show of the insolent Andong Kim. Now with the legitimately vested authority in him, he moved swiftly and resolutely to trim the government to his liking. In the process, the Kim and some of the long standing political and social ills were eliminated almost overnight.

Uppermost in his mind was understandably the strengthening of the royal authority, which was his. To create a new efficient bureaucracy loyal to himself, he tried, to an extent, to transcend party, regional, and even class lines in personnel appointment. As a result, many a man of merit, including descendants of the Koryŏ royalty and those of *chung'in* origin, came to occupy government posts vacated by the Kim. At the same time, he carried out, as in periods of royal assertion in the past, the readjustment of certain government organs, the compilation of a new law code, and related programs.

One of the most ambitious projects that he undertook in this connection was the reconstruction of the Kyŏngbok Palace, which had lain in ruins since the Japanese invasion of 1592. The Palace regained its former splendor in two years starting from 1865 but at the cost of 7,400,000 *yang* or taels * plus a series of inflationary spirals in the economy. The spirit and the basic method exemplified in the palace construction were typically the Taewŏn'gun's. As financial stress mounted from a lack of planning and preparation, he resorted to taxation, causing distress and resentment among the people of all classes. Moreover, fire reduced building materials to ashes twice during the construction period, engendering all sorts of distracting interpretations of the misfortune. In the face of such adversity, the Taewŏn'gun simply pushed the whole nation not only to the completion of the Palace but still further to the construction and repair of major defense facilities also.

Then, in 1871, he ordered, in a similar vein, the removal of the *sŏwŏn,* an extraordinary move which was comparable in difficulty of implementation to the rebuilding of the Kyŏngbok Palace. The removal order, however, was far sounder for the interest of the nation; it was also of historical significance. the importance of the *sŏwŏn* as an institution of higher learning as well as a sacred shrine of Confucianism had long been outweighed by the excessiveness of its extra-curricular activities in economic and political areas, which proved extremely pernicious to the central treasury and authority and also to the local populace. Overriding a fierce opposition offered by the Confucianists, the Taewŏn'gun boldly destroyed all but forty-seven *sŏwŏn* whose shrines were dedicated to truly outstanding scholars. Through this war upon the *sŏwŏn,* in which some of the hardcore Confucianists were executed, the Taewŏn'gun inflicted on himself the unmitigated animosity of local Confucianists, which worked for his eventual downfall in 1873.

Unruffled, the Taewŏn'gun went further to curb the economic power and social pretensions of the *yangban.* He enforced the payment of taxes upon the *yangban* who from now on might evade it at severe penalty or even pain of death. He standardized the *yangban* habiliments from the fradi-

---

* A *yang* was the monetary unit of account based on the value of a tael weight of silver.

tional flowery style to a more practical one. These domestic reforms, thought executed under the absolute, one-man dictatorship, constitute the positive precursor of the modernization of the country in many respects.

The Taewŏn'gun refuses to deal with the West

It was in the foreign area that the Taewŏn'gun met with stiffer challenges. The Western inroads in asia, as of the 1860's, had so deeply been made that the traditional concept of international order became irretrievably outmoded, without Korea's knowledge. The government was profoundly troubled by recent wars in China in which the Middle Kingdom was resoundingly defeated. Western powers and individual adventurers visibly stepped up their attempts at contact with Korea, which they came to call "the Hermit Kingdom." The steady expansion of Catholicism and the presence of British textile products and some other foreign goods in the domestic markets, which somehow made their way into the country, were extremely disturbing to the xenophobic government.

A chain of events involving Western powers that occurred under such volatile atmosphere drove the Taewŏn'gun bitterly defensive against the west. In 1865 a group of Russians crossed the Tuman River for the second time, requesting the border magistrate to establish trade relations. Even though they were turned away by the magistrate, the fact of the Russian advance by land seems to have wrought a ruder impact upon the Yi government than the "strange-looking ships" on the coastal seas had done. When the Taewŏn'gun was at great pains to find a means of blocking the Russian expansion southward, some Catholic believers, notably Nam Chong Sam, a former official, intimated that French and British forces might be introduced through French priests as intermediaries, who were thought to be able to induce the dispatchment of troops. The Taewŏn'gun found himself responsive to this idea and asked them to arrange a meeting with the missionaries. The Catholic failure to promptly realize the proposed meeting, however, aroused imperial displeasure in the Taewŏn'gun who then let himself be influenced by his ministers' express anti-Catholicism. In 1866 the Taewŏn'gun, probably to maintain the official consensus, or lest his flirtation with Catholics should lapse into a face-losing fiasco, moved to bring down upon the Catholics a bloody purge, which lasted for several months, claiming the lives of thousands of Catholics and nine off the twelve French missionary priests who had been working in the country.

Father Ridel, one of the three survivors who made it to China, aroused the feeling of the Western community in Peking, especially the personal ire of the French Charge d'Affaires, which culminated in the dispatchment of a fleet under admiral Roze. In the fall of 1866, a French squadron of seven men-of-war with 600 troopers and father Ridel aboard laid a month-long blockade to the mouth of the Han River, a strategy that seems to have been advised by the French priest. The numerically-superior defense forces that were deployed around the capital were ready for the first armed confrontation with the West. The decisive battles were fought on the island of Kanghwa. The French took the city after naval bombardments and engaged in burning and looting. But in the bitter contest at the mountain stronghold of Chŏngjok, twelve miles south of the city, a month later, 160 French attackers, pitted against 450 defenders positioned on the vantage ground, were beaten back, with as many as eighty wounded. In fact, this was the end of the invasion.

The French defeat enhanced the morale of the Koreans under the ill-informed Taewŏn'gun government. Then occurred a bizarre incident which added fuel to the flames of the Koreans' anti-foreignism. An assortment of Western adventurers in Peking thought it an uproarious idea to "snatch" from a royal tomb the corpse allegedly studded with precious metals and stones of Prince Namnyŏn, no less a personality than the father of the Taewŏn'gun himself. The professed purpose of this "body-snatching" expedition was "to retaliate [the religious persecution] without resorting to war," an idea that is said to have come from Father Feron, another one of the three survivors of the 1866 massacre. A Prussian adventurer named Ernest Oppert, a shady product of the era of Western scramble in Asia who had at least twice been frustrated in his attempt to "open" Korea before, immediately assumed the leadership of the expedition, no doubt, allured by the imaginary sparkles on the precious stone aspect of it. Oppert enlisted for the venture, beside Father Feron, an unemployed American named Jenkins for fund raising and, on the lower echelon, a crew of about 100 Chinese and Malaysians and a few Korean and European riffraff. In the summer of 1868, this thoroughly international task force, aboard a British steamship, *China*, left for its objective point in the coastal zone of Ch'ungch'ŏng Province.

The mission would have been neatly accomplished, had it not been for an extra layer protecting the sarcophagus below the ground. The upshot of this criminal undertaking was that, though ill-fated, it inflicted an irreparable damage on the Western image in the mind of not only the Taewŏn'gun but also all Koreans whose society was so firmly riveted to the father-son relationship. Not even the wholesale mobilization of the modern mass media could have aroused the Korean resistance to Western contact more effectively than this unfortunate incident. The incident such as this and those rampantly committed by the Japanese later helped delay the Yi government growing out its traditionalism. Indeed, "retaliate" they did in a far-reaching way.

The Taewŏn'gun's Korea was picked on again in 1871, this time by the

United states, as a climaxing result of a series of previous contacts. In early 1866 when the rough flames of the religious persecution were barely abated, an American schooner, *Surprise,* was washed ashore on the northwestern coast. The ship's captain and crew surrendered themselves to the local authorities, and to their surprise they were well treated with propriety (*ye*). When they were sent home via China, they were even given a farewell path at the border. A few months later came the *General Sherman,* a commercial vessel with a surreptitious intent which was surmised among the Western residents in Peking to be a treasure hunting in Korean tombs. Despite the warning given by the local authorities, the *General Sherman* sailed upstream the Taedong River to P'yŏngyang. Their shooting and unseemly conduct attracted the curiosity of Koreans which soon turned into a mob action. When the *General Sherman* was stranded as a heavy freshet subsided, they set it on fire with fire-rafts and destroyed the whole crew.

The American authorities in Peking, at some vague news about the demise of the *General Sherman,* dispatched a naval force twice to Korea's west coast on a fact-finding mission, while contacting the Taewŏn'gun government on the matter through the Ch'ing court, but without any satisfactory result. At this point, the Americans decided to push the matter further to establish some sort of trade relations with Korea, and they intended to apply the proven method of Commodore Perry as the last resort. In April, 1871 Admiral Rodgers, commanding a flotilla of five vessels with Frederick Low, the American minister to Peking, and 1,230 marines aboard, proceeded to Korea. But they failed in meeting the Korean government halfway. Instead, they exchanged bullets in the "forty-eight hour war" on Kanghwa Island which the invaders, though victorious, "did not want to remember." Indeed, the exchange of diplomatic papers and official errands between the two countries centering around the *General Sherman* question is a study in communication miscarried. When, for instance, the Taewŏn'gun sent a low-ranking official to prearrange the ministerial conference, the American admiral shouted, through his secretary, that the United States would not negotiate with a clerk. When the Americans, at their departure from Korean waters, condescended to return the wounded prisoners of war, the Koreans adamantly retorted that they might dispose of them as they pleased.

洋夷侵犯非戰則和主和賣國 戒我萬年子孫 丙寅作辛未立

Above left : Regent Taewŏngun.

Above right : A stone tablet on which anti-western policy was inscribed. The inscription said, "West- ern barbarians have invaded our land. If we do not fight and conclude peace with them, it wil lead to the selling of the country to them." Stone tablets with this inscription were placed throughout the country.

Epilogue

The Yi government under the Grand Prince became solvent and its army was functioning again. More important, the nation moved under one command. But the young Kojong now came of age. which suggested the end of the Taewŏn'gun as the regent. In 1873 he was eased out of power after ten years. Ironically, Queen Min, whom the Taewŏn'gun personally chose as his daughter-in-law, led the anti-Taewŏn'gun force which she had built up behind the screen. But the Taewŏn'gun remained a political force for another ten years. Kojong, who took the helm of the government, did not offer much in the way of enlightened leadership, which was extremely unfortunate. Even more unfortunate in many ways was the fact that Queen Min, two years older than Kojong, was highly astute in traditional politics, as shown in the overthrow of the Taewŏn'gun in which she was instrumental. The political base which she developed during the Taewŏn'gun period was a remarkable *tour de force*, but it remained hers, independent of Kojong. Thus, the helplessly anachronistic political leadership, further weakened by the three–way dispersion, was hardly expected to meet the extraordinary challenges, domestic and foreign, which are usually referred to as the modern transformation.

So it seemed that traditional Korea looked to the continued enjoyment of its own microcosm as long as possible, as that great sixteenth century philosopher Yi Hwang sang:

> Only I and the seagulls know
> > Ch'ŏngnyangsan's thirty–six peaks.
> The seagulls might chatter elysium is here
> > but falling flowers tells the most tales.
> Peach petals, do not fall, do not float down
> > The fishers will know where we are. *

But the fishers already knew, and they were coming. This time, Japan, having halfway transformed itself into a cocky modern state, took it upon itself to pry open "the clam shell." Backed by its military forces, the erstwhile "dwarf" nation, now a sophomoric giant of the Far East, was ready by 1875 to apply its own experience to Korea in reverse. This was no piratical attack but, as it turned out, the beginning of a much more destructive series.

---

* This is an assembled translation by the author. Its first, third, and fifth lines come from the *Hudson Review,* Vol. VIII, no. 4, p. 490, translated by Peter H. Lee and second, fourth, and sixth lines from the *Transactions of the Korea Branch of the Royal Asiatic Society,* Vol. XXXIV, p. 43, translated by Richard Rutt.

BIBLIOGRAPHY

A spate of publications in Korean Studies in the last decade did much to change the Korean historiographical makeup; many Korean histories written during the first half of the twentieth century, as they were written mostly by Japanese scholars, have been much politicized. Considering various publication and compilation plans announced by the government and private institutes of research and learning, the 1970's would witness another great step forward in the re-creation of Korea's past. And tens of thousands of still unread primary works are also expected to come under the critical investigations in this period.

Of the Korean histories produced during the traditional period, the *Samguk sagi (History of the Three Kingdoms)* by Kim Pu Sik and the *Samguk yusa(Memorabilia of the Three Kingdoms)* by Monk Iryŏn are the unique sources for the formative period of Korean culture (see pp. 199-200); these will be soon available in English. For other works written during the Yi dynasty, the reader may refer to "Printing and Practical Scholarship" (pp. 318-322) in Chapter Seven and "Intellectual Development" (pp. 377-397) in Chapter Eight.

The following list of select books, though mostly published works, is regarded as of primary importance in Korean Studies and served as the basis upon which this book is written.

General Surveys and Background Studies

Chang, To Pin 張道斌. Taehan yŏksa 大韓歷史 (*History of Korea*) (Seoul : Baehwasa, 1960).
Ch'oe, Nam Sŏn 崔南善. Kosat'ong 古事通 (*Discourses on the Ancient Matters*) (Seoul : Samjungdang, 1947).
_____. Chosŏn yŏksa 朝鮮歷史 (*History of Korea*) (Seoul : Tongamyŏngsa, 1931).
Chŏn, Hae Chong 全海宗 and Min, Tu Ki 閔斗基. Iibonsa 日本史 (*History of Japan*) (Seoul : Chimungak, 1964).
Han, Woo Kŭn 韓佑劤 and Kim, Ch'ŏl Chun 金哲埈. Kuksa Kaeron 國史概論 (*History of Korea*) (Seoul : Myŏnghaksa, 1954).

Han, Woo Kŭn 韓佑劤. Han'guk t'ongsa 韓國通史 *(General History of Korea)* (Seoul : Ŭlyumunhwasa, 1970).

Hatada, Takeshi 旗田巍. *A History of Korea,* trans. and ed. by Warren W. Smith, Jr. and Benjamin H. Hazard. (Santa Barbara, Calif.: Clio Press, 1969).

Hulbert, Homer B., *The History of Korea,* 2 vols. ed. by C. N. Weems. (New York : Hilary House, 1962).

Imanishi, Ryŭ 今西龍. Chōsensino shiori 朝鮮史の刊 *(Guide to Korean History)* (Seoul : Kanasawashoten, 1935).

Cho, Chwa Ho 曺佐浩. *Tong'yang munhwasa* 東洋文化史 *(Cultural History of Orient)* (Seoul : Pomun'gak, 1967)

Kim Tong Sŏng 金東成. *Chungguk munhwasa* 中國文化史 *(Cultural History of China)* (Seoul : Ŭlyumunhwasa, 1961).

Latourette, Kenneth Scot, *The Chinese : Their History and Culture.* 2 vols. (New York, Macmillan, 1946).

Lee, In Yŏng 李仁榮. *Kuksa yoron* 國史要論 *(History of Korea)* (Seoul : Kŭmnyong Book Co., 1950).

Lee, Pyŏng To 李丙燾. *Han'guksa taegwan* 韓國史大觀 *(General Survey of Korean History)* (Seoul : Pomun'gak, 1964).

Lee, Hong Chik 李弘植. *Kuksa taesajŏn* 國史大辭典 *(Encyclopedia of the Korean History)* (Seoul : Chimun'gak, 1968).

Lee, Ki Paek 李基白. *Han'guksa sinron* 韓國史新論 *(New History of Korea)* (Seoul : Ilchogak, 1967).

Li Dun J., *The Ageless Chinese* (New York : Charles Scribner's sons, 1965).

Reischauer, Edwin O and Fairbank, John K., *East Asia : The Great Tradition* (Boston : Houghton Mifflin Co., Tokyo : Charles E. Tuttle Co., 1962).

Sansom, G. B., *Japan : A Short Cultural History* (New York : Appleton-Century, 1944).

Sin, Ki Sŏk 申基碩. *Tong'yang wegyosa* 東洋外交史 *(Diplomatic History of East Asia* (Seoul : Tonggukmunhwasa, 1955).

Son, Chin T'ai 孫晋泰. *Han'gukminjoksa Kaeron* 韓國民族史槪論 *(General History of the Korena People)* (Seoul : Ŭlyumunhwasa, 1947).

Song, Sŏk Ha 宋錫夏. *Han'guk minsokko* 韓國民俗考 *(Studies in Korean Folklore* (Seoul : Ilsinsa, 1960).

Chindan Hak'hoe 震檀學會. *Han'guksa* 韓國史 *(History of Korea),* 7 vols. (Seoul : Ŭlyumunhwasa, 1959–65).

Kim, Chewŏn 金載元. and Lee, Pyŏng To 李丙燾. *Kodaep'yŏn* 古代篇 *(Ancient Period)* (1959).

Lee, Pyŏng To 李丙燾. *Chungsep'yŏn* 中世篇 *(Middle Period)* (1961).

Lee, Sang Paek 李相伯. *Kunsejŏn'gip'yŏn* 近世前期篇 *(Early Near Modern Period)* (1962).

Lee, Sang Paek 李相伯. *Kŭnsehugip'yŏn* 近世後期篇 *(Late Near*

Modern Period) (1965).

Lee, Sŏn Kun 李瑄根. *Ch'oegŭnsep'yŏn* 最近世篇 (*Very Near Modern Period*) (1961).

Lee, Sŏn Kun 李瑄根. *Hyŏndaep'yŏn.* 現代篇 (*Modern Period*) (1963).

Lee, Pyŏng To 李丙燾. *Yŏnp'yo* 年表 (*Chronological Table*) (1959).

Chŏsensi Gakukai 朝鮮史學會. *Chŏsensi taikei* 朝鮮史大系 (*Outline of the Korean History*), 5 vols. (Seoul : Chŏsensi Gakukai, 1927)

Ono, Shōgo 小野省吾. *Jōseisi* 上世史 (*Ancient Period*)

Seno, Umakuma 瀨野馬熊. *Chūseisi* 中世史 (*Middle Period*).

Seno, Umakuma 瀨野馬熊. *Kinseisi* 近世史 (*Near Modern Period*).

Sukimoto, Masasuke 杉本政助 and Oda, Shōgo 小田省吾. *Saikinseisi* 最近世史 (*Very Near Modern Period*).

Ōhara, Toshitake 大原年武. *Nenpyō* 年表 (*Chronological Table*).

Han'gukgyŏngjesa Hakhoe 韓國經濟史學會. *Han'guksa sidaegubunron* 韓國史時代區分論 (*On the Periodization of the Korean History*) (Seoul : Ulyumunhwasa, 1970).

Minjokmunhwa Yŏn'guso 民族文化研究所. *Han'gukmunhwasa taegye* 韓國文化史大系 (*Outline of the Korean Culture*), 6 vols. (Seoul : Minjokmunhwa Yŏn'guso, Korea University, 1964-70).

Yŏksa Hakhoe 歷史學會. *Han'guksaŭi Pansŏng* 韓國史의反省 (*Reflections on the Korean History*) (Seoul : Shin'gumunhwasa, 1969).

Korean Studies Guide, (Los Angeles and Berkeley : University of california Press, 1954).

Goverment and Historical Surveys

Chang, Yun Sik 張潤植. *Yijo amhyang'ŏsajedo ŭi yŏn'gu* 李朝暗行御使制度의 研究 (*Study of the Secret Envoy System of the Yi Dynasty) (Seoul : Korea Book Co., 1959).*

Ch'oe, Sŏk Nam 崔碩男. *Han'guk sugunsa yŏn'gu* 韓國水軍史研究 (*Study of theHistory of the Korean Traditional Navy*) (Seoul : Myŏngnyangsa, 1964).

Ch'oe, Tong 崔棟. *Chosŏn Sanggo minjoksa* 朝鮮上古民族史 (*History of the Korean People of the Ancient Period*) (Seoul : Tonggukmunhwasa, 1966).

Cho, In Pok 趙仁福. *Yi Sun Sin chŏnsa yŏn'gu* 李舜臣載史研究 (*Study on the Naval Operations of Yi Sun Sin*) (Seoul : Myŏngnyangsa, 1964).

Chŏng, In Po 鄭寅普. *Chosŏnsa yŏn'gu* 朝鮮史研究 (*Study of the Ancient History of Korea*), 2 vols. (Seoul : Seoul Sinmunsa, 1974).

Chŏng, Ch'ung Hwan 丁仲煥. *Karasach'o* 伽羅史草 (*Manuscript History of Kara* [Kaya]) (Pusan : Hanil Munhwayŏn'guso, Pusan National

University, 1962).

Ham, Pyŏng Ch'un 咸秉春. *Korean Political Tradition and Law* (Seoul : Hollymsa, 1965).

Hŏ, Sŏn To 許善道. *Han'guk hwagi paldalsa* 韓國火器發達史 (*History of Firearms Development in Korea*) (Seoul : Kunsapangmulgwan, 1969).

Hŏ, Sŏn To *et al.* 許善道外. *Han'guk Kunjesa* 韓國軍制史 (*History of the Korean Military System* [Yi period]) (Seoul : Army Headquarters, 1968).

Imanishi, Ryŭ 今西龍. *Paekchesi kenkyŭ* 百濟史研究 (*Study of the History of Paekche*) (Seoul : Chikasawashoten, 1936).

_____. *Sillasi kenkyŭ* 新羅史研究 (*Study of the History of Silla*) (Seoul : Chikasawashoten, 1933).

_____. *Koguryŏsi kenkyŭ* 高句麗史研究 (*Study of the History of Koguryŏ*) (Seoul : Chikasawashoten, 1944).

Kim, Sang Ki 金庠基. *Koryŏ sidaesa* 高麗時代史 (*History of the Koryŏ Period*) (Seoul : Tonggukmunhwasa, 1961).

_____. *Tongbang munhwagyoryusa yŏu'gu.* 東方文化交流研究 (*Study in the History of Cultural Exchanges in the East*) (Seoul : Ulyumunhwasa, 1948).

Lee, Sang Paek 李相伯. *Yijo kŏn'guk ui yŏn'gu* 李朝健國의 研究 (*Study on the Foundation of the Yi Dynasty*) (Seoul : Ulyumunhwasa, 1949).

Lee, Hyŏn Chong 李炫綜. *Chosŏnjŏn'gi taeilgyosŏpsa yŏn'gu* 朝鮮前基對日交涉史研究 (*Study in the Korea-Japan Relations during the Early Yi Period*) (Seoul : Han'guk Yŏn'guwŏn, 1964).

Lee, In Yŏng 李仁榮. *Han'guk Manju Kwan'gesa ŭi yŏn'gu* 韓國滿州關系史의 研究 (*Study in the Korea-Manchuria Relations* (Seoul : Ulyumunhwasa, 1954).

Lee, Ki Paek 李基白. *Koryŏ Pyŏngjesa Yŏn'gu* 高麗兵制史研究 (*Study in the Koryŏ Military System*) (Seoul : Ilchogak, 1968).

Lee, Chong Han 李鍾恒 *Han'guk chŏngch'isa* 韓國政治史 (*A Political History of Korea* [Yi period]) (Seoul : Pagyŏngsa, 1963).

No, Ke Hyŏn 盧啓鉉 *Han'guk Wegyosa yŏn'gu* 韓國外交史研究 (*Studies in the Diplomatic History of Korea*) (Seoul : Haemunsa, 1968).

Pak, Tong Sŏ 朴東緒 *Han'guk kwallyojedo ŭi yŏksajokjŏn'gae* 韓國官僚制度의 歷史的展開 (*Development of Korean Bureaucracy*) (Seoul : Han'guk Yŏn'guwŏn, 1961).

Sin, Ch'ae Ho 申采浩. *Chosŏn sanggosa* 朝鮮上古史 (*Ancient History of Korea*) (Seoul : Chongnosŏwŏn, 1948).

Suematsu, Masukasu 末松保和 *Sillasi no shomondai* 新羅史の諸問題 (*Problems in the Silla History*) (Tōkyō : Tōyōbungo, 1954).

_____. *Imna gŏbŏsi* 任那興亡史 (*The Rise and Fall of Imna*) (Tōkyō : Yoshikawagobunkan, 1956).

Minjokmunhwa Yŏn'guso 民族文化研究所. *Han'gukmunhwasa taegye* Ⅰ :
Minjok-Kukkasa ; Ⅲ : *Kwahak-Kisulsa* 韓國文化史大系
Ⅰ: 民族國家史 ; Ⅲ : 科學技術史 (*Outline of the Korean Culture* Ⅰ :
History of the Race and Governments ; Ⅲ : *History of science and
Technology*) (Seoul : Minjokmunhwa Yŏn'guso, Korea University, 1964-
70).

Economy and Social Organization

Cho, Ki Chun 趙璣濬. *Han'guk kyŏngjesa* 韓國經濟史 (*Economic History of
Korea*) (Seoul : Ilsinsa, 1962).
Ch'oe, Ho Chin 崔虎鎭. *Han'guk kyŏngjesa gaeron* 韓國經濟史概論
(*Introduction to the Korean Economic History*) (Seoul : Pomungak,
1962).
Ch'oe, Chae Sŏk 崔在錫. *Han'guk kajok yŏn'gu* 韓國家族研究 (*Studies of the
Korean Family*) (Seoul : Minjungsŏgwan, 1966).
Lee, Sang Paek 李相伯. *Han'guk munhwa yŏn'gunon'go* 韓國文化研究論考
(*Studies in the Korean Culture*) (Seoul : Ŭlyumunhwasa, 1974).
Lee, Ch'un Nyŏng 李春寧. *Yijo nong'ŏp kisulsa* 李朝農業技術史 (*History of
the Yi Dynasty Agricultural Technology*) (Seoul : Han'guk yŏn'guwŏn,
1964).
Lee, Sŏn Kŭn 李瑄根. *Hwarangdo yŏn'gu* 花郎道研究 (*Studies in the Way of
Hwarang*) (Seoul : Haedongmunhwasa, 1950).
Kim, Tu Hŏn 金斗憲. *Chosŏn kajokjedo yŏn'gu* 朝鮮家族制度研究 (*Studies
in the Korean Family System*) (Seoul : Ŭlyumunhwasa, 1949).
McCune, Shannon, *Korea's Heritage : A Regional and social Geography*
(Rutland : Charles E. Tuttle, 1956).
Osgood, Cornelius, *The Koreans and Their culture* (New York : The Ronald
Press, 1951).
Kerimsa 鷄林社. *Hwarangdo* 花郎道 (*The way of Hwarang*) (Seoul : Kerimsa,
1950).
Minjokmunhwa Yŏn'guso 民族文化研究所. *Han'guk munhwasa taegye* Ⅱ :
Chŏngch'i-kyŏngjesa 韓國文化史大系 Ⅱ: 政治經濟史 (*Outline of the
Korean Culture* Ⅱ : *History of Politics and Economics*) (Seoul :
Minjokmungwa Yŏn'guso, Korea University, 1964-70).

Religion and Philosophy

Cho, Chi Hun 趙芝薰. *Han'guk munhwasa sŏsŏl* 韓國文化史序說 (*Preface to the Korean Cultural History*) (Seoul : T'amgudang, 1964).

Cho, Myŏng Ki 趙明基. *Sillabulgyo ŭ uinyŏm gwa yŏksa* 新羅佛教의 理念과 歷史 (*History and Ideology of Silla Buddhism*) (Seoul : Sint'aeyangsa, 1962).

_____. *Koryŏ Taegakkuksa wa Ch'ŏnt'ae sasang* 高麗大覺國師와 天台思想 (*Koryŏ's National Teacher taegak and Ch'ŏnt'ae Thought*) (Seoul : Tonggukmunhwasa, 1964).

Ch'oe, Mun Hong 崔汶洪. *Han'guk ch'ŏlhak* 韓國哲學 (*Korean philosophy*) (Seoul : Sŏngmunsa, 1969).

Chung, P. G., *A Short History of Chinese Philosophy* (New York : Macmillan, 1960).

De Bary, Wm. Theodore, *et al*, *Sources of Chinese Tradition* (New York : Columbia University Press, 1960).

Fung, Yu-lan, *A Short History of Chinese Philosophy* (New York, Macmillan, 1948).

_____. *A History of Chinese Philosophy*, 2 vols., trans. by Derk Bodde (Princeton : Princeton University Press, 1952-3).

Han, Woo Kŭn 韓佑劤. *Yijo hungisahoe wa sasang* 李朝後期社會와 思想 (*Late Yi Dynasty Society and Thought*) (Seoul : Ŭlyumunhwasa, 1961).

Hong, I Sŏp 洪以燮. *Chŏng Tasan ŭ chŏngch'i kyŏngjesasang yŏn'gu* 丁茶山의 政治經濟思想研究 (*Studies in the Economic and Political Thought of Chŏng Tasan*) (Seoul : Han'guk Yŏn'guwŏn, 1960).

Hyŏn, Sang Yun 玄相允. *Chosŏn yugyosa* 朝鮮儒教史 (*History of Korean Confucianism*) (Seoul : Minjungsŏgwan, 1960).

Lee, Nŭng Hwa 李能和. *Chosŏn pulgyot'ongsa* 朝鮮佛教通史 (*General History of Korean Buddhism*), 2 vols. (Seoul : Sinmungwan, 1918).

_____. *Han'guk togyosa* 韓國道教史 (*History of Korean Taoism*) (Seoul : Dongguk University Press 1959).

Lee, Pyŏng To 李丙燾. *Koryŏ sidae ui yŏn'gu* 高麗時代의 研究 (*Study of the Koryŏ Period*) (Seoul : Ŭlyumunhwasa, 1948).

Kim, Tŭk Hwang 金得幌. *Han'guk chonggyosa* 韓國宗交史 (*Religious History of Korea)* (Seoul : Haemunsa, 1963).

_____. *Han'guk sasangsa* 韓國思想史 (*History of the Korean Thought*) (Seoul : Namsandang, 1958).

Kim, Sang Ki 金庠基. *Tonghak kwa tonghangnan* 東學과 東學亂 (*Tonghak and Tonghak Disturbances*) (Seoul : Taesŏngch'ul p'ansa, 1974).

Kim, Kyŏng T'ak 金敬琢. *Yulgok ŭ yŏn'gu* 栗谷의 研究 (*Study of Yulgok*) (Seoul : Han'guk Yŏn'guwŏn, 1960).

Moffett, Samuel H., *The Christians of Korea* (New York : Friendship Press, 1962).

Noss, John B., *Man's Religions* (New York, Macmillan, revised, 1956).

Pak, Chong Hong 朴鍾鴻. *Han'guk ŭ sasangjŏk Panghyang* 韓國의 思想的方

向 (*Ideological Direction of Korea*) (Seoul : Pagyŏngsa, 1968).

―――――――――. *Ch'ŏlhakgaesŏl* 哲學概說 (*Introduction to Philosophy*) (Seoul : Pagyŏngsa, 1964).

Palmer, Spencer J., *Korea and Christianity* (Seoul : Royal Asiatic Society Korea Branch, 1967).

Sŏ, Kyŏng Po 徐京保. *Tongyang pulgyomunhwasa* 東洋佛敎文化史 (*History of Buddhist Culture in East Asia*) (Seoul : Hoammunhwasa, 1964).

Yu, Hong Nyŏl 柳洪烈. *Han'guk ch'ŏnjugyohoesa* 韓國天主敎會史 (*History of the Catholic Church in Korea*) (Seoul : Catholic Press, 1962).

―――――――――. *Kojongch'iha ch'ŏnjugyosunan ŭi yŏn'gu* 高宗治下天主敎愛難의 硏究 (*Study of Catholic Persecutions under Kojong*) (Seoul : Ŭlyumunhwasa, 1963).

Ilsinsa 日新社. *Han'guk sasangsa : Kodaep'yŏn* 韓國思想史 : 高代篇 (*Intellectual History of Korea : Ancient Period*) (Seoul : Ilsinsa, 1966).

Minjokmunhwa Yŏn'guso 民族文化研究所. *Han'guk munhwasa taegye VI : Chonggyo-ch'ŏlhaksa* 韓國文化史大系 *VI* : 宗敎哲學史 (*Outline of the Korean Culture VI : History of Religion and Philosophy*) (Seoul : Minjokmunhwa Yŏn'guso, Korea University, 1964-70).

Literature and Biography

Cho, Yun Che 趙潤濟. *Han'guk munhaksa* 韓國文學史 (*History of Korean Literature*) (Seoul : Tonggukmunhwasa, 1949).

―――――――――. *Han'guk sigasagang* 韓國詩歌史綱 (*History of the Korean Poetry*) (Seoul : Ŭlyumunhwasa, 1954).

―――――――――. *Han'guksiga ŭi yŏn'gu* 韓國詩歌의 硏究 (*Studies in the Korean Poetry*) (Seoul : Ŭlyumunhwasa, 1948).

Ch'oe, Hyŏn Pae 崔鉉培. Han'gŭlgal 한글갈 (*Studies in the Han'gŭl*) (Seoul : Chŏng'ŭmgwan, 1941).

Hong, Ki Mun 洪起文. *Chŏng'ŭm paldalsa* 正音發達史 (*Development of the Chŏngŭm*), 2 vols. (Seoul : Sŏulsinmunsa, 1946).

Hoyt, James, *Songs of the Dragons Flying to Heaven*, (Seoul : Korean National Commission for Unesco : Royal Asiatic Society, Korea Branch, 1972).

Kim, Tong Uk 金東旭. *Kungmunhak gaesŏl* 國交學概論 (*Introduction to Korean Literature*) (Seoul : Minjungsŏgwan, 1961).

Kim, Min Su 金侮洙. *Sin'gug'ŏhaksa* 新國語學史 (*New History of the Korean Language*) (Seoul : Ilchogak, revised, 1968).

Kim, Sa Yŏp 金思燁. *Kungmunhaksa* 國交學史 (*History of Korean Literature*) (Seoul : Chŏng'ŭmsa, revised, 1956).

Lee, Ki Mun 李起文. *Kug'ŏsagaesŏl* 國語史槪論 (*General History of the Korean Language*) (Seoul : Minjungsŏgwan, 1961).

Lee, Pyŏng Ki 李丙岐. *Kungmunhakjŏnsa* 國文學全史 (*Complete History of Koeran Literature*) (Seoul : Sin'gumunhwasa, 1949).

Lee, Ka Wŏn 李家原. *Han'guk hanmunhaksa* 韓國漢文學史 (*History of Chines Literature in Korea*) (Seoul : Minjungsŏgwan, 1961).

Lee, T'ae Kŭk 李泰極. *Sijogaeron* 時調槪論 (*Introduction to the Sijo*) (Seoul : Saegŭlsa, 1961).

Lee, Sung Nyŏng 李崇寧. *Kug'ŏhak kaesŏl* 國語學槪論. (*Introduction to the Korean Language*) (Seoul : Chinmunsa, 1954).

Lee, Peter H., *Studies in the senaennorae : Old Korean Poetry* (Rome : Instituto Italiano Per Il Medio Estremo Orients, 1959).

─────────────────. *Korean Literature : Topics and Themes* (Tucson : University of Arizona Press, 1965).

Mun, Sŏn Kyu 文旋奎. *Han'guk hanmunhaksa* 韓國漢文學史 (*History of Chinese Literature in Korea*) (Seoul : Chŏng'ŭmsa, 1961).

Nam, Kwang U 南廣佑. *Sae chŏngsŏn kojŏn* 새 精選古典 (*Excerpts from Classical Literature*) (Seoul : Chinhakmunhaksa, 1967).

Pang, Chong Hyŏn 方鍾鉉. *Kosijo chŏnghae* 古時調精解 (*Interpretation of the Old Sijo*) (Seoul : Ilsŏngdangsŏjŏm, 1958).

Yang, Chu Tong 梁注東. *Koga yŏn'gu* 古歌研究 (*Studies in Old Poetry*) (Seoul : Pangmunch'ulp'ansa, 1955).

─────────────────. *Yŏyo chŏnju* 麗謠箋注 (*Interpretation of Koryŏ Poetry*) (Seoul : Ŭlyumunhwasa, 1954).

Korean Poets Association 韓國詩人協會. *Korean Verses* (Seoul : Korean Poets Association, 1961).

Minjokmunhwa Yŏn'guso 民族文化研究所. *Han'guk munhwasa taegye V : Ŏnŏ-munhaksa* 韓國文化史大系 V : 言語文學史 (*Outline of the Korean Culture V : History of Language and Literature*) (Seoul: Minjokmunhwa Yŏn'guk, Korea University, 1964-70).

Sin'gumunhwasa 新丘文化社. *Han'guk inmyŏng taesajŏn* 韓國人名大辭典 (*Dictionary of the Korean Biographies*) (Seoul : Sin'gumunhwasa, 1967).

─────────────────. *Han'guk ŭi in'gansang* 韓國의 人間像 (*Great men in the Korean History*), 6 vols. (Seoul : Sin'gunmunhwasa, 1965).

Pangmunsa 博文社. *Inmul han'guksa* 人物韓國史 (*Great Men in the Korean History*), 5 vols. (Seoul : Pangmunsa, 1965).

Art and Archeology

Chang, Sa Hun 張師勛. *Kug'ak non'go* 國樂論攷 (*Studies in Korean Music*)

(Seoul : Seoul National University Press, 1966).

Gompertz, Godfrey St. G. M., *Korean Celadon* (London : Faber and Faber, 1964).

Kim, Wŏn Yong 金元龍. *Studies on Silla Pottery* (Seoul : Ŭlyumunhwasa, 1960).

_____. *Han'guk sajŏnyujŏnhmul chimyŏngp'yo* 史前遺蹟物 地名表 (*List of Relics and Place Names of Prehistoric Korea*) (Seoul : Seoul National University Press, 1965).

_____. *Han'guk misula* 韓國美術史 (*History of Korean Art*) (Seoul : Kŭmsŏngdosŏ, 1966).

Kim, Chewŏn 金載元. and Kim, Wŏn Yong 金元龍. *Treasures of Korean Art* (New York : Harry N. Abrams, 1966).

Kim, Chewŏn 金載元. and Gompertz, Godfrey St. G. M., *The Ceramic Art of Korea*) (London : Faber and Faber, 1961).

Ko, Yu Sŏp 高裕燮. *Han'guk misulmunhwasa nonch'ŏng* 韓國美術文化史論 叢 (*Essays on the History of Korean Art and Culture*) (Seoul : T'ong-mungwan, 1966).

_____ *Han'guk misulsa mit mihak non'go* 韓國美術史及美學論攷 (*Essays on Korean Art History and Aesthetics*) (Seoul : T'ongmungwan, 1963).

_____. *Hanguk kŏnch'ukmisulsa ch'ogo* 韓國健築美術史草 稿 (*Draft History of Korean Architecture*) (Seoul : Kogomisudlong'inhoe, 1964).

_____. *Han'guk t'ap'a ŭi yŏn'gu* 韓國塔婆의 研究 (*Study of the Korean Pagodas*) (Seoul : Ŭlyumunhwasa, 1948).

_____. *Koryŏ ch'ŏngja* 高麗青磁 (*Koryŏ Celadon*) (Seoul : Ŭlyumunhwasa, 1954).

Lee, Hong Chik 李弘稙. *Han'guk kimunhwa non'go* 韓國古文化論攷 (*Studies in the Old Korean Culture*) (Seoul : Ŭlyumunhwasa, 1954).

Lee, Hye Ku 李惠求. *Han'guk ŭmak yŏn'gu* 韓國音樂研究 (*Studies in Korean Music*) (Seoul : Kungmunŭmak Yŏn'guhoe, 1957).

McCune, Eveline, *The Arts of Korea* (Rutland : Charles E. Tuttle, 1961).

Swann, Peter, *Art of China, Korea, and Japan* (London : Thames, and Hudson revised, 1967).

Minjokmunhwa Yŏn'guso 民族文化研究所. *Han'guk munhwasa taegye IV : P'ungsok-Yesulsa* 韓國文化史大系 IV : 風俗藝術史 (*Outline of the Korean Culture IV : History of Customs and Arts*) (Seoul : Minjokmunhwa Yŏn'guso, Korea University, 1964–70).

Mungyobu 文敎部. *Kukpo tohae* 國寶圖解 (*Pictures of the National Treasures*), 6 vols. (Seoul : Mungyobu, 1959–62).

Ŭlyumunhwasa 乙酉文化社. *Kungnip pangmulgwan kojŏkchosa pogo* 國立博

物館古蹟調査報告 (*Reports on the Cultural Remains by the National Museum*)
(Seoul : Ŭlyumunhwasa, 1948–63).

Periodicals

Asea yŏn'gu 亞細亞硏究. (*Journal of Asiatic Studies*) (Seoul : Institute of
  Asiatic Studies, Korea University, 1958–).

Chŏsen gakuhŏ 朝鮮學報. (*Journal of the Academic Association of
  Koreanology*) (Kyoto : Tenri University, 1961–).

Chindan hakpo 震檀學報. (*Chindan Historical Review*) (Seoul : Chindan Hak'oe,
  1934–).

Chŏnbuk taehakkyo nonmunjip 全北大學校論文集. (*Chŏnbuk University
  annual Essay Collection*) (Chŏnju : Chŏnbuk University, 1957–).

Chung'ang taehakkyo nonmunjip 中央大學校論文集. (*Chung'ang Unitersity,
  Annual Essay Collection* (Seoul : Chung'ang University, 1955–).

Han'guksa yŏn'gu 韓國史硏究 (*Journal of the Korean History*) (Seoul :
  Association for Korean Historical Studies, 1968–).

Han'guk sasang 韓國思想. (*Korean Thought*) (Seoul : Committee on
  Compilation of Korean Thought, 1959–).

Hyangt'o Seoul 鄕土서울 (*Review of Historic Seoul*) (Seoul : Committee on
  Compilation of History of the Special City of Seoul, 1957–).

Harvard Journal of Asiatic Studies (Cambridge : Harvard University)

Inmun kwahak 人文科學. (*Humanities and Sciences*) (Seoul : Yonsei
  University, 1957–).

Journal of Asian Studies (Ann Arbor, Michigan : Association for the Asian
  Studies, 1941–).

Journal of the Social Sciences and Humanities (Seoul : Korea Research Center,
  1960–).

Kyŏngbuk taehakkyo nonmunjip 慶北大學校論文集 (*Kyŏngbuk University
  Annual Essay Collection)* (Taegu : Kyŏngbuk University, 1956).

Kuksasang ŭi chemunje 國史上의 諸問題 (*Problems in the Korean History*)
  (Seoul : Committee on Compilation of National History, 1959–60).

Kug'ŏ kungmunhak 國語國文學 (*Korean Language and Literature*) (Seoul :
  Association for Koeran Language and Literature, 1952–).

Korea taehakkyo nonmunjip 高麗大學校論文集 (*Korea University Annual
  Essay Collection*) (Seoul : Korea University, 1955–).

Minjok munhwa yŏn'gu 民族文化硏究 (*Korean Classics Studies*) (Seoul :
  Minjokmunhwa Yŏn'guso Korea University, 1964–).

Nonch'ong 論叢 (*Essay Collection*) (Seoul : Korean Culture Research

Institute, Ehwa Womens University, 1960-).

Pulgyo hakpo 佛教學報 (*Journal of Buddhism*) (Seoul : Pulgyo Hakhoe, Dongguk University, 1963-).

Pusan taehakkyo nonmunjip 釜山大學校論文集 (*Pusan University Annual Essay Collection*) (Pusan : Pusan University, 1956-).

Sach'ong 史叢 (*Essay Collection*) (Seoul : Korea University Historical Society, 1955-).

Sahak yon'gu 史學研究 (*Studies in History*) (Seoul : Korean Historical Association, 1958-).

Sasanggye 思想界 (*The World of Thought*) (Seoul : Sasanggyesa, 1953-).

Seikyŭ gakusŏ 青丘學報 (*Essays in Korean Studies*) 1-30 (Seoul : Seikyŭ Gakukai, 1930-39).

Sindong'a 新東亞 (*New Asia*) (Tong'ailbosa, 1961-).

Seoul taehakkyo nonmunjip 서울大學校論文集 (*Seoul* National University Annual Essay Collection) (Seoul : Seoul National University, 1954-).

Sŏnggyungwan taehakkyo nonmunjip 成均館大學校論文集 (*Sŏnggyungwan University Annual Essay Collection*) (Seoul : Sŏnggyungwan University, 1954).

Sungmyŏng yŏja taehakkyo nonmunjip 淑明女子大學校論文集 (*Sungmyŏng Women's University Annual Essay Collection*) (Seoul : Sungmyŏng Women's University, 1961-).

Taedong munhwa yŏn'gu 大東文化研究 (*Korean Cultural Studies*) (Seoul : Taedong Culture Research Institute, Sŏnggyungwan University, 1962-).

Tōyōsi kenkyū 東洋史研究 (*Journal of the Oriental History*) (Kyoto : Kyoto University, 1935-).

Tang'a munhwa 東亞文化 (*Journal of the East Asian Culture*) (Seoul : Tong' amunhwa Yŏn'guso, Seoul National University, 1963-).

Transactions of the Korea Branch of the Royal Asiatic Society (Seoul : Korea Branch of the Royal Asiatic Society, 1900-).

Yŏksahak yŏn'gu 歷史學研究 (*Historical Studies*) (Seoul : Yŏksahakhoe 1949-).

Yŏksa hakpo 歷史學報 (*Korean Historical Review*) (Seoul : Korean Historical Association, 1952-).

Yŏksa kyoyuk 歷史教育 (*Korean Historical Education Review*) (Seoul : Association for Korean Historical Education, 1956-).

Index

Saengyuksin (Six Live Subjects), 242
Saganwŏn, 246
Sage–gentleman 85
Sahak (Four Schools), 254–256
Sahŏnbu, 246, 277
Sahwa (misfortunes of scholars), 273–277
Saja (rank), 62
Sakyamuni, 96, 97, granite, 119, relic of, 104
Salit'a, 201
Sallim kyŏngje (Management of Rural Economy), 333
Sallimp'a (Mountain and Forest School), 272
Sam Han, 21, 76, 90, component of, 22, construction of water reservoirs, 35, economic activities, 34, treatment of dead in, 36, location of, 21, political consciousness of, 22–23, social class distinction in, 34
Sambyolch'o (Three Special Units), 198, 201, 207, revolt of, 198–200
Samdaemok (Category of Three Generations), 109
Samguk sagi (History of the Three Kingdoms), 179, 180, 193
Samguk yusa (Memorabilia of the Three Kingdoms), 13, 179, 180, 215
Samnon (Trisāstravādin; Three Treatise), 101, 102, 106
Samsa (Finance Commission), 144
Samsa (Three Office), 246, 274, 275
Samsu (Three Hands), 313, 325
Sang'ambŏp (inlay method), 185
Sangdaedŭng, 65, 125
Sangga, 62
Sangsŏsŏng (Secretariat of State Affairs), 143
Sansang, King, 20, 30
Sanskrit, 97

Sansuhwa (Mountain and Water Painting), 301
Saro, 23
Sarvāstivādin (Sŏrilchŏryubu), 100, 101
Sasaek (Four Colors), 307, 320
Sasimgwan system, 135, 144
Sasŏl sijo, 339
Sassi namjŏng ki (Story of Lady Sa), 340
Sayuksin (Six Dead Subjects), 242
Scarlet Bird of South, 114
Scholastic Buddhism, 164
School of Ch'eng–Chu, 216
School of *Li(I)*, 216
School of Mind of Intuition, 216, 328–329
School of Northern Learning *(Pukhakp'a)*, 335
School of Principle or Reason, 216
Second Battle of Chinju, 313
Scripture of the Lotus of the Wonderful Law, 104
Sculpture, of Paekche, 115–116
Scytho–Siberian culture, 9, 11
Secret envoy *(amhyang ŏsa)*, 243, 341
Secretariat–Chancellery, 237
Secretariat of State Affairs *(Sangsŏsŏng)*, 143, 245
Sejo, 242–246, 248, 272, 273, 295
Sejong, 180, 238–241, 278, 281, as Confucian scholar, 282–283, commitment to Buddhism, 295, invention of the *Han'gul*, 239, invention of rain gouge, 240, private life, 240–241, trade arrangement with Tsushima, 269
Selections from Eastern Literature (Tongmunsŏn), 298
Seoul, 23, 144, 169, 256n
Seven sages of Bamboo Grove, 272